Design Methods and A.

MW01253135

Design Methods and Analysis of Algorithms

SECOND EDITION

S.K. BASU

Professor
Department of Computer Science
Banaras Hindu University
Varanasi

PHI Learning Private Limited

Delhi-110092
2015

₹ 350.00

DESIGN METHODS AND ANALYSIS OF ALGORITHMS, Second Edition
S.K. Basu

© 2013 by PHI Learning Private Limited, Delhi. All rights reserved. No part of this book may be reproduced in any form, by mimeograph or any other means, without permission in writing from the publisher.

ISBN-978-81-203-4746-5

The export rights of this book are vested solely with the publisher.

Sixth Printing (Second Edition) ... ... **February, 2015**

Published by Asoke K. Ghosh, PHI Learning Private Limited, Rimjhim House, 111, Patparganj Industrial Estate, Delhi-110092 and Printed by Raj Press, New Delhi-110012.

To the memory of my grandmother

Malati Lata Bose

CONTENTS

LIST OF FIGURES

Fig. No.   *Caption*

Fig. No.   Caption

LIST OF TABLES

PREFACE

In this second edition of the book, a few new sections, problems, and an altogether new chapter on Bioinformatics Algorithms have been added. In particular, the additions are: section 0.5 on BSP model in Chapter 0, section 1.8 on some examples of average complexity calculation, section 1.9 on amortization, and section 1.11 on a few more advance data structures in Chapter 1. A new section 2.6 on polynomial multiplication has been added in Chapter 2. New material on better-fit heuristic under section 7.3 on bin packing appears in Chapter 7. New section 9.8 on graph matching in Chapter 9 and section 12.4.5 on function optimization, neighbourhood annealing and implicit elitism have been added in Chapter 12. Considering the importance of bioinformatics computation, I have introduced a new Chapter 14 on Bioinformatics Algorithms. The earlier concluding Chapter 14 now becomes Chapter 15 in the new edition. I hope that the readers will benefit from this revised second edition. Any feedback on the revised edition of the book will be highly appreciated and the same may be sent to my email id swapankb@gmail.com.

S.K. BASU

PREFACE TO THE FIRST EDITION

The study of algorithms is at the core of all automatic problem-solving activities. How to design efficient algorithms to solve a given problem, is of primary concern to computer scientists and computer practitioners. Can we have a better algorithm to solve a given problem than what is already available? Given a new problem, how do we proceed to find a good algorithm to solve the problem? Is there still an opportunity to find a better algorithm for the problem? Which algorithm is good and which one is bad? There could also be some problems for which we cannot find algorithms that can be executed in reasonable time. What do we do for all these kinds of problems? These are the main issues that are studied in the area of design and analysis of algorithms.

Several excellent texts on design and analysis of algorithms are available from a number of international publishers. These are mostly advanced texts meant for postgraduate courses and to be used as handbooks for professionals. This book is basically designed to serve the needs of B.Tech students in computer science and engineering, B.Sc. (Honours) and M.Sc. students in computer science, and MCA students. It focuses on the standard algorithm design methods with examples. Elementary analysis of the time complexities is provided for each example-algorithm. The treatment throughout the book is primarily tailored to the curriculum needs of this group of students. In the author's view, there is a need for a suitable text that covers the essentials of the subject (without being highly specialized) for this segment of readers. The present book is meant to serve that purpose. From the author's experience over the last couple of years in teaching algorithms at the Banaras Hindu University, this book contains material that can be covered in approximately 50–55 hours of lectures.

The prerequisites for studying this book are that the students should have undergone undergraduate level courses in programming, data structures, and discrete mathematics.

There are fifteen chapters in the book and the examples chosen are mostly representative problems. Each chapter ends with a set of exercises. These exercises are of very simple to intermediate levels of hardness.

Chapter 0 deals with the models of computation. Chapter 1 reviews the preliminaries in the areas such as notions of algorithms, asymptotic complexity analysis, recurrence relation solution, and basic data structures. Chapter 2 deals with the divide-and-conquer method and its representative applications. Chapter 3 discusses the 'greedy method' and its representative applications. Chapter 4 presents the 'dynamic programming' technique and its applications. Chapter 5 gives some more divide-and-conquer applications. Chapter 6 deals with non-deterministic algorithms and NP-completeness. Chapters 7 and 8 discuss approximation algorithms and randomized algorithms respectively. Chapters 9 gives a brief introduction to graph algorithms. Chapter 10 deals with branch-and-bound and backtracking techniques. Chapter 11 provides an introduction to the lower bound techniques. Chapter 12 briefly discusses genetic algorithms. Chapter 13 is devoted to parallel algorithms. Chapter 14 concludes the book.

Each chapter is illustrated with suitable examples to reinforce the principles/methods involved.

The author will be happy to receive constructive criticisms and suggestions, or reports intimating the presence of errors and omissions in this book. The readers can email their comments to: **swapankb@bhu.ac.in.**

Finally, it is hoped that the students will find this book a useful companion for their courses of study.

S.K. BASU

ACKNOWLEDGEMENTS

I wish to express my sincere gratitude to the institutions whose facilities I have used at one time or the other for the preparation of this book. Notable among these institutions are: Banaras Hindu University, Korea University, Chennai Mathematical Sciences Institute, and Indian Statistical Institute, Kolkata.

Many individuals have encouraged and provided help during the preparation of the book. I wish to appreciate and acknowledge my gratitude to all of them. In particular, I would like to thank Dr. Debasis Majumdar, Ms. Aileen Svereika, Prof. Kamal Sheel, Prof. A.K. Srivastava, Dr. Avnish K. Bhatia, Mr. Frans van der Sommen and Prof. N. Prasad. I also acknowledge and express my gratitude to many authors and research workers whose papers/books I have freely consulted and referred to during the preparation of the book.

I must record and thank Sri M.R. Parida, acquisition editor, PHI Learning for putting persuasive pressure on me to complete this project and also the editorial staff including Sri Darshan Kumar for helping me to improve the presentation style.

I was fortunate to have the complete support of my wife, Nilanjana, and my son, Subhaditya, in my endeavour to write this book. I appreciate their commendable and sincere cooperation.

S.K. BASU

0

COMPUTATIONAL MODELS

0.0 INTRODUCTION

A computing model is an idealized or abstract description of real computers. Computing models are also prescriptions of how computers could or should be built. This aspect is more important in parallel processing where various paradigms are competing. A computing model is used to design and analyze algorithms for the class of computer architectures it describes. The model specifies the basic operations and the rules to compose valid programs. A cost function like *complexity measure* is used for performance evaluation. It is highly desirable to have the cost function defined in the same compositional way as the program semantics. A cost is associated with each basic operation, and rules are given to compute the cost of a composed program from the cost of its components. This second aspect of a computing model, namely the cost function, is usually not considered to be part of the formal specification of a computer architecture or a programming language. Yet, such cost function is essential for algorithm design because performance is an important issue here.

The goal of complexity theory is to determine the amount of computational resources needed to perform certain computational tasks. The efforts to achieve these goals have only been partly successful. The major shortcoming is our inability to prove lower bounds for general models of computation. However, by studying a simpler model of computation, it is sometimes possible to prove such lower bounds and give quite accurate estimates of the difficulty of a computational task.

0.1 RAM

RAM stands for Random Access Machine. It is one accumulator computer in which instructions are not permitted to modify itself. It has an input tape, an output tape, a program and a memory (see Figure 0.1). The input tape consists of a sequence of squares, each of which can store an integer. Whenever one square is read from the tape, the tape head moves one square to the right. The output tape is also a sequence of squares; in each square an integer can be written.

1

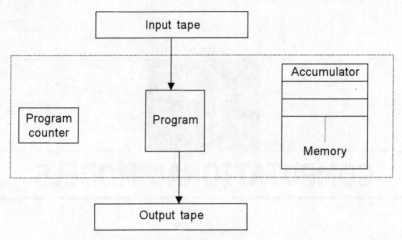

FIGURE 0.1 RAM.

Initially, the tape is blank. Output is written on the square under the tape head and after the writing, the tape head moves one square to the right. Over-writing on the same square is not permitted. The memory consists of a sequence of registers, each of which is capable of holding an integer of arbitrary size. The program for RAM is not stored in the memory and so is not subject to modification. A program for RAM contains a sequence of labeled instructions resembling those found in assembly language programs. All computations take place in the first register called accumulator. The program counter determines the next instruction to be executed. A RAM program defines a mapping from the input tape to the output tape. Since the program may not halt on all input tapes, the mapping may be undefined for certain inputs.

The worst-case complexity of a RAM program is the function $f(n)$ which is the maximum over all inputs of size n of the sum of the time taken by each instruction executed. The expected time complexity is the average over all inputs of size n of the same sum. The space complexity is defined in an analogous manner. It is basically the sum total of the registers (memory) used by the instructions. To specify the time and space complexities precisely, we must know the time required to execute each RAM instruction and the space used by each register. There are mainly two cost criteria: *uniform* and *logarithmic*. In the uniform cost criterion—which is more frequently used—each RAM instruction requires one unit of time and each register requires one unit of space. In the logarithmic cost, each instruction is charged for the sum of the lengths of all the data manipulated implicitly or explicitly by the instruction. This is more realistic, but sometimes less convenient to use.

0.2 TURING MACHINE

Alan Turing[1] introduced this model in 1936. It has a finite control, an input tape that is divided into a sequence of squares, and a tape head that scans one cell of the tape at a time.

---

[1] Alan Mathison Turing (1912–1954) invented the Turing machine to solve a decision problem posed by Hilbert. He worked towards the development of the theory of computation, was instrumental in breaking the German naval code during World War II, and proposed the test of machine intelligence (popularly known as the Turing test).

The tape has a left-most square but there is no right-most square, that is, the tape is infinite to the right (see Figure 0.2). Each square can store a tape symbol. Initially, the left-most n squares (assuming input length is n) contain tape symbols and the remaining squares are blank. In one move of the Turing machine (which is dependent on the current input symbol and the state of the finite control), it changes state, writes a symbol on the tape square replacing what was written there, and then the tape head moves one square left or right.

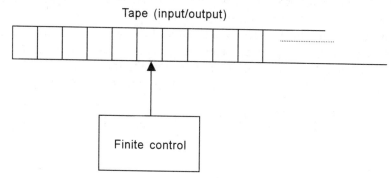

FIGURE 0.2 Basic Turing machine.

Formally, a *deterministic Turing machine* (DTM) is denoted by a 7-tuple $(Q, T, B, \Sigma, \delta, q_0, F)$, where

Q: a finite set of states
T: a finite set of tape symbols
$B \in T$: blank symbol
$\Sigma \subseteq T - \{B\}$: a finite set of input symbols
$\delta: Q \times T \to Q \times T \times \{Left, Right\}$, transition function
$q_0 \in Q$: the distinguished start state
$F \subseteq Q$: a set of final states

The single tape Turing machine is a variant of the general Turing machine. In fact, a Turing machine can have multiple tapes. A single tape Turing machine is capable of computing what a multi-tape Turing machine can. A Turing machine can simulate a RAM, provided that the elementary RAM instructions can themselves be simulated by a Turing machine.

If for every input of length n, a Turing machine makes $T(n)$ moves before halting, then the Turing machine is said to be a $T(n)$ time-bounded Turing machine, or one of complexity $T(n)$. The language recognized by the Turing machine is said to be of time complexity $T(n)$. If for every input of length n, the Turing machine scans at most $S(n)$ squares, then the Turing machine is said to be a $S(n)$ space-bounded Turing machine, or one of space complexity $S(n)$. The language recognized by the machine is also said to be of space complexity $S(n)$.

Alternative definitions of Turing machines abound, including versions with multi-tapes or non-determinism. The original model and its reasonable variants all have the same power, that is, they recognize the same class of languages.

A *non-deterministic Turing machine* (NTM) is, in a way similar to the above except that at any point in a computation, the machine may proceed according to several possibilities, which means that, for a given state and an input symbol, the machine may move to one of the possible next states. The computation of an NTM may be thought to have the structure of a rooted tree, whose branches correspond to the different possibilities for the machine. If some branch of the computation leads to one of the final states, the machine accepts its input. There is an alternative, but equivalent description of an NTM. In this description, we augment the standard DTM with a guessing module having its own write-only head as shown in Figure 0.3. The guessing module writes down the guess on the tape. The computation proceeds in two stages. In the first stage (guessing stage), the guessed string is written on a suitable area of the tape. In the second stage (checking stage), the computation proceeds as in the case of a DTM. The guessed string is examined during the checking stage. The computation stops when the finite control enters one of the final states. DTM and NTM may be used to define the complexity classes (refer Chapter 6) *P* and *NP* respectively.

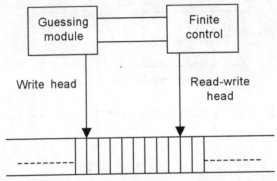

FIGURE 0.3   Non-deterministic Turing machine.

0.3   CIRCUIT MODEL

Since all real computers are built from circuits, the general Boolean circuits represent a more fundamental model than the others usually considered. A Boolean circuit is a finite, directed graph without cycle (see Figure 0.4). A function f is computed by a sequence of circuits, one for each length of the input. One individual circuit has n inputs, m outputs, AND, OR and NOT gates configured to compute the m binary outputs given the n binary inputs. From every input node, there is at least one path to some operation node. The *depth* of a circuit is defined to be the length of the longest path from some input to the output. The total number of nodes in the circuit is called the *size* of the circuit. The number of operation nodes at depth i is called the width of the circuit at depth i, assuming that the inputs are at depth 0. The maximum of the width at all levels is called the *width*, w, of the circuit. The *size* of a circuit is a measure of its hardware content while its *depth* measures the time required in parallel processing to compute the output assuming unit delay at each gate. The *width* represents the maximum degree of parallelism.

Let $f = < f_N >$ be a family of functions with $\{0, 1\}^{g(N)}$ as domain and $\{0, 1\}^{h(N)}$ as the range where $g(N)$ is a monotonically increasing function of N. Let $C = <C_N>$ be a family of Boolean circuits, where C_N computes f_N. C_N has $g(N)$ inputs and $h(N)$ outputs. A family $C = <C_N>$ of circuits is said to be uniform if for a given N there is an algorithm to generate

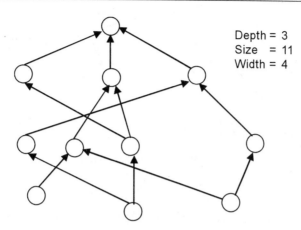

Depth = 3
Size = 11
Width = 4

FIGURE 0.4 Boolean circuit.

the Nth member, C_N, of the family C. Uniform circuit families, introduced by Borodin, have played a key role in the definition of various parallel complexity classes. It has helped in establishing relations between the various parallel complexity classes and the complexity classes based on time and space using the Turing machine model. We now quote some important results from the literature without giving the proofs. This relates computations on Boolean circuit model with those on Turing machine model. Pippenger and Fisher proved that for every deterministic Turing machine that computes the solution to a problem in time $T(N)$ $(\geq N)$, there corresponds a circuit computing the solution to the same problem with size bounded above by $dT(N)\log T(N)$ for some constant $d > 0$. Borodin proved the correspondence between the (extra) space needed to compute a function using a non-deterministic Turing machine to the depth of the circuit computing the same function. More specifically, if a problem is solvable by a non-deterministic Turing machine using $S(N)$ $(\geq \log N)$ extra space, then there exists a circuit for solving the same problem with the depth bounded above by $dS^2(N)$ for some constant $d > 0$. The first result relates sequential time with space in parallel computation and the second result relates space in sequential computation with time in parallel computation.

0.4 PRAM

PRAM is an acronym for *parallel random access machine*. It is the most popular model for parallel algorithm design. Fortune and Wyllie introduced this model. The PRAM model provides an abstraction that strips away problems of synchronization, reliability and communication delays, thereby permitting algorithm designers to focus first and foremost on the structure of the computational problem at hand, rather than the architecture of a currently available machine. An N-processor PRAM consists of N processors that access a globally shared memory as shown in Figure 0.5. During each step of a PRAM computation, each processor is allowed to read from, or write to, an arbitrary location in the shared memory and to perform some computation according to its local memory and local control. There are many variants of PRAM models depending upon the discipline imposed on concurrent read and write. Most important among them are EREW, CREW and CRCW.

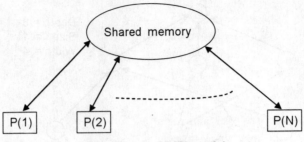

FIGURE 0.5   PRAM model.

EREW PRAM

This is exclusive read and exclusive write PRAM. In this model, at most one processor can read from or write to any location in the shared memory during each step. Processors can read (from) or write (to) different locations at the same time.

CREW PRAM

This is concurrent read but exclusive write PRAM. In this, multiple processors are allowed to read from the same memory location at the same time; but only one processor is allowed to write to any particular location during a step. Processors can write concurrently at different locations.

CRCW PRAM

This is concurrent read and concurrent write PRAM. In this model, any number of processors can read from any memory location at the same time and any number of processors can write into any memory location at the same time. Simultaneous reading from the same memory location by many processors is understandable. But simultaneous writing into the same memory location by many processors leads to unpredictable state of the memory cell. To resolve the situation arising out of simultaneous writing by many processors, a number of disciplines are imposed. Some of them are: (i) all simultaneous writes store the same value to the memory location, (ii) any one of the values written may remain, the others are lost, (iii) the value written by the processor with the minimum index will remain, (iv) the values being written are combined using some associative functions, such as summation or minimum or maximum, and this remains in the cell.

0.5   BSP MODEL

Designers of parallel algorithms use parallel models with unlimited parallelism assumptions ignoring communication and synchronization issues. A parallel computer more realistically is viewed as a collection of sequential processors, each having its own local memory and interconnected by a network allowing communication through sending and receiving of messages.

The *Bulk-Synchronous Parallel* (BSP) model has been used to address these limitations of parallel computing models. It is a theoretical scheme for the design, analysis and programming of general purpose parallel computers. It involves processor-memory modules, network for communication among the processors, facility for synchronization. A piece of computation is divided into what is known as *large* or *super steps*. Processors carry out computation on locally available data, receive, and send messages during a large step.

A 3-tuple (*n*, *MinLat*, *r*) is used to describe the behaviour and performance of a parallel computer under this model. Here *n* represents the number of processors, *MinLat* the minimum time between two successive synchronization operations (dependent on the diameter of the underlying interconnection network), and *r* is the ratio of the total computational and message delivery throughputs of the system. Message sizes are not considered in this model. When all the processors send or receive at most *k* (greater than some machine-dependent value) messages of fixed size, the cost for this communication is *nk*. Otherwise, the cost of communication is *MinLat*.

The objective in programming endeavour is to maximize the size of *large steps*, and increase processor utilization. To find the performance of a parallel algorithm *P*, we have to mention a sequential algorithm *S* with which the comparison is to be made. Two scalars π and μ are specified for this purpose. π ($\pi = C_{BSP}/(C_{Seq}/n)$) is the ratio of the computation time C_{BSP} of the BSP algorithm and the comparing sequential algorithm time C_{Seq} divided by *n*. μ ($\mu = M_P/(C_{Seq}/n)$) is the ratio of the communication time of the BSP algorithm (M_p) and the computation time of the sequential algorithm divided by *n*.

BSP model introduced the notion of *large step*, and that all remote memory accesses occur between *large steps* as part of a global operation among the processors; the results of these accesses become effective at the end of the current *large step*. Many attempts have been made to extend BSP for predicting performance of parallel computers more realistically.

SUMMARY

In this chapter, we have presented a brief discussion on the basic theoretical models used for analysis of algorithms. These include RAM, Turing machine (including its non-deterministic version), circuit model, PRAM, and BSP. RAM and Turing machines are used for analysis of sequential algorithms. Logarithmic cost RAMs and Turing machines can simulate each other with polynomial overheads. Computation on non-deterministic Turing machine corresponds to execution of non-deterministic algorithm. Non-deterministic Turing machine is used to define a complexity class called *NP*. Circuit model, PRAM, and BSP are used for the analysis of parallel algorithms.

1

BASICS OF ALGORITHM

1.0 INTRODUCTION

Suppose we have to find the greatest common divisor (GCD) of two positive integers A and B. Euclid[1] gave the following procedure to compute it.

    Step 0: Input A and B.

    Step 1: If A and B are equal, then either is the GCD.

    Step 2: If A is greater than B, replace A by the difference of
             A and B, otherwise replace B by the difference of B and A.

    Step 3: Go to Step 1.

Suppose $A = 45$ and $B = 15$. The sequence of computations is:

	A	B
Step 0	45	15
Step 1	30	15
Step 2	15	15
Step 3	GCD = 15	

The above is a well-ordered sequence of precise arithmetic actions. It requires finite input. Each action takes finite time, the output is finite and the actions are guaranteed to terminate. The above is an example of an algorithm. The above algorithm requires time logarithmic with respect to the value of the numbers and is linear with respect to the input length.

---

[1] The great Greek mathematician gave the first non-trivial algorithm sometime between 400 and 300 B.C.

An algorithm is a procedure that can be executed on a Turing machine. An algorithm has the following characteristics:

(1) It is a finite sequence of instructions to achieve some particular output.
(2) It requires finite input.
(3) It produces finite output.
(4) It terminates after a finite time.

The word algorithm comes from the name of a Persian mathematician, A.J.M ibn Musa al Khowarizmi. In computer science 'algorithm' refers to a method that can be used by a computer for the solution of a problem.

Algorithms can be broadly classified into deterministic and non-deterministic algorithms.

Deterministic algorithm: The output for the same input is always the same irrespective of place and time.

Non-deterministic algorithm: Different output can be obtained with the same set of input while using the same algorithm. Action corresponding to one or more steps of the algorithm is dependent on a number of alternatives. It is basically a definitional device for capturing the notion of verifiability.

There are a number of standard methods for designing an algorithm. The most important among them are:

(1) Divide-and-conquer method
(2) Greedy method
(3) Dynamic programming method
(4) Branch-and-bound method
(5) Approximation methods, etc.

In addition, we have the brute-force method based on a problem's statement and definitions of the concepts involved. This method is the easiest to apply. Sometimes, this strategy is quite useful but in most of the cases, it leads to inefficient algorithms.

The quality of an algorithm is decided by two parameters: how much extra space it requires other than the input, and the time it requires for execution for a given input of size n. An algorithm is generally considered to be a good one if its time complexity is of the form of a polynomial in 'n', where n is the size of input (size of input is defined differently for different cases). We analyze algorithms in terms of their time complexities.

For analysis of time complexity, we consider the performance of the algorithm in the following cases:

(1) *Best case:* Inputs are provided in such a way that the minimum time is required to process them.

(2) *Average case:* Average behaviour of the algorithm is studied for various kinds of inputs. Let $Prob(I)$ be the probability of occurrence of problem instance I. Let $t(I)$ be the time required for the processing of this instance. The average time complexity of the algorithm is then the sum of the product $Prob(I)*t(I)$ for all possible problem instances of the given size. $Prob(I)$ is determined from experience or from simplifying

assumption like that all inputs of size n are equally likely to occur. If finding $Prob(I)$ is complicated, the computation of average behaviour is difficult.

(3) *Worst case:* Input is given in such a way that maximum time is required to process them. If $t(I)$ is the time for processing of the problem instance I of size n, the worst case complexity for problems of size n is the maximum of all such $t(I)$.

A single operation can be more time consuming in some situations, though the total time for a sequence of n such operations is always better than the worst-case time of that operation multiplied by n. The high cost of such a worst-case occurrence over the entire sequence can be amortized in a way similar to the way a business house amortizes the cost of an expensive product over the years of the product's production cycle.

Let us consider the problem of searching an element in a given array of N elements. In the best case, we will make one comparison, in the worst case we will make $N - 1$ comparisons, in the average case we will make $N/2$ comparisons under the assumption that the element we are looking for is equally likely to be present at any of the N positions in the array.

We can have the following situations with algorithms:

(1) Different algorithms for the same problem may take different amounts of time. For example, the problem of searching can be solved by both linear search algorithm and binary search algorithm. But the binary search is much faster than the linear search.

(2) Some algorithms require different amounts of time for different input. As an example, consider bubble sort that has different time complexities for the best, the average and the worst-case input.

In algorithms, we may have to follow a set of instructions repeatedly. For implementing this, we have two approaches: (a) recursion and (b) iteration. For programming purpose, they are different. However, for analysis purpose, they are the same except that the analysis is more straightforward and easier in the iterative case than in the recursive case. We will give two examples to show both the iterative and recursive implementations.

EXAMPLE 1.1   Fibonacci series: $F_0 = F_1 = 1$, $F_i = F_{i-1} + F_{i-2}$, $i \geq 2$.

(a) Recursion
```
Fib(n)  /* n terms */
    If (n = 0 or n = 1) Then Return(1);
    Else
    Return (Fib(n - 1) + Fib(n - 2));
    Endif
End Fib
```
(b) Iteration:
```
Fib(n)
    If (n = 0 or n = 1) Then Return(1); Endif
    F0 = 1;
    F1 = 1;
```

```
         For i = 2 to n Step 1 Do
            F = F0 + F1;
            F0 = F1;
            F1 = F;
         Endfor
         Return(F)
      End Fib
```

We can see that it is much easier to count the number of steps (operations that can be assumed to take constant/unit amount of time) in the iterative case than in the recursive case. Similarly, for the next example, we find that the same is true.

EXAMPLE 1.2 Factorial of a number.

(a) Iterative
```
      Fac(n)
      If (n < 0) Then Return('error');
         Else If (n < 2) Then Return(1);
            Else
               PROD = 1; Endif Endif
      For i = n down to 1 Step 1 Do
         PROD = PROD * i;
      Endfor
      Return (PROD);
      END Fac
```

(b) Recursive
```
      Fac(n)
      If (n < 0) Then Return('error');
         Else if (n < 2) Then Return(1);
            Else
               Return (n * Fac(n - 1)); Endif Endif
      END Fac
```

We now give some examples of algorithms with different forms of time complexities.

EXAMPLE 1.3 Trace of a matrix (sum of diagonal elements).

```
   Procedure Trace (A, n)
      Array A(n)
      T = 0;
      For i = 1 to n in Step 1 Do
         T = T + A(i, i);    /* A is n × n matrix */
      Endfor
   End Trace
```

Here $Time = (K1 + n * K2) \propto n$,

where $K1$ and $K2$ are two constants, $K1$ is the time taken for the assignment $T = 0$, and $K2$ is the time taken for the assignment $T = T + A(i, i)$. Thus, the algorithm takes linear time.

EXAMPLE 1.4 Maximum element of a matrix (square matrix).

```
Procedure Maxelement (A, n)
  Array A(n)
  Max = -∞ /* initialization */
  For i = 1 to n Step 1 Do
    For j = 1 to n Step 1 Do
      If(A(i,j) > Max) Then Max = A(i,j); Endif
    Endfor /* j */
  Endfor /* i */
End Maxelement
```

Here, the time required is of the form $(k_1 + k_2 * n * n) \propto n^2$, where k_1 and k_2 are constants; k_1 is the time for the assignment $Max = -\infty$ and k_2 is the time taken by the operations inside the loop. Thus, the algorithm takes quadratic time.

EXAMPLE 1.5 Product of two matrices A and B.

```
Procedure Matmul(A, B, n)
  Array A(n), B(n), C(n)
  For i = 1 to n Step 1
    For j = 1 to n Step 1
      C(i,j) = 0;   /* initialization */
      For k = 1 to n in Step 1
        C(i,j) = C(i,j) + A(i,k) * B(k,j);
      Endfor /* k */
    Endfor /* j */
  Endfor /* i */
End Matmul
```

Here the time required is of the form:

$\{(k_3 * n + k_2) * n\} * n$, where k_2 and k_3 are constants. This expression is proportional to n^3. Thus, the algorithm takes cubic time.

1.1 UPPER BOUND OF POLYNOMIAL FORM OF TIME COMPLEXITY

Let x be the size of data (according to the problem) and let the algorithm take time of the form:

$$T = A_n x^n + A_{n-1} x^{n-1} + \cdots + A_0$$

$$\Rightarrow T \le |A_n| \, x^n + |A_{n-1}| \, x^{n-1} + |A_{n-2}| \, x^{n-2} + |A_0|$$

$$= \left(|A_n| + \frac{|A_{n-1}|}{x} + \frac{|A_{n-2}|}{x^2} + \cdots + \frac{|A_0|}{x^n} \right) x^n$$

$$\le (|A_n| + |A_{n-1}| + |A_{n-2}| + \cdots + |A_0|)x^n \quad (\because x \ge 1)$$

$$= Kx^n, \; K = (|A_n| + |A_{n-1}| + |A_{n-2}| + \cdots + |A_0|)$$

That is, Kx^n bounds the time from the above. We say that the time requirement is of the order of x^n. For this, we use the 'Big Oh' notation and write $T \in O(x^n)$.

Big O: $f(n)$ is said to be $O(g(n))$ iff there exist two constants c and n_o such that $f(n) \le c*g(n), \; \forall \; n \ge n_o$.
Let $f(n) = 4n^2 + 3n, \; g(n) = 2n^3$.

$$g(n) > f(n), \; \forall \; n \ge 3 \Rightarrow f(n) \sim O(g(n)) \Rightarrow f(n) \sim O(n^3).$$

Algorithms taking constant time are said to be of $O(1)$. The order of dominance of some common time complexities is:

$$O(1) < O(\log n) < O(n) < O(n \log n) < O(n^2) < O(n^3) < O(k^n), \; k \text{ is a constant.}$$

Table 1.1 shows how a few of the common functions grow with the increase in argument values. We note that the growth rates of $T5$ and $T6$ are very very fast compared to the others. After some small values of N, these two functions become unmanageably large.

TABLE 1.1   Growth of functions

N	$T1 = N$	$T2 = N \log_2 N$	$T3 = N^2$	$T4 = N^3$	$T5 = 2^N$	$T6 = N!$
1	1	0	1	1	2	1
10	10	33.21928095	100	1000	1024	3628800
20	20	86.4385619	400	8000	1048576	2.4329E+18
30	30	147.2067179	900	27000	1073741824	2.65253E+32
40	40	212.8771238	1600	64000	1.09951E+12	8.15915E+47
50	50	282.1928095	2500	125000	1.1259E+15	3.04141E+64
60	60	354.4134357	3600	216000	1.15292E+18	8.32099E+81
70	70	429.0498112	4900	343000	1.18059E+21	1.1979E+100
80	80	505.7542476	6400	512000	1.20893E+24	7.1569E+118
90	90	584.2667787	8100	729000	1.23794E+27	1.4857E+138
100	100	664.385619	10000	1000000	1.26765E+30	9.3326E+157
110	110	745.9495685	12100	1331000	1.29807E+33	1.5882E+178
120	120	828.8268715	14400	1728000	1.32923E+36	6.6895E+198
130	130	912.9078157	16900	2197000	1.36113E+39	6.4669E+219
140	140	998.0996224	19600	2744000	1.3938E+42	1.3462E+241
150	150	1084.322804	22500	3375000	1.42725E+45	5.7134E+262

Problems whose best known algorithms require exponential (k^n) time or more, where k is a constant, is also known as *hard* or *intractable* problems.

There are other asymptotic notations like *Big Oh*. Some of these are:

Ω-notation: It deals with the minimum time (best cases) required by the algorithm. $f(n)$ is said to be $\Omega(g(n))$ iff there exist positive constants c and n_o such that $|f(n)| \geq c * |g(n)|$, $\forall \ n \geq n_o$.

Ω gives the lower bound while O gives the upper bound of time required by the algorithm. We say an algorithm to be *optimal* if $f(n)$ is $O(g(n))$ as well as $f(n)$ is $\Omega(g(n))$.

Θ-notation: $f(n)$ is $\Theta(g(n))$ iff there exist positive constants c_1, c_2 and n_o such that $c_1|g(n)| \leq |f(n)| \leq c_2|g(n)|$, $\forall \ n \geq n_o$. $\Theta(g(n))$ deals with the optimum time.

o-notation (small *o*): $f(n)$ *is* $o(g(n))$ iff:

$$\text{Limit}_{n\to\infty} \ \frac{f(n)}{g(n)} = 0$$

The function $f(n)$ becomes insignificant relative to $g(n)$ as $n \to \infty$.

Now we consider some more examples for evaluating time complexities.

EXAMPLE 1.6   Suppose we have a programme having outline as given below. Let one time execution of the statements between the i-loop and the j-loop require K_1 units of time and those within the j-loop require K_2 units of time.

```
Do 10 i = 1 to N
   ...
   K₁
   ...
Do 10 j = 1 to i
   K₂
   ...
10 Continue
```

The time-complexity of the above algorithm may be expressed as:

$$T(N) = K_1 * N + K_2 * 1 + K_2 * 2 + K_2 * 3 + \cdots + K_2 * N$$
$$= K_1N + K_2(1 + 2 + 3 + \cdots + N)$$
$$= K_1N + K_2N(N + 1)/2$$

So, $T(N)$ is $O(N^2)$.

EXAMPLE 1.7   Suppose we have a programme having outline as given below. Let one time execution of the statements between the i-loop and the j-loop require K_1 units of time and those within the j- and l-loops require K_2 units of time.

```
Do 10 i = 1 to N
   ...
   K₁
   ...
Do 10 j = 1 to i
Do 10 l = 1 to i
   ...
   K₂
   ...
10 Continue
```

The time complexity for the above algorithm may be written as:

$$T(N) = K_1 N + K_2 1^2 + K_2 2^2 + \cdots + K_2 N^2$$
$$= K_1 N + K_2 (1^2 + 2^2 + \cdots + N^2)$$
$$= K_1 N + K_2 \frac{N(N+1)(2N+1)}{6}$$

So, $T(N)$ is $O(N^3)$.

EXAMPLE 1.8 Suppose we have a programme having the outline given below. Let one time execution of the statements between the i- and j-loops require K_1 units of time and those within the j-, l- and m-loops require K_2 units of time.

```
Do 10 i = 1 to N
   ...
   K₁
   ...
Do 10 j = 1 to i
Do 10 l = 1 to i
Do 10 m = 1 to i
   ...
   K₂
   ...
10 Continue
```

The time complexity of the above algorithm may be written as:

$$T(N) = K_1 N + K_2 (1^3 + 2^3 + \cdots + N^3)$$
$$= K_1 N + K_2 \left(\frac{N(N+1)}{2}\right)^2$$

So, $T(N)$ is $O(N^4)$.

Some of the useful relations involving O-notation that help in finding time complexities are:

- $f(n) \sim O(f(n))$, that is, $f(n)$ is dominated by its own time.
- $C * O(f(n)) = O(f(n))$, that is, constants are absorbed in O-notation.

- $O(f(n)) + O(f(n)) = O(f(n))$
- $O(O(f(n))) = O(f(n))$
- $O(f(n)) * O(g(n)) = O(f(n) * g(n))$
- $O(f(n) * g(n)) = f(n) * O(g(n))$

EXAMPLE 1.9   Show that $n \log n \in \Theta(\log(n!))$.

We have, $\log(n!) = \log(1 \times 2 \times \dots \times n)$

$$= \log(1) + \log(2) + \dots + \log(n)$$

$$\leq \log(n) + \log(n) + \dots + \log(n)$$

$$= n \log n$$

So, $n \log n \in \Omega(\log(n!))$

Similarly,

$$\log(n!) \geq \log(n/2) + \log(n/2 + 1) + \dots + \log(n)$$

Therefore, $\log(n!) \geq (n/2) \dfrac{1}{2} \log(n/2)$

$$= (n/2) \dfrac{1}{2} \log(n) - (n/2) \dfrac{1}{2} \log(2)$$

That is, $\log(n!) \geq n \log(n)/4, \ n > 10$

So, $n \log(n) \in O(\log(n!))$

Hence, $n \log n \in \Theta(\log(n!))$

EXAMPLE 1.10   Show that if $f \in O(g)$ and $g \in O(h)$, then $f \in O(h)$.

From the definition, there exists N_1, N_2, K_1, K_2 such that

$$f(n) \leq K_1 g(n), \ n > N_1 \quad \text{and} \quad g(n) \leq K_2 h(n), \ n > N_2$$

Therefore, $f(n) \leq K_1 K_2 h(n), \ n > \max(N_1, N_2)$

With $K_1 K_2 = K \quad \text{and} \quad N_3 = \max(N_1, N_2)$, we have

$$f(n) \leq K h(n), \ n > N_3$$

Thus, $f \in O(h)$

1.2   SOLUTION OF SOME COMMON RECURRENCE RELATIONS

(i) Let the form of the recurrence be:

$$t_N = t_{N-1} + N, \ N \geq 2, \ t_1 = 1$$

$$t_N = t_{N-1} + N$$

$$= t_{N-2} + (N - 1) + N$$

$$= t_{N-3} + (N - 2) + (N - 1) + N$$

$$= t_1 + 2 + 3 + \cdots + N$$
$$= 1 + 2 + 3 + \cdots + N$$
$$\therefore \ t_N = O(N^2)$$

Let N be of the form 2^K for some positive integer K in the examples (ii), (iii) and (iv) below.

(ii) Let the form of the recurrence be:

$$t_N = t_{N/2} + 1, \ N \geq 2, \ t_1 = 1$$
$$t_N = t_{N/2} + 1$$
$$= t_{N/4} + 1 + 1$$

$$\cdots$$

$$= t_1 + 1 + 1 + \cdots + 1$$
$$= \log N$$
$$\therefore \ t_N = O(\log N)$$

(iii) Let the form of the recurrence be:

$$t_N = t_{N/2} + N, \ N \geq 2, \ t_1 = 0.$$

Then, $t_N = O(N)$.

The derivation is similar to (ii) above.

(iv) Let the form of the recurrence be:

$$t_N = 2t_{N/2} + N, \ N \geq 2, \ t_1 = 0.$$

Then $\dfrac{t_N}{N} = \dfrac{2\,t_{N/2}}{N} + 1$, whereby

$$\frac{t_{2^K}}{2^K} = \frac{2\,t_{2^{K-1}}}{2^K} + 1$$

$$= \frac{t_{2^{K-1}}}{2^{K-1}} + 1$$

$$= \frac{t_{2^{K-2}}}{2^{K-2}} + 1 + 1$$

$$\cdots$$

$$= 1 + 1 + 1 + 1 \cdots \ (\text{to } K \text{ terms})$$
$$= K$$

Then, $\dfrac{t_N}{N} = K \implies t_N = NK \implies t_N = N \log N \implies t_N = O(N \log N)$

1.3 HOMOGENEOUS RECURRENCES

A recurrence relation is said to be a homogeneous linear recurrence relation with constant coefficients if it has the form:

$$a_0 t_n + a_1 t_{n-1} + \cdots + a_k t_{n-k} = 0$$

where a_i's are constants. An example is the recurrence: $t_n - t_{n-1} - 3t_{n-2} = 0$. We now discuss a general method for solving any such recurrence.

Let $t_n = x^n$, where x is a constant, as yet unknown. Then, we may write,

$$a_0 x^n + a_1 x^{n-1} + \cdots + a_k x^{n-k} = 0$$

The equation is satisfied if $x = 0$ (a trivial solution of no interest) or else if, $a_0 x^k + a_1 x^{k-1} + \cdots + a_k = 0$.

This is an equation of degree k in x and is called the *characteristic equation* of the recurrence.

Suppose for the time being that the k roots $r_1, r_2, \ldots, r_k$ of this characteristic equation are all distinct (they could be complex numbers). It is then easy to verify that any linear combination of r_i's, is a solution of the characteristic equation and so of the recurrence, where the k constants $c_1, c_2, \ldots, c_k$ are determined by the initial condition.

$$t_n = \sum_{i=1}^{k} c_i r_i^n$$

Theorem 1.1 Let $f(x)$ be the characteristic equation of the recurrence:

$$a_0 t_n + a_1 t_{n-1} + \cdots + a_k t_{n-k} = 0$$

where the a_i are constants. Let the roots of f, over the complex numbers, be r_i, $i = 1, \ldots, m$, and let their respective multiplicities be q_i, $i = 1, \ldots, m$. Then any solution to the recurrence

is of the form $\displaystyle\sum_{i=1}^{i=m} \left(r_i^n \sum_{j=0}^{q_i-1} c_{ij} n^j \right)$, where c_{ij} are constants to be determined from initial

conditions.

EXAMPLE 1.11 Consider the recurrence $t_n - 3t_{n-1} - 4t_{n-2} = 0$, $n \geq 2$, subject to $t_0 = 0$, $t_1 = 1$.

The characteristic equation is $x^2 - 3x - 4 = 0$ whose roots are -1 and 4. The general solution has the form:

$$t_n = c_1(-1)^n + c_2 4^n$$

The initial conditions give:

$$c_1 + c_2 = 0 \quad \text{and} \quad -c_1 + 4c_2 = 1$$

which gives

$$c_1 = -1/5, \qquad c_2 = 1/5$$

$$\therefore \qquad t_n = \frac{4^n + (-1)^{n+1}}{5}$$

EXAMPLE 1.12 Fibonacci numbers.

$$t_n = t_{n-1} + t_{n-2}, \ n \geq 2, \quad \text{subject to } t_0 = 0, \ t_1 = 1.$$

The recurrence may be written as:

$$t_n - t_{n-1} - t_{n-2} = 0$$

The characteristic equation is $x^2 - x - 1 = 0$. The roots[2] are: $\dfrac{1 + \sqrt{5}}{2}, \dfrac{1 - \sqrt{5}}{2}$

The general solution is of the form:

$$t_n = c_1 \left(\frac{1 + \sqrt{5}}{2} \right)^n + c_2 \left(\frac{1 - \sqrt{5}}{2} \right)^n$$

Initial conditions give:

$$0 = c_1 + c_2, \qquad 1 = c_1 \left(\frac{1 + \sqrt{5}}{2} \right) + c_2 \left(\frac{1 - \sqrt{5}}{2} \right)$$

The values of c_1 and c_2 are:

$$c_1 = \frac{1}{\sqrt{5}}, \quad c_2 = -\frac{1}{\sqrt{5}}$$

$$\therefore \qquad t_n = \frac{1}{\sqrt{5}} \left(\frac{1 + \sqrt{5}}{2} \right)^n - \frac{1}{\sqrt{5}} \left(\frac{1 - \sqrt{5}}{2} \right)^n$$

1.4 INHOMOGENEOUS RECURRENCES

A recurrence relation is said to be inhomogeneous, if it has the form:

$$a_0 t_n + a_1 t_{n-1} + \cdots + a_k t_{n-k} = F(n),$$

where $F(n)$ is a non-zero function of n.

As an example, the following is an inhomogeneous linear recurrence with constant coefficients:

$$t_n - 5t_{n-1} + 6t_{n-2} = 6$$

---

[2] $(1+\sqrt{5})/2 \approx 1.61803$ is known as the golden ratio or the golden mean. This number is regarded as the most pleasing ratio in the art world since ancient times and is important in many parts of mathematics.

Any sequence t_n which satisfies the recurrence is called a particular solution; any sequence which makes the left-hand side identically zero is called a homogeneous solution. Sometimes, we can guess a particular solution, but cannot easily find one which satisfies the boundary conditions.

Theorem 1.2 If we start with any particular solution t_n and add any homogeneous solution, we obtain another particular solution. Moreover, the difference between any two particular solutions is always a homogeneous solution.

The above theorem suggests the following approaches for solving inhomogeneous recurrences.

(1) Guess a particular solution t_n.
(2) Write a formula for t_n plus the general homogeneous solution with unknown constants.
(3) Use the boundary conditions to solve for the constants.

However, the above method has the disadvantage in the sense that we need to guess a particular solution. A fairly general technique for producing solutions to inhomogeneous equations with constant coefficients is to transform the inhomogeneous equation into a homogeneous equation through algebraic manipulations and then solve it employing the method used for solving homogeneous equations. This is illustrated through the next two examples.

EXAMPLE 1.13 Solve the following recurrence relation:

$$t_n = 2t_{n-1} + n$$

Rewriting, we have
$$t_n - 2t_{n-1} = n \tag{1.1}$$

Replacing n by $n + 1$, we get
$$t_{n+1} - 2t_n = n + 1$$

$$\Rightarrow \qquad 2t_{n+1} - 4t_n = 2n + 2 \tag{1.2}$$

Replacing n by $n + 2$, we get
$$t_{n+2} - 2t_{n+1} = n + 2 \tag{1.3}$$

Adding Eqs. (1.1) and (1.3), we get
$$t_{n+2} - 2t_{n+1} + t_n - 2t_{n-1} = 2n + 2 \tag{1.4}$$

Subtracting Eq. (1.2) from Eq. (1.4), we get
$$t_{n+2} - 4t_{n+1} + 5t_n - 2t_{n-1} = 0$$

The characteristic equation is
$$x^3 - 4x^2 + 5x - 2 = 0$$

or
$$x^3 - 2x^2 - 2x^2 + 4x + x - 2 = 0$$

or
$$x^2(x - 2) - 2x(x - 2) + 1(x - 2) = 0$$

or
$$(x - 1)^2 (x - 2) = 0$$

The general solution is

$$t_n = c_1 2^n + c_2 1^n + c_3 n 1^n$$

whereby
$$t_n = O(2^n)$$

EXAMPLE 1.14   Solve the following recurrence relation:

$$t_n = 2t_{n-1} + n + 2^n, \ n \geq 1, \text{ subject to } t_0 = 0.$$

Here,
$$t_n - 2t_{n-1} = n + 2^n \tag{1.5}$$

Replacing n by $n + 1$, we get

$$t_{n+1} - 2t_n = n + 1 + 2^{n+1} \tag{1.6}$$

Replacing n by $n + 2$, we get

$$t_{n+2} - 2t_{n+1} = n + 2 + 2^{n+2} \tag{1.7}$$

Replacing n by $n + 3$, we get

$$t_{n+3} - 2t_{n+2} = n + 3 + 2^{n+3} \tag{1.8}$$

Multiplying Eq. (1.5) by –2, Eq. (1.6) by 5, Eq. (1.7) by –4 and Eq. (1.8) by 1 and then adding, we get

$$t_{n+3} - 6t_{n+2} + 13t_{n+1} - 12t_n + 4t_{n-1} = 0$$

The characteristic equation is

$$x^4 - 6x^3 + 13x^2 - 12x + 4 = 0$$

or
$$x^4 - 4x^3 + 4x^2 - 2x^3 + 8x^2 - 8x + x^2 - 4x + 4 = 0$$

or
$$(x^2 - 4x + 4)(x^2 - 2x + 1) = 0$$

or
$$(x - 2)^2(x - 1)^2 = 0$$

This equation has roots 1 and 2, both of multiplicity 2. The general solution of the recurrence is of the form:

$$t_n = (c_1 + c_2 n)1^n + (c_3 + c_4 n)2^n$$

$\therefore$
$$t_n \in O(n2^n)$$

1.5   CHANGE OF VARIABLE

It is sometimes possible to solve more complicated recurrences by making a change of variable. The following three examples illustrate this.

EXAMPLE 1.15 Solve the recurrence: $T(n) = 4T(n/2) + n$, where $n \geq 1$, and is a power of 2.

Replacing n by 2^k and $T(2^k) = t_k$, we get

$$T(2^k) = 4T(2^{k-1}) + 2^k$$

or
$$t_k = 4t_{k-1} + 2^k \tag{1.9}$$

Replacing k by $k - 1$, we get

$$t_{k-1} = 4t_{k-2} + 2^{k-1} \tag{1.10}$$

Multiplying Eq. (1.10) by 2 and subtracting the result from Eq. (1.9), we get

$$t_k - 2t_{k-1} = 4t_{k-1} - 8t_{k-2} \quad \text{or} \quad t_k - 6t_{k-1} + 8t_{k-2} = 0$$

Putting $t_k = x^k$, we get

$$x^k - 6x^{k-1} + 8x^{k-2} = 0$$

or
$$x^2 - 6x + 8 = 0$$

or
$$(x - 2)(x - 4) = 0$$

$\therefore$
$$t_k = c_1 2^k + c_2 4^k$$

Putting back n, we get

$$T(n) = c_1 n + c_2 n^2$$

$\therefore$
$$T(n) \in O(n^2)$$

EXAMPLE 1.16 Solve the following recurrence relation

$$T(n) = 4T(n/2) + n^2$$

where $n > 1$ and is a power of 2.

Put $n = 2^k$ and $T(2^k) = t_k$ to get

$$t_k = 4t_{k-1} + 2^{2k} \tag{1.11}$$

and replacing k by $k - 1$, we get $t_{k-1} = 4t_{k-2} + 2^{2(k-1)}$ $\qquad$ (1.12)

Multiplying Eq. (1.12) by 4 and subtracting the result from the Eq. (1.11), we get

$$t_k - 4t_{k-1} = 4t_{k-1} - 16t_{k-2}$$

or
$$t_k - 8t_{k-1} + 16t_{k-2} = 0$$

Putting $t_k = x^k$, we get

$$x^k - 8x^{k-1} + 16x^{k-2} = 0$$

Thus, the characteristic equation is

$$x^2 - 8x + 16 = 0 \quad \text{or} \quad (x - 4)^2 = 0$$

$\therefore$
$$t_k = (c_1 + c_2 k)4^k$$

Putting back n, we get

$$T(n) = c_1 n^2 + c_2 n^2 \log n$$

$\therefore$
$$T(n) \in O(n^2 \log n)$$

EXAMPLE 1.17 Solve the recurrence: $T(n) = 7T(n/2) + 3n^2$, where n is a power of 2 and is greater than 1.

Let us put $n = 2^k$ and $T(2^k) = t_k$, to get

$$t_k = 7t_{k-1} + 3 \times 2^{2k} \qquad (1.13)$$

Putting $k = k - 1$ in Eq. (1.13), we get

$$t_{k-1} = 7t_{k-2} + 3 \times 2^{2(k-1)} \qquad (1.14)$$

Multiplying Eq. (1.14) by 4 and subtracting the result from Eq. (1.13), we get

$$t_k - 4t_{k-1} = 7t_{k-1} - 28t_{k-2}$$

or
$$t_k - 11t_{k-1} + 28t_{k-2} = 0$$

Putting $t_k = x^k$ in the above equation, we get $x^k - 11x^{k-1} + 28x^{k-2} = 0$. Thus, the characteristic equation is:

$$x^2 - 11x + 28 = 0$$

or
$$(x - 4)(x - 7) = 0$$

Hence,
$$t_k = c_1 4^k + c_2 7^k = c_1 n^2 + c_2 7^{\log_2 n}$$

$\therefore$
$$T(n) = c_1 n^2 + c_2 7^{\log_2 n}$$

1.6 GENERATING FUNCTIONS

Generating functions transform a problem from one conceptual domain to another, in the hope that the problem will be easier to solve in the new domain. We demonstrate how generating functions can be used to solve some simple recurrence relations.

EXAMPLE 1.18 Suppose we have a recurrence: $t_n = 2t_{n-1} + 1$, $n \geq 1$ and $t_0 = 1$.

Let
$$A(z) = \sum_{n=0}^{\infty} t_n z^n.$$

From the given recurrence this sum can be written as

$$A(z) = t_0 z^0 + \sum_{n=1}^{\infty} t_n z^n = 1 + \sum_{n=1}^{\infty} t_n z^n$$

$$= 1 + \sum_{n=1}^{\infty} (2t_{n-1} + 1) z^n$$

$$= 1 + 2zA(z) + \sum_{n=1}^{\infty} z^n$$

$$= 1 + 2zA(z) + \left(\frac{1}{1 - z} - 1 \right)$$

Simple algebraic manipulation yields

$$A(z) = \frac{1}{(1 - z)(1 - 2z)}$$

$$= \frac{2}{1 - 2z} - \frac{1}{1 - z} \quad \text{(breaking into partial fractions)}$$

The corresponding sequence is given by $t_n = 2^{n+1} - 1$, since $1/(1 - 2z)$ generates the sequence 1, 2, 2^2, ... and $1/(1 - z)$ generates the sequence 1, 1, 1, ...

Note that initially, we had a problem to be solved for t_n and we converted it into a simpler problem to be solved for A. In tackling a problem, we can choose a domain that makes the problem easier to solve.

EXAMPLE 1.19   Consider the recurrence relation

$$t_n - 5t_{n-1} + 6t_{n-2} = 2^n + n, \, n \geq 2 \text{ with } t_0 = 1 \text{ and } t_1 = 1.$$

Let $A(z) = \sum_{n=0}^{\infty} t_n z^n$. Since $\sum_{n=2}^{\infty} t_n z^n - 5 \sum_{n=2}^{\infty} t_{n-1} z^n + 6 \sum_{n=2}^{\infty} t_{n-2} z^n = \sum_{n=2}^{\infty} 2^n z^n + \sum_{n=2}^{\infty} nz^n$,

we may write

$$A(z) - t_0 - t_1 z - 5z[A(z) - t_0] + 6z^2 A(z) = \frac{4z^2}{1 - 2z} + z \left[\frac{1}{(1 - z)^2} - 1 \right]$$

Solving the above equation for $A(z)$, we get

$$A(z) = \frac{1 - 8z + 27z^2 - 35z^3 + 14z^4}{(1 - z)^2 (1 - 2z)^2 (1 - 3z)}$$

Breaking into partial fractions, we get

$$A(z) = \frac{5}{4(1 - z)} + \frac{1}{2(1 - z)^2} - \frac{3}{1 - 2z} - \frac{2}{(1 - 2z)^2} + \frac{17}{4(1 - 3z)}$$

The corresponding sequence is given by

$$t_n = \frac{5}{4} + \frac{1}{2}(n+1) - 3 \times 2^n - 2(n+1) \times 2^n + \frac{17}{4} \times 3^n$$

$$= \frac{7}{4} + \frac{n}{2} - n \times 2^{n+1} - 5 \times 2^n + \frac{17}{4} \times 3^n$$

since $1/(1-z)$ generates the sequence 1, 1, 1, ...

$1/(1-z)^2$ generates the sequence 1, 2, 3, ...

$1/(1-2z)$ generates the sequence 1, 2, 2^2, ...

$1/(1-2z)^2$ generates the sequence 1, 2 × 2, 3 × 2^2, ...

$1/(1-3z)$ generates the sequence 1, 3, 3^2, ...

EXAMPLE 1.20 Solve the following recurrence using the generating function

$$t_n = t_{n-1} + t_{n-2}, \; n \geq 2, \text{ subject to } t_0 = 0, \; t_1 = 1.$$

Let
$$A(z) = \sum_{n=0}^{\infty} t_n z^n$$

Now,
$$t_n z^n = t_{n-1} z^n + t_{n-2} z^n$$

Therefore,
$$\sum_{n=2}^{\infty} t_n z^n = \sum_{n=2}^{\infty} t_{n-1} z^n + \sum_{n=2}^{\infty} t_{n-2} z^n$$

or
$$\sum_{n=2}^{\infty} t_n z^n = z \sum_{n=2}^{\infty} t_{n-1} z^{n-1} + z^2 \sum_{n=2}^{\infty} t_{n-2} z^{n-2}$$

or
$$\sum_{n=2}^{\infty} t_n z^n = z \sum_{n=1}^{\infty} t_n z^n + z^2 \sum_{n=0}^{\infty} t_n z^n$$

whereby,
$$A(z) - t_0 - t_1 z = z(A(z) - t_0) + z^2 A(z)$$

or
$$A(z) - z = zA(z) + z^2 A(z)$$

or
$$A(z)(1 - z - z^2) = z$$

or
$$A(z) = \frac{z}{1 - z - z^2}$$

$$= \frac{z}{\left(1 - \dfrac{1 - \sqrt{5}}{2}z\right)\left(1 - \dfrac{1 + \sqrt{5}}{2}z\right)}$$

$$= \frac{1}{\sqrt{5}}\left\{\frac{1}{1 - \dfrac{1 + \sqrt{5}}{2}z} - \frac{1}{1 - \dfrac{1 - \sqrt{5}}{2}z}\right\}$$

The corresponding sequence is given by

$$t_n = \frac{1}{\sqrt{5}}\left[\left(\frac{1 + \sqrt{5}}{2}\right)^n - \left(\frac{1 - \sqrt{5}}{2}\right)^n\right]$$

since $1/(1 - cz)$ generates the sequence $1, c, c^2, \ldots$

1.7 A FAMOUS PROBLEM

We now look at the complexity of the Tower of Hanoi[3] problem. The problem is to move n discs from the first peg A (stacked in decreasing size) to the third peg C. The middle peg B may be used to hold discs during the transfer. The discs are to be moved one at a time under the condition that at any time, a disc of larger size cannot rest on a disc of smaller size on any of the pegs. For simplicity, let us consider that we have 3 discs on peg A initially as shown in Figure 1.1.

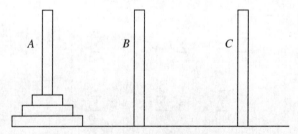

FIGURE 1.1   Tower of Hanoi.

The following sequence of moves ($A \rightarrow C$ means that the topmost disc from peg A is moved to peg C) will solve this instance of the Tower of Hanoi problem.

$$A \rightarrow C, A \rightarrow B, C \rightarrow B, A \rightarrow C, B \rightarrow A, B \rightarrow C, A \rightarrow C$$

---

[3] The legend says that the world will come to an end when 64 discs are moved from peg A to peg C. Refer Édouard Lucas, *Récréations Mathématiques*, Vol. 3, pp. 55–59, Albert Blanchard, Paris, 1960.

What about larger size problems? The problem admits a nice recursive solution. To move n discs from A to C, one can move $n - 1$ discs from A to B, the remaining disc from A to C and then move the $n - 1$ discs from B to C. The time complexity may be expressed in the form of the following recurrence relation:

$$T(n) = 2T(n - 1) + 1 \text{ with } T(1) = 1 \text{ and } T(2) = 3.$$

The solution of the above recurrence relation is $T(n) = A * 2^n + B$. Putting the boundary conditions, we get $T(n) = 2^n - 1$. For $n = 64$, $2^n - 1 \approx 1.8 \times 10^{19}$, a large number indeed.

1.8   SOME EXAMPLES OF AVERAGE COMPLEXITY CALCULATION

Finding the average time complexity of an algorithm is, in general, difficult. However, for some problems, this is not so. In this section, we take two simple examples to demonstrate this. The first problem is about deciding whether a given binary string is a *palindrome* or not. A string is a palindrome when it reads the same from the left and the right ends. For example, "110010011" is a palindrome. We give a pseudocode for an algorithm to decide whether a given binary string is a palindrome or not.

```
Procedure Palindrome (X)
   Array X(n) /* X is a binary string of length n */
   Leftend = 1;
   Rightend = n;
   While(Leftend < Rightend and(X(Leftend)= X(Rightend)) Do
      {
      Leftend = Leftend + 1;
      Rightend = Rightend - 1;
      }
Endwhile
If (Leftend ≥ Rightend) Then
      Print("Yes");
   Else
      Print("No");
End Palindrome
```

The loop in the above algorithm is executed at most $n/2$ times when X is a palindrome. The computation within the loop body takes constant time. The condition testing in the while loop $X(Leftend)= X(Rightend)$ fails when the first and the last characters of X are different; the loop body is not executed at all. So the best case performance of the algorithm is $O(1)$ and the worst case time complexity is $\Theta(n)$. To find the average running time, we have to consider all possible binary strings of length n. Let us first consider that n is even. Only 2^{n-1} binary strings out of 2^n possibilities differ in the first and the last characters leading to zero repetition of the while loop. 2^{n-2} binary strings differ in the second and the last but one position leading to execution of the while loop only once. Proceeding this way, we find that only $2^{n/2}$ strings differ in the $n/2$ and $1 + n/2$ positions giving rise to $n/2 - 1$ repetitions of the while loop. So the average number of repetitions of the while loop for even length strings becomes after some manipulations

$$\frac{0*2^{n-1} + 1*2^{n-2} + 2*2^{n-3} + \cdots + (n/2-1)*2^{n/2}}{2^n} + \frac{n}{2}*2^{n/2} = 1 - \frac{1}{2^{n/2}}$$

When the string X is of odd length, the average number of repetitions of the while loop may be found as $1 - 1/2^{(n-1)/2}$. Hence, we may write that the average execution time of the algorithm is $\Theta(1)$, as for large values of n, the second term becomes almost zero.

The second problem we now discuss is the selection sorting of n distinct numbers in ascending order. In selection sort, we scan through the array of elements and find the least element and place it in the first position. We then find the next minimum element and place it in the second position. At the ith iteration, the algorithm finds the ith smallest element out of the remaining $n - i + 1$ elements and places it in the ith position. In the worst case, the algorithm will make $(n - 1) + (n - 2) + \cdots + 1$ comparisons, which is quadratic. We give a pseudocode for this problem here.

```
Procedure S_Sort(X)
   Array X(n)  /* X contains n numbers */
     For i = 1 to n-1 Do
        t = X(i);
        k = i;
        For j = i + 1 to n Do
          If (X(j) < t) Then
          t = X(j);
          k = j;
       Endif
     Endfor
     X(k)=X(i);
     X(i)= t;
     Endfor
   End S_Sort
```

To find the average case complexity of the algorithm, we assume that every possible instance of n numbers has the same probability of occurrence. The total number of possible instances of n distinct numbers is $n!$. At each iteration i, the algorithm searches for the minimum from $n - i + 1$ elements. Let $M(l)$ denote the number of moves needed to select the minimum among l elements. Expect $M(l)$ be the expected value of $M(l)$. The time function $T(n)$ may

be written as $T(n) = \sum_{i=1}^{i=n-1} \text{Expect}(M(n-i+1))$ where expectations are taken over $n!$ and

$(n - i + 1)!$, $i = 1, 2, \ldots, n - 1$ possible cases, respectively. For the sake of convenience, we define $m = n - i + 1$. So the elements i through n may be referred as i through m. So the possible cases for the ith iteration of the outer loop is $m!$. Out of $m!$ cases, in only $(m - 1)!$ cases the minimum is located at the last position. The number of times the instruction is executed for all these instances is $\alpha(m - 1) + (m - 1)!$, where $\alpha(m)$ is the total number of times the instruction is executed for all $m!$ possible instances of m elements, because the minimum is effectively found in the last position. For the $(m - 1)(m - 1)!$ remaining cases, the minimum is selected while searching the first $m - 1$ elements and the corresponding number of times is $(m - 1) * \alpha(m - 1)$. The total number of times of instruction execution for all possible cases can be expressed as $\alpha(m) = m * \alpha(m - 1) + (m - 1)!$.

Bringing a new variable $\beta(m) = \dfrac{\alpha(m)}{m!}$, we may write $\beta(m) = 0$ if $m \leq 1$, otherwise $\beta(m) = \beta(m - 1) + 1/m$. The solution for this recurrence relation may be written as

$$\beta(m) = \sum_{p=2}^{p=m} \frac{1}{p} = H_m - 1, \text{ where } H_m \text{ is the } m^{th} \text{ harmonic number.}$$

The average number of times the instruction is executed, therefore, is:

$$T(n) = \sum_{i=1}^{i=n-1} (H_{n-i+1} - 1) = \sum_{i=2}^{i=n} (H_i - 1) = \sum_{i=2}^{i=n} \sum_{j=2}^{i} \frac{1}{j}$$

$$= \left(\frac{1}{2}\right) + \left(\frac{1}{2} + \frac{1}{3}\right) + \cdots + \left(\frac{1}{2} + \frac{1}{3} + \cdots + \frac{1}{n}\right)$$

$$= (n + 1) \sum_{i=2}^{i=n} \frac{1}{i} - \sum_{i=2}^{i=n} 1 = (n + 1)(H_n - 1) - n + 1$$

$$= (n + 1) H_n - 2n = O(n \log n)$$

1.9 AMORTIZATION

The worst-case time complexity of an algorithm may not be attractive, but on closer look, one may realize that many a times the worst situation occurs less frequently. Many good instances also occur along with the worst instances. The good instances may outweigh the bad instances. The cost of the bad instances is amortized over the good instances. So a reexamination of the behaviour of the algorithm is needed. This can be done with *credit analysis*.

In credit analysis, we do not keep track of time only but also of a *potential*, defined as one wishs it to be. The amortized time is the sum of the actual time and the potential. How to define the potential? We should define the potential so that the total amortized time increases slowly with the problem size; the total potential should also be bounded. If one can find the potential successfully, the instances that take a lot of computation time will also reduce the potential so that the amortized time will be reasonably small. The good instances will take small amounts of time but increase the potential by small amounts. The amortized time for the good instances will still be small, although not as small as the original time. If the good instances can build up enough potential to cover the bad instances, the long-term performance of the algorithm would be good. This type of analysis may not be suitable for every algorithm. This may be applied to those algorithms where there is a favourable balance between the occurrences of good and bad instances.

In the potential method, we start with a data structure (say DS_0) and a potential function V that maps the data structure to a real number. Let n operations be successively applied on DS_0. Operation i, $1 \leq i \leq n$ with actual cost t_i transforms DS_{i-1} to DS_i. The amortized cost ac_i of the ith operation with respect to the potential function V is defined as $ac_i = t_i + V(DS_i)$

$- V(DS_{i-1})$ and the total amortized cost may be written as $\sum_{i=1}^{i=n} ac_i = \sum_{i=1}^{i=n} t_i + V(DS_n) - V(DS_0)$.

Let us illustrate this method with a very simple example. We consider the example of stack with three operations: PUSH, POP, and MULTIPOP (multiple objects are removed from the stack). V is defined as the number of objects in the stack. Initially, the stack is empty and $V(DS_0) = 0$, and $V(DS_i) \geq 0$. If the ith operation on the stack containing k objects is a PUSH operation, then $V(DS_i) - V(DS_{i-1}) = (k + 1) - k = 1$. Amortized cost of this PUSH operation is $ac_i = t_i + V(DS_i) - V(DS_{i-1}) = 1 + 1 = 2$. Suppose that the ith operation on the stack is MULTIPOP with m objects to be removed from the stack. The number of objects actually removed is the minimum of m and the number of objects actually present in the stack (say l). The actual cost of this operation is l and the potential difference is $-l$. The amortized cost of MULTIPOP operation is $ac_i = l - l = 0$. Proceeding in a similar way, one can show that the amortized cost of an ordinary POP operation is 0.

The amortized cost of each of the three operations is $O(1)$, and, thus, the total amortized cost of a sequence of n operations is $O(n)$. The total amortized cost of n operations is an upper bound on the total actual cost.

1.10 BASIC DATA STRUCTURES

In a programming language, the data type of a variable is the set of values that the variable may assume. For example, a variable of type character can assume values from the set, $\{x \mid x$ is an alphabetic character, any digit 0 through 9, and any of the permitted special symbols$\}$. A string type is constructed out of character type. An abstract data type (ADT) is a mathematical model, together with various operations defined on the model. To implement an algorithm in a given programming language, we have to find some way of representing the ADTs in terms of the data types and operators supported by the programming language. Data structures that are collection of variables of several data types aggregated in various ways, are used to represent the mathematical model underlying an ADT.

1.10.1 Array

The simplest data structure is an array. It is a collection of data storage cells of a particular type and may be accessed randomly through the use of a finite index set. Figure 1.2 shows a 1-dimensional character array and a 2-dimensional integer array.

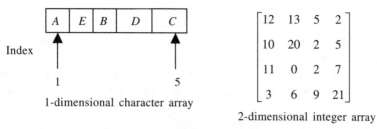

Index

1   5

1-dimensional character array

2-dimensional integer array

FIGURE 1.2   Array.

1.10.2   Linked List

The linked list consists of a series of cells (records) that are not necessarily adjacent in the memory. Each cell (record) contains the element and a pointer to a cell (record) containing its successor. A record is a group of fields. The common functions defined on a list include: deletion of a record, addition of a record, searching for a record, determining the length of the list, etc. There are many variations of linked lists, such as, two-way linked lists, circular lists, multi-lists, etc. Figure 1.3 shows one-way linked list.

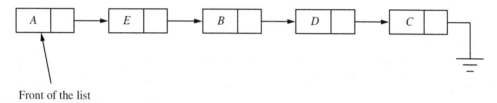

Front of the list

FIGURE 1.3   Linked list.

1.10.3   Stack

A stack is a list with the restriction that insertions and deletions can be performed at one end of the list. The fundamental operations on a stack are PUSH and POP. PUSH inserts an element at the designated end and POP deletes an element from the same end. Applying POP on an empty stack and applying PUSH to a full stack (implementation dependent) leads to an error situation. Stack is also called LIFO (last in first out list). A stack can be implemented using a linked list or an array. Figure 1.4 shows the effect of push and pop operations on a stack.

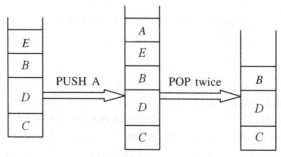

FIGURE 1.4   Stack.

1.10.4   Queue

Like stacks, queues are lists but have insertion done at one end and deletion at the other end. Queues follow the 'first in first out' (FIFO) discipline. The basic operations on a queue are 'enque' which inserts an element at the end of the list (the rear end) and 'dequeue' which deletes the element at the start of the list (the front of the queue). Figure 1.5(a) schematically shows a queue.

After insertion of element *A*, the queue becomes as shown in Figure 1.5(b) and after deletion of element *E*, it becomes as shown in Figure 1.5(c).

Queues may also be implemented using arrays. Dequeing from an empty queue leads to error. So also, enqueing in a full queue (implementation limitation) leads to implementation error.

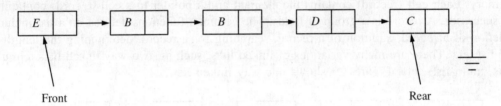

FIGURE 1.5(a)   A queue.

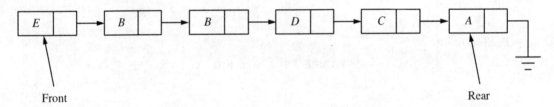

FIGURE 1.5(b)   Insertion of an element.

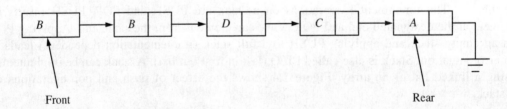

FIGURE 1.5(c)   Deletion of an element.

1.10.5   Set

A set is a collection of non-repetitive elements where each element of a set is either a set or atomic. The atoms are usually integers, characters, strings, etc. and all elements in a set are usually of the same type. The most common operations on sets are union, intersection, difference, membership checking, insertion of a new element, deletion of an element, finding the extremal element, checking for equality of two sets, etc.

Sets can be implemented using linked lists, bit vectors, various kinds of trees, such as binary search trees, tries and balanced trees. We show how to represent disjoint sets by using trees. Suppose, we have two sets $S_1 = \{1, 3, 5, 9\}$ and $S_2 = \{6, 7, 8\}$. Each set has a representative that is a member of the set. For example, in Figure 1.6(a), 1 is a representative of S_1 and 6 is a representative of S_2.

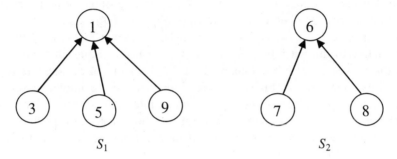

FIGURE 1.6(a) Disjoint sets.

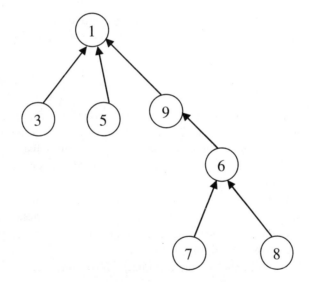

FIGURE 1.6(b) Set union.

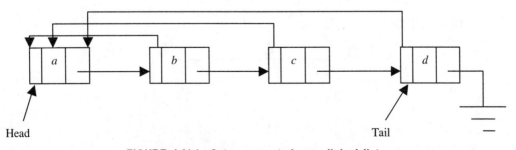

FIGURE 1.6(c) Set represented as a linked list.

Two important operations on sets are FIND and UNION. FIND(8) will give us 6 (the representative). The UNION of S_1 and S_2 will give us a set as represented in Figure 1.6(b).

A simple way to implement a disjoint-set structure is to represent each set by a linked list. The first object in each linked list serves as the set's representative. Each object in the linked list contains a set member, a pointer to the node containing the next member of the set, and a pointer back to the representative. We have two other pointers: one to the head of the list (first object) another to the tail (last object) of the list. Thus, the linked list representation for S, where $S = \{a, b, c, d\}$ will be as shown in Figure 1.6(c).

An alternative to the list representation is the bit-vector representation of sets. Let us assume that the universal set has n linearly ordered members. A subset S is represented as a vector of n bits, where the ith bit is 1 if the ith element of the universal set is a member of S. The bit-vector representation has the advantage that one can determine whether the ith element of the universal set is a member of a set in time independent of the size of the set. The basic operations on sets such as union and intersection can be carried out through the bit operations OR, AND.

A set can also be represented by an array A such that $A(i) = 1$ if and only if the ith member of the universal set is in S. With an array representation, it is easy to determine whether an element is a member of a set. The disadvantage is that union and intersection require time proportional to n rather than the sizes of the sets involved. The space required to store S is proportional to n.

1.10.6 Graph

A graph $G = (V, E)$ is a set of vertices V and a set of edges E, where $E \subseteq V \times V$. A graph may be represented in two ways: (i) adjacency list (ii) adjacency matrix. Two vertices are adjacent if there is an edge between them. In the case of adjacency list, we maintain, as many lists as there are vertices in the graph. For each vertex of the graph, we maintain a list containing the vertices that are adjacent to the vertex.

For the graph in Figure 1.7(a), the adjacency lists are shown in Figure 1.7(b).

The alternative representation uses a matrix. The $(i, j)^{th}$ element of the matrix is 1 if there is an edge from vertex i to vertex j, and is 0 otherwise. For the graph in Figure 1.7(a), the adjacency matrix is shown in Figure 1.7(c).

For the undirected graph, the adjacency matrix is symmetric.

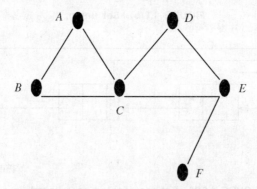

FIGURE 1.7(a) A sample graph.

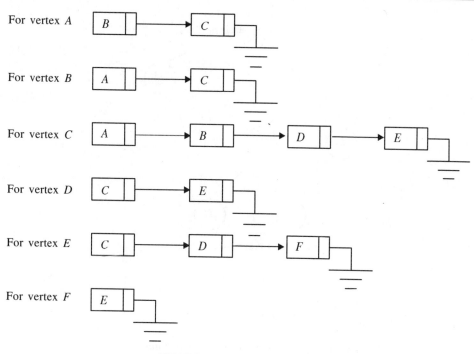

FIGURE 1.7(b) Adjacency lists.

	A	B	C	D	E	F
A	0	1	1	0	0	0
B	1	0	1	0	0	0
C	1	1	0	1	1	0
D	0	0	1	0	1	0
E	0	0	1	1	0	1
F	0	0	0	0	1	0

FIGURE 1.7(c) Adjacency matrix.

1.10.7 Tree

A tree is a connected graph without cycle. There are many alternative definitions of a tree. For example, a tree may be defined as a graph where there is exactly one path between any pair of vertices. We are more interested in rooted binary trees. A rooted binary tree has a distinguished vertex called the root (A in Figure 1.8(b)) of the tree and if the tree is also binary, then each vertex has at most two children: the left child and the right child. Leaf

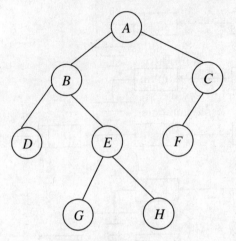

FIGURE 1.8(a)   Binary tree.

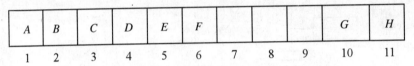

FIGURE 1.8(b)   Array representation of binary tree.

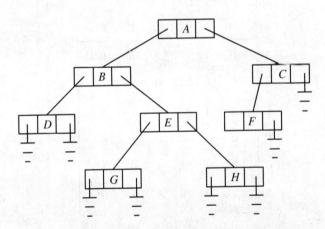

FIGURE 1.8(c)   Linked list representation of binary tree.

vertices have no children. The root vertex has no parent; all other vertices have unique parents. A binary tree may be represented using an array or a linked list.

The binary tree may be represented in the form of an array as shown in Figure 1.8(b).

The left-child of vertex (i) is stored in the location $2i$, if it exists and the right child is stored in the location $2i + 1$, if it exists. The parent of vertex i is stored in location $\lfloor i/2 \rfloor$. The above tree may be represented in the form of a linked list as shown in Figure 1.8(c).

1.10.8 Priority Queue (Heap)

A priority queue is a data structure for maintaining a set S of elements, each with an associated value called a *key*. A priority queue supports the operations: insertion of an element into the set S, searching maximum (minimum) element in the set S, and deletion of maximum (minimum) element from the set S. Priority queues are used in many applications such as job scheduling on a shared computer, event-driven simulation, etc. The name 'priority

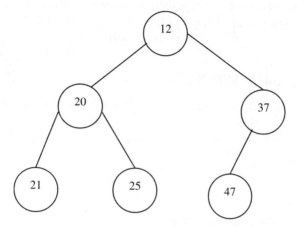

FIGURE 1.9(a) Heap.

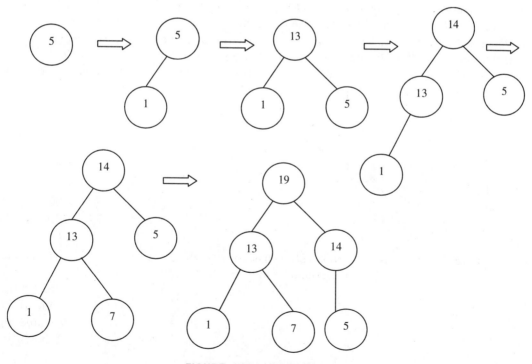

FIGURE 1.9(b) Heap creation.

queue' comes from the fact that the keys determine the 'priority' used to pick elements to be removed from the set S. We can use a heap to implement a priority queue.

A max (min) heap is a complete binary tree with the property that the key value at each node is at least as large (small) as the values at its children. A binary tree with height h is called *complete* if the levels 0, 1, 2, ..., $h - 1$ have the maximum number of nodes possible and in level h all the nodes are towards left. Figure 1.9(a) shows a min-heap.

The important operations involving heaps are creation of heap, deletion from a heap and addition to a heap. Creation of a heap with n elements requires $O(n)$ time. Addition and deletion operations each requires $O(\log n)$ time. We illustrate in Figure 1.9(b) how a max-heap is created for the elements {5, 1, 13, 14, 7, 19}.

1.11 SOME MORE DATA STRUCTURES

We introduce a few advance data structures in this section. They are balanced tree, red-black tree, splay tree, suffix tree, B-tree, binomial heap, and Fibonacci heap. Some of these data structures allow faster and efficient operation and information storage, others are of theoretical importance.

1.11.1 Balanced Trees

Balanced trees can be constructed in different ways such as left and right sub-trees of any node in the tree should be of the same height or every node except the leaves must have left and right sub-trees of the same height, etc. Adelson-Velskii and Landis introduced one such tree called AVL tree. In an AVL tree, the difference in the heights of the left and right sub-trees could be at most 1. The condition imposed for balancing a tree should be easy to maintain, otherwise the advantage of using such a tree would be lost. An example AVL tree is shown in Figure 1.10. The difference in the heights of the left and the right sub-trees for

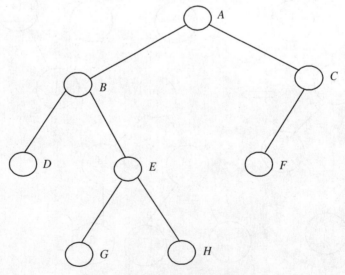

FIGURE 1.10 AVL Tree.

each node in the tree is at most 1. All nodes in the tree have this property regarding its sub-trees. An AVL tree containing n nodes has height at most 1.44 log n roughly.

If a new node is inserted into an AVL tree, the inserted node may disturb the balance of the tree. We have to carry out modification of the tree through rotations to maintain the balance in the tree. This imbalance can always be fixed by either a single or a double rotation. Deletion in AVL trees is more complex than insertion because deletion may require more than one rebalancing step unlike insertion operation. Most of the usual operations can be done in $O(\log n)$ time for an AVL tree containing n nodes.

1.11.2 Red-Black Trees

Red-Black trees are augmented binary trees. The augmentation is done by adding fictitious nodes at the vertices having null links. Figure 1.11 shows an example of red-black tree. There are 7 null links in this tree. These null links are replaced by links to 9 square boxes. These are the fictitious nodes added to the tree. Every vertex (both original and fictitious) are now coloured either *red* or *black.* Some restrictions are put on the way these nodes are coloured. These are: root and every leaf in the augmented tree are coloured black, both the children of a red coloured node are black coloured, every path from the root to a leaf contains the same number of black nodes. In the figure, every path from the root to any leaf has 3 black nodes. We define black-height of a node (x) as the number of black nodes (excluding x) on any path originating at x and terminating at any descendant leaf. So the *black height* of root of the tree in the figure is 2. A red-black tree with n nodes (excluding the fictitious nodes) has height $2\log(n + 1)$ at most.

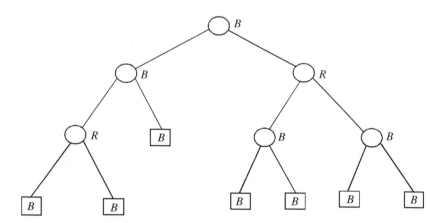

FIGURE 1.11 Red-Black tree.

If a new node is inserted into or deleted from a red-black tree, some adjustments may be needed to maintain the red-black property of the tree. The worst-case cost of these adjustments is $\Theta(\log n)$. So, insertion and deletion operations in a red-black tree can be done in $\Theta(\log n)$ worst-case time.

1.11.3 Splay Trees

Splay trees are special type of binary search trees used for dictionary problems. We have to maintain a set of elements in the tree under a sequence of dictionary operations. Every node in the tree contains a key, along with other necessary information. The keys are totally ordered. The usual operations on a splay tree are accessing an element, deletion of an element, or insertion of a new element. The tree has a restructuring rule that modifies the tree after each operation. After a node is accessed, it is moved to the root and the tree is reorganized. This reorganization of the tree is known as *splaying*. Balancing the height of the tree is not important here. Amortized time of each operation is $O(\log n)$ for a splay tree with n nodes. Access and update operations in splay trees are simple. Splay trees perform well on insertion and deletion operations. However, the main disadvantage is that rotations are required for every access operation.

When a node containing an element (x) is accessed, it is moved to the root through a sequence of rotations. There are three situations to consider as shown in Figures 1.12(a), (b), and (c), where triangles (A, B, C, D) represent sub-trees and circles represent nodes. Figure 1.12(a) shows the reorganized tree after x is accessed. Here parent of x was the root of the tree. Figure 1.12(b) shows the reorganized tree after x is accessed when parent of x was not the root of the tree, x and its parent were each left child of their parents. Finally, Figure 1.12(c) shows the reorganized tree after x is accessed where parent of x was not the root of the tree, x was a left child and parent of x was a right child.

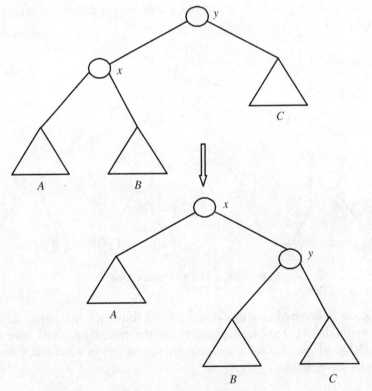

FIGURE 1.12(a)   Splay tree.

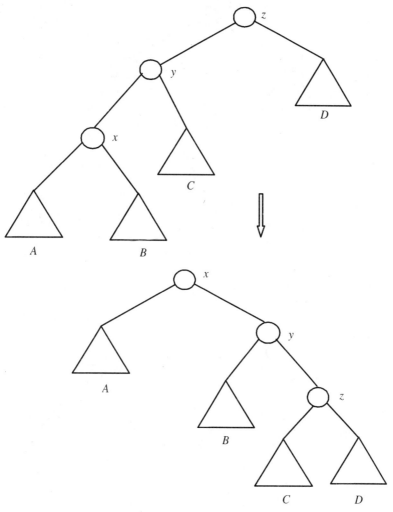

FIGURE 1.12(b)　Splay tree.

1.11.4　Suffix Trees

Suffix trees allow one to preprocess a text in such a way that for any pattern of length n, one can answer whether or not it occurs in the text, using only $O(n)$ time, regardless of how long the text is. Their real utility is their linear time solutions to many string matching problems more complex than exact matching. The suffix tree for a text $t = t_1 t_2 \ldots t_m$ is a rooted labelled tree with m leaves (numbered 1 through m) satisfying the following conditions:

(i) Each edge is labelled with a substring of the text.
(ii) Each internal node (except possibly the root) has at least two children.
(iii) Any two edges out of the same node start with a different letter.
(iv) Every suffix of text t is spelt out on a path from the root to some leaf.

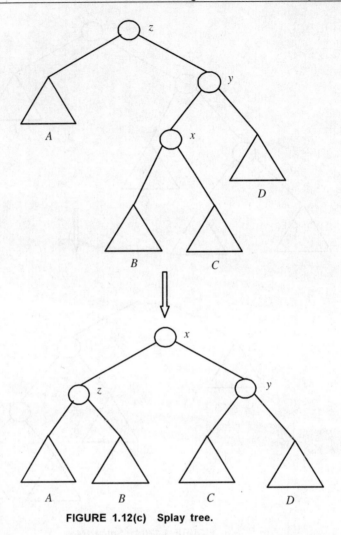

FIGURE 1.12(c)   Splay tree.

Consider the string *atcatg*. The suffixes are *g*, *tg*, *atg*, *catg*, *tcatg*, and *atcatg*. The corresponding suffix tree is shown in Figure 1.13. The end of suffixes is indicated by a special symbol $ in the tree.

There are many applications of suffix trees. Some of these are: the longest common substring problem, longest prefix repeat problem, lowest common ancestor, approximate string matching, etc. We will discuss some of them in Chapter 14.

1.11.5   B-Trees

A B-tree of order *b* (also known as the branching factor) contains internal nodes having number of children between *b* and *b*/2. The root of a B-tree can be a leaf or has 2 to *b* children. All leaves of a B-tree lie on the same level. When we insert a new key *K* to a

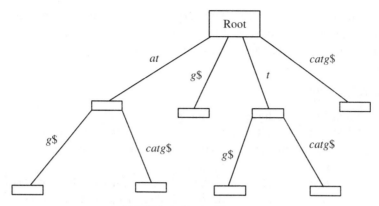

FIGURE 1.13 Suffix tree.

B-tree node, and the node overflows, we split the node. The median key is put in the parent node; two new nodes created accommodate the lower and the upper halves of the keys in increasing sorted order. What is the maximum number of keys in a B-tree *BT* containing *n* keys and *p* nodes? $p = n/(b - 1)$, since each node of *BT* contains $b - 1$ keys. The total number of nodes *p* can be written as $p = (b^{l+1} - 1)/(b - 1)$, assuming there are *l* levels in the B-tree. Combining these two expressions, we get $l = \log_b(n + 1) - 1$. A full B-tree of order 64 can store about 16 million records in just four levels 0, 1, 2, 3. It requires accessing 4 nodes to find a given key. The use of trees with high branching factors is more useful when we store the tree nodes on external storage devices. Figure 1.14 shows one example of B-tree with branching factor 4. The root contains three integers, which are used to select one child of the root during searching for a key. Suppose, we are looking for information associated with the key 69. We reach the third child of the root from the left, as 69 is more than 65 but less than 90. The information in this node is 75 indicating that the sought after key may be present in the leftmost child of this node. After reaching this grand child of the root we find 69. The internal nodes stores pointers to at most four sub-trees and they also store maximum three keys. These are the smallest keys in the three rightmost sub-trees of the node, used to determine which sub-tree needs to be searched.

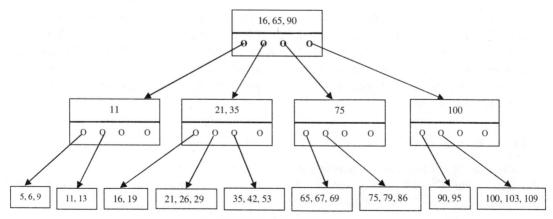

FIGURE 1.14 B-tree.

B-trees are quite useful for storage of large amount of data on the secondary storage. With this structuring of data, any record can be retrieved by traversing through a few levels of the tree and doing linear search in the selected leaf.

1.11.6 Binomial Heap

To define a binomial heap, we have to define binomial trees first. A single vertex tree is a binomial tree (B_0) of order 0. A binomial tree $B_i(i > 0)$ is made up of two binomial trees of order B_{i-1} trees. One of the two B_{i-1} trees is attached to the root of the other as the rightmost child.

B_0 has height 0, B_1 has height 1, and B_i has height i for all values of i. How many nodes does B_i contain? To find this, we first find the number of children in B_i at depth $j(0 \leq j \leq i)$.

It is $\dfrac{i(i-1) \dots (i-j+1)}{j!}$. This is basically the binomial coefficient ${}^iC_j$. The name binomial tree is derived from this fact. A *binomial heap* is defined as a forest of binomial trees with the restriction that a particular binomial tree appears at most once, and each binomial tree is partially ordered. Figure 1.15 shows a binomial heap made of B_0, B_1, B_2, and B_3. To search for the minimum in a binomial tree, one has to search through the roots of these trees. This requires $O(\log n)$ time using binary search for a binary heap with n nodes. However, we can do it in $O(1)$ time with the overhead of a pointer to the root of the tree containing the least element.

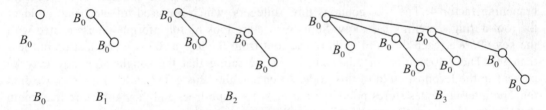

FIGURE 1.15 Binomial heap.

The worst case time complexity for building a binomial heap is $\Theta(1)$. Node insertion and finding minimum in the heap each requires $O(\log n)$ time in the worst case. Deleting the minimum key node from the heap in the worst case requires $\Theta(\log n)$ time. Unification of two heaps requires $O(\log n)$ time in the worst case. Binomial heaps have been used in the problems of single-source shortest paths, all-pair shortest paths, weighted bipartite matching, minimum spanning tree, and others.

1.11.7 Fibonacci Heap

A collection of rooted trees, where all these trees are organized as heaps is known as a Fibonacci heap. These trees are unordered. Figure 1.16 shows an example containing three trees organized as a Fibonacci heap.

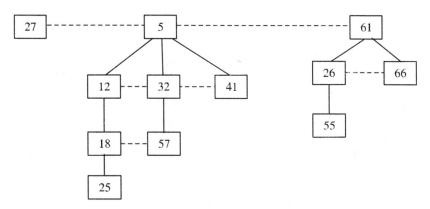

FIGURE 1.16 Fibonacci heap.

Roots of the trees in a Fibonacci heap are connected in an arbitrary manner through a doubly-linked list (shown as dotted line in the Figure). The children of a node are connected similarly through doubly-linked lists. The siblings appear in a list in an arbitrary manner. The Fibonacci heap is accessed through a pointer. The pointer points to the root of the tree containing the minimum key. Root of any other tree can then be accessed by using the pointers of the doubly-linked list of the roots of the trees.

The general operations supported by this data structure are: building_heap, node_insertion, minimum_finding, deleting the minimum key node from the heap, unifying two heaps. The amortized time complexities of these operations are: $\Theta(1)$, $\Theta(1)$, $\Theta(1)$, $O(\log n)$, $\Theta(1)$, respectively. Fibonacci heaps are especially desirable when the number of minimum extraction and deletion operations is small compared to the number of other operations performed. Theoretically, many graph problems may exploit Fibonacci heap for faster execution. It is less attractive compared with ordinary heap in practice, because of programming and other reasons.

1.12 PSEUDOCODE CONVENTION

Several conventions are used for the description of algorithms. These are mixtures of natural and programming language-like constructs.

In this book, we follow the following conventions for the description of algorithms:

(i) An algorithm is described within a pair of lines:

Procedure Name

...

...

End Name

(ii) Assignment is denoted as:

Variable_name = Expression;

(iii) *If statement* is shown as:

```
If Condition Then          │
   Statement(s);           │
   Else                    │   If Condition Then Statement(s); Endif
   Statement(s);           │
Endif                      │
```

(iv) *Do loop* is shown as:

```
For Variable = Initial Value to Final Value {Step Step-size} Do
...
...
Endfor
```

(v) *Repeat construct* is shown as:

```
Repeat
...
...
Until condition
```

(vi) *Returning results* is shown as:

```
Return(Value(s))
```

(vii) *While construct* is used as:

```
While condition Do
...
...
Endwhile
```

(viii) *Case construct* is used as:

```
Case
...
Endcase
```

(ix) *Comment* is shown as:

```
/*   Text   */
```

(x) *Parallel activities* by different computing elements are shown through the following constructs in the pseudocode for parallel algorithms:

```
For each processor i, Do in parallel
...
...
Enddo
```

```
For all k Do in parallel
...

...
Enddo

For i = 0 to n - 1 and j = 0 to n - 1, Do in parallel
...

...
Enddo
```

SUMMARY

In this chapter, we have introduced the general notion of algorithms and the means to characterize asymptotic complexities of algorithms. Linear recurrence relations are quite common in complexity analysis of algorithms. We have indicated how these recurrences are solved using the standard techniques. The basic data structures, used in the algorithm design methods were also briefly described. This chapter also described the conventions used in the representation of algorithms through pseudocode.

EXERCISES

1.1 Develop an algorithm to construct the first N rows of Pascal's triangle. The first four rows of Pascal's triangle are given by:

$$
\begin{array}{ccccccc}
 & & & 1 & & & \\
 & & 1 & & 1 & & \\
 & 1 & & 2 & & 1 & \\
1 & & 3 & & 3 & & 1
\end{array}
$$

Analyze the algorithm for time complexity.

1.2 Which of the following statements are true? Prove your answers.

$$n^2 \in O(n^3),\ n^2 \in \Omega(n^3),\ 2^n \in \Theta(2^{n+1}),\ n! \in \Theta((n + 1)!)$$

1.3 If the Fibonacci sequence, defined as: $f(i) = f(i - 1) + f(i - 2)$, $(n > 1)$ and $f(0) = f(1) = 1$ is computed by recursion, how many additions will be performed when computing $f(n)$?

1.4 Solve the following recurrence:

$T(N) = T(N - 1) + 2T(N - 2) - 2T(N - 3)$, $N \geq 3$ and

$T(N) = 9N^2 - 15N + 106$, $N = 0, 1, 2$.

1.5 Solve the following recurrence assuming N as an integer power of 2:

$T(N) = 4T(N/2) + N$, $N \geq 2$ and

$T(N) = 1$, $N = 1$.

1.6 Ackermann's function is defined as

$Ack(i, j) = j + 1, i = 0$
$\qquad = Ack(i - 1, 1), i > 0, j = 0$
$\qquad = Ack(i - 1, Ack(i, j - 1))$, otherwise.

Calculate Ack(2,3), Ack(3,3).

1.7 Given $K = K_1 + K_2$, find the minimum value of $K_1 \log_2 K_1 + K_2 \log_2 K_2$.

1.8 Consider the following recursive procedure:

```
Procedure Comb (N, K)
   If K = 0 or K = N Then Return(1);
      Else Return(Comb(N - 1, K - 1) + Comb(N - 1, K));
   Endif
End Comb
```

Show that the total number of recursive invocations of Comb( ) is $2 {}^N C_K - 2$ for computation of Comb(N, K).

1.9 Show that: $f_1(x) = 7.2x^2 + 78x + 10^6$ is $O(x^2)$, $f_2(x) = 2^x/(10^5) - 10$ is $O(2^x)$, and $f_3(x) = x!$ is $O(x^x)$.

1.10 Algorithm A requires n^2 days and algorithm B requires n^3 seconds to solve a problem. Which algorithm would you prefer for a problem instance with $n = 10^6$?

1.11 Sorting method A runs in $8n^2$ steps while sorting method B runs in $64n \log n$ steps. For which values of n does method A run faster than method B?

1.12 Consider the following algorithm:

```
Procedure Test(N)
   For i = 1 to N Do
     For j = 1 to i
       Write i, j, N;
     Endfor
   Endfor
   If N > 0 Then Do
     For i = 1 to 8 Do
       Call Test(N/2);
     Endfor
   Endif
End Test
```

Let $T(N)$ denote the number of lines written by Test(N). Formulate a recurrence relation for $T(N)$.

1.13 Show that $\log^3 n$ is $o(n^{1/3})$.

1.14 What is the time complexity of the following algorithm in terms of 'Big Oh' notation?

```
Procedure Test(N)
  S = 0;
  For I = 1 to N³ Do
    For J = 1 to I Do
      S = S + I;
    Endfor
  Endfor
End Test
```

1.15 Show that $(n + 1)^5$ is $O(n^5)$, 2^{n+1} is $O(2^n)$, $n^3 \log n$ is $\Omega(n^3)$.

1.16 If the space is at a premium, would you use the adjacency list or the adjacency matrix representation to store (i) a graph with 10^4 vertices and 10^4 edges, (ii) a graph with 10^4 vertices and 10^7 edges?

1.17 Solve the recurrence relation, where N is an integer power of 3:

$$T(N) = 6T(N/3) + 2N - 1, \ N > 1 \text{ and } T(N) = 2 \text{ for } N = 1.$$

1.18 Write an algorithm to check whether every sequence of consecutive ones in a 1-dimensional Boolean array is even. Determine the time complexity as well.

1.19 Write an algorithm to generate all permutations of 1, 2, 3, ..., n. What is the time complexity of the algorithm?

1.20 Arrange the following functions from the lowest asymptotic order to the highest asymptotic order:

$7n$, 2^n, $10n \log n$, $4n^3$, $5n^2$, $2 \log n$, $10n - n^3 + 9n^5$, $n^2 + 7 \log n$.

1.21 Solve the following recurrence where N is an integer power of 2:

$$T(N) = 2T(N/2) + \log N, \ N > 1 \text{ and } T(N) = 1 \text{ for } N = 1.$$

1.22 Develop and analyze an algorithm to determine whether a given $N \times N$ matrix A has the metric property (that is, for all values of $1 \le i, j, k \le N$, $a_{ij} \le a_{ik} + a_{kj}$) or not.

1.23 Solve the recurrence relation: $T(N) = 4T(N/2) + N^3$.

1.24 For two sequences a_n, b_n consider the statements: $a_n = O(b_n)$, $a_n = o(b_n)$. Which one implies the other?

1.25 Find the complexity of the following algorithm:

```
Procedure Test2(n)
  Integer n;
  If n ≤ 1 Then Return(n);
    Else Return(Test2(n - 1) + Test2(n - 2));
  Endif
End Test2
```

1.26 Find the complexity of the following algorithm:

```
Procedure Test3(m, n)
  Integer m, n;
  If n = 0 Then Return(m);
    Else Return(Test3(n, m mod n));
  Endif
End Test3
```

1.27 Given a polynomial, $P = (a_n, a_{n-1}, ..., a_0)$, write an algorithm to find $P(x)$ for $x = 2^i$, $0 \le i \le n - 1$. Find the time complexity as well.

1.28 Find the solution of the following recurrence relation in O-notation

$$T(n) = 8T(n/2) + 3n^2$$

where n is an integer power of 2 and greater than 1.

1.29 Show that the solution to the following recurrence is bounded from the lower side by $n \log n$. A tree structure may be used for the proof.

$$T(n) = T(n/3) + T(2n/3) + n$$

1.30 Solve the recurrence: $T(n) = T(n - 1) + T(n - 3) - T(n - 4)$, $n \ge 4$ subject to $T(n) = n$ for $0 \le n \le 3$.

1.31 Solve the recurrence: $T(n) = 3T^2(n - 1)$, for $n \ge 1$ and $T(0) = 1$ using change of variable.

1.32 Show the steps in the construction of a heap of records with the following key values: 13, 7, 32, 12, 39, 5, 40, 11.

1.33 Solve the following recurrence relation by using the method of generating function: $h_n = h_{n-1} + h_{n-2}$, $n \ge 2$, $h_0 = 1$, $h_1 = 3$.

1.34 Prove that the GCD algorithm requires time logarithmic with respect to the value of the numbers and is linear with respect to the input length.

1.35 The stirling number of the second kind, $S(n, k)$, is the number of partitions of an n-element set into k classes. $S(n, k)$ is recursively defined as

$$S(n + 1, k) = S(n, k - 1) + kS(n, k)$$

with $S(n, k) = 0$ for $k > n$,

$S(n, 1) = 1$ for $n \ge 1$,

$S(0, 0) = 1$,

$S(n, 0) = 0$ for $n \ge 1$.

Write an algorithm to compute $S(l, r)$ for the given values of l and r where $l, r \ge 0$. Formulate the time complexity of the algorithm in terms of l and r.

1.36 Write an algorithm to compute the LCM of two given integers using the GCD algorithm of Euclid.

1.37 Suppose the elements of an array are stored in row-major fashion starting from the location l_0 of the main memory.

   (i) What would be the address of the (i, j)th element of a 2-dimensional array in the memory?

   (ii) What would be the address of the (i, j, k)th element of a 3-dimensional array?

   (iii) Generalize the above results for an array of d-dimensions.

1.38 Build a max-heap on an array containing the elements: 5, 2, 7, 1, 9, 10, 8, 15, 3, 17.

1.39 Solve the inhomogeneous recurrence relation:

   $T(N) = 2T(N - 1) + 1$ with $T(1) = 1$ and $T(2) = 3$.

1.40 For the following trees, decide which choice is valid.

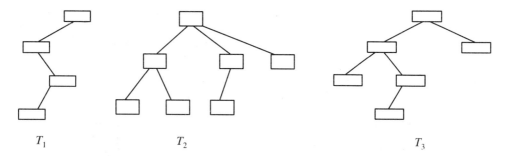

T_1 T_2 T_3

   (i) T_1 is not a binary tree, T_2 is not a binary tree, T_3 is a balanced binary tree.

   (ii) T_1 is a binary tree, T_2 is not a binary tree, T_3 is a balanced binary tree.

   (iii) T_1 is a binary tree, T_2 is a binary tree, T_3 is a balanced binary tree.

   (iv) T_1 is a binary tree, T_2 is not a binary tree, T_3 is not a balanced binary tree.

1.41 Let us consider a stack which stores either a byte (PushB) or a word (PushW). Similary, it can retrieve a byte (PopB) or a word (PopW). Each word consists of two bytes. Push inserts in the least significant byte, if it is free, otherwise it inserts in the most significant bytes. A word when being pushed into the stack cannot be split; if some byte is free, it remains so. PopB retrieves the most significant byte, if it is present; otherwise it retrieves the least significant byte. Stack pointer either points to the most significant byte from the top of the stack or to the least significant byte depending on the data stored in the stack. What would be the outcome when the following sequence of operations is applied on the following stack:

   Assume $X = 5$, $Y = 503$, and $Z = 19$. PushB X, PushW Y, PushB Z, PopB, PopB, PopB, PopW. The contents of the stack are:
   (i) 14, 42; (ii) 42, 19, 34; (iii) 5, 503, 42; (iv) 42, 14, 19

1.42 A queue of characters is implemented using a linear array, and by treating it as if it were circular, i.e., the queue wraps around. One character is deleted, and then two are added to the queue shown below. What would be the values of the front and rear pointers?

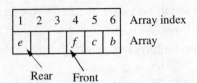

1.43 A binary tree is to be used to sort positive integers 5, 2, 17, 1, 4, 14, 25, 15, 21, 24, 13. The partial tree shown below is formed. The next number in the file is 13. Where should this be placed such that in order traversal of the tree yields the sorted file? Numbers in the rectangles show how the successive numbers of the input are inserted in the tree.

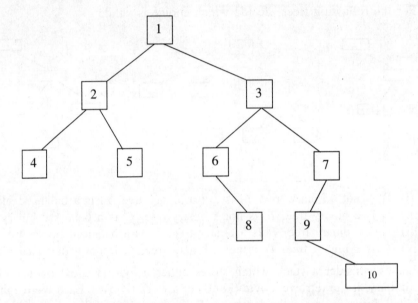

1.44 A queue of characters currently contains: *a, b, c, d*. The following operations are performed on the queue: one deletion, addition of *w*, addition of *x*, one deletion, addition of *y*. What would be the contents of the queue after these operations?

1.45 What is the number of nodes to be accessed for finding a given key in a B-tree with branching factor $b = 256$, and number of keys $n = 16,777,215$?

1.46 16,777,215 keys are stored in a completely balanced binary tree. What is the maximum number of accesses required to find a given key in such a tree?

1.47 Find the average time complexity of finding palindromes in strings of length n where the characters in the strings are from the set $\{0, 1, 2\}$.

1.48 Make an amortized analysis of queue data structure.

DIVIDE AND CONQUER

2.0 INTRODUCTION

Sometimes it is easier to solve a problem by breaking up the problem into smaller problems, finding solutions of the smaller problems, and combining the solutions of the smaller problems to obtain the solution for the original problem. Often, the smaller problems generated by breaking up the bigger problem are of the same nature as the original problem except that the size is reduced because of the split. This method is known as *divide and conquer*. Some of the problems that are solved by using divide-and-conquer method are binary search, merge-sort, quick-sort, multiplication of large numbers, etc. These problems are discussed in this chapter. We solve some more problems using this method in Chapter 5.

2.1 MULTIPLICATION OF TWO *n*-BIT NUMBERS

The traditional method of multiplication of two *n*-bit numbers requires $O(n^2)$ bit operations. The divide-and-conquer method provides a solution of complexity $O(n^{\log 3}) \cong O(n^{1.59})$. Let X and Y be two *n*-bit numbers. Assume n is a power of 2. We partition X and Y each into two halves as shown below. Each half is of $n/2$ bits.

X	A	B
Y	C	D

We may write the product as:

$$Z = XY = (A2^{n/2} + B)(C2^{n/2} + D)$$
$$= AC2^n + (AD + BC)2^{n/2} + BD$$

This requires 4 multiplications of *n*/2 bit numbers plus some additions and shifts (multiplication by powers of 2). This way of dividing the problem and carrying out 4 multiplications will lead to $O(n^2)$ complexity. Let us try to find a faster way by reducing the number of multiplications of $n/2$ bit numbers through rearrangement in the computation process.

The product Z of X and Y can also be computed by the following program:

Procedure Multiply (A, B, C, D)

    $U = (A + B) * (C + D)$;

    $V = A * C$;

    $W = B * D$;

    $Z = V * 2^n + (U - V - W) * 2^{n/2} + W$;

End Multiply

We assume that $A + B$ and $C + D$ have only $n/2$ bits, ignoring the fact that due to carry, $A + B$ and $C + D$ may be $(n/2 + 1)$ bit numbers. The scheme requires only three multiplications of $n/2$ bit numbers, plus some additions and shifts, to multiply two n-bit numbers. One can use the multiplication routine recursively to evaluate the products U, V and W. The addition and shifts require time $O(n)$. Thus the time complexity of multiplying two n-bit numbers is bounded from above by:

$$T(n) = k, \text{ for } n = 1$$

$$= 3T(n/2) + kn, \text{ for } n > 1,$$

where k is a constant reflecting the costs of additions and shifts.

$$T(n) = 3T(n/2) + kn$$

$$= 3\{3T(n/4) + kn/2\} + kn$$

$$= 3^2 T(n/4) + 3 \, kn/2 + kn$$

$$= 3^2\{3T(n/2^3) + kn/4\} + 3kn/2 + kn$$

$$= 3^3 T(n/2^3) + (3/2)^2 kn + (3/2)kn + kn$$

Let $n = 2^p$, then we may write $T(n)$ as:

$$T(n) = 3^p T(1) + (3/2)^{p-1} kn + \cdots + (3/2)^3 kn + (3/2)^2 kn + (3/2)kn + kn$$

$$= k3^p + kn\{(3/2)^{p-1} + \cdots + (3/2)^2 + (3/2) + 1\}$$

$$= k3^p + 2kn\{(3/2)^p - 1\}$$

$$= k3^{\log_2 n} + 2kn\{(3^{\log_2 n}/2^{\log_2 n}) - 1\}$$

$$= k3^{\log_2 n} + 2kn\{(3^{\log_2 n}/n) - 1\}$$

$$= 3k3^{\log_2 n} - 2kn \quad (\text{since } 3^{\log_2 n} = n^{\log_2 3})$$

$$= 3kn^{\log_2 3} - 2kn$$

Therefore, $T(n)$ is $O(n^{\log_2 3}) = O(n^{1.59})$

Suppose $X = 0101$, $Y = 0110$. Then $A = 01$, $B = 01$, $C = 01$, $D = 10$

$U = (A + B)(C + D) = 110$, $V = AC = 001$, $W = BD = 010$.

$W = V * 2^4 + (U - V - W) * 2^2 + W = 00010000 + 1100 + 010 = 00011110$

2.2 MERGE-SORT

Given a sequence of n elements $A(1)$, $A(2)$, ..., $A(n)$, the general idea is to split them into two parts. $A(1)$, ..., $A(\lfloor n/2 \rfloor)$ and $A(\lfloor n/2 \rfloor + 1)$, ..., $A(n)$. Each part is individually sorted and the resulting sequences are merged to produce a single sorted sequence of n elements. The following pseudocode achieves this.

```
Procedure Merge_sort(low,high)
  Array A(n)
If low < high Then
  mid = ⌊(low + high)/2⌋;
  call Merge_sort(low,mid);
  call Merge_sort(mid + 1,high);
  call Merge(low,mid,high);
Endif
End Merge_sort

Procedure Merge(low,mid,high)
  /*Array A is global, Array B is local */
  Array B(n), A(n)
  h = low; i = low; j = mid + 1;
  While h ≤ mid and j ≤ high Do
    If A(h) ≤ A(j) Then
      B(i) = A(h);
      h = h + 1;
    Else
      B(i) = A(j);
      j = j + 1;
    Endif
    i = i + 1;
  Endwhile
  If h > mid Then
    For k = j to high Do
      B(i) = A(k);
      i = i + 1;
    Endfor
  Else
```

```
For k = h to mid Do
    B(i) = A(k);
    i = i + 1;
Endfor
Endif
For k = low to high Do
    A(k) = B(k);
Endfor
End Merge
```

Figure 2.1 gives a snapshot of the merge-sort of 8 elements.

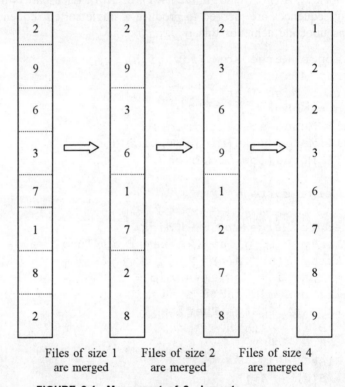

Files of size 1   Files of size 2   Files of size 4
are merged   are merged   are merged

FIGURE 2.1 Merge-sort of 8 elements.

If the time for the merging operation is proportioned to n, then the computing time for merge-sort is described by:

$$T(n) = \begin{cases} 0, & n = 1 \\ 2T\left(\dfrac{n}{2}\right) + cn, & n > 1, c \text{ is a constant}. \end{cases}$$

When n is a power of 2, that is, $n = 2^k$, we proceed as follows:

$$T(n) = 2T\left(\frac{n}{2}\right) + cn$$

$$= 2\left(2T\left(\frac{n}{4}\right) + c\frac{n}{2}\right) + cn$$

$$= 4T\left(\frac{n}{4}\right) + 2cn$$

$$= 4(2T(n/8) + cn/4) + 2cn$$

$$= 8T(n/8) + 3cn$$

$$\cdots$$

$$= 2^k T\left(\frac{n}{2^k}\right) + kcn$$

$$= 2^k T(1) + kcn$$

$$= kcn = cn \log_2 n.$$

It is easy to see that if $2^k < n < 2^{k+1}$ then $T(n) \leq T(2^{k+1})$.
Therefore, $T(n) = O(n \log n)$.

2.3 BINARY SEARCH

Given an integer x and an array $A(i)$, $i = 1$ to n, of sorted integers in ascending (descending) order, we have to find an index j, $1 \leq j \leq n$ such that $A(j) = x$, if x appears in A, otherwise we return -1. A pseudocode may be written for the binary search as:

```
Procedure Binary_search(A,n,x)
  /* A is an array of n elements A(0), A(1), ..., A(n-1) */
  Array A(n)
  int low, mid, high;
  low = 0;
  high = n - 1;
  While (low ≤ high)
    mid = ⌊(low + high)/2⌋;
    If (A(mid) < x) Then low = mid + 1;
        Else
      If (A(mid) > x) Then high = mid - 1;
        Else
        Return(mid);
      Endif
```

```
        Endif
     Endwhile
     Return(-1);
  End Binary_search
```

Suppose we have an array with the 8 elements: 10, 20, 30, 41, 55, 77, 80 and 85 and we are looking for 35 in the array. We first compare 35 with the element at position 4 in the array, that is, with 41. But 35 is less than 41, so we restrict our search to the first half of the array. We then compare 35 with the element at position 2, that is, with 20 and find that 35 is greater than this element. We finally compare 35 with 30 and declare that 35 is not present in the array.

The time complexity for this problem may be written as:

$$T(n) = \begin{cases} k, & n = 1 \\ T\left(\dfrac{n}{2}\right) + k, & n > 1 \end{cases}$$

$$T(n) = T(n/2) + k$$

$$= T\left(\frac{n}{2^2}\right) + 2k$$

$$= T\left(\frac{n}{2^3}\right) + 3k$$

$$. . .$$

$$= T(1) + rk, \quad \text{where } 2^r = n, \ r \text{ is a positive interger.}$$

$$= (r + 1)k$$

$$= (1 + \log_2 n)k \approx O(\log n)$$

2.4 QUICK-SORT

In quick-sort, we divide the list of input elements into two lists by choosing a partitioning element. One list contains all elements less than or equal to the partitioning element and the other list contains all elements greater than the partitioning element. These two lists are recursively partitioned in the same way till the resulting lists become trivially small to sort by comparison. We then go on combining the sorted smaller lists to produce the sorted list of all the input elements. Suppose the input consists of 10, 2, 7, 23, 34, 8, 1, 9, 11, 5. The recursive partitioning goes as shown in Figure 2.2. We use the first element of the list as the partitioning element. Other choices are also possible.

The sorted list consists of the concatenation of the smaller sorted lists in order along with the partitioning elements in the appropriate places: 1, 2, 5, 7, 8, 9, 10, 11, 23, 34. The following description gives an outline of the working of quick-sort.

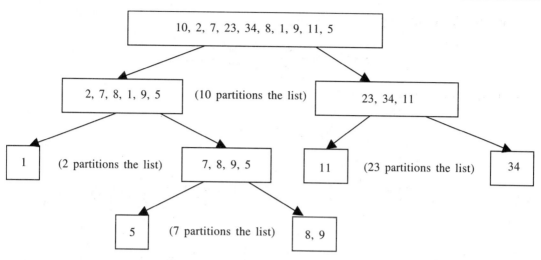

FIGURE 2.2 Partitioning in quick-sort.

```
Procedure Quick-sort(A)
/* A is an array of input elements */
   Array A(n), A₁(n), A₂(n)
   If A contains one element Then Return(A);
      Else
      Choose an element a randomly from A; Let A₁, A₂ be the sub-files
of elements in A less than equal to and greater than a, respectively;
      Endif
      Return {Quick-sort(A₁) followed by a followed by Quick-sort(A₂)};
   End Quick-sort
```

Average case time requirement

Let $T(n)$ be the expected time required by quick-sort to sort a sequence of n elements. Clearly $T(0) = T(1) = b$, for some constant b. Suppose the element 'a' chosen for partitioning is the ith smallest element of the n elements of A. Then the two recursive calls of quick-sort have expected times $T(i - 1)$ and $T(n - i)$ respectively. Since i is equally likely to take on any value between 1 and n, and the balance of quick-sort(A) requires time cn for some constant c, we have,

$$T(n) \leq cn + \frac{1}{n} \sum_{i=1}^{i=n} \{T(i - 1) + T(n - i)\}, n \geq 2$$

or

$$T(n) \leq cn + \frac{2}{n} \sum_{i=0}^{i=n-1} T(i)$$

We solve this inequality through induction. For $n \geq 2$, we assume that $T(n) \leq kn\log_e n$, where $k = 2c + 2b$ and $b = T(0) = T(1)$. For the basis case $n = 2$, $T(2) \leq 2c + 2b$ follows immediately.

For the induction step, we write

$$T(n) \leq cn + \frac{4b}{n} + \frac{2}{n} \sum_{i=2}^{i=n-1} ki \log_e i$$

Since $(i \log_e i)$ is concave upwards,

$$\sum_{i=2}^{n-1} i \log_e i \leq \int_2^n x \log_e x \, dx$$

But $\int_2^n x \log_e x \, dx = \left| \frac{x^2 \log_e x}{2} \right|_2^n - \int_2^n (\frac{1}{x} \int x \, dx) \, dx = \left| \frac{x^2 \log_e x}{2} \right|_2^n - \int_2^n \frac{1}{x} \frac{x^2}{2} \, dx$

$$= \left| \frac{x^2 \log_e x}{2} \right|_2^n - \frac{1}{2} \int_2^n x \, dx = \left| \frac{x^2 \log_e x}{2} \right|_2^n - \left| \frac{x^2}{4} \right|_2^n = \frac{n^2 \log_e n}{2} - \frac{n^2}{4} - (2 \log_e 2 - 1)$$

Thus, $$\int_2^n x \log_e x \, dx \leq \frac{n^2 \log_e n}{2} - \frac{n^2}{4}$$

$\therefore$ $$T(n) \leq cn + \frac{4b}{n} + kn \log_e n - \frac{kn}{2}$$

Since $n \geq 2$ and $k = 2c + 2b$, it follows that,

$$cn + \frac{4b}{n} \leq cn + bn \leq \frac{kn}{2} \quad \text{and} \quad T(n) \leq kn \log_e n.$$

So the average-case time complexity of the quick-sort is $O(n \log n)$.

Worst-case time requirement

In the worst case, one sub-file (A_1 or A_2) is empty after every partitioning. Hence, the time complexity for the worst case may be written as:

$$T(n) = cn + T(n - 1)$$
$$= cn + c(n - 1) + T(n - 2)$$
$$= cn + c(n - 1) + c(n - 2) + T(n - 3)$$
$$= cn + c(n - 1) + c(n - 2) + \ldots c.1 + T(1)$$
$$= c(1 + 2 + \cdots + n) + T(1)$$
$$= c \left\{ \frac{n(n + 1)}{2} \right\} + b, \quad \therefore T(n) \in O(n^2)$$

In the worst-case, the quick-sort requires quadratic time.

2.5 STRASSEN'S MATRIX MULTIPLICATION

Multiplication of two $n \times n$ matrices requires $O(n^3)$ operations because the product matrix contains n^2 elements and computing each element of the product matrix requires $O(n)$ operations. Suppose the matrices A and B are each partitioned into four square sub-matrices, each sub-matrix having dimension $n/2 \times n/2$.

$$\begin{bmatrix} A_{11} & A_{12} \\ A_{21} & A_{22} \end{bmatrix} \times \begin{bmatrix} B_{11} & B_{12} \\ B_{21} & B_{22} \end{bmatrix} = \begin{bmatrix} C_{11} & C_{12} \\ C_{21} & C_{22} \end{bmatrix}$$

$$C_{11} = A_{11}B_{11} + A_{12}B_{21}$$

$$C_{12} = A_{11}B_{12} + A_{12}B_{22}$$

$$C_{21} = A_{21}B_{11} + A_{22}B_{21}$$

$$C_{22} = A_{21}B_{12} + A_{22}B_{22}$$

In order to compute AB using the above decomposition, we need to perform 8 multiplications of $n/2 \times n/2$ matrices and 4 additions of $n/2$ matrices. Since two $n/2 \times n/2$ matrices may be added in time cn^2 for some constant c, the overall computing time, $T(n)$, of the resulting divide and conquer algorithm is given by the recurrence:

$$T(n) = \begin{cases} b & n \leq 2 \\ 8T\left(\dfrac{n}{2}\right) + an^2, & n > 2 \end{cases} \qquad \text{where } a \text{ and } b \text{ are constants.}$$

This recurrence has solution $T(n) = O(n^3)$; so there is no improvement. Since matrix multiplication ($O(n^3)$ operations) is more expensive than matrix addition ($O(n^2)$ operations), one may attempt to reformulate the equations for C_{ij} so as to have fewer multiplications and possibly more additions. V. Strassen has discovered a way to compute C_{ij}'s using only 7 multiplications and 18 additions and subtractions:

$$D = (A_{11} + A_{22})(B_{11} + B_{22})$$

$$E = (A_{21} + A_{22})B_{11}$$

$$F = A_{11}(B_{12} - B_{22})$$

$$G = A_{22}(B_{21} - B_{11})$$

$$H = (A_{11} + A_{12})B_{22}$$

$$M = (A_{21} - A_{11})(B_{11} + B_{12})$$

$$P = (A_{12} - A_{22})(B_{21} + B_{22})$$

$$C_{11} = D + G - H + P$$

$$C_{12} = F + H$$

$$C_{21} = E + G$$

$$C_{22} = D + F - E + M$$

The resulting recurrence relation for $T(n)$ may be written as:

$$T(n) = \begin{cases} b & n \le 2 \\ 7T(n/2) + an^2, & n > 2, \text{ and } a \text{ and } b \text{ are constants.} \end{cases}$$

$$T(n) = an^2 + 7T(n/2)$$

$$= an^2 + 7[a(n/2)^2 + 7T(n/4)]$$

$$= an^2 + 7an^2/4 + 7^2 T(n/4)$$

$$= an^2 + 7an^2/4 + 7^2[a(n/4)^2 + 7T(n/8)]$$

$$= an^2 + 7an^2/4 + (7/4)^2 an^2 + 7^3 T(n/8)$$

$$= an^2 \{1 + 7/4 + (7/4)^2 + \cdots + (7/4)^{k-1}\} + 7^k T(n/2^k)$$

(assuming $n = 2^k$, where k is a positive integer).

$$= an^2 \frac{\{(7/4)^k - 1\}}{(7/4) - 1} + 7^k b$$

$$= \frac{4}{3} an^2 \{(7/4)^{\log n} - 1\} + 7^{\log_2 n} b$$

$$\le cn^{\log 4 + \log 7 - \log 4} + bn^{\log_2 7}, \text{ where } c = 4a/3$$

$$= cn^{\log 7} + bn^{\log 7}$$

$$= (c + b)n^{2.81}$$

$$\therefore \qquad T(n) \in O(n^{2.81})$$

The complexity of Strassen's[1] method of matrix multiplication is $O(n^{2.81})$. Let us consider the multiplication of the matrices A and B as given below:

$$A = \begin{bmatrix} 4 & 2 & 0 & 1 \\ 3 & 1 & 2 & 5 \\ 3 & 2 & 1 & 4 \\ 5 & 2 & 6 & 7 \end{bmatrix} \quad B = \begin{bmatrix} 2 & 1 & 3 & 2 \\ 5 & 4 & 2 & 3 \\ 1 & 4 & 0 & 2 \\ 3 & 2 & 4 & 1 \end{bmatrix}$$

---

[1] Coppersmith and Winograd's method has complexity $O(n^{2.496})$. Refer D. Coppersmith and S. Winograd, "On the Asymptotic Complexity of Matrix Multiplication", *SIAM J. Computing*, **11**(1982), 472–492.

Finding the product matrix C by the usual way, will require $16 \times 4 = 64$ multiplications. We partition the input matrices into sub-matrices as given below:

$$A = \begin{bmatrix} A_{11} & A_{12} \\ A_{21} & A_{22} \end{bmatrix} \qquad B = \begin{bmatrix} B_{11} & B_{12} \\ B_{21} & B_{22} \end{bmatrix} \text{ where}$$

$$A_{11} = \begin{bmatrix} 4 & 2 \\ 3 & 1 \end{bmatrix}, \quad A_{12} = \begin{bmatrix} 0 & 1 \\ 2 & 5 \end{bmatrix}, \quad A_{21} = \begin{bmatrix} 3 & 2 \\ 5 & 2 \end{bmatrix}, \quad A_{22} = \begin{bmatrix} 1 & 4 \\ 6 & 7 \end{bmatrix}$$

$$B_{11} = \begin{bmatrix} 2 & 1 \\ 5 & 4 \end{bmatrix}, \quad B_{12} = \begin{bmatrix} 3 & 2 \\ 2 & 3 \end{bmatrix}, \quad B_{21} = \begin{bmatrix} 1 & 4 \\ 3 & 2 \end{bmatrix}, \quad B_{22} = \begin{bmatrix} 0 & 2 \\ 4 & 1 \end{bmatrix}$$

$$D = (A_{11} + A_{22})(B_{11} + B_{22})$$

$$= \begin{bmatrix} 5 & 6 \\ 9 & 8 \end{bmatrix} \begin{bmatrix} 2 & 3 \\ 9 & 5 \end{bmatrix} = \begin{bmatrix} 64 & 45 \\ 90 & 67 \end{bmatrix}$$

$$E = (A_{21} + A_{22})B_{11}$$

$$= \begin{bmatrix} 4 & 6 \\ 11 & 9 \end{bmatrix} \begin{bmatrix} 2 & 1 \\ 5 & 4 \end{bmatrix} = \begin{bmatrix} 38 & 28 \\ 67 & 47 \end{bmatrix}$$

$$F = A_{11}(B_{12} - B_{22})$$

$$= \begin{bmatrix} 4 & 2 \\ 3 & 1 \end{bmatrix} \begin{bmatrix} 3 & 0 \\ -2 & 2 \end{bmatrix} = \begin{bmatrix} 8 & 4 \\ 7 & 2 \end{bmatrix}$$

$$G = A_{22}(B_{21} - B_{11})$$

$$= \begin{bmatrix} 1 & 4 \\ 6 & 7 \end{bmatrix} \begin{bmatrix} -1 & 3 \\ -2 & -2 \end{bmatrix} = \begin{bmatrix} -9 & -5 \\ -20 & 4 \end{bmatrix}$$

$$H = (A_{11} + A_{12})B_{22}$$

$$= \begin{bmatrix} 4 & 3 \\ 5 & 6 \end{bmatrix} \begin{bmatrix} 0 & 2 \\ 4 & 1 \end{bmatrix} = \begin{bmatrix} 12 & 11 \\ 24 & 16 \end{bmatrix}$$

$$M = (A_{21} - A_{11})(B_{11} + B_{12})$$

$$= \begin{bmatrix} -1 & 0 \\ 2 & 1 \end{bmatrix} \begin{bmatrix} 5 & 3 \\ 7 & 7 \end{bmatrix} = \begin{bmatrix} -5 & -3 \\ 17 & 13 \end{bmatrix}$$

$$P = (A_{12} - A_{22})(B_{21} + B_{22})$$

$$= \begin{bmatrix} -1 & -3 \\ -4 & -2 \end{bmatrix} \begin{bmatrix} 1 & 6 \\ 7 & 3 \end{bmatrix} = \begin{bmatrix} -22 & -15 \\ -18 & -30 \end{bmatrix}$$

Finding the elements of each of the matrices D, E, F, G, H, M and P requires 7 multiplications. So all the elements of these 7 matrices are found with 49 multiplications.

$$C_{11} = D + G - H + P$$

$$= \begin{bmatrix} 64 & 45 \\ 90 & 67 \end{bmatrix} + \begin{bmatrix} -9 & -5 \\ -20 & 4 \end{bmatrix} + \begin{bmatrix} -12 & -11 \\ -24 & -16 \end{bmatrix} + \begin{bmatrix} -22 & -15 \\ -18 & -30 \end{bmatrix} = \begin{bmatrix} 21 & 14 \\ 28 & 25 \end{bmatrix}$$

$$C_{12} = F + H = \begin{bmatrix} 8 & 4 \\ 7 & 2 \end{bmatrix} + \begin{bmatrix} 12 & 11 \\ 24 & 16 \end{bmatrix} = \begin{bmatrix} 20 & 15 \\ 31 & 18 \end{bmatrix}$$

$$C_{21} = E + G = \begin{bmatrix} 38 & 28 \\ 67 & 47 \end{bmatrix} + \begin{bmatrix} -9 & -5 \\ -20 & 4 \end{bmatrix} = \begin{bmatrix} 29 & 23 \\ 47 & 51 \end{bmatrix}$$

$$C_{22} = D + F - E + M$$

$$= \begin{bmatrix} 64 & 45 \\ 90 & 67 \end{bmatrix} + \begin{bmatrix} 8 & 4 \\ 7 & 2 \end{bmatrix} + \begin{bmatrix} -38 & -28 \\ -67 & -47 \end{bmatrix} + \begin{bmatrix} -5 & -3 \\ 17 & 13 \end{bmatrix} = \begin{bmatrix} 29 & 18 \\ 47 & 35 \end{bmatrix}$$

Finding the elements of $C_{11}, C_{12}, C_{21}, C_{22}$ from the elements of D, E, F, G, H, M, P does not involve any multiplication. Strassen's method requires 49 multiplications while the usual method of matrix multiplication requires 64 multiplications for multiplying two 4×4 matrices.

2.6 POLYNOMIAL MULTIPLICATION

Consider the problem of finding the product of two polynomials A and B. Suppose

$$A(x) = \sum_{j=0}^{n-1} a_j x^j$$

$$B(x) = \sum_{j=0}^{n-1} b_j x^j$$

then

$$C(x) = \sum_{j=0}^{2n-2} c_j x^j$$

where
$$c_j = \sum_{k=0}^{j} a_k b_{j-k}$$

The straightforward method for multiplying polynomials using these equations require $O(n^2)$ time. However, by using the divide and conquer technique, we can lower the asymptotic complexity. We assume that n is a positive integer power of 2. We follow a technique similar to that used in Section 2.1. We split $A(x)$ into two parts $A_1(x)$ and $A_2(x)$, where

$$A_1(x) = \sum_{j=k}^{n-1} a_j x^{j-k} \quad \text{and} \quad A_2(x) = \sum_{j=0}^{k-1} a_j x^j, \text{ where } k = n/2$$

Similarly, we can write

$$B_1(x) = \sum_{j=k}^{n-1} b_j x^{j-k} \quad \text{and} \quad B_2(x) = \sum_{j=0}^{k-1} b_j x^j$$

where, $k = n/2$. We express $A(x)$ in terms of $A_1(x)$ and $A_2(x)$, and $B(x)$ in terms of $B_1(x)$ and $B_2(x)$ as

$$A(x) = x^k A_1(x) + A_2(x) \quad \text{and} \quad B(x) = x^k B_1(x) + B_2(x)$$

The product of the polynomials $A(x)B(x)$ may be expressed as

$$A(x)B(x) = x^{2k} A_1(x)B_1(x) + x^k(A_2(x)B_1(x) + A_1(x)B_2(x)) + A_2(x)B_2(x)$$

The smaller polynomials $A_1(x)$, $A_2(x)$, $B_1(x)$, and $B_2(x)$ have half the number of terms compared to those of polynomials $A(x)$ and $B(x)$. The original problem of multiplying $A(x)$ and $B(x)$ is reduced to multiplying $A_1(x)B_1(x)$, $A_2(x)B_1(x)$, $A_1(x)B_2(x)$ and $A_2(x)B_2(x)$. If we purse this further, we shall land up with quadratic algorithm for matrix multiplication. In the above, we have to do four polynomial multiplications and three polynomial additions with polynomials of half the original degree. If we can reduce the number of polynomial multiplications at the cost of a few more polynomial additions, we shall arrive at reduced time complexity. We have to do it a bit cleverly. Let us rearrange the multiplication of $A(x)B(x)$ as:

$$A(x)B(x) = x^{2k} A_1(x) B_1(x) + x^k ((A_2(x) + A_1(x))(B_2(x) + B_1(x))$$
$$- A_2(x) B_2(x) - A_1(x) B_1(x)) + A_2(x) B_2(x)$$

We have now only three polynomial multiplications and six polynomial additions of half the original degree. The recurrence relation of the time complexity may be written as $T(n) = 3T(n/2)$, $n > 1$ and $T(1) = 1$. The solution is $O(n^{\log_2 3})$. A simple pseudocode for the recursive procedure of polynomial multiplication may be written as

```
Procedure Poly_mult(P, Q, n)
    /* P and Q are the polynomials each with n terms */
    /* A₁, A₂, B₁, B₂, A₁₂, B₁₂ are polynomials each with n/2 terms */
    /* C, D, E are polynomials each with n terms */
```

```
/* CC is a polynomial with 2n terms */
/* DCE is a polynomial with (3/2)n terms */
/* F is a polynomial with 2n terms */

If (n = 1) Then
    Return (a₀b₀);
Else
  K = n/2;
  Divide(A, A₁, A₂);
  Divide(B, B₁, B₂);
/* Divide splits the polynomial into two smaller size polynomials
as described in the text*/
  C = Poly_mult(A₁,B₁,k);
  A₁₂ = A₁+ A₂;
  B₁₂ = B₁+ B₂;
  D = Poly_mult(A₁₂,B₁₂,k);
  E = Poly_mult(A₂,B₂,k);
  CC = Each coefficient of C is shifted right by n places;
/* This amounts to multiplying C by x²ᵏ */
  DCE = Each coefficient of D - C - E is shifted right by n/2 places;
/* This amounts to multiplying D - C - E by xᵏ */
  F = CC + DCE + E;
  Return(F);
Endif
End Poly_mult
```

SUMMARY

In this chapter, we have shown how some standard problems such as the multiplication of two n-bit numbers, merge-sorting, binary searching, quick-sorting, polynomial multiplication can be done using the approach of divide and conquer. Mere equal size divisions of the original problem may not always lead to reduction of time complexity as is evident from the matrix, n-bit number, and polynomial multiplication problems. We will further illustrate the divide-and-conquer method with some more problems in Chapter 5.

EXERCISES

2.1 Modify the binary search so that at each stage instead of halving the remaining list, we divide it using a uniform random number in the appropriate range. How does this modified algorithm compare with the original algorithm in terms of performance?

2.2 Prove that quick-sort takes $O(N \log N)$ time to sort N elements on the average.

2.3 Formulate integer multiplication algorithm using the divide-and-conquer technique but dividing each integer into 4 pieces instead of 2. What would be the complexity of the resulting algorithm?

2.4 Show how matrix multiplication is carried out using the Strassen's method. Find the complexity of the Strassen's method.

2.5 Show how the following matrices would be multiplied using the Strassen's algorithm.

$$\begin{bmatrix} 7 & 9 \\ 2 & 5 \end{bmatrix} \text{ and } \begin{bmatrix} 3 & 2 \\ 6 & 5 \end{bmatrix}$$

2.6 Given a file which is partially sorted as $x_1 \geq x_2 \geq \ldots \geq x_m$ and $x_{m+1} \geq x_{m+2} \geq \ldots \geq x_n$, is it possible to sort the entire file in $O(n)$ time using some extra storage?

2.7 Show the snapshots of lexicographically sorting the strings *abc, acb, bbca, bb, aac, baa, abca, cab* using quick-sort.

2.8 Decide empirically, the minimum size of the input two-dimensional matrices for which the Strassen's method should be preferred over the traditional way of multiplying matrices on your computer.

2.9 Heap-sort, merge-sort, or quick-sort—which one would you prefer for implementation on your machine? Justify through empirical results.

2.10 How many key comparisons are made in the quick-sort if the input data is already sorted?

2.11 Use the steps of $O(n^{1.59})$ algorithm given in this chapter for carrying out multiplication of the following 8-bit numbers: 01101010, 00110101.

2.12 You are given a list of positive and negative numbers. Use binary search to find out the number of members in the list having absolute value K. Analyze the time complexity as well.

2.13 Show the snapshots of sorting the following using quick-sort:

$$2, -1, 5, 13, 55, 22, 77, 3, 17, 50.$$

Find the number of comparisons made.

2.14 Use the divide-and-conquer technique to find a^n, where $a > 0$, and n is a positive integer. Compare the efficiency of this algorithm with the brute-force method.

2.15 A problem can be directly solved in n^3 time. The problem can be divided into r sub-problems of size $n/2$ in unit time. How small must r be so that it is better to divide a large problem into sub-problems rather than to solve it directly?

2.16 Suppose there is a method for multiplying 3×3 matrices with k multiplications and this method can be used recursively to multiply larger matrices. How small should k be so that this method is faster than the traditional method of matrix multiplication?

GREEDY METHOD

3.0 INTRODUCTION

This is a simple method used to solve optimization problems. The problems that are solved using the greedy method include finding the best order to execute a certain set of jobs on a computer, finding the shortest path in a graph, etc.

To solve an optimization problem, we look for a set of candidates constituting a solution that optimizes (minimizes or maximizes, as the case may be) the value of the objective function. A greedy algorithm proceeds step by step. Initially the set of chosen candidates is empty. Then at each step, we try to add to this set the best remaining candidates, our choice being guided by the *selection function*. The selection function is dependent on the problem at hand. For example, the selection function in the case of minimum weight spanning tree picks an edge of minimum weight from the remaining edges, an object with maximum profit per unit weight out of the remaining objects is chosen for putting in the knapsack in the case of knapsack problem. If the enlarged set of chosen candidates is no longer feasible, we remove the candidate we just added; the candidate we tried and removed is never considered again. However, if the enlarged set is still feasible, then the candidate we just added stays in the set of chosen candidates from then on. Each time we enlarge the set of chosen candidates, we check whether the set now constitutes a solution to our problem. When a greedy algorithm works correctly, the first solution found in this way is always optimal. The following is a generic pseudocode for the greedy method.

```
Procedure Greedy(C) /* C is the set of all candidates */
    S = φ;/* S is the set in which we construct the solution */
    While not solution (S) and C ≠ φ Do
        Select x ∈ C based on the selection criterion;
        C ← C - {x};
```

```
     If feasible(S ∪ {x}) Then
        S = S ∪ {x};
     Endif
  Endwhile
  If solution (S) Then
                    Return(S);
                    Else
                    Return("No solution");
     Endif
  End Greedy
```

It is easy to see why such algorithms are called 'greedy'. At every step, the procedure chooses the best candidate from the remaining, without worrying about the future. Once a candidate is included in the solution, it is there for good; once a candidate is excluded from the solution, it is never reconsidered.

The selection function is usually based on the objective function; they may even be identical. At times there may be several possible selection functions, so that we have to choose the right one if we want our algorithm to work properly.

Suppose we want to give change to a customer using the smallest possible number of coins. The elements of the problem are as follows: the candidates are a finite set of coins, representing for instance, 1, 5, 10, and 25 units, and containing at least one coin of each type. The solution is a subset of the coins whose value is the amount we have to pay. A feasible set is the total value of the chosen subset whose value does not exceed the amount to be paid. The selection function is, choosing the highest valued coin remaining in the set of candidates, and the objective function is the number of coins used in the solution.

3.1 MINIMUM COST SPANNING TREE

The spanning tree (T) of a connected graph $G = (V, E)$ is an acyclic, connected sub-graph of G containing all the nodes of G. The minimum spanning tree is a spanning tree of a weighted graph having the least sum of the edge weights, that is, no other spanning tree of the weighted graph will have sum of the edge weights less than that of the minimum spanning tree. Connected component C of a graph G is the maximally connected sub-graph of G, that is, there is no sub-graph B of G which is connected and includes C as a sub-graph. We describe two algorithms for finding the minimum cost spanning tree: Kruskal's algorithm and Prim's algorithm.

3.1.1 Kruskal's Algorithm

Let $G = (V, E)$ be a connected, undirected graph where V is the set of nodes and E is the set of edges. Each edge has a given non-negative length (cost). The problem is to find a subset T of the edges of G such that all the nodes remain connected without forming cycle when only the edges in T are used, and the sum of the lengths (cost) of the edges in T is as small as possible.

The set T of edges is initially empty. With the progress of the algorithm, edges are added to T. At every instant, the partial graph formed by the nodes of G and the edges in T consists of several connected components. (Initially, when T is empty, each node of G forms an initial connected component.) The elements of T that are included in a given connected component form a minimal spanning tree for the nodes in this component. At the end of the algorithm, only one connected component remains, so that T is then a minimal spanning tree for all the nodes of G.

To build bigger and bigger connected components, we examine the edges of G in the order of increasing length. If an edge joins two nodes in different connected components, we add it to T, and consequently the two connected components now form only one component. Otherwise, the edge is rejected; it joins two nodes in the same connected component and cannot therefore be added to T without forming a cycle since the edges in T form a minimal spanning tree for each component. The algorithm stops when only one connected component remains.

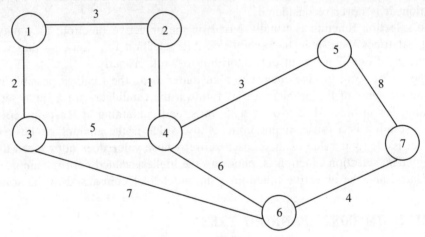

FIGURE 3.1 Weighted graph.

To illustrate how the algorithm works, we consider the edges (refer Figure 3.1) in increasing order of length (cost): {2,4}, {1,3}, {1,2}, {4,5}, {6,7}, {3,4}, {4,6}, {3,6}, {5,7}. The edge considered at each step and the connected components are shown in Table 3.1.

TABLE 3.1   Illustration of Kruskal's algorithm

Step	Edge considered	Connected components
Initialization	—	{1},{2},{3},{4},{5},{6},{7}
1	{2,4}	{1}{2, 4},{3},{5},{6},{7}
2	{1,3}	{1,3},{2, 4},{5},{6},{7}
3	{1,2}	{1,2,3,4},{5},{6},{7}
4	{4,5}	{1,2,3,4,5}, {6},{7}
5	{6,7}	{1,2,3,4,5}, {6,7}
6	{3,4}	Rejected because of cycle creation
7	{4,6}	{1,2,3,4,5,6,7}

The minimum spanning tree found has cost 19 as shown in Figure 3.2.

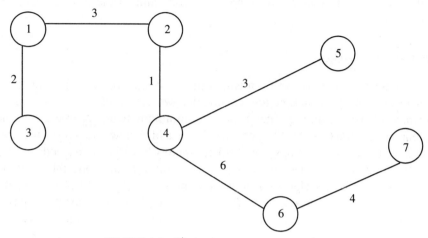

FIGURE 3.2 Minimal cost spanning tree.

The algorithm is:

```
Procedure Kruskal(G = (V,E),f:E→R⁺)
  Sort E by increasing length;
  n = |V|;
  T = φ;
  Repeat
    (u,v) = Shortest edge not yet considered;
    ucomp = find(u);
  /* find(u) tells us in which component the node u is to be
found */
    vcomp = find(v);
    If ucomp ≠ vcomp Then
      Merge(ucomp,vcomp);
      T = T ∪ {(u,v)};
    Endif
  Until |T| = n - 1;
  Return(T);
End Kruskal
```

Complexity analysis

Let $|V| = n$ and $|E| = a$. We observe that $O(a \log a)$ time is needed to sort the edges which is $O(a \log n)$ time, since $(n - 1) \leq a \leq n(n - 1)/2$, $O(n)$ time is required to initialize the n disjoint sets, there are at most $2a$ find operations and $(n - 1)$ merge operations. Using efficient data structure, this can be done in $O((2a + n - 1)\log n)$ time. $O(a)$ time is needed for the remaining operations.

For a sparsely connected graph, a is $O(n)$ and so the total time for the algorithm is $O(n \log n)$. For a densely connected graph, a is $O(n^2)$ and so the total time in such a case will be $O(n^2 \log n)$.

3.1.2 Prim's Algorithm

In Kruskal's algorithm, we choose promising edges without worrying too much about their connection to previously chosen edges, except that we are careful never to form a cycle.

In Prim's algorithm, on the other hand, the minimum spanning tree grows 'naturally', starting from an arbitrary root. At each stage, we add a new branch to the tree already connected, and the algorithm stops when all the nodes have been reached.

Initially, the set B of nodes contains a single arbitrary node, and the set T of edges is empty. At each step, Prim's algorithm looks for the shortest possible edge (u, v) such that $u \in V - B$ and $v \in B$. It then adds u to B and (u, v) to T. In this way the edges in T form at any instant, a minimal spanning tree for the nodes in B. We continue as long as $B \neq V$.

```
Procedure Prim(G = (V,E,W))
  T = φ;
  B = {An arbitrary member of V};
  While B ≠ V Do
    Find(u, v) of minimum length such that u ∈ V - B and v ∈ B;
      T = T ∪ {(u,v)};
      B = B ∪ {u};
  Endwhile
  Return(T);
End Prim
```

Complexity analysis

As before, let $|V| = n$ and $|E| = a$. The *while loop* is repeated $|V| - 1 = n - 1$ times. For each repetition of the *while loop*, the inside statements require $O(n)$ time. Hence, Prim's algorithm requires $O(n^2)$ time. If the graph is represented by its adjacency lists and a min-priority queue of the edges is implemented, the running time of the algorithm will be $O(a \log n)$. This is because the algorithm makes $n - 1$ deletions of the smallest elements and makes a insertions in the priority queue. Each of these operations takes *logarithmic* time. Hence, the running time of the algorithm is in $(n - 1 + a)O(\log n) = O(a \log n)$ because in a connected graph, $a \geq n - 1$.

Let us find the minimum cost spanning tree of the graph shown in Figure 3.3 using Prim's algorithm. Table 3.2 shows the progress of the algorithm on the input graph of Figure 3.3.

3.2 KNAPSACK PROBLEM

We are given n objects and a knapsack. Object i has a weight w_i and the knapsack has a capacity M. If a fraction x_i, $0 \leq x_i \leq 1$, of object i is placed into the knapsack then a profit

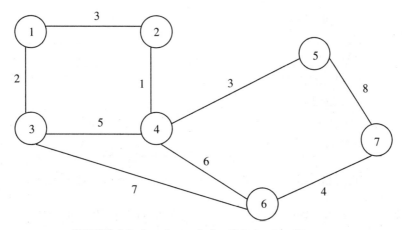

FIGURE 3.3 Input graph for Prim's algorithm.

TABLE 3.2 Minimal cost spanning tree using Prim's algorithm

Step	(u, v)	B	V – B
Initialization	—	{1}	{2,3,4,5,6,7}
1	(1,3)	{1,3}	{2,4,5,6,7}
2	(1,2)	{1,2,3}	{4,5,6,7}
3	(2,4)	{1,2,3,4}	{5,6,7}
4	(4,5)	{1,2,3,4,5}	{6,7}
5	(4,6)	{1,2,3,4,5,6}	{7}
6	(6,7)	{1,2,3,4,5,6,7}	ϕ

of $p_i x_i$ is earned. Since the knapsack capacity is M, we require that the sum of weights of all the chosen objects to be at most, M. Formally:

$$\text{Maximize} \sum_{i \le i \le n} p_i x_i, \tag{3.1}$$

subject to

$$\sum_{1 \le i \le n} w_i x_i \le M \tag{3.2}$$

and

$$0 \le x_i \le 1, \quad 1 \le i \le n \tag{3.3}$$

The profits and weights are positive numbers. A feasible solution is any set $(x_1, x_2, \ldots, x_n)$ satisfying the conditions of (3.2) and (3.3). An optimal solution is a feasible solution for which the value of (3.1) is maximum.

EXAMPLE 3.1 With usual notations, let

$M = 20, n = 3$

$(p_1, p_2, p_3) = (25, 24, 20)$ and $(w_1, w_2, w_3) = (18, 15, 10)$

Four feasible solutions are as tabulated:

x_1, x_2, x_3	$\Sigma w_i x_i$	$\Sigma p_i x_i$
1/2, 1/3, 1/4	16.5	25.5
1, 2/15, 0	20	28.2
0, 2/3, 1	20	36
0, 1, 1/2	20	34

Of the four feasible solutions, the third one yields the maximum profit.

EXAMPLE 3.2 Let us consider the following knapsack problem:

$M = 25, n = 3$
$P = (25, 24, 17)$
$W = (16, 14, 9)$

We find the P/W vector as $(25/16, 24/14, 17/9) = (1.562, 1.714, 1.888)$. The highest profit per unit weight is achieved by selecting the third item, hence $x_3 = 1$. The remaining capacity is 16. We can now select the second item, so that, $x_2 = 1$ and the remaining capacity is 2. We now select $2/16 = 1/8^{\text{th}}$ of the first item and thus, $x_1 = 1/8$. Hence the solution vector for this instance of the knapsack is $(1/8, 1, 1)$ and the profit earned is $17 + 24 + 25/8 = 44.125$.

The following pseudocode solves a fractional knapsack problem:

```
Procedure Knapsack (P,W,M,X,n)
   /* P(1:n) is profit array, W(1:n) the weights array of the n
objects ordered so that
```

$$\frac{P(i)}{W(i)} \geq \frac{P(i+1)}{W(i+1)}$$

```
   M is the knapsack size and X(1:n) is the solution vector */
   Array P(n), W(n), X(n)
   For i = 1 to n Do
     X(i) = 0; /* Initial solution */
   Endfor
   RC = M; /* Remaining capacity of knapsack */
   For i = 1 to n Do
     If W(i) > RC Then
        Exit;
     Endif
     X(i) = 1;
     RC = RC - W(i);
   Endfor
```

```
If i ≤ n Then
    X(i) = RC/W(i);
Endif
End Knapsack
```

Complexity analysis

Arranging the array so that $(P(i)/W(i)) \geq (P(i + 1)/W(i + 1))$, $1 \leq i < n$ requires $O(n \log n)$ time. The two *for loops* in the procedure each requires $O(n)$ time. So solving the fractional knapsack problem requires $O(n \log n)$ time.

Theorem 3.1   If $P_1/W_1 \geq P_2/W_2 \geq ... \geq P_n/W_n$, the previous procedure knapsack generates an optimal solution to the given instance of the knapsack problem.

Proof: Let $X = (x_1, ..., x_n)$ be the solution generated by the algorithm. If all the x_i are equal to one, clearly the solution is optimal.

Let j be the least index such that $x_j \neq 1$. From the algorithm it follows that:

$x_i = 1$ for $1 \leq i < j$ and $x_i = 0$ for $j < i \leq n$ and $0 \leq x_j < 1$.

Let $Y = (y_1, ..., y_n)$ be an optimal solution. Without loss of generality, we may assume $\Sigma y_i w_i = M$.

Let k be the least index such that $y_k \neq x_k$. Clearly, such a value of k must exist. Let us consider the three possibilities.

(i) If $k < j$, then $x_k = 1$ and $y_k \neq x_k$, so $x_k > y_k$.
(ii) If $k = j$, then since $\Sigma w_i x_i = M$ and $y_i = x_i$ for $1 \leq i < j$, it follows that either $x_k > y_k$ or $\Sigma w_i y_i > M$.
(iii) If $k > j$ then $\Sigma w_i y_i > M$ which is not possible.

Therefore, $x_k > y_k$.

Now suppose we increase y_k to x_k and decrease as many of $(y_{k+1}, ..., y_n)$ as is necessary so that the total capacity used is still M. This results in a new solution $Z = (z_1, z_2, ..., z_n)$ with

$z_i = x_i$, $1 \leq i \leq k$ and $\displaystyle\sum_{k < i \leq n} w_i(y_i - z_i) = w_k(z_k - y_k)$.

Then for the solution Z, we have:

$$\sum_{1 \leq i \leq n} p_i z_i = \sum_{1 \leq i \leq n} p_i y_i + (z_k - y_k) w_k \frac{p_k}{w_k} - \sum_{k < i \leq n} (y_i - z_i) w_i p_i / w_i$$

$$\geq \sum_{1 \leq i \leq n} p_i y_i + \left[(z_k - y_k) w_k - \sum_{k < i \leq n} (y_i - z_i) w_i \right] \frac{p_k}{w_k} \quad /* \text{ Since } \frac{p_k}{w_k} \geq \frac{p_i}{w_i} \ \forall \ k < i \ */$$

$$= \sum_{1 \leq i \leq n} p_i y_i \quad /* \text{ The two terms within the rectangular brackets cancel each other } */$$

If $\Sigma p_i z_i > \Sigma p_i y_i$, then Y could not have been an optimal solution. If these sums are equal, then either $Z = X$ and X is optimal, or $Z \neq X$. In the latter case, repeated use of the above argument will either show that Y is not optimal or will transform Y into X, showing that X too is optimal.

3.3 DIJKSTRA'S SINGLE SOURCE SHORTEST PATH ALGORITHM

The problem is to find the shortest path from a given node to all other nodes in a weighted directed graph. The algorithm of Dijkstra based on greedy approach is described below. The algorithm progressively labels the nodes of the graph permanently starting from the designated start node. The permanent label of a node is the shortest distance of the node from the designated start node. By making each node of the graph as the starting node, we can find the shortest distance among all pairs of nodes of the graph by repetitively applying the Dijkstra's algorithm. The algorithm is as follows:

```
Procedure Dijk(u, Cost(N,N), Dist(N), N)
   /* Cost(i,j) = weight of edge (i,j), u = source vertex, Dist(i)
= Shortest distance of vertex i from u, N = number of vertices in
the graph */
   Array Cost(N,N), Dist(N)
   For i = 1 to N Do
     S(i) = 0; /* i is not included in the shortest path */
     Dist(i) = Cost(u,i);
        /* weight of edge (u, i) or ∞ if no edge exists, 0 if i = u */
   Endfor
   S(u) = 1; /* Vertex u is put in set S */

   For k = 2 to N Do
     Choose v such that Dist(v) = min{Dist(w)} and S(w)=0;
     S(v) = 1; /* put vertex v in set S */
   For all w with S(w) = 0 Do
     Dist(w) = min(Dist(w), Dist(v) + Cost(v,w));
   Endfor
   Endfor
End Dijk
```

Complexity analysis

The time taken by Dijkstra's algorithm on a graph with N vertices is $O(N^2)$ because the *k-loop* is repeated $N - 1$ times and for each repetition of *k-loop* v is searched from a list which is decreasing in length starting from $N - 1$ with every iteration of k. The time $T(N)$ may be expressed as $T(N) = (N - 1) + (N - 2) + \cdots + 1 = N(N - 1)/2$.

Let us apply Dijkstra's algorithm to find the shortest distance between A and E in the directed graph of Figure 3.4. Snapshot of the computation is shown in Table 3.3. A node permanently labelled is shown with double under-score and the latest permanently labelled node, with an asterisk. The shortest distance between A and E is 6, that between A and D is 9, that between A and C is 3, and that between A and B is 2 as shown in the last row of

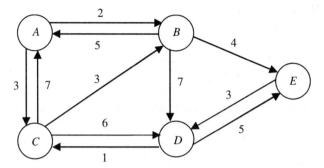

FIGURE 3.4 Directed weighted graph.

Table 3.3. The shortest path can be retrieved from the table as follows. Node *E* was permanently labelled using node *B*. So the shortest path from *A* to *E* passes through *B*. Node *B* was permanently labelled using node *A*. So the shortest path from *A* to *E* consists of the edges *AB, BE*.

TABLE 3.3 Illustration of Dijkstra's algorithm

A	B	C	D	E	S(A)	S(B)	S(C)	S(D)	S(E)
0	2	3	∞	∞	1	0	0	0	0
0	2*	3	∞	∞	1	1	0	0	0
0	2	3*	9	6	1	1	1	0	0
0	2	3	9	6*	1	1	1	0	1
0	2	3	9	6	1	1	1	1	1

3.4 HUFFMAN CODE

This is a variable length, prefix code (prefix-free code would be a better name) used for compression of data. A prefix code is a code where, for no two code words, one is the prefix of the other. This prefix freeness helps in decoding uniquely. We assume that *C* is a set of *n* characters and that each character $c \in C$ is an object with a given frequency $f[c]$. A priority queue *Q*, based on *f*, is used to identify the two least-frequent objects to merge together. A priority queue arranges the elements in the queue according to priority or key value of the elements. Min (max.) heap is an example of priority queue where the element with the least (maximum) key value is at the root of the heap. The following algorithm builds the tree *T* corresponding to the optimal code in a bottom-up manner. It begins with a set of |*C*| leaves and performs a sequence of |*C*| − 1 merging operations to create the final tree. The result of the merger of two objects is a new object whose frequency is the sum of the frequencies of the two objects that were merged.

```
Procedure Huffman (C, f)
  Character Array C(n), f(n)
  n = |C|;
  Build a priority queue Q containing the elements of C;
  For i = 1 to n - 1 Do
  z = Get_node( ); /* Allocates space */
    x = Extract_min(Q); /* Extracts the minimum element from Q */
    y = Extract_min(Q);
    Make x as the left-child and y as the right-child of z;
    f[z] = f[x] + f[y];
    Insert z into Q;
  Endfor
End Huffman
```

Complexity analysis

Q is implemented as a binary heap. The initialization of Q can be performed in $O(n)$ time using the heap building procedure. The *for loop* is executed $(n - 1)$ times and since each heap operation requires $O(\log n)$ time, the loop contributes $O(n \log n)$ time to the complexity. The overall complexity of the above algorithm is $O(n \log n)$.

Suppose we have a file with 100,000 characters consisting of $s1, s2, s3, s4, s5, s6$. Fixed-length code requires 300,000 bits. Variable-length Huffman code as shown in Table 3.4 requires 254,000 bits. It has a saving of about 15.33%.

TABLE 3.4 Symbols and their frequency of occurrence

Character	Frequency of occurrence (in %)	Fixed length code word	Variable length code word
S1	18	000	111
S2	25	001	10
S3	21	010	01
S4	17	011	110
S5	5	100	000
S6	14	101	001

Let us see how the variable length Huffman code is designed. The creation of the leaf nodes is shown through Figures 3.5(a) to 3.5(d) and the full tree is shown in Figure 3.5(e). First, we create two leaf nodes corresponding to the characters with the lowest frequencies;

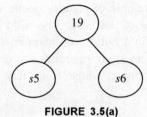

FIGURE 3.5(a)

the smaller one is attached as the left child and the larger one as the right child of a third node created with weight equal to the sum of the children's frequencies. So *s5* becomes the left child and *s6*, the right child.

We now pick up *s4* and *s1* having the least frequencies 17 and 18 respectively. We make a new node with weight (35) equal to the sum of the frequencies of *s4*, *s1* and make *s4* as the left child and *s1* as the right child of this newly created node.

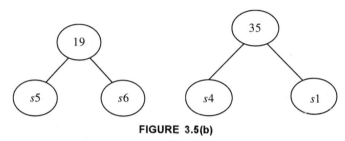

FIGURE 3.5(b)

Next we pick up *s3* as the character with the least frequency (21) and create a new node with weight 40 whose left sub-tree with weight 19 contains *s5* and *s6* while the right sub-tree contains *s3*.

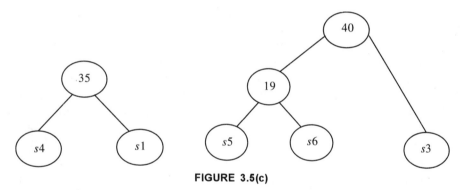

FIGURE 3.5(c)

We then pick up *s2* with weight 25 and create a node with weight 60 whose left sub-tree contains *s2* and the right sub-tree with weight 35 contains *s4* and *s1*.

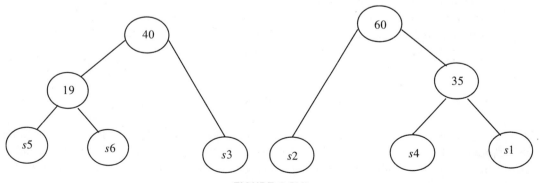

FIGURE 3.5(d)

No more symbols are left out. We now create a node with weight 100, whose left sub-tree with weight 40 contains the symbols $s5$, $s6$, $s3$ and the right sub-tree with weight 60 contains $s2$, $s4$, $s1$.

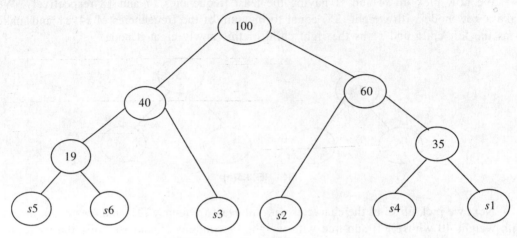

FIGURE 3.5(e)   Tree for Huffman code.

Let us see how variable length code is assigned to the different characters. To find the code for any character, we start from the root and after traversing along the left and right branches we reach the leaf corresponding to the character. We build the code by concatenating 0's and 1's depending on whether we have traversed a left branch or a right branch from a node. We take 0 for the left branch and 1 for the right branch. Let us see what would be the code for $s4$. To reach $s4$ from the root we take the right branch two times followed by a left branch. Hence the code for $s4$ would be 110 as shown in Table 3.4. By following the same argument, we find the codes for $s1$ as 111, $s2$ as 10, $s3$ as 01, $s4$ as 110, $s5$ as 000 and $s6$ as 001. The weighted average code length is 2.54.

Let us now see how given a code string, the actual characters are found. This can be done in an unambiguous manner because of the prefix freeness of Huffman code. Suppose we are given the code string 1101001. We scan the string one character at a time and take the left branch if the character is 0 and the right branch if it is 1. This is continued till we reach a leaf node. After scanning 110, we reach $s4$ and this is output. Next we find 1 and we take the right branch and then a 0 and we take the left branch reaching $s2$ and this is output. Next we find 0 and so take the left branch and then 1 and take the right branch to reach $s3$. So the given code represents $s4$, $s2$, $s3$.

SUMMARY

In this chapter, we have introduced the basic steps of greedy approach to algorithm design. The approach has been used to find algorithms for minimal cost spanning tree using Kruskal's and Prim's algorithms, solving fractional knapsack problem, single-source shortest paths problem using Dijkstra's algorithm and variable-length Huffman code design. The greedy method is quite simple, but the approach may not always yield the optimal solution; for example, in the case of TSP problem. The theory of matroids is used in determining when the greedy method produces optimal solutions. The theory of matroids does not cover all cases for which a greedy method is useful, but it does cover many cases of practical interest.

EXERCISES

3.1 What are the general characteristics of greedy algorithms and the problems solved by these algorithms?

3.2 Construct an example and show that the Dijkstra's algorithm does not work correctly if some of the edge weights are negative.

3.3 Examine whether the following procedure gives a minimum-weight spanning tree T for a given connected graph $G = (V, E)$.

Step 1: Take T as an arbitrary spanning tree of G.

Step 2: Examine each edge not in T in turn. The edge is added to T forming a cycle and then the heaviest edge in the cycle is deleted.

3.4 Show the snapshots of Prim's and Kruskal's algorithms for finding the minimum-weight spanning tree for the following graph.

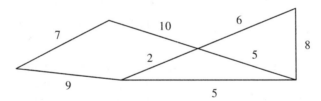

3.5 Design a greedy algorithm for the coin-changing problem. Under what condition, the greedy algorithm always yields an optimal solution?

3.6 Prove that the edge with the smallest weight will be part of every minimum spanning tree.

3.7 Prove that if all the edge weights are distinct, there is only one minimum spanning tree.

3.8 Design Huffman codes for the following symbols: a, b, c, d, e, f, and i having relative frequencies 2, 4, 6, 8, 10, 12, 16 respectively.

3.9 Suppose we have n programs of lengths L_1, L_2, ..., L_n on a tape. Program i is to be retrieved with frequency f_i. Show that the expected retrieval time is minimized when the programs are stored in non-increasing order of f_i/L_i.

3.10 Show how Prim's algorithm can be implemented using heap. What would be the time complexity of the algorithm?

3.11 Show that if the symbols are sorted by frequency, algorithm for the generation of Huffman code can be implemented in linear time.

3.12 Does any greedy approach to the chained matrix multiplication work?

3.13 Make a comparative study of the greedy, exhaustive and heuristic approaches to TSP problem on your computer using different problem instances.

3.14 What is spanning tree? What is the importance of finding minimal spanning tree?

3.15 (i) Design Huffman code for the following characters:

Character: *a*   *b*   *c*   *d*   *e*

Frequency: 40%   18%   12%   16%   14%

(ii) Suppose we have to transmit 10^8 characters. Sending each bit requires 10^{-9} seconds. How much saving in transmission time can be achieved using Huffman code compared to the fixed-length code?

3.16 Suppose we have a set of coins of denominations c^{n-1}, c^{n-2}, ..., c^0, for some $c > 1$. Coins of each denomination are available in unlimited quantity. The problem is to make up an exact amount A using a minimum total number of coins. Devise a greedy solution for this problem and analyze the time complexity of the algorithm.

3.17 Describe Huffman's algorithm with an example for generation of prefix code. Modify the algorithm of Section 3.4 to incorporate the code symbols {0, 1, 2} instead of {0, 1}.

3.18 What is the maximal length of a code word possible in Huffman encoding of an alphabet of n characters?

3.19 (i) We have to assign n jobs to n workers, one job per worker. There is a definite cost of assigning worker i to job j, $1 \leq i, j \leq n$. Design a greedy algorithm so that workers are assigned jobs with the minimum total cost.

(ii) Does the greedy approach always succeed in the assignment problems?

(iii) What is the complexity of the algorithm?

DYNAMIC PROGRAMMING

4.0 INTRODUCTION

Richard Bellman invented the technique of dynamic programming in the 1950s as a general method for optimizing multistage decision processes. The word 'programming' here stands for 'planning' and does not refer to computer programming. It is often possible to divide an instance of a problem into sub-instances, to solve these sub-instances, and then combine the solutions of the sub-instances to solve the original instance. The natural way of dividing an instance may lead us to consider several overlapping sub-instances. If we solve each of these sub-instances independently, they will in turn create a large number of identical sub-instances. It is likely that we will be duplicating certain pieces of computation, resulting in an inefficient algorithm. If, on the other hand, we take advantage of the duplication and solve each sub-instance only once, saving the solution for later use, then a more efficient algorithm will result.

The underlying idea of dynamic programming is: avoid calculating the same thing twice, usually by keeping a table of known results, which we fill up as the sub-instances are solved. Dynamic programming is a bottom-up technique. We usually start with the smallest, and hence the simplest sub-instances. By combining their solutions, we obtain answers to sub-instances of increasing size, until finally we arrive at the solution of the original instance. Divide and conquer, on the other hand, is a top-down method; we immediately attack the complete instance, which we then divide into smaller and smaller sub-instances as the algorithm progresses. The main advantage of dynamic programming is that it solves every sub-instance exactly once, while the divide-and-conquer may compute a solution to the same sub-instance many times.

Let us consider the computation of the nth Fibonacci number $F(n)$ using the recurrence relation: $F(n) = F(n - 1) + F(n - 2)$, $n \geq 2$, $F(0) = 0$ and $F(1) = 1$. The dynamic programming approach computes in the following sequence: $F(2) = F(1) + F(0)$, $F(3) = F(2) + F(1)$, $F(4) = F(3) + F(2)$, ..., $F(n) = F(n - 1) + F(n - 2)$. A divide-and-conquer approach will recursively compute $F(n - 1)$ and $F(n - 2)$. Computation of $F(n - 1)$ will involve recursive computation of $F(n - 2)$, $F(n - 3)$ while recursive computation of $F(n - 2)$ will involve recursive computation of $F(n - 3)$, $F(n - 4)$, and so on. The divide-and-conquer approach needs to tackle exponential number of sub-instance calls while it is linear in the case of dynamic programming approach.

Dynamic programming is often used to solve optimization problems that satisfy the principle of optimality. The principle states that *in an optimal sequence of decisions or choices, each sub-sequence must also be optimal.* In this chapter, we show how a number of problems can be solved using the dynamic programming technique.

4.1 CHAIN MATRIX MULTIPLICATION

Let us consider the problem of chain matrix multiplication. The problem is to find the product of a given collection of matrices in the indicated manner. Let us suppose that we have to find the product:

$$M = M_1 \times M_2 \times ... \times M_n$$

where M_i has r_{i-1} rows and r_i columns.

The order in which matrices are multiplied together can have significant effect on the total number of operations required to evaluate M, no matter what matrix multiplication method is used. Let us consider an example:

$$M = \quad M_1 \quad \times \quad M_2 \quad \times \quad M_3 \quad \times \quad M_4$$
$$[20 \times 50] \quad [50 \times 3] \quad [3 \times 50] \quad [50 \times 2]$$

Evaluating M in the order:

$M_1 \times (M_2 \times (M_3 \times M_4))$ requires 2600 operations as detailed below:

$M_3 \times M_4$ requires 300 operations

$M_2 \times (M_3 \times M_4)$ requires an additional 300 operations

$M_1 \times (M_2 \times (M_3 \times M_4))$ requires an additional 2000 operations, that is, a total of 2600 operations is required.

While evaluating M in the order:

$(M_1 \times (M_2 \times M_3)) \times M_4$ requires 59500 operations as detailed below.

$M_2 \times M_3$ requires 7500 operations.

$M_1 \times (M_2 \times M_3)$ requires an additional 50000 operations.

$(M_1 \times (M_2 \times M_3)) \times M_4$ requires an additional 2000 operations so that the total operations count is 59500.

The number of ordering of a chain of $n + 1$ matrix multiplication is the Catalan number,

$\dfrac{1}{n+1} \binom{2n}{n}$. Trying all possible orderings in which to evaluate the product of n matrices so as to minimize the number of operations is an exponential process, which is impractical when n is large.

However, dynamic programming provides an $O(n^3)$ algorithm.

Let $c(i, j)$ be the minimum cost of computing $M_i \times M_{i+1} \times ... \times M_j$ for $1 \leq j \leq n$. Clearly:

$$c(i, j) = \begin{cases} 0 & \text{if } i = j \\ \min_{i \leq k < j} (c(i,k) + c(k + 1, j) + r_{i-1} r_k r_j) & \text{if } j > i \end{cases}$$

The term $c(i, k)$ gives the minimum cost of evaluating $A = M_i \times M_{i+1} \times ... \times M_k$. The second term, $c(k + 1, j)$ is the minimum cost of evaluating $B = M_{k+1} \times M_{k+2} \times ... \times M_j$. The third term is the cost of multiplying A by B. We note that A is a $r_{i-1} \times r_k$ matrix and B is a $r_k \times r_j$ matrix. The previous equation states that $c(i, j)$, $j > i$, is the minimum value of the sum for all possible values of k between i and $(j - 1)$.

The algorithm may be written as:

```
Procedure Chain-matrix(M₁, M₂, ..., Mₙ, r₀, r₁, ..., rₙ)
   Array c(n,n), M₁(r₀,r₁), M₂(r₁,r₂), ... Mₙ(rₙ₋₁, rₙ)
   For i = 1 to n Do
     c(i,i) = 0;
   Endfor
   For p = 1 to n - 1 Do
     For i = 1 to n - p Do
       j = i + p;
       c(i,j) = ∞;
       For ik = i to j - 1 Do
         S = c(i,ik) + c(ik + 1,j) + rᵢ₋₁rᵢₖrⱼ;
         If s < c(i,j) Then
                         c(i,j) = s;
                         k = ik;
         Endif
       Endfor
     Endfor
   Endfor
   Write c(1,n);
End Chain-matrix
```

Let us see how the algorithm is used to find the optimal way of multiplying the above sequence of matrices for minimum operation count. The computational result is given in Table 4.1.

TABLE 4.1   Chain matrix multiplication

$c(1,1) = 0$	$c(2,2) = 0$	$c(3,3) = 0$	$c(4,4) = 0$
$c(1,2) = 3,000$	$c(2,3) = 7500$	$c(3,4) = 300$	
$c(1,3) = 6000$	$c(2,4) = 600$		
$k = 2$	$k = 2$		
$c(1,4) = 2600$			
$k = 1$			

Thus, we find that the minimum cost of finding the product of the example chain matrix multiplication $M = M_1 \times M_2 \times M_3 \times M_4$ is 2600. This minimum is based on multiplying $M_2 \times M_3 \times M_4$ which, in turn, is based on multiplying $M_3 \times M_4$. The sequence of multiplication for minimum cost is as follows:

First we multiply M_3 and M_4 producing matrix A at a cost of 300. We then find $M_2 \times A$ producing matrix B at a cost of 300. Finally, we multiply M_1 and B producing M at an additional cost of 2000.

The dynamic programming approach calculates the $c(i, j)$s in the order of increasing difference in the subscripts. We begin by calculating $c(i, i)$ for all i, then $c(i, i + 1)$ for all i, next $c(i, i + 2)$, and so on. In this way, the terms $c(i, ik)$ and $c(ik + 1, j)$ will be available when we calculate $c(i, j)$. This follows since $j - i$ must be strictly greater than either of $ik - i$ and $j - (ik + 1)$ if ik is in the range $i \leq ik < j$. Table 4.1 gives the optimal count of operations but it is a simple extension of the above algorithm to find the sequence of multiplication. If at each stage of computation of $c(i, j)$, we keep record of ik that produced the minimum value of $c(i, j)$, we will be able to decide the optimal sequence of the chain matrix multiplication.

4.2   FLOYD'S ALGORITHM FOR ALL PAIR SHORTEST PATHS

Let $G = (V, E)$ be a directed graph; V is the set of vertices and E is the set of edges. Each edge has an associated non-negative length. We want to calculate the length of the shortest path between each pairs of nodes.

Suppose that the nodes of G are numbered 1 through n, $V = \{1, 2, ..., n\}$ and that a matrix C gives the length of each edge, with $C(i, i) = 0$, $C(i, j) \geq 0$ if $i \neq j$, and $C(i, j) = \infty$, if the edge (i, j) does not exist.

The principle of optimality is applicable and it says that if k is a node on the shortest path from i to j, parts of the path from i to k, and from k to j must also be optimal.

We construct a matrix D iteratively that gives the length of the shortest path between each pair of nodes. The algorithm initializes D to C. It then does n iterations. After iteration k, D gives the length of the shortest paths that use only nodes in the set $\{1, 2, ..., k\}$ as intermediate nodes. After n iterations we obtain the result we want.

At iteration k, the algorithm checks for each pair of nodes (i, j) whether or not there exists a path passing through node k that is better than the present optimal path passing though the nodes in $\{1, 2, ..., k - 1\}$. Let D_k be the matrix D after the kth iteration.

The necessary check can be written as:

$$D_k(i, j) = \min(D_{k-1}(i, j), D_{k-1}(i, k) + D_{k-1}(k, j))$$

We use the principle of optimality to compute the length of the shortest path passing through k. We have also implicitly made use of the fact that an optimal path through k does not visit k twice.

At the kth iteration, the values in the kth column of D do not change; $D(k, k)$ is always zero. It is therefore not necessary to preserve these when updating D. This allows us to manage with a two-dimensional matrix D only, whereas at first sight a matrix $n \times n \times 2$ (or even $n \times n \times n$) seems necessary. If we are also interested in knowing the shortest path and not just its length, we use a second matrix P initialized to null.

The algorithm is known as Floyd's algorithm.

```
Procedure Floyd(C(n,n))
  Array D(n,n), P(n,n), C(n,n)
  For i = 1 to n Do
    For j = 1 to n Do
      D(i,j) = C(i,j);
      P(i,j) = Null;
    Endfor
  Endfor
  For k = 1 to n Do
    For i = 1 to n Do
      For j = 1 to n Do
        If D(i,k) + D(k,j) < D(i,j) Then
          D(i,j) = D(i,k) + D(k,j);
          P(i,j) = k;
        Endif
      Endfor
    Endfor
  Endfor
  Return(D,P);
End Floyd
```

It is obvious that this algorithm takes time $O(n^3)$ because there are three nested loops, each repeated n times. We can also use Dijkstra's algorithm to solve the same problem. In this case we have to apply Dijkstra's algorithm n times, each time choosing a different node as the source. Dijkstra's algorithm applied n times will require $n \times O(n^2) = O(n^3)$ time. However, the simplicity of Floyd's algorithm probably implies that it will be faster in practice.

When the algorithm stops, $P(i, j)$ contains the number of the last iteration that caused a change in $D(i, j)$. To recover the shortest path from i to j, we look at $P(i, j)$. If $P(i, j) = 0$, the shortest path is directly along the edge (i, j); otherwise, if $P(i, j) = k$, the shortest path from i to j passes through k. We look recursively at $P(i, k)$ and $P(k, j)$ to find other intermediate nodes along the shortest path.

Let us find all pair shortest paths for the directed graph in Figure 4.1 using Floyd's algorithm. In the P matrices below, an entry x represents null.

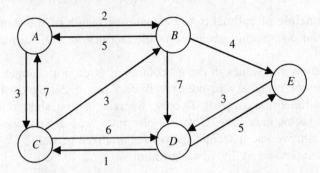

FIGURE 4.1 Example graph for all pair shortest paths.

$$D_0 = \begin{array}{c} \\ A \\ B \\ C \\ D \\ E \end{array} \begin{array}{ccccc} A & B & C & D & E \\ \left[\begin{array}{ccccc} 0 & 2 & 3 & \infty & \infty \\ 5 & 0 & \infty & 7 & 4 \\ 7 & 3 & 0 & 6 & \infty \\ \infty & \infty & 1 & 0 & 5 \\ \infty & \infty & \infty & 3 & 0 \end{array}\right] \end{array} \qquad P_0 = \begin{array}{c} \\ A \\ B \\ C \\ D \\ E \end{array} \begin{array}{ccccc} A & B & C & D & E \\ \left[\begin{array}{ccccc} x & x & x & x & x \\ x & x & x & x & x \\ x & x & x & x & x \\ x & x & x & x & x \\ x & x & x & x & x \end{array}\right] \end{array}$$

When the shortest path between i and j (i and j could be any of A, B, C, D or E) is allowed to include A as an intermediate node, we have the following distance and path matrices:

$$D_1 = \begin{array}{c} \\ A \\ B \\ C \\ D \\ E \end{array} \begin{array}{ccccc} A & B & C & D & E \\ \left[\begin{array}{ccccc} 0 & 2 & 3 & \infty & \infty \\ 5 & 0 & 8 & 7 & 4 \\ 7 & 3 & 0 & 6 & \infty \\ \infty & \infty & 1 & 0 & 5 \\ \infty & \infty & \infty & 3 & 0 \end{array}\right] \end{array} \qquad P_1 = \begin{array}{c} \\ A \\ B \\ C \\ D \\ E \end{array} \begin{array}{ccccc} A & B & C & D & E \\ \left[\begin{array}{ccccc} x & x & x & x & x \\ x & x & A & x & x \\ x & x & x & x & x \\ x & x & x & x & x \\ x & x & x & x & x \end{array}\right] \end{array}$$

When the shortest path between i and j (i and j could be any of A, B, C, D or E) is allowed to include A and B as intermediate nodes, we have the following distance and path matrices:

$$
D_2 = \begin{array}{c} \\ A \\ B \\ C \\ D \\ E \end{array}
\begin{array}{ccccc}
A & B & C & D & E \\
\hline
0 & 2 & 3 & 9 & 6 \\
5 & 0 & 8 & 7 & 4 \\
7 & 3 & 0 & 6 & 7 \\
\infty & \infty & 1 & 0 & 5 \\
\infty & \infty & \infty & 3 & 0
\end{array}
\qquad
P_2 = \begin{array}{c} \\ A \\ B \\ C \\ D \\ E \end{array}
\begin{array}{ccccc}
A & B & C & D & E \\
\hline
x & x & x & B & B \\
x & x & A & x & x \\
x & x & x & x & B \\
x & x & x & x & x \\
x & x & x & x & x
\end{array}
$$

When the shortest path between i and j (i and j could be any of A, B, C, D or E) is allowed to include A, B and C as intermediate nodes, we have the following distance and path matrices:

$$
D_3 = \begin{array}{c} \\ A \\ B \\ C \\ D \\ E \end{array}
\begin{array}{ccccc}
A & B & C & D & E \\
\hline
0 & 2 & 3 & 9 & 6 \\
5 & 0 & 8 & 7 & 4 \\
7 & 3 & 0 & 6 & 7 \\
8 & 4 & 1 & 0 & 5 \\
\infty & \infty & \infty & 3 & 0
\end{array}
\qquad
P_3 = \begin{array}{c} \\ A \\ B \\ C \\ D \\ E \end{array}
\begin{array}{ccccc}
A & B & C & D & E \\
\hline
x & x & x & B & B \\
x & x & A & x & x \\
x & x & x & x & B \\
C & C & x & x & x \\
x & x & x & x & x
\end{array}
$$

When the shortest path between i and j (i and j could be any of A, B, C, D or E) is allowed to include A, B, C and D as intermediate nodes, we have the following distance and path matrices:

$$
D_4 = \begin{array}{c} \\ A \\ B \\ C \\ D \\ E \end{array}
\begin{array}{ccccc}
A & B & C & D & E \\
\hline
0 & 2 & 3 & 9 & 6 \\
5 & 0 & 8 & 7 & 4 \\
7 & 3 & 0 & 6 & 7 \\
8 & 4 & 1 & 0 & 5 \\
11 & 7 & 4 & 3 & 0
\end{array}
\qquad
P_4 = \begin{array}{c} \\ A \\ B \\ C \\ D \\ E \end{array}
\begin{array}{ccccc}
A & B & C & D & E \\
\hline
x & x & x & B & B \\
x & x & A & x & x \\
x & x & x & x & B \\
C & C & x & x & x \\
D & D & D & x & x
\end{array}
$$

When the shortest path between i and j (i and j could be any of A, B, C, D or E) is allowed to include A, B, C, D and E as intermediate nodes, we have the following distance and path matrices:

$$
D_5 = \begin{array}{c} \\ A \\ B \\ C \\ D \\ E \end{array}
\begin{array}{ccccc}
A & B & C & D & E \\
\hline
0 & 2 & 3 & 9 & 6 \\
5 & 0 & 8 & 7 & 4 \\
7 & 3 & 0 & 6 & 7 \\
8 & 4 & 1 & 0 & 5 \\
11 & 7 & 4 & 3 & 0
\end{array}
\qquad
P_5 = \begin{array}{c} \\ A \\ B \\ C \\ D \\ E \end{array}
\begin{array}{ccccc}
A & B & C & D & E \\
\hline
x & x & x & B & B \\
x & x & A & x & x \\
x & x & x & x & B \\
C & C & x & x & x \\
D & D & D & x & x
\end{array}
$$

   To find the length of the shortest path, we look at the entries of D_5 and to find the actual path, we examine the entries of P_5. As an example, let us find the shortest path between E and A. $D_5(E, A)$ is 11 and so the length of the shortest path between E and A is 11. To find the actual path, we examine the $P_5(E, A)$ entry which is D. So the shortest path between E and A passes through D. We then examine the entries $P_5(E, D)$ and $P_5(D, A)$. We find that there is no intermediate node in the shortest path between E and D but C is an intermediate node on the shortest path between D and A. There is neither any intermediate node between D and C nor between C and A.

   Hence the shortest path from E to A is: $E \rightarrow D \rightarrow C \rightarrow A$, having length: $3 + 1 + 7 = 11$.

4.3   BINARY SEARCH TREE

A binary tree is a tree where each node has atmost two children: a left child and a right child. A binary search tree for a set S is a labelled binary tree in which each vertex v is labeled by an element $L(v) \in S$ such that:

   (1) For each vertex u in the left sub-tree of v, $L(u) < L(v)$,
   (2) For each vertex u in the right sub-tree of v, $L(u) > L(v)$, and
   (3) For each element $a \in S$, there is exactly one vertex v such that $L(v) = a$.

   In the binary search tree of Figure 4.2, $L(A) = 40$, $L(B) = 17$, $L(C) = 10$, $L(D) = 30$, $L(E) = 35$, $L(F) = 45$, $L(G) = 42$, $L(H) = 52$ and $L(I) = 50$. For any node in the search tree, L-values of the nodes in its left sub-tree are less than the L-value at the node. Similarly, L-values of the nodes in its right sub-tree are greater than the L-value at the node. This holds good for any node in the search tree.

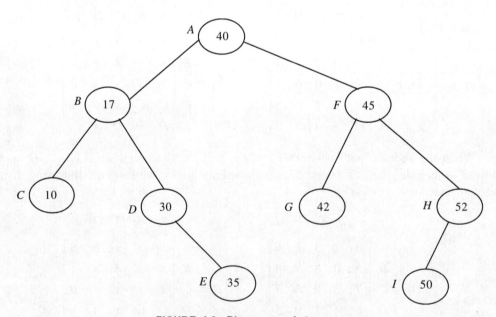

FIGURE 4.2 Binary search tree.

The binary search algorithm is as follows:

```
Procedure Search (a,v)
    /*a is the element to be searched, v is the root node of the
tree */
    If a = L(v) Then Return("Yes");
        Else
      If a < L(v) Then
        If v has a left child w Then Return(Search(a,w));
          Else Return("No");
        Endif
          Else
        If v has a right child w Then Return(Search(a,w));
          Else Return("No");
        Endif
      Endif
    Endif
End Search
```

Let us consider the set of reserved words: S = {for, end, if, do, loop, while}. Figure 4.3 shows two binary search trees based on this set of reserved words.

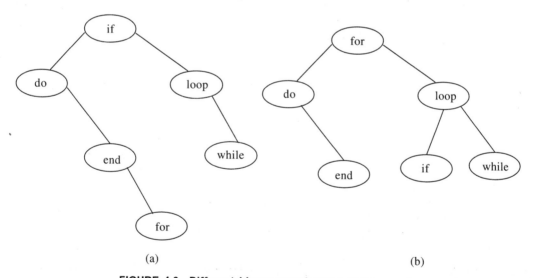

(a)   (b)

FIGURE 4.3 Different binary search trees of key words.

These two trees have different performance characteristics. If each node is equally likely to be searched, the average comparisons required in the tree of Figure 4.3(a) is 15/6 and that in the tree of Figure 4.3(b) is 14/6. In a general situation, one may expect different identifiers to be searched for with different frequencies (probabilities). In addition, we may expect unsuccessful searches (i.e. searches for identifiers not in the tree) also to be made.

Brute force approach for checking all possible binary search trees on n nodes is not practical for large values of n. Let $BST(n)$ denote the number of different binary search trees on n nodes, then we may write

$$BST(n) = \sum_{i=0}^{i=n-1} BST(i) * BST(n - i - 1)$$

where the left sub-tree has i nodes, $0 \le i \le n - 1$ and the right sub-tree has $n - i - 1$ nodes.

The solution of the above recurrence relation is $BST(n) = \dfrac{1}{n+1}\dbinom{2n}{n}$, the Catalan numbers. This implies that the number of binary search trees is exponential in the number of nodes. So we have to look for a better way to find the optimal binary search tree. Dynamic programming approach requires much less time. We assume that the search involves both successful and unsuccessful cases.

Let $a_1 < a_2 < ... < a_n$ be the elements in the set S, and p_i be the probability of the instruction $MEMBER(a_i, S)$ in θ, the sequence of $MEMBER$ instructions. Also, let q_o be the probability that an instruction of the form $MEMBER(a, S)$, for some $a < a_1$ appears in θ. Let q_i be the probability that an instruction of the form $MEMBER(a, S)$, for some $a_i < a < a_{i+1}$ appears in θ and q_n be the probability that an instruction of the form $MEMBER(a, S)$, for some $a > a_n$ appears in θ. To define the cost of a binary search tree, we add $(n + 1)$ fictitious leaves $e_0, e_1, ..., e_n$ to the binary tree to reflect the elements in $U - S$, where U is the universal set. Leaf e_3 in Figure 4.4 represents those elements 'a' such that 'for' $< a <$ 'if'. To construct an optimal binary search tree, we have to define a cost criterion.

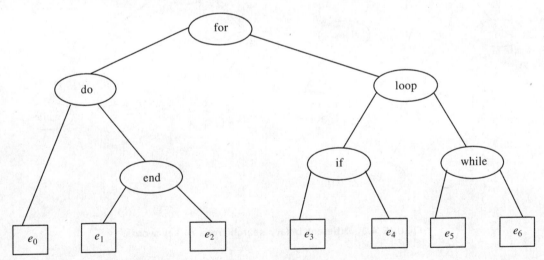

FIGURE 4.4 Binary search tree with fictitious leaves.

Cost of a binary search tree

If element a is the label $L(v)$ of some vertex v, then the number of vertices visited when we process the instruction $MEMBER(a, S)$ is one more than the depth of vertex v; depth of root is zero and it increases with each level of the tree. If $a \notin S$, and $a_i < a < a_{i+1}$, then the number of vertices visited to process the instruction $MEMBER(a, S)$ is equal to the depth of the fictitious leaf e_i.

Thus, the cost of a binary search tree can be defined as

$$\sum_{i=1}^{n} p_i (\text{Depth}(a_i) + 1) + \sum_{i=0}^{n} q_i \text{Depth}(e_i)$$

Minimum cost tree

Let $Tree_{i,j}$ be the minimum cost tree for the subset of elements $\{a_{i+1}, a_{i+2}, ..., a_j\}$. Let $c_{i,j}$ be the cost of $Tree_{i,j}$. The weight of $Tree_{i,j}$ is $w_{i,j}$ and $r_{i,j}$ is the root of $Tree_{i,j}$. The weight $w_{i,j}$ of $Tree_{i,j}$ is defined as $q_i + (p_{i+1} + q_{i+1}) + \cdots + (p_j + q_j)$. A possible approach to find a minimum cost tree is to make a decision as to which of the a_i's should be the root of the tree. A tree $Tree_{i,j}$ consists of a root a_k, plus a left sub-tree $Tree_{i,k-1}$ which is a minimum cost tree for $\{a_{i+1}, a_{i+2}, ..., a_{k-1}\}$, plus a right sub-tree $Tree_{k,j}$ which is a minimum cost tree for $\{a_{k+1}, a_{k+2}, ..., a_j\}$. This is shown in Figure 4.5.

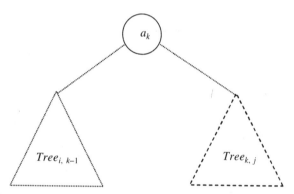

FIGURE 4.5 Sub-tree $Tree_{i,r}$

If $i = k - 1$, the left sub-tree is empty and if $k = j$, the right sub-tree is empty. $Tree_{i,i}$ denotes the empty tree. The weight $w_{i,i}$ of $Tree_{i,i}$ is q_i and its cost $c_{i,i}$ is 0. The depth of every vertex in the left and right sub-trees of $Tree_{i,j}$, $i < j$, has increased by one from what depths were in $Tree_{i,k-1}$ and $Tree_{k,j}$. Thus $c_{i,j}$, the cost of $Tree_{i,j}$ can be expressed as:

$$c_{i,j} = (w_{i,k-1} + c_{i,k-1}) + p_k + (w_{k,j} + c_{k,j})$$
$$= (w_{i,k-1} + p_k + w_{k,j}) + c_{i,k-1} + c_{k,j}$$
$$= w_{i,j} + c_{i,k-1} + c_{k,j}$$

The value of k to use is that which minimizes the sum $c_{i,k-1} + c_{k,j}$. Thus, to find an optimal tree $Tree_{i,j}$ we compute the cost for each k, $i < k \leq j$, of the tree with the root a_k, the left sub-tree $Tree_{i,k-1}$ and the right sub-tree $Tree_{k,j}$, and then select a tree of minimum cost.

The following pseudocode gives an algorithm to compute roots of optimal sub-trees:

```
Procedure Find_root(a₁,a₂,…,aₙ,p₁,p₂,…,pₙ,q₀,q₁,…,qₙ)
  For i = 0 to n Do
    wᵢ,ᵢ = qᵢ;
    cᵢ,ᵢ = 0;
  Endfor
  For L = 1 to n Do
  For i = 0 to n - L Do
    j = i + L;
    wᵢ,ⱼ = wᵢ,ⱼ₋₁ + pⱼ + qⱼ;
    minc = ∞;
    For k = i + 1 to j Do
      If minc > cᵢ,ₖ₋₁ + cₖ,ⱼ Then
          minc = cᵢ,ₖ₋₁ + cₖ,ⱼ;
          m = k;
      Endif
    Endfor
    cᵢ,ⱼ = wᵢ,ⱼ + minc;
    rᵢ,ⱼ = aₘ;
  Endfor
  Endfor
  Call Form_tree(1,n);
End Find_root
```

After finding the roots of all possible optimal sub-trees, we need to form the optimal binary search tree spanning all the nodes. The following pseudocode gives an algorithm to construct an optimal binary search tree:

```
Procedure Form_tree (i,j)
  Create a vertex and label it aₘ,the root of Treeᵢ,ⱼ;
  If i < m - 1 Then
    Call Form_tree (i, m - 1) to form the left sub-tree;
  Endif
  If m < j Then
    Call Form_tree (m,j) to form the right sub-tree;
  Endif
  Return(Treeᵢ,ⱼ);
End Form_tree
```

EXAMPLE 4.1 Consider the four elements $a_1 < a_2 < a_3 < a_4 < a_5$ with $q_0 = 0$, $q_1 = 0.1875$, $q_2 = q_3 = q_4 = q_5 = 0.0625$ and $p_1 = p_2 = 0.125$, $p_3 = p_4 = 0.0625$, $p_5 = 0.1875$.

The roots of optimal sub-trees are as found in Table 4.2 while the optimal binary search tree is as shown in Figure 4.6. In Table 4.2, the column header represents the value of i and the row header represents the value of $L = j - i$.

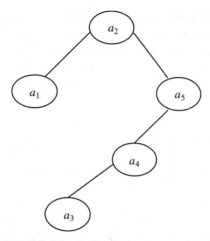

FIGURE 4.6   Optimal binary search tree.

TABLE 4.2   Finding roots of optimal sub-trees

	0	1	2	3	4	5
0	$w_{00} = 0$ $c_{00} = 0$	$w_{11} = 0.1875$ $c_{11} = 0$	$w_{22} = 0.0625$ $c_{22} = 0$	$w_{33} = 0.0625$ $c_{33} = 0$	$w_{44} = 0.0625$ $c_{44} = 0$	$w_{55} = 0.0625$ $c_{55} = 0$
1	$w_{01} = 0.3125$ $c_{01} = 0.3125$ $r_{01} = a_1$	$w_{12} = 0.375$ $c_{12} = 0.375$ $r_{12} = a_2$	$w_{23} = 0.1875$ $c_{23} = 0.1875$ $r_{23} = a_3$	$w_{34} = 0.1875$ $c_{34} = 0.1875$ $r_{34} = a_4$	$w_{45} = 0.3125$ $c_{45} = 0.3125$ $r_{45} = a_5$	
2	$w_{02} = 0.5$ $c_{02} = 0.8125$ $r_{02} = a_2$	$w_{13} = 0.5$ $c_{13} = 0.6875$ $r_{13} = a_2$	$w_{24} = 0.3125$ $c_{24} = 0.5$ $r_{24} = a_3(a_4)$	$w_{35} = 0.4375$ $c_{35} = 0.625$ $r_{35} = a_5$		
3	$w_{03} = 0.625$ $c_{03} = 1.125$ $r_{03} = a_2$	$w_{14} = 0.625$ $c_{14} = 1.125$ $r_{14} = a_2$	$w_{25} = 0.5625$ $c_{25} = 1.0625$ $r_{25} = a_4(a_5)$			
4	$w_{04} = 0.75$ $c_{04} = 1.5625$ $r_{04} = a_2$	$w_{15} = 0.875$ $c_{15} = 1.875$ $r_{15} = a_3(a_4)$				
5	$w_{05} = 1$ $c_{05} = 2.375$ $r_{05} = a_2$					

Complexity analysis

Once we have computed the table, construction of an optimal tree from this table will require $O(n)$ time using Form_tree. There are only n calls of the procedure and each call requires constant time. The first part of the Find-root procedure requires $O(n)$ time because of the i-loop. The second part consists of two nested loops: L-loop and i-loop. Within these two loops, optimum value of k is to be found from the $O(j - i)$ values. The other steps in this part require constant time. Thus, the total cost of binary search tree creation requires $O(n^3)$ time. With some modification in the Find_root procedure, we can construct optimal binary search tree in $O(n^2)$ time using a result of Knuth. The result shows that if the search is restricted to the range between the roots of $Tree_{i,j-1}$ and $Tree_{i+1,j}$, the same optimal value of k is obtained minimizing the sum $c_{i,k-1} + c_{k,j}$.

4.4 TRAVELING SALESPERSON (TSP)

Let G be a directed graph with n vertices. Let $length(u, v)$ be the length of the edge (u, v). A path starting at a given vertex v_0, going through every other vertex exactly once, and finally returning to v_0 is called a *tour*. The length of a tour is the sum of the lengths of the edges on the path defining the tour. We are interested in finding a tour of minimum length. A mail van starting from the head post-office collecting letters from different post offices of the town and returning to the head post-office is an example of this problem. The objective is to plan a tour of the different post-offices starting and ending at the head post-office having minimum length.

4.4.1 Greedy Method

Let (P, v) represent the path constructed; it starts at v_0 and ends at v. Initially, P is empty and $v = v_0$. If all vertices in G are on P, then include the edge (v, v_0) and stop. Otherwise, include an edge (v, w) of minimum length among all edges from v to a vertex w not on P.

Does the greedy approach give shortest path in the traveling salesperson problem (TSP of Figure 4.7)? It does not. The example graph for the TSP problem of Figure 4.7 confirms this.

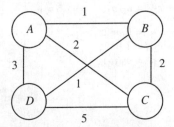

FIGURE 4.7   Example graph for TSP.

The greedy method will select the edges in the sequence AB, BD, DC, CA resulting in a tour of length 9, though we have a shorter length tour consisting of the edges AC, CB, BD, DA having length 8. Thus greedy algorithm fails in this example.

4.4.2 Dynamic Programming

Let the vertices of the graph be numbered 1 through n. Without loss of generality, we regard a tour to be a simple path that starts and ends at the vertex 1. Every tour consists of an edge

(1, k) for some $k \in V - \{1\}$ and a path from vertex k to vertex 1. The path from vertex k to vertex 1 goes through each vertex in $V - \{1, k\}$ exactly once.

If the tour is optimal, then the path from k to 1 must be a shortest k to 1 path going through all vertices in $V - \{1, k\}$. Hence the principle of optimality holds. Let $sp(i, S)$ be the length of a shortest path starting at vertex i, going through all vertices in S, and terminating at the vertex 1.

The function $sp(1, V - \{1\})$ is the length of an optimal salesperson tour. From the principle of optimality, it follows that

$$sp(1, V - \{1\}) = \min_{2 \le k \le n} \{W_{1k} + sp(k, V - \{1, k\})\} \tag{4.1}$$

where W_{ij} represents the length/cost of the edge (i, j) and n is the number of cities.

Generalizing, we obtain (for $i \notin S$),

$$sp(i, S) = \min_{j \in S} \{W_{ij} + sp(j, S - \{j\})\} \tag{4.2}$$

Equation (4.1) can be solved for $sp(1, V - \{1\})$ if we know $sp(k, V - \{1, k\})$ for all choices of k. The sp values are obtained by using Eq. (4.2). Clearly, $sp(i, \phi) = W_{i,1}$, $1 \le i \le n$. Hence, we can use Eq. (4.2) to obtain $sp(i, S)$ for all S of size 1. Then we can obtain $sp(i, S)$ for S with $|S| = 2$ and so on. When $|S| < n - 1$, the values of i and S for which $sp(i, S)$ is needed are such that $i \ne 1$, $1 \notin S$, and $i \notin S$.

Complexity analysis

Let M be the number of $sp(i, S)$'s that have to be computed before Eq. (4.1) can be used to compute $sp(1, V - \{1\})$. For each value of $|S|$ there are $n - 1$ choices for i. The number of distinct sets S of size k not including 1 and i is $^{n-2}C_k$. Hence:

$$M = \sum_{k=0}^{n-2} (n - 1) \binom{n-2}{k} = (n - 1)2^{n-2}$$

The computation of $sp(i, S)$ with $|S| = k$ requires $k - 1$ comparisons when solving Eq. (4.2). The time T required to find an optimal tour using Eqs. (4.1) and (4.2) is

$$T = \sum_{k=1}^{k=n-2} (k - 1)(n - 1)\, ^{n-2}C_k = (n - 1) \sum_{k=1}^{k=n-2} (k - 1)\, ^{n-2}C_k$$

But

$$\sum_{k=1}^{k=n-2} (k - 1)\, ^{n-2}C_k = \sum_{k=1}^{k=n-2} k\, ^{n-2}C_k - \sum_{k=1}^{k=n-2} {}^{n-2}C_k$$

$$= \sum_{k=1}^{k=n-2} (n - 2)\, ^{n-3}C_{k-1} - \sum_{k=1}^{k=n-2} {}^{n-2}C_k,$$

since for integer k, $k\, ^rC_k = r\, ^{r-1}C_{k-1}$

$$= (n - 2) \sum_{k=1}^{k=n-2} {}^{n-3}C_{k-1} - (2^{n-2} - 1), \text{ since } \sum_{k=0}^{k=n} {}^{n}C_k = 2^n$$

$$= (n - 2)2^{n-3} - 2^{n-2} + 1$$

Hence, $T = (n - 1) \left\{ \dfrac{(n - 2)2^n}{8} - \dfrac{2^n}{4} + 1 \right\} = \dfrac{(n - 1)(n - 2)2^n}{8} - \dfrac{(n - 1)2^n}{4} + (n - 1)$

$$= O(n^2 2^n)$$

This method is better than enumerating all the $n!$ permutations to find the best one. The most serious drawback of this dynamic programming solution is the $O(n2^n)$ space requirement (value of M) which is too large even for modest values of n.

EXAMPLE 4.2 Let us consider the graph of Figure 4.8 (the input graph for a traveling salesperson problem). We assume that the tour starts at A and goes through the other nodes and terminates at A.

$$
\begin{array}{c}
\quad\quad A \quad B \quad C \quad D \\
\begin{array}{c} A \\ B \\ C \\ D \end{array}
\left[
\begin{array}{cccc}
\infty & 12 & 5 & 7 \\
11 & \infty & 13 & 6 \\
4 & 9 & \infty & 18 \\
10 & 3 & 2 & \infty
\end{array}
\right]
\end{array}
$$

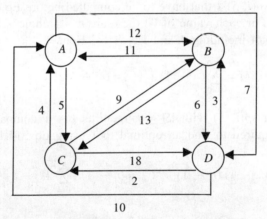

FIGURE 4.8 Input graph for TSP.

$sp(B, \phi) = W_{BA} = 11$
$sp(C, \phi) = W_{CA} = 4$
$sp(D, \phi) = W_{DA} = 10$

$sp(A, \{B\}) = W_{AB} + sp(B, \phi) = 12 + 11 = 23$
$sp(C, \{B\}) = W_{CB} + sp(B, \phi) = 9 + 11 = 20$
$sp(D, \{B\}) = W_{DB} + sp(B, \phi) = 3 + 11 = 14$

$sp(A, \{C\}) = W_{AC} + sp(C, \phi) = 5 + 4 = 9$
$sp(B, \{C\}) = W_{BC} + sp(C, \phi) = 13 + 4 = 17$
$sp(D, \{C\}) = W_{DC} + sp(C, \phi) = 2 + 4 = 6$

$sp(A, \{D\}) = W_{AD} + sp(D, \phi) = 7 + 10 = 17$
$sp(B, \{D\}) = W_{BD} + sp(D, \phi) = 6 + 10 = 16$
$sp(C, \{D\}) = W_{CD} + sp(D, \phi) = 18 + 10 = 28$

$sp(A, \{B, C\}) = \min\{W_{AB} + sp(B, \{C\}), W_{AC} + sp(C, \{B\})\}$
$\qquad\qquad = \min\{12 + 17, 5 + 20\} = 25$
$sp(B, \{C, D\}) = \min\{W_{BC} + sp(C, \{D\}), W_{BD} + sp(D, \{C\})\}$
$\qquad\qquad = \min\{13 + 28, 6 + 6\} = 12$
$sp(C, \{B, D\}) = \min\{W_{CB} + sp(B, \{D\}), W_{CD} + sp(D, \{B\})\}$
$\qquad\qquad = \min\{9 + 16, 18 + 14\} = 25$
$sp(D, \{B, C\}) = \min\{W_{DB} + sp(B, \{C\}), W_{DC} + sp(C, \{B\})\}$
$\qquad\qquad = \min\{3 + 17, 2 + 20\} = 20$

$sp(A, \{B, C, D\}) = \min\{W_{AB} + sp(B, \{C, D\}), W_{AC} + sp(C, \{B, D\}),$
$\qquad\qquad\qquad W_{AD} + sp(D, \{B, C\})\}$
$\qquad\qquad = \min\{12 + 12, 5 + 25, 7 + 20\} = 24$

An optimal tour of the graph in Figure 4.8 has length 24. A tour of this length can be constructed if we retain with each $sp(i, S)$ the value of j that minimizes the R.H.S. of Eq. (4.2). Let $J(i, S)$ be the value. Then, $J(A, \{B, C, D\}) = B$. Thus the tour starts from A and goes to B. The remaining tour can be obtained from $sp(B, \{C, D\})$. $J(B, \{C, D\}) = D$. Thus the next edge is (B, D). The remaining tour is for $sp(D,\{C\})$. So $J(D, \{C\}) = C$. The optimal tour is thus: $A \to B \to D \to C \to A$.

4.5   0/1 KNAPSACK THROUGH DYNAMIC PROGRAMMING

The problem is to select objects out of n total number of objects such that $\sum_{1 \le i \le n} p_i x_i$ is maximum subject to $\sum_{1 \le i \le n} w_i x_i \le m$, where $[p_1, p_2, ..., p_n]$ is the profit vector, $[w_1, w_2, ..., w_n]$ is the weight vector, x_i is either 0 or 1 for $1 \le i \le n$ and m is the capacity of the knapsack.

A solution to the 0/1 knapsack problem can be obtained by making a sequence of decisions on the variables $x_1, x_2, ..., x_n$. A decision on the variable x_i involves assigning a value 0 or 1 to it. Without loss of generality, let us assume that decisions on the variables x_i are made in the order $x_n, x_{n-1}, ..., x_1$. Following a decision on x_n, we may be in one of the two possible states: the capacity remaining in the knapsack is m and no profit is accrued or the capacity remaining is $m - w_n$ and a profit of p_n has accrued. For the solution to be optimal the remaining decisions about the variables $x_{n-1}, ..., x_1$ must be optimal with respect to the problem state resulting from the decision about the variable x_n.

Let $KNAPSACK(1, j, y)$ represent the problem:

$$\text{maximize} \sum_{1 \le i \le j} p_i x_i$$

$$\text{subject to } \sum_{1 \le i \le j} w_i x_i \le y$$

$$x_i = 0 \text{ or } 1, 1 \le i \le j$$

Our objective is to solve $KNAPSACK(1, n, m)$. Let $f_j(y)$ be the value of an optimal solution to $KNAPSACK(1, j, y)$. Since the principle of optimality holds, we obtain,

$$f_n(m) = \max\{f_{n-1}(m), f_{n-1}(m - w_n) + p_n\} \tag{4.3}$$

For arbitrary $f_i(y)$, $i > 0$, Eq. (4.3) generalizes to:

$$f_i(y) = \max\{f_{i-1}(y), f_{i-1}(y - w_i) + p_i\} \tag{4.4}$$

Equation (4.4) can be solved for $f_n(m)$ by beginning with $f_0(y) = 0$ for all y and $f_i(y) = -\infty$, $y < 0$. $f_1, f_2, ..., f_n$ can then successively be computed using Eq. (4.3). When the w_i's are integers, we need to compute $f_i(y)$ for integer y, $0 \le y \le m$. Since $f_i(y) = -\infty$ for $y < 0$, these function values need not be computed explicitly. As each f_i can be computed from f_{i-1} in $\Theta(m)$ time, it takes $\Theta(mn)$ time to compute f_n. This algorithm is not strictly speaking a polynomial time algorithm as its running time depends on both the size (n) of the input and a given number (m). This type of algorithm is commonly referred as *pseudo-polynomial* time algorithm. When the w_i's are real numbers, $f_i(y)$ is needed for real numbers y such that $0 \le y \le m$. f_i cannot be explicitly computed for all y in this range. Even when the w_i's are integer, the explicit $\Theta(mn)$ computation of f_n may not be the most efficient.

EXAMPLE 4.3A   Consider $n = 3$, $(w_1, w_2, w_3) = (2, 3, 3)$, $(p_1, p_2, p_3) = (1, 2, 4)$ and $m = 6$. For this problem, we may write

$$f_0(y) = f_1(y) = f_2(y) = f_3(y) = -\infty, \ \forall \ y < 0$$

$$f_0(y) = 0, \ \forall \ y \ge 0 \text{ and } f_1(0) = f_2(0) = f_3(0) = 0$$

$f_1(1) = \max\{f_0(1), f_0(-1) + 1\} = \max\{0, -\infty + 1\} = 0$
$f_1(2) = \max\{f_0(2), f_0(0) + 1\} = \max\{0, 0 + 1\} = 1$
$f_1(3) = \max\{f_0(3), f_0(1) + 1\} = \max\{0, 0 + 1\} = 1$
$f_1(4) = \max\{f_0(4), f_0(2) + 1\} = \max\{0, 0 + 1\} = 1$
$f_1(5) = \max\{f_0(5), f_0(3) + 1\} = \max\{0, 0 + 1\} = 1$
$f_1(6) = \max\{f_0(6), f_0(4) + 1\} = \max\{0, 0 + 1\} = 1$

$f_2(1) = \max\{f_1(1), f_1(-2) + 2\} = \max\{0, -\infty + 2\} = 0$
$f_2(2) = \max\{f_1(2), f_1(-1) + 2\} = \max\{1, -\infty + 2\} = 1$
$f_2(3) = \max\{f_1(3), f_1(0) + 2\} = \max\{1, 0 + 2\} = 2$
$f_2(4) = \max\{f_1(4), f_1(1) + 2\} = \max\{1, 0 + 2\} = 2$
$f_2(5) = \max\{f_1(5), f_1(2) + 2\} = \max\{1, 1 + 2\} = 3$
$f_2(6) = \max\{f_1(6), f_1(3) + 2\} = \max\{1, 1 + 2\} = 3$

$f_3(1) = \max\{f_2(1), f_2(-2) + 4\} = \max\{0, -\infty + 4\} = 0$
$f_3(2) = \max\{f_2(2), f_2(-1) + 4\} = \max\{1, -\infty + 4\} = 1$

$$f_3(3) = \max\{f_2(3), f_2(0) + 4\} = \max\{2, 0 + 4\} = 4$$
$$f_3(4) = \max\{f_2(4), f_2(1) + 4\} = \max\{2, 0 + 4\} = 4$$
$$f_3(5) = \max\{f_2(5), f_2(2) + 4\} = \max\{3, 1 + 4\} = 5$$
$$f_3(6) = \max\{f_2(6), f_2(3) + 4\} = \max\{3, 2 + 4\} = 6.$$

The maximum profit is 6. By tracing back, we can find the objects included in the solution. The value 6 is obtained by including the 3rd object with profit 4 leaving capacity $6 - 3 = 3$ and profit $6 - 4 = 2$ to be acquired from the remaining objects. The value of $f_2(3)$ is 2 and this value is obtained by including the 2nd object. The capacity remaining for the 1st object is 0. So the optimal solution is (0, 1, 1).

Considering all subsets of the set of n items, computing the total weight of each subset and finding a feasible subset (not all subsets are feasible) of maximum profit leads to a $O(2^n)$ algorithm as described hereafter. Let S^i represent the possible states resulting from the 2^i decision sequences for $x_1, \ldots, x_i$. A state refers to a pair (P_j, W_j), where W_j is the total weight of objects included in the knapsack and P_j is the corresponding profit. We note that $S^0 = \{(0, 0)\}$. To obtain S^{i+1}, we note that the possibilities for x_{i+1} are $x_{i+1} = 0$ or $x_{i+1} = 1$. When $x_{i+1} = 0$, the resulting states are the same as for S^i. When $x_{i+1} = 1$, the resulting states are obtained by adding (P_{i+1}, W_{i+1}) to each state in S^i. We call this set of additional states S_1^i. Now, S^{i+1} can be computed by merging the states in S^i and S_1^i together. If S^{i+1} contains two pairs (P_j, W_j) and (P_k, W_k) with the property that $P_j \leq P_k$ and $W_j \geq W_k$, then the pair (P_j, W_j) can be discarded because the other pair gives more profit with no additional weight.

Complexity analysis

Each S^i, $i > 0$ is obtained by merging S^{i-1} and S_1^{i-1}. $|S_1^{i-1}| \leq |S^{i-1}|$ because of the presence of dominated pairs in S_1^{i-1}, $|S^i| \leq 2 |S^{i-1}|$. In the worst-case no pair is removed. The time required to generate S^i from S^{i-1} is $|S^{i-1}| + |S_1^{i-1}| = O(|S^{i-1}|)$. So the time required to compute all the S^is, $1 \leq i \leq n$, is $O(\Sigma|S^{i-1}|) = O(2^n)$, since in the worst-case $|S^i| = 2^i$.

EXAMPLE 4.3B Consider $n = 3$, $(w_1, w_2, w_3) = (2, 3, 3)$, $(p_1, p_2, p_3) = (1, 2, 4)$ and $m = 6$. For these data we have:

$$S^0 = \{(0,0)\}; \ S_1^0 = \{(1,2)\}$$
$$S^1 = \{(0,0), (1,2)\}; \ S_1^1 = \{(2,3), (3,5)\}$$
$$S^2 = \{(0,0), (1,2), (2,3), (3,5)\}; \ S_1^2 = \{(4,3), (5,5), (6,6)\}$$
$$S^3 = \{(0,0), (1,2), (4,3), (5,5), (6,6)\}$$

Note that the pair (3,5) has been eliminated from S^3 as a result of the purging rule. When generating the S^i's, we can also purge all pairs (P, W) with $W > m$ as these pairs determine the value of $f_n(y)$ only for $y > m$. Since the knapsack capacity is m, we are not interested in the behavior of f_n for $y > m$. When all pairs (P_j, W_j) with $W_j > m$ are purged from the S^i's, $f_n(m)$ is given by the P value of the last pair in S^n (note that S^i's are ordered sets). By computing S^n, we can find the solutions to all the knapsack problems $KNAPSACK(1, n, y)$, $0 \leq y \leq m$ and not just $KNAPSACK(1, n, m)$. Since, we want a solution only to $KNAPSACK(1, n, m)$, we can dispense with the computation of S^n. The last pair in S^n is either the last one in S^{n-1} or it is $(P_j + p_n, W_j + w_n)$, where $(P_j, W_j) \in S^{n-1}$ such that $W_j + w_n \leq m$ and W_j is maximum. If $(P1, W1)$ is the last tuple in S^n, a set of 0/1 values for the x_i's such that $\Sigma p_i x_i = P1$ and $\Sigma w_i x_i = W1$ can be determined by carrying out a search through the S^i's. We can set $x_n = 0$ if $(P1, W1) \in S^{n-1}$. If $(P1, W1) \notin S^{n-1}$, then $(P1 - p_n, W1 - w_n) \in S^{n-1}$ and we can set $x_n = 1$. This leaves us to determine how either $(P1, W1)$ or $(P1 - p_n, W1 - w_n)$ was obtained in S^{n-1}. This can be done recursively. With $m = 6$, the value of $f_3(6)$ is given by the tuple $(6, 6)$ in S^3. The tuple $(6, 6) \notin S^2$, and so we must set $x_3 = 1$. The pair $(6, 6)$ came from the pair $(6 - p_3, 6 - w_3) = (2, 3)$ and hence, $(2, 3) \in S^2$. Since $(2, 3) \notin S^1$, we can set $x_2 = 1$ and $x_1 = 0$. Hence the optimal solution is $(x_1, x_2, x_3) = (0, 1, 1)$.

4.6 RELIABLE MACHINE DESIGN USING DYNAMIC PROGRAMMING

The problem we are attempting now is to design a machine that functions with maximum reliability. The machine consists of n devices connected in series (see Figure 4.9). For each device d_i, $1 \leq i \leq n$ in the machine, we use redundant devices (see Figure 4.10) at each stage subject to maximizing overall reliability of the machine. The reliability of the machine is the product of the reliabilities of the devices in the machine. This is an example of multiplicative function optimization.

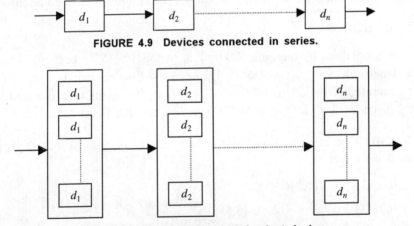

FIGURE 4.9   Devices connected in series.

FIGURE 4.10   Machine with redundant devices.

When n devices d_i, $1 \leq i \leq n$ are connected in series, the reliability $= \Pi r_i$, where $r_i =$ reliability of device d_i. Even if the individual devices are very reliable, the reliability of the system may not be good.

If stage i contains m_i copies of device d_i, then the probability that all the m_i devices are malfunctioning is: $(1 - r_i)^{m_i}$. Hence, the reliability of the stage i is: $1 - (1 - r_i)^{m_i}$.

Let us assume that the reliability of stage i is given by a function $\Phi(m_i)$, $i \leq n$. The reliability of the system is:

$$\prod_{1 \leq i \leq n} \Phi_i(m_i)$$

Our objective is to use device redundancy to maximize reliability under a cost constraint. Let c_i be the cost of each unit of d_i and let C be the maximum allowable cost of the system being designed. The problem is mathematically formulated as:

$$\text{Maximize} \prod_{1 \le i \le n} \Phi_i(m_i)$$

$$\text{subject to} \sum_{1 \le i \le n} c_i m_i \le C$$

where m_i is an integer ≥ 1, and $1 \le i \le n$.

Each $c_i > 0$ and m_i is in the range $1 \le m_i \le u_i$, where

$$u_i = \left\lfloor (C + c_i - \sum_1^n c_j)/c_i \right\rfloor$$

An optimal solution $m_1, m_2, \ldots, m_n$ is the result of a sequence of decisions for each m_i. Let

$$f_i(x) = \max(\prod_{1 \le j \le i} \Phi_j(m_j))$$

$$\text{subject to} \sum_{1 \le j \le i} c_j m_j \le x \quad \text{and} \quad 1 \le m_j \le u_j, 1 \le j \le i$$

The value of an optimal solution is $f_n(C)$. The last decision made requires one to choose m_n from $\{1, 2, \ldots, u_n\}$. Once a value for m_n has been chosen, the remaining decisions must be taken to use the remaining funds $C - c_n m_n$ in an optimal way.

Using the principle of optimality, we can write:

$$f_n(C) = \max_{1 \le m_n \le u_n} \{\Phi_n(m_n) f_{n-1}(C - c_n m_n)\} \tag{4.5}$$

For any $f_i(x)$, $i \ge 1$ this generalizes to

$$f_i(x) = \max_{1 \le m_i \le u_i} \{\Phi_i(m_i) f_{i-1}(x - c_i m_i)\} \tag{4.6}$$

Clearly, $f_0(x) = 1$ for all x, $0 \le x \le C$. Let $S^i = \{(f_i(x), x)\}$, where $x \le C$. There is at most one tuple for each different x that results from a sequence of decisions on $m_1, m_2, \ldots, m_n$. The dominated tuples are discarded from S^i. (f_1, x_1) dominates (f_2, x_2) iff $f_1 \ge f_2$ and $x_1 \le x_2$. Moreover, there is no need to retain any tuple (f, x) in S^i with x value greater than $C - \Sigma c_j$, $i \le j \le n$, as such a tuple will not leave adequate funds to construct the system.

EXAMPLE 4.4 Consider a 4-stage system with device types d_1, d_2, d_3, d_4. Let $c_1 = 30$, $c_2 = 15$, $c_3 = 20$, $c_4 = 10$. The cost of the system is $C \le 135$. The reliabilities of the devices are:

$$r_1 = 0.9, \ r_2 = 0.8, \ r_3 = 0.5, \ r_4 = 0.6$$

Subject to the budget constraint, the allowable maximum number of devices at different stages are:

$$u_1 = \lfloor (165 - 75)/30 \rfloor = 3$$
$$u_2 = \lfloor (150 - 75)/15 \rfloor = 5$$
$$u_3 = \lfloor (155 - 75)/20 \rfloor = 4$$
$$u_4 = \lfloor (145 - 75)/10 \rfloor = 7$$

We use S^i to represent the set of all undominated tuples $(f_i(x), x)$ that may result from the various decision sequences for $m_1, m_2, ..., m_i$. Beginning with $S^0 = \{(1, 0)\}$, we can construct S^i from S^{i-1} by trying out all possible values for m_i and combining the resulting tuples together. S^i_j represents all tuples obtainable from S^{i-1} by choosing $m_i = j$. Some tuples below are shown in bold. These are the entries that are used for finding the solution through backtracing as explained later.

$S^1_1 = \{(\mathbf{0.9, 30})\}$, $S^1_2 = \{(0.9, 30), (.99, 60)\}$, $S^1_3 = \{(0.9, 30), (.99, 60), (0.999, 90)\}$.

$S^1 = \{(\mathbf{0.9, 30}), (.99, 60), (0.999, 90)\}$.

$S^2_1 = \{(0.72, 45), (0.792, 75), (0.7992, 105)\}$.

$S^2_2 = \{(\mathbf{0.864, 60}), (0.9504, 90), (0.95904, 120)\}$.

$S^2_3 = \{(0.8928, 75), (0.98208, 105), (0.991008, 135)\}$.

$S^2_4 = \{(0.89856, 90), (0.988416, 120)\}$.

$S^2_5 = \{(0.899712, 105), (0.9896832, 135)\}$.

Removing dominated tuples, we get

$S^2 = \{(0.72, 45), (\mathbf{0.864, 60}), (0.8928, 75), (0.9504, 90), (0.98208, 105), (0.988416, 120), (0.991008, 135)\}$.

$S^3_1 = \{(0.36, 65), (0.432, 80), (0.4464, 95), (0.4752, 110), (0.49104, 125)\}$.

$S^3_2 = \{(0.54, 85), (\mathbf{0.648, 100}), (0.6696, 115), (0.7128, 130)\}$.

$S^3_3 = \{(0.63, 105), (0.756, 120), (0.7812, 135)\}$.

$S^3_4 = \{(0.675, 125)\}$.

Removing dominated tuples, we get

$S^3 = \{(0.36, 65), (0.432, 80), (0.54, 85), (\mathbf{0.648, 100}), (0.6696, 115), (0.756, 120), (0.7812, 135)\}$.

$S^4_1 = \{(0.216, 75), (0.2592, 90), (0.324, 95), (0.3888, 110), (0.40176, 125), (0.4536, 130)\}$.

$S^4_2 = \{(0.3024, 85), (0.36288, 100), (0.4536, 105), (0.54432, 120), (0.562464, 135)\}$.

S_3^4 = {(0.33696, 95), (0.404352, 110), (0.50544, 115), (**0.606528, 130**)}.

S_4^4 = {(0.350784, 105), (0.4209408, 120), (0.526176, 125)}.

S_5^4 = {(0.3563136, 115), (0.4275763, 130), (0.5344704, 135)}.

S_6^4 = {(0.3585254, 125)}.

S_7^4 = {(0.3594101, 135)}.

Removing dominated tuples, we get

S^4 = {(0.216, 75), (0.3024, 85), (0.33696, 95), (0.36288, 100), (0.4536, 105), (0.54432, 120), (**0.606528, 130**)}.

We find that 0.606528 is the highest reliability attainable within the given budget at a cost of 130. (0.606528, 130) appears in S_3^4 and it does not appear in S^3. So $m_4 = 3$. (0.606528, 130) has come from (0.648, 100) in S^3. (0.648, 100) appears in S_2^3 and it does not appear in S^2. So $m_3 = 2$. (0.648, 100) has come from (0.864, 60). (0.864, 60) appears in S_2^2 and it does not appear in S^1. So $m_2 = 2$. (0.864, 60) has come from (0.9, 30) in S^1. (0.9, 30) appears in S_1^1. So $m_1 = 1$. So the optimal design of the machine is as shown in Figure 4.11.

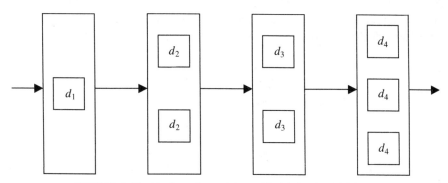

FIGURE 4.11 Designed machine with highest reliability.

The reliability of the machine is $0.9 \times (1 - 0.2 \times 0.2) \times (1 - 0.5 \times 0.5) \times (1 - 0.4 \times 0.4 \times 0.4) = 0.9 \times 0.96 \times 0.75 \times 0.936 = 0.606528$ and the cost of the machine is $1 \times 30 + 2 \times 15 + 2 \times 20 + 3 \times 10 = 130$. The machine will have reliability 0.216 without redundant devices.

4.7 LONGEST COMMON SUBSEQUENCE

Given two strings X and Y of lengths n and m respectively, we have to find the longest common subsequence. Subsequence of X is any string of the form $X(i_1) X(i_2) X(i_3) \ldots X(i_k)$, $i_j < i_{j+1}$ for $j = 1, 2, \ldots, k - 1$. Subsequence is a sequence of characters that are not necessarily contiguous but are taken in order. Suppose X = "aabcdafacd", then "acdcd" is a subsequence of X. Substring is a subsequence if $i_2 - i_1 = i_3 - i_2 = i_4 - i_3 = \ldots = i_k - i_{k-1} = 1$. The problem we are interested here is to find the longest string S that is a subsequence of both X and Y. The brute-force approach for this problem yields an exponential algorithm. By using dynamic programming, we can solve the problem much faster.

Let $L(i, j)$ be the length of the longest common subsequence of $X(0)X(1) \ldots X(i)$ and $Y(0)Y(1) \ldots Y(j)$. We distinguish between two cases.

(1) The last character is the same in the two strings, that is, $X(i) = Y(j) = $ 'c'. The longest common subsequence of $X(0)X(1) \ldots X(i)$ and $Y(0)Y(1) \ldots Y(j)$ ends with 'c'. So we write:

$$L(i, j) = L(i - 1, j - 1) + 1 \qquad (4.7)$$

(2) The last characters are different in the two strings, that is $X(i) \neq Y(j)$. In this case $L(i, j)$ is the maximum of $L(i - 1, j)$ and $L(i, j - 1)$. So we write:

$$L(i, j) = \max\{L(i - 1, j), L(i, j - 1)\} \qquad (4.8)$$

For Eqs. (4.7) and (4.8) to make sense in the boundary cases when $i = 0$ or $j = 0$. we write:

$$L(i, -1) = 0 \text{ for } i = -1, 0, \ldots, n - 1 \text{ and } L(-1, j) = 0 \text{ for } j = -1, 0, \ldots, m - 1.$$

The problem satisfies the principle of optimality. We cannot have the longest common subsequences without also having the longest common subsequences for the sub-problems. We give pseudocode for the problem based on the above formulation.

```
Procedure LCSS(X,Y,n,m)
   Character Array X(n),Y(m)
   For i = -1 to n - 1 Do
      L(i,-1)=0;
   Endfor
   For j = -1 to m - 1 Do
      L(-1,j)=0;
   Endfor
   For i = 0 to n - 1 Do
      For j = 0 to m - 1 Do
         If X(i) = Y(j)Then
               L(i,j) = L(i - 1, j - 1) + 1;
         Else
               L(i,j) = Max{L(i - 1,j), L(i,j - 1)};
         Endif
      Endfor
   Endfor
End LCSS
```

The time complexity of the above procedure is dominated by the two nested *for* loops. The *if* statement within the nested loop requires constant time and so the time complexity of the algorithm is $O(length(X)$ times $length(Y)) = O(nm)$.

EXAMPLE 4.5 Find the longest common subsequence of X = 'aabcdacdbb', Y = 'abacdabd' using dynamic programming.

Using Table 4.3, we find that the common longest subsequence has length 6. To find a longest subsequence we work back through the table. We start with $L(n - 1, m - 1)$, that is, with the cell (9, 7). We find that the characters are different. We can now move to either the cell (9, 6) or the cell (8, 7). We examine the cell (9, 6) and find that the common character is b. So the last character of a longest common subsequence is **b**. From the cell (9, 6), we move to the cell (8, 5) and find that the characters are different. We can now move to the cell (8, 4) or the cell (7, 5). If the characters corresponding to a cell (i, j) are identical, then we move to cell $(i - 1, j - 1)$; otherwise to the cell $(i - 1, j)$ or $(i, j - 1)$ whichever is having the greater value. The possible traces through the table for the example strings are shown in the directed graph of Figure 4.12. The algorithm produces five longest common subsequences each of length 6: **abacdb, abcdab, aacdab, aacdad, abcdad** as shown in Figure 4.12.

TABLE 4.3 Finding the length of the longest common subsequence

L		a	b	a	c	d	a	b	d
	−1	0	1	2	3	4	5	6	7
−1	0	0	0	0	0	0	0	0	0
a 0	0	1	1	1	1	1	1	1	1
a 1	0	1	1	2	2	2	2	2	2
b 2	0	1	2	2	2	2	2	3	3
c 3	0	1	2	2	3	3	3	3	3
d 4	0	1	2	2	3	4	4	4	4
a 5	0	1	2	3	3	4	5	5	5
c 6	0	1	2	3	4	4	5	5	5
d 7	0	1	2	3	4	5	5	5	6
b 8	0	1	2	3	4	5	5	6	6
b 9	0	1	2	3	4	5	5	6	6

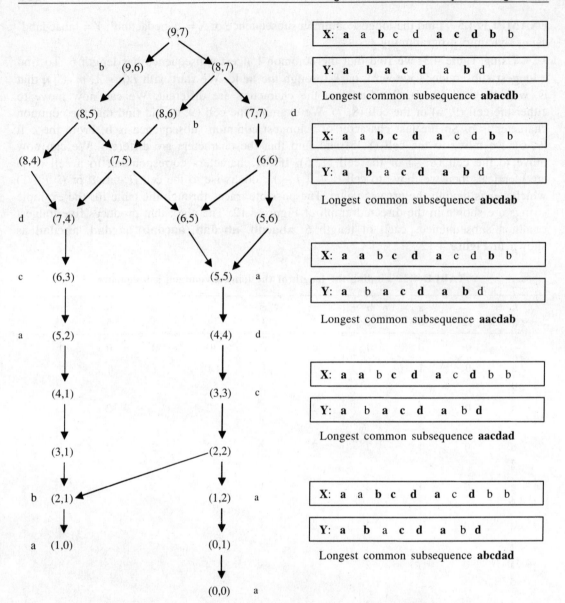

FIGURE 4.12 Finding the longest common subsequences.

SUMMARY

The dynamic programming approach can be applied to situations where the principle of optimality holds. By keeping record of the previous partial results, it is possible to economize the computation and get a reasonably efficient algorithm for many practical problems. We have used the method to solve the problems of chain matrix multiplication, all-pair shortest paths, constructing optimal binary search tree, TSP, 0/1 knapsack problem, and reliable machine design within cost constraint.

EXERCISES

4.1 Construct a binary search tree for the list of keys: 17, 12, 21, 5, 91, 12, 37, 19.

4.2 Give a dynamic programming approach to solve the all-pair shortest path problem.

4.3 Use the dynamic programming method to find the sequence in which the following chain of matrices should be multiplied to minimize the computation time.

$$A(10,5) \times B(5,8) \times C(8,10) \times D(10,10)$$

4.4 Find one problem for which the principle of optimality does not hold. Explain why the principle does not hold.

4.5 Develop a dynamic programming algorithm to evaluate ^nC_k, where $^nC_k = \dfrac{n!}{k!(n-k)!}$.

4.6 Give a dynamic programming solution for the subset sum problem. Analyze the complexity of the algorithm.

4.7 Demonstrate empirically which one is better on your computer: Dijkstra's algorithm or Floyd's algorithm for the all-pair shortest paths problem.

4.8 Consider the problem of finding minimum cost binary search tree of 5 nodes $S = \{a_1, a_2, a_3, a_4, a_5\}$. The nodes are such that $a_1 < a_2 < a_3 < a_4 < a_5$. Let P_i be the probability of the instruction $MEMBER(a_i, S)$, Q_0 be the probability that an instruction of the form $MEMBER(a, S)$ for some $a < a_1$, Q_i be the probability that an instruction of the form $MEMBER(a, S)$ for some $a_i < a < a_{i+1}$ appears in the sequence of $MEMBER$ instructions. Given the following values of the probabilities, find the minimal cost binary search tree.

$P_1 = 1/16$ $P_2 = 3/16$ $P_3 = 1/16$ $P_4 = 1/32$ $P_5 = 1/16$

$Q_0 = 1/32$ $Q_1 = 3/16$ $Q_2 = 1/16$ $Q_3 = 1/16$ $Q_4 = 3/16$ $Q_5 = 1/16$.

4.9 Find the minimum number of operations required for the following chain matrix multiplication using dynamic programming:

$$A(30, 40) * B(40, 5) * C(5, 15) * D(15, 6)$$

4.10 Solve the following 0/1 knapsack problem using dynamic programming:

$$P = (11, 21, 31, 33), \ W = (2, 11, 22, 15), \ C = 40, \ n = 4.$$

4.11 Using dynamic programming method, find the maximum number of operations possible for the following chain matrix multiplication and also the sequence of multiplications that will require this maximum number of operations. $A(20, 30) * B(30, 5) * C(5, 12) * D(12, 5)$.

4.12 Design a machine with the highest reliability, given that the machine has 3 stages with device types d_1, d_2, d_3, cost of one $d_1 = 25$, cost of one $d_2 = 20$, cost of one $d_3 = 22$ and the maximum cost of the machine could be 100. For proper functioning of the machine, at least one device at each stage should be functioning. Assume that the reliabilities of the devices are $r_1 = 0.7$, $r_2 = 0.8$, $r_3 = 0.6$.

4.13 Find the shortest paths between all pairs of nodes in the following graph using Floyd's algorithm.

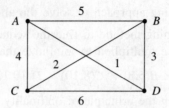

4.14 Find the shortest tour of a TSP for the following graph using dynamic programming.

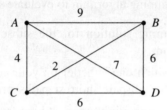

4.15 What is dynamic programming technique? How does it differ from the divide-and-conquer technique?

4.16 Consider a two-team game where teams A and B play a series of games until one of the teams win n games. Assume that the probability of team A winning a game is p and losing it, $q = 1 - p$. We also assume that there is no tie in a game. Let $P(i, j)$ be the probability of team A winning the series if A needs i more games to win the series and B needs j more games to win the series. After setting a recurrence relation for $P(i, j)$, write pseudocode for solving this problem using dynamic programming. What is the time complexity of the algorithm?

4.17 Find the longest common subsequences of the strings "addaacacdbac" and "aadccadba" using dynamic programming technique.

4.18 $^{n}C_k$ can be computed using the formula $^{n-1}C_k + {}^{n-1}C_{k-1}$. Compare the performances of divide-and-conquer and dynamic programming approaches for computing $^{n}C_k$ using this formula.

4.19 Consider the computation of Fibonacci number $(F(n))$ using divide-and-conquer approach. Estimate how many times the sub-problem $F(n - i)$, $1 \leq i \leq n - 1$ is solved in the approach.

4.20 In how many ways, the following chain of matrices may be multiplied?

$$A \times B \times C \times D$$
$$[2 \times 5] \ [5 \times 3] \ [3 \times 6] \ [6 \times 4]$$

Find the number of multiplications required in each case.

4.21 Let A be the adjacency matrix of a weighted connected graph containing n nodes. Hedetniemi sum $\oplus$ is defined as

$$A^1 = A$$

$$A^n = A^{n-1} \oplus A, \; n \geq 2$$

where $(A^n)_{ij} = \min\{(A^{n-1})_{i1} + (A)_{1j}, \; (A^{n-1})_{i2} + (A)_{2j}, \; ..., \; (A^{n-1})_{in} + (A)_{nj}\}$

$(A^{n-1})_{ij}$ represents the length of the shortest path between i and j of $(n - 1)$ or fewer edges. Develop an algorithm using the above formulation to find all pair shortest paths in a weighted connected graph. Analyze the time complexity of the algorithm.

4.22 Modify the algorithm developed for Exercise 4.21 to find the actual shortest path from one point to another. How does this algorithm compare with that given in section 4.2 of this book?

4.23 In how many ways, the following chain of matrices can be multiplied? Enumerate them

$$A(2, 5) \times B(5, 3) \times C(3, 6) \times D(6, 4) \times E(4, 3).$$

5

FURTHER DIVIDE AND CONQUER

5.0 INTRODUCTION

In this chapter, we discuss some more applications of the divide-and-conquer technique of algorithm design. Specifically, we discuss Fast Fourier Transform, finding convex hull of a finite collection of points on a plane, and the median problem.

5.1 DISCRETE FOURIER TRANSFORM (DFT)

Given the sample points $X(0)$, $X(1)$, $X(2)$, ..., $X(n-1)$, the DFT of this sequence is defined as:

$$Y(I) = \sum_{\substack{J=0 \\ 0 \le I \le n-1}}^{J=n-1} X(J)\,\omega_n^{IJ}$$

where $\omega_n = e^{2\pi i/n}$ is the primitive n^{th} root of unity and $i = \sqrt{-1}$.

The DFT may be written as a matrix vector product.

$$Y = V_n X$$

where $Y = (y_0, y_1, ..., y_{n-1})$, $X = (x_0, x_1, ..., x_{n-1})$ and V_n is a Vandermonde matrix containing the appropriate powers of ω_n.

The $(k, j)^{\text{th}}$ entry of V_n is ω_n^{kj} for $j, k = 0, 1, ..., n-1$, where ω_n is the nth primitive root of unity.

$$
\begin{bmatrix} y(0) \\ y(1) \\ \vdots \\ y(n-1) \end{bmatrix}
=
\begin{bmatrix}
\omega_n^0 & \omega_n^0 & ... & \omega_n^0 \\
\omega_n^0 & \omega_n^1 & ... & \omega_n^{n-1} \\
\vdots & & & \\
\omega_n^0 & \omega_n^{n-1} & ... & \omega_n^{(n-1)(n-1)}
\end{bmatrix}
\begin{bmatrix} x(0) \\ x(1) \\ \vdots \\ x(n-1) \end{bmatrix}
$$

For the inverse operation, we write $X = V_n^{-1} Y$, where V_n^{-1} is the inverse of V_n.

Theorem 5.1   For j, $k = 0, 1, \ldots, n-1$, the $(j, k)^{\text{th}}$ entry of V_n^{-1} is ω_n^{-Kj}/n.

Proof: We will show that $V_n^{-1} V_n = I_n$, the $n \times n$ identity matrix. Let us consider the (j, j') entry of $V_n^{-1} V_n$.

$$\left[V_n^{-1} V_n \right]_{jj'} = \sum_{K=0}^{K=n-1} \frac{\omega_n^{-Kj}}{n} \, \omega_n^{Kj'}$$

$$= \sum_{K=0}^{K=n-1} \frac{\omega_n^{-K(j'-j)}}{n}$$

This summation equals 1 if $j' = j$, and is 0 otherwise. We note that $-(n-1) \le j' - j \le n-1$, so that $j'-j$ is not divisible by n.

Given the inverse matrix V_n^{-1}, we have the DFT$^{-1}(Y)$ given by

$$x_j = \frac{1}{N} \sum_{K=0}^{n-1} y_k \omega_n^{-Kj} \quad \text{for } j = 0, 1, \ldots, n-1$$

The inverse DFT has a form similar to that of DFT except that (i) the roles of vectors X and Y are interchanged, (ii) ω_n is replaced by ω_n^{-1}, and (iii) each element of the result is divided by n.

The DFT can be thought of as the evaluation of a polynomial with coefficients $x(0)$, $x(1)$, $\ldots$, $x(n-1)$ at the points ω_n^0, ω_n^1, $\ldots$, ω_n^{n-1}. The vector $Y = \langle y(0), y(1), \ldots, y(n-1) \rangle$ is the DFT of the coefficient vector $X = \langle x(0), x(1), \ldots, x(n-1) \rangle$. This means that the value of the polynomial at ω_n^0 is $y(0)$, at ω_n^1 is $y(1)$, and so on. The inverse DFT may be thought of as the transformation that produces the coefficient vector $\langle x(0), x(1), \ldots, x(n-1) \rangle$ given the values of the polynomial $y(0)$, $y(1)$, $\ldots$, $y(n-1)$ at the pre-selected points which are the n complex n^{th} roots of unity.

The inverse of Discrete Fourier Transform is defined as:

$$x(I) = \frac{1}{n} \sum_{J=0}^{J=n-1} y(J) \, \omega^{-IJ}$$

The polynomial with coefficients $x(0)$, $x(1)$, $\ldots$, $x(n-1)$ has the following point-value representation:

$$\left\{ (\omega_n^0, y(0)), (\omega_n^1, y(1)), \cdots, (\omega_n^{n-1}, y(n-1)) \right\}$$

The Fourier transform of a continuous function $a(t)$ is given by:

$$A(f) = \int_{-\infty}^{+\infty} a(t) e^{2\pi i f t} \, dt, \quad \text{where } i = \sqrt{-1}$$

The inverse transform is given by:

$$a(t) = \frac{1}{2\pi} \int_{-\infty}^{+\infty} A(f)\, e^{-2\pi i f t}\, df$$

$$\text{Time} \xrightarrow{\text{FT}} \xleftarrow{\text{IFT}} \text{Frequency}$$

For the sake of illustration, we first find the DFT of the vector (0, 1, 2, 3) and then perform the inverse DFT to get back the vector.

The four complex roots of unity are:

$$\omega_4^0, \omega_4^1, \omega_4^2, \omega_4^3 = 1,\, i,\, -1,\, -i$$

We note that $\omega_4 = e^{2\pi i/4} = \cos\dfrac{\pi}{2} + i \sin\dfrac{\pi}{2} = i$

Hence $Y = V_4 X$

$$= \begin{bmatrix} 1 & 1 & 1 & 1 \\ 1 & \omega_4^1 & \omega_4^2 & \omega_4^3 \\ 1 & \omega_4^2 & \omega_4^4 & \omega_4^6 \\ 1 & \omega_4^3 & \omega_4^6 & \omega_4^9 \end{bmatrix} \begin{bmatrix} 0 \\ 1 \\ 2 \\ 3 \end{bmatrix} = \begin{bmatrix} 1 & 1 & 1 & 1 \\ 1 & i & -1 & -i \\ 1 & -1 & 1 & -1 \\ 1 & -i & -1 & i \end{bmatrix} \begin{bmatrix} 0 \\ 1 \\ 2 \\ 3 \end{bmatrix} = \begin{bmatrix} 6 \\ -2-2i \\ -2 \\ 2i-2 \end{bmatrix}$$

To carry out the inverse transform we proceed as:

$$X = V_4^{-1} Y = \frac{1}{4} \begin{bmatrix} 1 & 1 & 1 & 1 \\ 1 & -i & -1 & i \\ 1 & -1 & 1 & -1 \\ 1 & i & -1 & -i \end{bmatrix} \begin{bmatrix} 6 \\ -2-2i \\ -2 \\ 2i-2 \end{bmatrix}$$

$$= \frac{1}{4} \begin{bmatrix} 0 \\ 4 \\ 8 \\ 12 \end{bmatrix} = \begin{bmatrix} 0 \\ 1 \\ 2 \\ 3 \end{bmatrix}$$

The DFT and IDFT may be carried out as a simple matrix multiplication requiring $O(n^2)$ time. We need to look for a better method. Here comes the Fast Fourier Transform (FFT) and the Inverse Fast Fourier Transform (IFFT).

5.2 FOURIER TRANSFORM AND POLYNOMIAL ARITHMETIC

Fourier transform has applications in many fields of science and engineering. It is sometimes convenient to transform a difficult problem into an easier problem through such transformations. The easier problem is then solved and the results are transformed back to find solution of the original problem. Consider the problem of finding the product of two polynomials. It is computationally convenient first to apply a linear transformation to the coefficient vectors of the polynomials, then to perform an operation which is simpler than convolution on the images of the coefficients, and finally to apply the inverse transformation to the result to get the desired product. An appropriate linear transformation for this situation is the discrete Fourier transformation.

Suppose

$$A(x) = \sum_{j=0}^{n-1} a_j x^j$$

$$B(x) = \sum_{j=0}^{n-1} b_j x^j$$

then

$$C(x) = \sum_{j=0}^{2n-2} c_j x^j$$

where

$$c_j = \sum_{k=0}^{j} a_k b_{j-k}$$

The straightforward method for multiplying polynomials using these equations require $O(n^2)$ time when the polynomials are represented in coefficient form but $O(n)$ time when they are represented in point-value form.

A polynomial can be represented either in coefficient or point-value form. Polynomial A can be represented as $(a_0, a_1, ..., a_{n-1})$ or by $\{(x_0, y_0), (x_1, y_1), ..., (x_{n-1}, y_{n-1})\}$. Given a polynomial in the coefficient representation, it is more convenient to transform it into the point-value representation through a transformation cheaper than the $O(n^2)$ cost and do the multiplication and then using the inverse transformation, produce the coefficient representation. A point-value representation of a polynomial $A(x)$ is a set of n point-value pairs: $\{(x_0, y_0), (x_1, y_1), ..., (x_{n-1}, y_{n-1})\}$ such that all of the x_k are distinct and $y_k = A(x_k)$ for $k = 0, 1, ..., n - 1$. A polynomial has many different point-value representations, since any set of n distinct points $x_0, x_1, ..., x_{n-1}$ can be used as the basis for its representation. Computing a point-value representation for a polynomial given in coefficient form is straightforward, since all we have to do is select n distinct points $x_0, x_1, ..., x_{n-1}$ and then evaluate $A(x_k)$ for $k = 0, 1, ..., n - 1$. With the Horner's method, this n-point evaluation takes $O(n^2)$ time. If we choose x_k cleverly, this computation time can be reduced.

The inverse of evaluation, that is, determining the coefficient form of a polynomial from a point-value representation is called interpolation. n-point interpolation using Lagrange's method requires $O(n^2)$ time. The n-point evaluation and interpolation are inverse operations that transform between the coefficient representation of a polynomial and a point-value representation. The point-value representation is quite convenient for many operations on polynomials.

Addition

If $C(x) = A(x) + B(x)$, then $C(x_k) = A(x_k) + B(x_k)$ for any point x_k. More precisely, if we have a point-value representation for A, $\{(x_0, y_0), (x_1, y_1), ..., (x_{n-1}, y_{n-1})\}$, and for B, $\{(x_0, y'_0), (x_1, y'_1), ..., (x_{n-1}, y'_{n-1})\}$, then a point-value representation for C is: $\{(x_0, y_0 + y'_0), (x_1, y_1 + y'_1), ..., (x_{n-1}, y_{n-1} + y'_{n-1})\}$.

The time to add two polynomials of degree n in point-value form is $O(n)$.

Multiplication

If $C(x) = A(x)B(x)$, then $C(x_k) = A(x_k)B(x_k)$ for any point x_k and we can, point-wise multiply the point-value representations for A and B to obtain a point-value representation for C. The degree of C is the sum of the degrees of A and B. So we need $2n$ point-value pairs for a point value representation of C. We must begin with point-value representations of A and B consisting of $2n$ point-value pairs each.

Given $2n$ point-value representation for A, $\{(x_0, y_0), (x_1, y_1), ..., (x_{2n-1}, y_{2n-1})\}$, and a corresponding point-value representation for B, $\{(x_0, y'_0), (x_1, y'_1), ..., (x_{2n-1}, y'_{2n-1})\}$, a point-value representation for C is: $\{(x_0, y_0y'_0), (x_1, y_1y'_1), ..., (x_{2n-1}, y_{2n-1}y'_{2n-1})\}$.

The time to multiply the above two polynomials to obtain point-value form of the result is $O(n)$, which is much less than the time required to multiply polynomials in the coefficient form.

Fast multiplication of polynomials in coefficient form

We can use the linear-time multiplication method for polynomials in point-value form to expedite polynomial multiplication if we have a method to convert a polynomial quickly from the coefficient-form to the point-value form and vice-versa. Any set of points may be used, but by choosing the evaluation points carefully, we can convert between the representations in only $O(n \log n)$ time. If we choose *complex roots of unity* as the evaluation points, we can produce a point-value representation by taking the Discrete Fourier Transform (or DFT) of the coefficient vector. The inverse operation (interpolation) can be performed by taking the *inverse* DFT (IDFT) of point-value pairs, yielding a coefficient vector. Using DFT and inverse DFT, we can covert any signal representation in the time domain to its representation in the frequency domain. Figure 5.1 shows how DFT and IDFT are used for inter-conversion of polynomial representations. Figure 5.2 shows how polynomials can be multiplied efficiently. For this, we make a transformation from the coefficient representation to the point-value

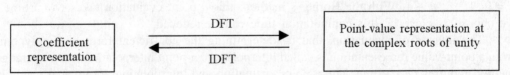

FIGURE 5.1 Inter-convertibility of representation.

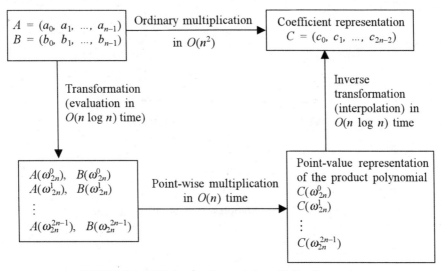

FIGURE 5.2 Efficient polynomial multiplication scheme.

representation at the complex roots of unity, carry out point-wise multiplication to find point-value representation of the product polynomial and then make inverse transformation to find the coefficient representation of the product polynomial. The total time required is $O(n \log n) + O(n) + O(n \log n) = O(n \log n)$ which is better than the straightforward method requiring $O(n^2)$ time.

5.3 COMPLEX ROOTS OF UNITY

A complex n^{th} root of unity is a complex number ω such that $\omega^n = 1$. There are exactly n complex n^{th} roots of unity. These are given by:

$$e^{2\pi i k/n} \qquad \text{for } k = 0, 1, ..., n - 1$$

Figure 5.3(a) shows the 4th roots of unity while Figure 5.3(b) shows the 8th roots of unity. The value $\omega_n = e^{2\pi i/n}$ is called the principal n^{th} root of unity, all the other complex n^{th} roots of unity are powers of ω_n. The n complex n^{th} roots of unity $\omega_n^0, \omega_n^1, ..., \omega_n^{n-1}$ form *a group* under multiplication.

Some properties of complex roots of unity

(1) For integers $n \geq 0$, $k \geq 0$, and $d > 0$

$$\omega_{dn}^{dk} = \omega_n^k$$

   Proof:

$$\omega_{dn}^{dk} = (e^{2\pi i/dn})^{dk} = (e^{2\pi i/n})^k = \omega_n^k$$

This is called the cancellation lemma.

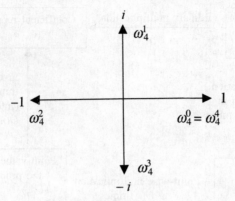

FIGURE 5.3(a)   Complex 4th roots of unity.

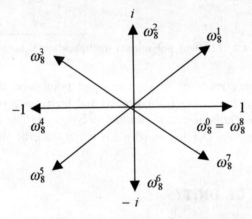

FIGURE 5.3(b)   Complex 8th roots of unity.

(2) For any even integer $n > 0$, $\omega_n^{n/2} = \omega_2 = -1$.

We have $\omega_n^{n/2} = (e^{2\pi i/n})^{n/2} = (e^{2\pi i/2}) = \omega_2 = e^{\pi i} = \cos \pi + i \sin \pi = -1$

(3) If n is even and $n > 0$, then the squares of the n complex n^{th} roots of unity are the $n/2$ complex $(n/2)^{th}$ roots of unity.

Proof:

$$(\omega_n^k)^2 = \omega_{2.n/2}^{2k} = \omega_{n/2}^k$$

We note that if we square all of the nth roots of unity, then each $(n/2)^{th}$ root of unity is obtained exactly twice, since

$$(\omega_n^{k+n/2})^2 = \omega_n^{2k+n} = \omega_n^{2k} = (\omega_n^k)^2$$

Thus, ω_n^k and $\omega_n^{k+n/2}$ have the same square. This can be proved from the previous result

$$\omega_n^{n/2} = -1 \implies \omega_n^{n/2+k} = -\omega_n^k$$

thus $(\omega_n^{n/2+k})^2 = (\omega_n^k)^2$ where $k = 1, 2, ..., (n-1)$

$$= \omega_n^{2k} = (\omega_{n/2})^k, \quad \text{since } \omega_{n/2}^k = (\omega_{n/2}^{k/2})^2 = (\omega_n^k)^2.$$

This is known as the halving lemma and is quite useful in the conversion between the coefficient and point-value representations of polynomials.

(4) For any integer $n \geq 1$ and non-negative integer k not divisible by n, $\displaystyle\sum_{j=0}^{j=n-1} (\omega_n^k)^j = 0$

   Proof:

$$\sum_{j=0}^{j=n-1} (\omega_n^k)^j = \frac{(\omega_n^k)^n - 1}{\omega_n^k - 1}$$

$$= \frac{(\omega_n^n)^k - 1}{\omega_n^k - 1} = \frac{(1)^k - 1}{\omega_n^k - 1} = 0$$

The requirement that k is not divisible by n ensures that the denominator is not 0, since $\omega_n^k = 1$ only when k is divisible by n.

5.4 FAST FOURIER TRANSFORM (FFT)

This is a fast way to carry out Fourier transform using the divide-and-conquer method that exploits properties of the complex roots of unity.

Let $N = 2^k$, where k a positive integer and ω is a primitive N^{th} root of unity. If $N = 2n$, then (a) $\omega^j = -\omega^{j+n}$ and (b) ω^2 is a primitive nth root of unity. From these two results and using the divide-and-conquer strategy, we can derive a faster version of Fourier transform which runs in $O(N \log N)$ time.

Let $X = (a_{N-1}, a_{N-2}, ..., a_0)$ be the coefficient vector to be transformed and let

$$A(x) = a_{N-1}x^{N-1} + a_{N-2}x^{N-2} + \cdots + a_0$$

$$= (a_{N-1}x^{N-1} + a_{N-3}x^{N-3} + \cdots + a_1x) + (a_{N-2}x^{N-2} + a_{N-4}x^{N-4} + \cdots + a_0)$$

Let $y = x^2$, then,

$$A(x) = x(a_{N-1}x^{N-2} + a_{N-3}x^{N-4} + \cdots + a_1) + (a_{N-2}x^{N-2} + a_{N-4}x^{N-4} + \cdots + a_0)$$

$$= x(a_{N-1}y^{n-1} + a_{N-3}y^{n-2} + \cdots + a_1) + (a_{N-2}y^{n-1} + a_{N-4}y^{n-2} + \cdots + a_0)$$

$$= A^{(0)}(x^2) + xA^{(1)}(x^2) \tag{5.1}$$

Evaluation of $A(x)$ at $\omega_N^0, \omega_N^1, ..., \omega_N^{N-1}$ reduces to evaluation of the polynomials $A^{(0)}$ and $A^{(1)}$ (of degree $N/2$) at the points $(\omega_N^0)^2, (\omega_N^1)^2, ..., (\omega_N^{N-1})^2$ and then combining the results according to Eq. (5.1).

The list of values consists not of N distinct values but only of the n complex n^{th} roots unity with each root occurring exactly twice. Therefore, the polynomials $A^{(0)}$ and $A^{(1)}$ of degree at most $N/2 = n$ are recursively evaluated at the n complex n^{th} roots of unity. These sub-problems have exactly the same form as the original problem, but are half the size. We have now successfully divided an N-element DFT computation into two n-element DFT computations, where $N = 2n$. This decomposition is the basis for a recursive FFT algorithm as given below.

```
Procedure  FFT(A(0 : N - 1), N)
           Array A(N), Y(N)
/*1*/  If N = 1 Then
           Return(A);
           Endif
/*2*/  WN = e↑(2πi/N);
/*3*/  W = 1;
/*4*/  A⁽⁰⁾ = (a₀, a₂, ..., a_{N-2});
/*5*/  A⁽¹⁾ = (a₁, a₃, ..., a_{N-1});
/*6*/  Y⁽⁰⁾ = FFT(A⁽⁰⁾(0 : (N/2) - 1), N/2);
/*7*/  Y⁽¹⁾ = FFT(A⁽¹⁾(0 : (N/2) - 1), N/2);
/*8*/  For k = 0 to (N/2) - 1 Do
/*8A*/ B = Wy_k^{(1)} /*y_k^{(1)} are the elements of Y⁽¹⁾*/
/*9*/ Y_k = y_k^{(0)} + B;  /*y_k^{(0)} are the elements of Y⁽⁰⁾*/
/*10*/ Y_{k+N/2} = y_k^{(0)} - B;
/*11*/ W = W * WN;
           Endfor
RETURN(y₀, y₁, ..., y_{N-1});
End FFT
```

Line (1) of the algorithm represents the basis of the recursion; DFT of one element is the element itself, since $y_0 = a_0\omega_0^1 = a_0.1 = a_0$.

Lines (4) and (5) define the coefficient vectors $A^{(0)}$ and $A^{(1)}$. Lines (2), (3) and (11) ensure that W is updated proportionally so that whenever statements 9 and 10 are executed, $W = (WN)^k$. Lines (6) and (7) perform recursive $DFT_{N/2}$ computations. Lines (9) and (10) combine the results of the recursive $DFT_{N/2}$ calculations.

Let us now illustrate how we can find FFT of the vector (0, 1, 2, 3) using the recursive procedure. The computation is shown in the form of a tree in Figure 5.4.

Running time

The recurrence equation for the running time of FFT may be written as: $T(N) = 2T(N/2) + CN/2$, where $T(1) = d$, a constant and $2T(N/2)$ accounts for two recursive calls for FFT of size $N/2$. C is a constant and $CN/2$ accounts for combining the results in the lines (8) through (11).

$$T(N) = 2T\left(\frac{N}{2}\right) + C\frac{N}{2}$$

$$= 2\left\{2T\left(\frac{N}{2^2}\right) + C\frac{N}{2^2}\right\} + C\frac{N}{2}$$

$$= 2^2 T\left(\frac{N}{2^2}\right) + 2\frac{CN}{2}$$

$$= 2^3 T\left(\frac{N}{2^3}\right) + 3\frac{CN}{2}$$

$$\cdots$$

$$= 2^{\log_2 N} T(1) + \log_2 N \frac{CN}{2}$$

$$= dN + \frac{1}{2}CN \log_2 N = O(N \log_2 N)$$

Hence, recursive version of FFT runs in $O(N \log N)$ time whereas the direct matrix-vector multiplication technique requires $O(N^2)$ time.

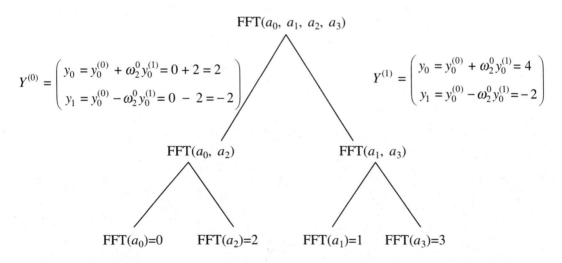

$$Y = (6, -2 - 2i, -2, -2 + 2i)$$

$$y_0 = y_0^{(0)} + \omega_4^0 y_0^{(1)} = 2 + 4 = 6$$

$$y_2 = y_0^{(0)} - \omega_4^0 y_0^{(1)} = 2 - 4 = -2$$

$$y_1 = y_1^{(0)} + \omega_4^1 y_1^{(1)} = -2 - 2i$$

$$y_3 = y_1^{(0)} - \omega_4^1 y_1^{(1)} = -2 + 2i$$

FFT(a_0, a_1, a_2, a_3)

$$Y^{(0)} = \begin{pmatrix} y_0 = y_0^{(0)} + \omega_2^0 y_0^{(1)} = 0 + 2 = 2 \\ y_1 = y_0^{(0)} - \omega_2^0 y_0^{(1)} = 0 - 2 = -2 \end{pmatrix}$$

$$Y^{(1)} = \begin{pmatrix} y_0 = y_0^{(0)} + \omega_2^0 y_0^{(1)} = 4 \\ y_1 = y_0^{(0)} - \omega_2^0 y_0^{(1)} = -2 \end{pmatrix}$$

FFT(a_0, a_2)   FFT(a_1, a_3)

FFT(a_0)=0   FFT(a_2)=2   FFT(a_1)=1   FFT(a_3)=3

Note: $\omega_2^1 = e^{2\pi i/2} = -1$, $\omega_2^0 = 1$, $\omega_4^1 = e^{2\pi i/4} = i$, $\omega_4^0 = 1$

FIGURE 5.4   FFT computation.

5.5 INTERPOLATION AT THE COMPLEX ROOTS OF UNITY (IFFT)

We now show how to interpolate at the complex roots of unity, that is, given the point-value representation, (ω_N^0, y_0), (ω_N^1, y_1), ..., $(\omega_N^{N-1}, y_{N-1})$, how we find the polynomial in coefficient representation, $(a_0, a_1, ..., a_{N-1})$. This is achieved through inverse FFT. Pseudocode for inverse FFT is given below. The returned result vector should be divided by N.

```
Procedure IFFT(Y(0 : N - 1), N)
        Array Y(N), A(N)
/*1*/ IF N = 1 Then
          Return(Y);
        Endif
/*2*/ WN = e↑(-2πi/N);
/*3*/ W = 1;
/*4*/ Y^(0) = (y_0, y_2, ..., y_{N-2});
/*5*/ Y^(1) = (y_1, y_3, ..., y_{N-1});
/*6*/ A^(0) = IFFT(Y^(0)(0 : (N/2) - 1), N/2);
/*7*/ A^(1) = IFFT(Y^(1)(0 : (N/2) - 1), N/2);
/*8*/ For K = 0 to (N/2) - 1 Do
/*8A*/B = Wa_k^(1)   /*a_k^(1) are the elements of A^(1)*/
/*9*/ a_K = a_K^(0) + B; /*a_k^(0) are the elements of A^(0)*/
/*10*/ a_{K+N/2} = a_K^(0) - B;
/*11*/W = W * WN;
        Endfor
Return(a_0, a_1, ..., a_{N-1});
End IFFT
```

How the recursive IFFT calls are made is illustrated for an example in Figure 5.5. Obviously, this inverse FFT requires $O(N \log N)$ time, the same as in the FFT case.

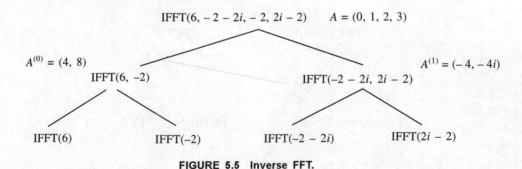

FIGURE 5.5 Inverse FFT.

5.6 ITERATIVE VERSION OF FFT

Figure 5.6 shows how recursive FFT calls are made in the case of 8-point FFT. Looking at the tree in Figure 5.6, we observe that if we arrange the elements of the initial vector A into the order in which they appear in the leaves, we can easily simulate the execution of the recursive FFT procedure. We take the elements in pairs, compute the DFT of each pair using one butterfly operation (Figure 5.7), and replace the pair with its DFT. For the N-point case,

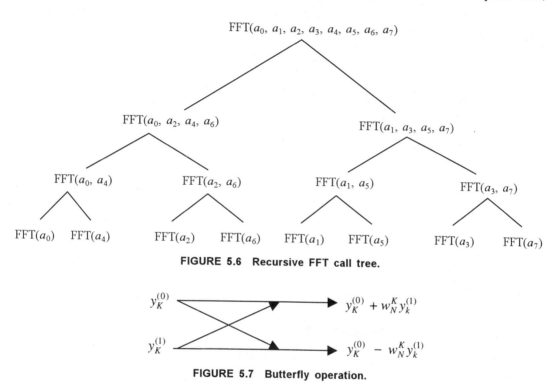

FIGURE 5.6 Recursive FFT call tree.

FIGURE 5.7 Butterfly operation.

we now have $N/2$ 2-element DFTs (one level above the leaves in the tree). Next, we take these $N/2$ DFTs in pairs and compute the DFT of the four vector elements they come from by executing two butterfly operations, replacing two 2-element DFTs with one 4-element DFT. We have now $N/4$ 4-element DFTs. We continue in this manner until we have two $N/2$ element DFTs which we then combine using $N/2$ butterfly operations into the final N-element DFT.

    We use an auxiliary array $B(0{:}N - 1)$ to arrange the elements of the input vector in the order in which they appear in the leaves of the tree, variable S is used to denote the level—which ranges from 1 (at the leaves) to $\log N$ (at the root)—and temporary variables U and T to perform the butterfly operation. We identify $Y^{(0)}$ with $A(K{:}K + 2^{S-1} - 1)$ and $Y^{(1)}$ with $A(K + 2^{S-1}{:} K + 2^S - 1)$ where K will have values 0, 2, 4, 6, ..., for $S = 1$, 0, 4, 8, ..., for $S = 2$, 0, 8, 16, ..., for $S = 3$, and so on.

```
Procedure IterFFT(A(0:N - 1), N)
   Array A(N), B(N)
   For K = 0 to N - 1 Do
      B(K) = A(K);                              /* 0*/
   Endfor
      For K = 0 to N - 1 Do
      A(Reverse(K)) = B(K);                     /*1*/
      /*Reverse(K) means the number obtained by reversing the binary
representation of K*/
      Endfor
      For S = 1 to log N Do                     /*2*/
         M = 2^S;                               /*3*/
         WM = e↑(2πi/M);                        /*4*/
         W = 1;                                 /*5*/
      For J = 0 to M/2 - 1 Do                   /*6*/
         For K = J to N - 1 Step M Do           /*7*/
            U = A(K);                           /*8*/
            T = W*A(K + M/2);                   /*9*/
            A(K) = U + T;                       /*10*/
            A(K + M/2) = U - T;                 /*11*/
         Endfor
            W = W*WM;                           /*12*/
      Endfor
   Endfor
End IterFFT
```

Complexity analysis of iterative FFT

For each value of J, loop labeled /*7*/ is repeated $(N - 1 - J + 1)/2^s$ times; that is, $(N - J)/2^s$ times.

Hence statements /*8*/ through /*12*/ are repeated $\displaystyle\sum_{J=0}^{2^{S-1}-1} \frac{N-J}{2^S}$ times for each value

of S. Thus the statements are repeated $\displaystyle\sum_{S=1}^{\log N}\left(\sum_{J=0}^{2^{S-1}-1} \frac{N-J}{2^S}\right)$ times in all.

Therefore, the total time is:

$$= \sum_{S=1}^{\log N}\left(\sum_{J=0}^{2^{S-1}-1}\left(\frac{N}{2^S} - \frac{J}{2^S}\right)\right) = \sum_{S=1}^{\log N}\left(2^{S-1}\frac{N}{2^S} - \sum_{J=0}^{2^{S-1}-1}\frac{J}{2^S}\right)$$

$$= \sum_{S=1}^{\log N}\left(\frac{N}{2} - \frac{1}{2^S}\frac{(2^{S-1} - 1)\,2^{S-1}}{2}\right) = \frac{N}{2}\log N - \sum_{S=1}^{\log N}\left(\frac{(2^{S-1} - 1)}{4}\right)$$

$$= \frac{N}{2} \log N + \frac{1}{4} \log N - \sum_{S=1}^{\log N} \frac{2^S}{8} = \frac{N}{2} \log N + \frac{1}{4} \log N - \frac{1}{8} \sum_{S=1}^{\log N} 2^S$$

$$= \frac{N}{2} \log N + \frac{1}{4} \log N - \frac{1}{8} \left[\frac{2(2^{\log N} - 1)}{2 - 1} \right]$$

$$= \frac{1}{4} (2N + 1) \log N - \frac{1}{8} \left[2(N - 1) \right]$$

$$= \frac{1}{4} (2N + 1) \log N - \frac{1}{4} (N - 1)$$

$$\equiv O(N \log N)$$

5.7   SELECTION

Finding the maximum or the minimum of a list of items is an example of selection problem. The general problem is to find the kth smallest (largest) element from a collection of n elements, where $1 \leq k \leq n$. When $k = \lceil n/2 \rceil$, the selection problem becomes the same as the median finding problem. If we sort the n elements and pick up the kth smallest (largest) element, the selection process will require $O(n \log n)$ time. By using divide-and-conquer algorithm, we can find the kth smallest (largest) element in $O(n)$ time as explained below.

The basic idea behind the divide-and-conquer method for selection is to partition the given elements into three groups G_1, G_2, G_3 based on some pivot element m such that G_1 contains all the elements less than m, G_2 contains all the elements equal to m and G_3 contains all the elements greater than m. By counting the number of elements in G_1 and G_2, we can determine the group to which the kth smallest element belongs. This process may be applied recursively. To obtain a linear algorithm, we must be able to find the pivot element in linear time such that the sizes of the groups G_1 and G_3 are each bounded from the above by a fixed fraction of n. Success in finding a linear time algorithm depends on how the pivot element m is chosen. The given elements are partitioned into groups of 5 elements each. Each group is then sorted and the median is selected from each group to form a subgroup M containing $\lfloor n/5 \rfloor$ elements. We sort M (subgroup of medians) and the median of M is used as the pivot element m, that is, m is the median of medians.

From Figure 5.8, it is obvious that at least one-fourth of the elements are less than or equal to m and at least one-fourth of the elements are greater than or equal to m. We have divided the elements into groups of 5 but division into groups of certain other numbers will also work. We give below a pseudocode for the algorithm.

```
Procedure Select(G, K)
   Array G(n), G₁(n), G₂(n), G₃(n)
   If |G| < 50 Then /* |G| denotes the number of elements in G */
      Sort G; /* It is assumed that problems of size less than 50*/
      Return (kth smallest element in G); /*will be solved through*/
   Endif /*sorting and picking at a cheaper cost */
```

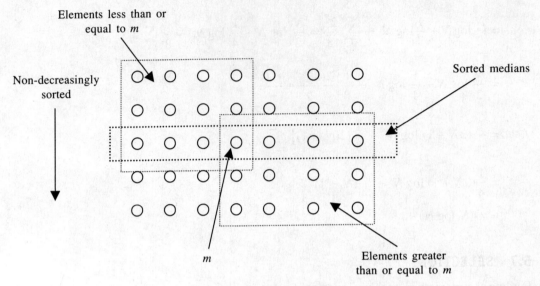

FIGURE 5.8 Median finding.

```
    Divide G into ⌊|G|/5⌋ groups of 5 elements each with up to 4
leftover elements;
    Sort each 5-element group;
    M = Set of medians of the groups;
    m = Select(M, ⌈|M|/2⌉); /* m is assigned the value returned
by Select */
    G₁ = {Elements < m};/*Elements less than m are put in G₁*/
    G₂ = {Elements = m};
    G₃ = {Elements > m};
    If |G₁| ≥ k Then Return(Select(G₁,k));
      Else If (|G₁| + |G₂| ≥ k) Then
                                Return(m);
                         Else
                                Return(Select(G₃,
                                k - |G₁| - |G₂|));
        Endif
    Endif
End Select
```

Complexity analysis

Worst case

Let $T(n)$ be the time to select the kth smallest element from a group of n elements. The subgroup M is of size $n/5$ and the $Select(M, \lceil |M|/2 \rceil)$ requires at most $T(n/5)$ time. Groups G_1 and G_3 are each of size $3n/4$ (at most). So the two recursive invocation of $Select(\ )$

requires at most $T(3n/4)$ time. All other statements require at most $O(n)$ time. From these considerations, we may write the following inequalities:

$T(n) \leq cn$, for $n \leq 49$ (c is a constant)

$T(n) \leq T(n/5) + T(3n/4) + cn$, for $n \geq 50$.

By using induction on n, it can be shown that $T(n)$ is $O(n)$.

Average case

Let $T(n)$ denote the expected time to select the kth smallest element from a group of n elements. Suppose that the pivot element m chosen at random is the ith smallest element in G. The probability of i being one of 1, 2, ..., n is uniform. If $i > k$, we call *select* from a group of $i - 1$ elements, and if $i < k$, we call *select* from a group of $n - i$ elements. The expected time of the recursive calls may be written as:

$$\frac{1}{n} \left[\sum_{i=1}^{i=k-1} T(n - i) + \sum_{i=k+1}^{i=n} T(i - 1) \right]$$

Putting i for $n - i$ in the 1st term and i for in $i - 1$ in the 2nd term, we get

$$\frac{1}{n} \left[\sum_{i=n-k+1}^{i=n-1} T(i) + \sum_{i=k}^{i=n-1} T(i) \right]$$

The rest of the procedure *select* requires cn time for some constant c so that we have,

$$T(n) \leq cn + \max_k \left\{ (1/n) \left[\sum_{i=n-k+1}^{i=n-1} T(i) + \sum_{i=k}^{i=n-1} T(i) \right] \right\}$$

Using induction on n, it can be shown that $T(n)$ is $O(n)$.

So, we have an algorithm for the selection problem which takes linear time both in the worst and the average cases.

5.8 CONVEX HULL

Given a finite set of points in the plane, the problem is to find the convex polygon with the smallest area that includes all the points, either as its vertices or as interior points. A polygon is convex (see Figure 5.9(a)) when the line segment connecting any two interior points remains entirely inside the polygon. Intuitively, imagine surrounding the set of points by a large, stretched rubber band. When the band is released, it will assume the shape of a convex hull.

We consider the problem of finding the convex hull in 2-dimensions using the divide-and-conquer technique. Given a set of points on a plane, we have to find the vertices of the smallest bounding convex polygon such that the points of the set either lie inside the polygon or are vertices of the polygon. The smallest bounding convex polygon is called convex hull (*CH*) and the vertices are called the hull points.

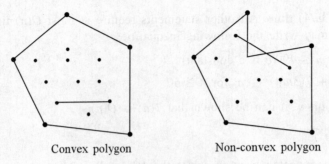

Convex polygon   Non-convex polygon

FIGURE 5.9(a) Polygons.

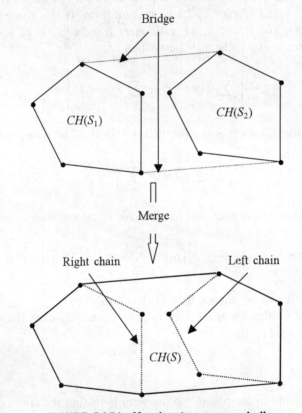

FIGURE 5.9(b) Merging two convex hulls.

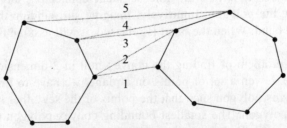

FIGURE 5.9(c) Snapshots of upper bridge finding.

The idea of a divide-and-conquer algorithm for finding convex hull is to partition the set of points S into more or less equal-sized subsets S_1 and S_2 (points of S_1 are assumed to lie to the left of the points of S_2), and then recursively construct the $CH(S_1)$ and $CH(S_2)$ and merge them to form $CH(S)$. The points belonging to S_1 have x-coordinates less than those of the points belonging to S_2. To merge $CH(S_1)$ and $CH(S_2)$, we remove the right chain of $CH(S_1)$ and the left chain of $CH(S_2)$ and replace them by an upper bridge and a lower bridge as shown in Figure 5.9(b).

A line is a supporting line (tangent) of a convex polygon P if the line passes through a vertex of P and the interior of P lies entirely to one side of the line. A line is said to be a bridge (common tangent) of two convex polygons if it is a supporting line (tangent) of both the polygons. The line is an upper bridge if both the polygons lie below the line, and it is a lower bridge if both the polygons lie above the line. The computation of bridge begins with a segment connecting the rightmost point of the left convex polygon to the leftmost point of the right convex polygon. Advancing (retracting) the endpoints of this segment in a zigzag manner, we can reach the top (or the bottom) bridge such that the entire set of points lies on one side of the line containing the bridge. This is shown in Figure 5.9(c).

To merge $CH(S_1)$ and $CH(S_2)$, we find the upper bridge which connects some vertex $s_{1u} \in S_1$ to some vertex $s_{2u} \in S_2$, and the lower bridge which connects $s_{1l} \in S_1$ and $s_{2l} \in S_2$. Vertices s_{1u} and s_{1l} divide the boundary of $CH(S_1)$ into a left chain and a right chain. Similarly, u_{2u} and u_{2l} divide the boundary of $CH(S_2)$ into left and right chains. To merge $CH(S_1)$ and $CH(S_2)$ into $CH(S)$, we replace S_1's right chain and S_2's left chain by the upper and lower bridges.

Let the array $A(1, N)$ contain the N input points; obviously $N \geq 3$, otherwise we cannot have a polygon. We sort the input array A on the basis of x-coordinates using either quick-sort or merge-sort. Pseudocode for a divide-and-conquer approach to the convex hull problem may be written as follows. DCHull(A, a, b) is recursively called and the output of these calls are merged using the procedure Merge$(B_l, N1, B_r, N2)$.

```
Procedure DCHull(A, low, high)
    Array B(high), B_l(high), B_r(high), A(high);
    If ((high - low) ≤ 2) Then
        Store the elements of A in B in clockwise order;
        Return(B);
    Endif;
    mid = ⌈(low + high)/2⌉;
    B_l = DCHull(A, low, mid); /*N1 is the number of Hull vertices
in B_l */
    B_r = DCHull(A, mid + 1, high); /*N2 is the number of Hull
vertices in B_r */
    B = Merge(B_l, N1, B_r, N2);
    Return(B);
End DCHull
```

The procedure Merge$(B_l, N1, B_r, N2)$ creates the convex hull from the input arrays B_l and B_r as follows:

```
Procedure Merge(B_l,N1,B_r,N2)

Array M(N1 + N2),B_l(N1), B_r(N2);

Curr_left1=(x1,y1) such that (x1,y1)∈ B_l and (x1,y1) is the rightmost
element in B_l, in case of a tie we choose the lowest y-value point;

Curr_right1=(x2,y2) such that (x2,y2)∈ B_r and (x2,y2) is the leftmost
element in B_r, in case of a tie we choose the lowest y value point;

Curr_left2=Curr_left1;

Curr_right2=Curr_right1;

While(NOT(Lower_tan(B_l,Curr_left1, Curr_right1))OR
NOT(Lower_tan(B_r,Curr_right1,Curr_left1))) Do

     While(NOT(Lower_tan(B_l,Curr_left1,Curr_right1)) Do
       Advance Curr_left1; /* in clockwise order */
     Endwhile;
     While(NOT(Lower_tan(B_r,Curr_right1,Curr_left1)) Do
         Retract Curr_right1; /* in anticlockwise order */
     Endwhile;

Endwhile;


While(NOT(Upper_tan(B_l,Curr_left2,Curr_right2))OR
NOT(Upper_tan(B_r,Curr_right2,Curr_left2))) Do
     While(NOT(Upper_tan(B_l,Curr_left2,Curr_right2)) Do
         Retract Curr_left2;
     Endwhile;
     While(NOT(Upper_tan(B_r, Curr_right2,Curr_left2)) Do
         Advance Curr_right2;
     Endwhile;
Endwhile;
I = 1;
While(Curr_left1 ≠ Curr_left2) Do
       M(I) = B_l(Curr_left1);
       Advance Curr_left1;
       I = I + 1;
Endwhile;
M(I) = B_l(Curr_left2);
I = I + 1;
While(Curr_right2 ≠ Curr_right1) Do
       M(I) = B_r(Curr_right2);
       Advance Curr_right2;
       I = I + 1;
```

```
Endwhile;
M(I) = B_r(Curr_right1);
Return (M);
End Merge
```

The procedure Lower_tan(B, $p1$, $p2$) returns the value *true* if the line joining the points $p1$, $p2$ is a lower tangent to B. Similarly, Upper_tan(B, $p1$, $p2$) returns the value *true* if the line joining $p1$, $p2$ is a upper tangent to B. The final array returned by the procedure DCHull( ) contains the boundary points of the convex hull for the given point set A in the clockwise order.

Complexity analysis

Polygons $CH(S_1)$ and $CH(S_2)$ can be merged in time proportional to the number of points in $CH(S_1)$ and $CH(S_2)$ together. To find each bridge, we alternately advance past vertices in $CH(S_1)$ and $CH(S_2)$. Once a vertex is passed, we do not visit it again. Hence, each of the two bridges is found in $O(|CH(S_1)| + |CH(S_2)|)$ time, that is, in linear time in the number of hull vertices. So we may write the recurrence relation for the time complexity of finding convex hull of n points as:

$$T(n) = 2T(n/2) + Cn, \ n > 1$$

$$= k, \ n = 1, \ C \text{ and } k \text{ are constants.}$$

For the case, $n > 1$, $2T(n/2)$ represents the time to construct two convex hulls, each containing $n/2$ points and Cn represents linear time for the merging of two convex hulls of $n/2$ points. The recurrence relation has the same form as that of the merge-sort (section 2.2). The solution of the above recurrence is $T(n) \in O(n \log n)$.

SUMMARY

In this chapter we have shown how the divide-and-conquer method is used to develop faster algorithms for a few more problems like Fourier transform, finding median, and convex hull of a set of points on a plane. The divide-and-conquer approach has reduced the complexity for Fourier transform from $O(n^2)$ to $O(n \log n)$, for the median problem from $O(n \log n)$ to $O(n)$. For the convex hull problem, the complexity remains at $O(n \log n)$ as is found through other methods like Graham's scan.

EXERCISES

5.1 Find the Fourier transform of the vector $(-4, 2, 0, 1)$.

5.2 Find the FFT of the vector $(1, 0, -1, 2)$.

5.3 Compute the product of the polynomials using FFT: $4x^2 + 4x + 2$, $x^3 + 3x^2 + 3$.

5.4 Given two lists of sorted integers, each containing n elements, develop an algorithm that finds the median of the $2n$ elements combined.

5.5 Develop an algorithm to find the median of five keys with only six comparisons in the worst case.

5.6 Compute the discrete Fourier transform of (0, 2, 1, 4).

5.7 Develop an efficient algorithm to find any one of the k smallest keys. How many key comparisons are required?

5.8 Show how the FFT of the vector, (0, 0, –1, 3, 4, 2, 5, –2) will be computed using recursion.

5.9 Determine how the convex hull of the following points on a plane may be found: (–3, 2), (8, 3), (4, 3), (–5, –6), (9, 4), (7, 7), (0, 0), (6, 1), (–9, –9).

5.10 Use the divide-and-conquer method to solve the closest pair problem, that is, given a set of points on a plane find the pair of points which are the closest.

5.11 Suppose we want to search for an element y in an array A of n sorted elements in ascending order. We compare y with the element at the position

$$x = i + \lfloor (y - A(i)) * (j - i)/(A(j) - A(i)) \rfloor$$

where $A(i)$, $A(j)$ are the elements at the positions i and j in the array and $A(i) \leq y \leq A(j)$. If $A(x) = y$, we stop. If $A(x) > y$, we search in the same way between positions $x - 1$ and i, otherwise between positions $x + 1$ and j. Develop an algorithm for this search and show that it requires on the average log log $n + 1$ key comparisons.

5.12 Analyze the worst-case time complexity of the search algorithm in Problem 5.11. Is it linear?

5.13 When should one prefer the search algorithm of Problem 5.11 over the binary search?

5.14 Devise an algorithm that produces the values of a polynomial and its derivatives of all possible orders.

5.15 How much time is needed to find the coefficients of the polynomial $(1 + x)^n$ using FFT?

5.16 Describe a $O(n \log n)$ time method to multiply the derivatives of $p(x)$ and $q(x)$, where both p and q are n-degree polynomials.

5.17 Describe a modified FFT that works when n is a power of 3 by dividing the input vector into three sub-vectors, recursing on each one, and then merging the solutions of the subproblems.

5.18 Show how a k-dimensional DFT can be computed, where $n_1 \times n_2 \times \ldots \times n_k = n$. What is the order of time required for solving this problem? Is it dependent on k?

A BIT OF THEORY

6.0 NON-DETERMINISTIC ALGORITHMS

A non-deterministic algorithm involves some kind of choice at some stage in its execution. The algorithms we use to solve problems in reality using computers belong to the deterministic category. Every step of a deterministic algorithm is uniquely determined. On the otherhand, in the non-deterministic algorithms, action corresponding to one or more steps of the algorithm is dependent on a number of alternatives. The algorithm is assumed to have the (magical!) power to make the correct choice. Non-deterministic algorithm is basically a definitional device for capturing the notion of verifiability, rather than a realistic method for solving problems.

To reconcile this situation with our experience with deterministic algorithms, we may assume (for the sake of conceptual understanding) that each time a choice is to be made in a non-deterministic algorithm, several copies of the algorithm are brought into action. Each copy tries with a separate choice. The copy that reaches success first terminates all other copies. A non-successful copy does not affect other copies. We may simply assume that a non-deterministic algorithm always makes a correct choice whenever it is asked to make selection out of a number of alternatives, provided such a correct choice exists in the alternatives. Further, when successful termination is possible, a non-deterministic algorithm makes a sequence of choices that is a shortest sequence of choices leading to a successful termination.

Let us give a simple algorithmic description of non-deterministic algorithms for a number of problems. A non-deterministic algorithm works in two steps: first it guesses a solution from the feasible set of solutions and then it verifies whether the guessed solution is indeed a correct solution.

Non-deterministic searching

Let us consider the problem of searching for an element e in a one-dimensional array $A[i]$, $1 \le i \le n$. We are looking for an index j such that $A[j] = e$ or $j = 0$ if e is not in A. The pseudocode looks like:

```
Procedure Nds
  Array A(n)
  j = Select one element from the set {1,2, ...., n};
  If A[j] = e Then
            Print("Found at index =", j);
            Else
            Print("Not present in the array", 0);
  Endif
End Nds
```

Obviously, this algorithm requires constant time, that is, its time complexity is $O(1)$.

Non-deterministic sorting

We can sort a one-dimensional array $A(i)$, $1 \leq i \leq n$ in non-decreasing order using a non-deterministic algorithm. We use an auxiliary array B for this.

```
Procedure Ndsort
  Array A(n), B(n)
  For i = 1 to n Do
    B(i) = 0;
  Endfor
  For i = 1 to n Do
    j = Select one element from the set {1,2, ...., n};
    If B(j) ≠ 0  Then
              Print("Failure");
              Exit;
    Endif
    B(j) = A(i); /* Array A contains the input */
  Endfor

  For i = 1 to n - 1 Do
    If B(i) > B(i + 1) Then
              Print("Failure");
              Exit;
    Endif
  Endfor
  Print("Sorted Array");
  For i = 1 to n Do
    Print(B(i));
  Endfor
End Ndsort
```

The complexity of this non-deterministic algorithm is $O(n)$.

Non-deterministic Knapsack decision problem

This problem is to decide if there is a 0/1 assignment of values to $x(i)$, $1 \leq i \leq n$ such that $\sum p(i)x(i) \geq k$ and $\sum w(i)x(i) \leq M$, where $p(i)$ are the components of the profit vector, k is a given number, $w(i)$ are the components of the weight vector and M is the capacity of the knapsack. The values of $p(i)$, $w(i)$ and M are positive numbers. The algorithm is:

```
Procedure Ndknap
  Array p(n), w(n), x(n)
  For i = 1 to n Do
    x(i) = Select one element from the set {0,1};
  Enddo

  If  Σ (w(i)x(i)) > M or  Σ (p(i)x(i)) < k Then
     1≤i≤n                 1≤i≤n
                      Print("Failure");
                      Exit;
                      Else
                      Print("Success");
  For i = 1 to n Do
    Print(x(i));
  Endfor
  Endif
End Ndknap
```

The complexity of the above non-deterministic algorithm is $O(n)$.

Non-deterministic satisfiability

Here we discuss about satisfiability problem in conjunctive normal form (CNF). The problem is to determine if a Boolean expression in CNF is true for some assignment of truth-values to the variables. A Boolean expression in CNF is the conjunction of a number of OR terms. It is easy to obtain a non-deterministic polynomial time algorithm that terminates successfully if and only if a given Boolean expression $F(x_1, x_2, ..., x_n)$ is satisfiable. The algorithm may be described as:

```
Procedure Ndsat
  For i = 1 to n Do
    x_i = Select one element from the set {True, False};
  Endfor
  If F(x_1, x_2, ..., x_n) is True Then
                      Print("Satisfied");
                      Else
                      Print("Not Satisfied");
  Endif
End Ndsat
```

The complexity of this algorithm is $O(n)$, assuming that evaluation of F requires at most $O(n)$ time.

Non-deterministic compositeness testing

The following pseudocode is to determine whether a given number is composite or not:

```
Procedure  Ndct
  Input  n;
  Select  two  natural  numbers  n₁  and  n₂  less  than  n;
  If  n  =  n₁ * n₂  Then
                         Print("Yes");
                         Else
                         Print("No");
  Endif
End  Ndct
```

The complexity of this algorithm is $O(1)$.

Non-deterministic primality testing

The following pseudocode decides whether a given number is prime or not.

```
Procedure  Ndpt
  Input  n;
  If  (n = 1)  OR  (n is an even integer)  AND  (n > 2)  Then
                         Print("No");
  Endif
  If  n = 2  Then
      Print("Yes");
  Endif
  If  (n is odd)  AND  (n > 2)  Then
    Select  x  such that  1 < x < n;
    If  xⁿ⁻¹ ≡ 1(mod n)  Then  y = 1;
    Endif
    Select  prime numbers  p₁,  p₂,  p₃,  ...,  pₖ;
    If  (n - 1 = p₁p₂p₃ ... pₖ)  AND  (NOT(xⁿ⁻¹/pᵢ = 1 mod n))  for
    all  i,  1 ≤ i ≤ k  Then  z = 1;
    Endif
    If  (y = 1)  AND  (z = 1)  Then
                         Print("Yes");
    Endif
  Endif
End  Ndpt
```

This algorithm has complexity $O(w^5)$, where w is the length of the input n.

6.1 PROBLEM TAXONOMY

The universe of problems may broadly be divided into the categories of undecidable problems, intractable problems and tractable problems as shown in Figure 6.1. Examples of undecidable problems are the halting problem of Turing machine, tiling a rectangular area with given tiles with certain conditions imposed on the juxtaposition of tiles, word correspondence problems, etc. The halting problem is to tell whether a given program (X) will terminate for a given input (Y), that is, whether we can have a program which when supplied with X and Y will

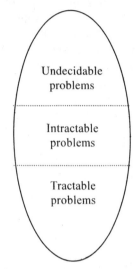

FIGURE 6.1 Problem categories.

tell us in finite amount of time that X terminates for the input Y. The word correspondence problem is: given two groups of words $X(1)$, $X(2)$, ..., $X(n)$ and $Y(1)$, $Y(2)$, ..., $Y(n)$ on some alphabet Σ, whether there is a finite ordered index set $\{i_1, i_2, ..., i_k\}$, where $1 \leq i_j \leq n$, $\forall j$, $1 \leq j \leq k$, such that concatenation of the words $X(i_1)$, $X(i_2)$, ..., $X(i_k)$ gives the same result as the concatenation of $Y(i_1)$, $Y(i_2)$, ..., $Y(i_k)$. The intractable problems include finding Hamiltonian cycle in a given graph, finding clique of a given minimum size, the set partitioning problem, etc. Tractable problems include sorting, searching, matrix multiplication, etc. The tractable problems have polynomial[1] time complexity. The intractable problems have super-polynomial time complexity, whereas undecidable problems do not have algorithms of any known complexity, polynomial or super-polynomial. The algorithms of tractable problems are also called good algorithms irrespective of the degree of the polynomial. In this section, we will discuss decidable problems.

There are different types of decidable problems. These include:

(1) *Decision problems:* In this class of problems, the output is either 'yes' or 'no'. For example, whether a given number is prime is a decision problem.

---

[1] The degree of these polynomials is not high.

(2) *Counting problem:* The output of this class of algorithms is a natural number. For example, given a number how many distinct factorization of the number are there.

(3) *Optimization problem:* This class of algorithms optimizes some objective function based on the problem instance. For example, given a weighted connected graph, finding a minimal spanning tree is an optimization problem.

For every optimization problem, we have corresponding decision and counting problems. For example, given the description of a minimal spanning tree problem, we can have a decision problem like finding whether the given weighted graph has a minimum spanning tree with weight less than a given value k. The corresponding counting problem could be: how many spanning trees can be constructed for the given graph with weight less than k.

Let us consider the knapsack problem. Given a profit vector $P = (p_1, p_2, ..., p_n)$ and a weight vector $W = (w_1, w_2, ..., w_n)$ and a knapsack of capacity C, the decision, counting and optimization problems may be formulated as:

Decision: Does there exist an n-tuple, $(x_1, x_2, ..., x_n) \in \{0,1\}^n$ such that $\sum_{i=1}^{i=n} p_i x_i \geq k$, where k is a given profit value and $\sum_{i=1}^{i=n} w_i x_i \leq C$?

Counting: How many n-tuples are there such that $\sum_{i=1}^{i=n} p_i x_i \geq k$, where k is a given profit value and $\sum_{i=1}^{i=n} w_i x_i \leq C$?

Optimization: Find an n-tuple $(x_1, x_2, ..., x_n) \in \{0,1\}^n$ such that $\sum_{i=1}^{i=n} p_i x_i$ is maximized subject to $\sum_{i=1}^{i=n} w_i x_i \leq C$.

A solution of either the optimization or the counting problem constitutes a solution of the related decision problem. However, many decision and counting problems are no less easy than the related optimization problems.

A decision problem can be recast as a language recognition problem. We can encode each instance of such a problem as a string and the original problem can be reformulated as one of recognizing the language consisting of all strings representing those instances of the problem whose answer is 'yes'. For example, the graph in the Figure 6.2 can be encoded as a decimal string. The string contains a list of nodes of the graph followed by a list of the edges of the graph. Each node is a decimal number, and each edge is a pair of decimal numbers that represents the endpoints of the edge. The graph of the Figure 6.2 is encoded as the string: (1, 2, 3, 4, 5)(1, 2)(2, 3)(3, 4)(4, 5)(5, 2).

Whether a graph has a k-clique can be formulated as a language L of the form: $L=\{(k)$ (1, 2, ..., n)(i_1, j_1) (i_2, j_2) ..., (i_m, j_m)$\}$, where k is a decimal number representing the size of the clique, (1, 2, ..., n) are decimal numbers representing the nodes of the graph and the (i, j) pairs represent edges between nodes i and j.

Two important classes amongst the decidable problems are P and NP problems.

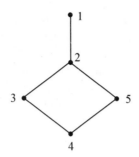

FIGURE 6.2   Graph for encoding.

P-problems

This is the class of problems for which we have deterministic polynomial time algorithms. The notion of polynomial time computability is robust. It does not depend on whether we select Turing machine, counter program or the circuit model of computation. This means that if we have a polynomial time algorithm on one model, we will have a polynomial time algorithm on the other models. Membership in P for a problem implies membership in P for its complement. Tens of thousands of polynomial time algorithms have been designed to solve problems arising in many different areas. Some of the examples are sorting, searching, matrix multiplication, shortest path finding, primality[2] testing, linear programming, etc.

NP-problems

This is the class of problems solvable by a non-deterministic algorithm in polynomial time. The class NP corresponds to the decision problems that have an efficient proof system, which means that each 'yes' instance must have at least one succinct certificate, whose validity can be verified quickly. This definition is asymmetric. We require the existence of succinct certificates for each 'yes' instance but there is no such requirement for 'no' instances.

Are all the problems in NP class of the same complexity? Is there any single problem in NP such that if we showed it to be in P, then that would imply that all the problems in NP will be in P also? This would mean that $NP - P = \phi$. The P versus NP problem is to determine whether every language accepted by some non-deterministic algorithm in polynomial time is also accepted by some deterministic algorithm in polynomial time. Alternative definitions of P and NP in terms of language are given below:

$P = \{L|\ L = L(M)$ for some Turing machine M which runs in polynomial time$\}$.

The language accepted by M, denoted by $L(M)$, has an associated alphabet Σ and is defined as $L(M) = \{w \in \Sigma^* \mid M$ accepts $w\}$.

NP: A language over Σ is in NP iff there is a $k \in N$ and a polynomial time checking relation R such that for all $w \in \Sigma^*$, $w \in L \Leftrightarrow \exists\ y\ \{|y| \le |w|^k$ and $R(w,y)\}$, where $|y|$ and $|w|$ denote the lengths of y and w respectively. A checking relation is simply a binary relation $R \subseteq \Sigma^* \times \Sigma_1^*$ for some finite alphabets Σ and Σ_1. A language L_R over $\Sigma \cup \Sigma_1 \cup \{\#\}$ is

---

[2] M. Agrawal, N. Kayal and N. Saxena researchers from IIT Kanpur proved that PRIMES is in P.

associated with each such relation R defined by $L_R = \{w\#y \mid R(w, y)\}$, where the symbol $\#$ is not in Σ. We say that R is polynomial time iff $L_R \in P$.

Unlike the P-class, membership of a problem in NP does not imply membership of its complement in NP. Many practical problems such as Hamiltonian cycle, traveling salesperson, independent set, satisfiability, 3-colorability of a graph, etc. for which no deterministic polynomial time algorithm has been found, belong to NP.

Co-NP

A language L belongs to this class if $\overline{L}$, the complement of L belongs to NP. The complement of a language L is defined as $\overline{L} = \{\Sigma^* - x \mid x \in L\}$. Thus for each problem in NP, we have a corresponding problem in Co-NP, with the same set of valid instances, but with *yes* and *no* instances reversed by negating the question. For example, unsatisfiability of Boolean formula, non-3-colorability of a graph, etc. are in Co-NP.

The relationship amongst the P, NP and Co-NP class of problems is shown schematically in Figure 6.3.

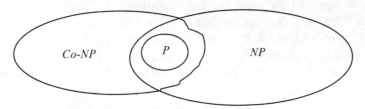

FIGURE 6.3 *P, NP* and *Co-NP* problems.

S.A. Cook[3] showed in 1971 that satisfiability is in P if and only if $P = NP$. The problem of satisfiability is that given a Boolean formula in conjunctive normal form, is there a truth assignment to the Boolean variables so that the formula is *true*? The Boolean formula $E = C_1 \wedge C_2 \wedge C_3 \wedge C_4$ over the Boolean variables x_1 and x_2, where $C_1 = (x_1 + x_2)$, $C_2 = x_1$, $C_3 = x_2$, and $C_4 = (\overline{x}_1 + \overline{x}_2)$ is not satisfiable. For E to be satisfied, all the four clauses C_1, C_2, C_3, and C_4 should be *true*. For C_1 to be *true* one of x_1 and x_2 should be *true*. For C_4 to be *true* one of x_1 and x_2 should be *false* but for C_2 and C_3 to be *true* both of x_1 and x_2 should be *true*. So the four clauses cannot be simultaneously satisfied.

We now introduce the concept of reducibility of one problem to another (refer Figure 6.4). This helps us in deciding the complexity class and solving one problem using the known algorithm for another problem. We are interested in reductions that can be carried out in polynomial time. Let L_1 and L_2 denote two problems. We say L_1 reduces to L_2, written as $L_1 \le L_2$, if and only if there is a way to solve L_1 by a deterministic polynomial time algorithm that solves L_2 in polynomial time after converting an instance of L_1 into an instance of L_2

---

[3] S.A. Cook, "The Complexity of Theorem-Proving Procedures", *Proc. the Third Annual ACM Symposium on the Theory of Computing,* ACM, pp. 151–158, 1971. Cook gave the first *NP*-completeness proof for satisfiability. L.A. Levin independently discovered the notion and gave an *NP*-completeness proof for a tiling problem in 1973.

FIGURE 6.4 Problem reduction.

and the conversion takes polynomial time. The relation $\leq$ is transitive, that is, if $L_1 \leq L_2$ and $L_2 \leq L_3$, then $L_1 \leq L_3$.

Let us consider the problems of squaring and multiplication. Multiplication of x and y can be carried out as $xy = \{(x + y)^2 - (x - y)^2\}/4$. So the squaring algorithm can be used for multiplication. Any significant algorithmic improvement of the method of squaring would yield a better multiplication algorithm. The method of reduction can be used to solve a number of problems after reducing them to linear programming problem. In linear programming, we maximize or minimize an objective function expressed as a linear combination of certain variables subject to a number of restrictions on linear combinations of those variables. The knapsack problem trivially reduces to the linear programming problem. The single-source shortest-path problem can be formulated as a linear programming problem. Given a weighted directed graph, $G = (V, E, w)$, where w is a mapping from E to R^+, the set of positive real numbers, we have to find the length (L) of the shortest-path from a source s to the destination t. The problem can be formulated as a linear programming problem as:

Minimize $L(t)$
subject *to*
$\qquad L(v) \leq L(u) + w(u, v)$ for each $(u, v) \in E$, $L(s) = 0$

The maximum-flow problem can also be expressed as a linear programming problem. Given a directed graph, $G = (V, E, c)$, where c is a mapping from E to R^+, the set of positive real numbers, and two distinguishing vertices, source s and sink t, we have to find the maximum flow (f) from s to t without violating the capacity (c) constraints of the edges, where $f: V \times V \rightarrow R^+$. The reduced problem is:

Maximize $\sum_{v \in V} f(s, v)$

subject to
$\qquad f(u, v) \leq c(u, v)$ for each $u, v \in V$
$\qquad f(u, v) = -f(v, u)$ for each $u, v \in V$

$\qquad \sum_{v \in V} f(u, v) = 0$ for each $u \in V - \{s, t\}$. /* Flow in = Flow out */

If L_1 is a decision problem and L_2 is the corresponding optimization problem, then it is quite possible that $L_1 \leq L_2$. It is not difficult to show that the knapsack decision problem reduces to the knapsack optimization problem. Suppose A is an algorithm that solves the knapsack optimization problem. Let $I = (p_1, p_2, ..., p_n; w_1, w_2, ..., w_n; C, K)$ be an instance of the knapsack decision problem. We construct an algorithm B as follows. Let us define an instance $II = (p_1, p_2, ..., p_n; w_1, w_2, ..., w_n; C)$. Run A on II obtaining an optimal n-tuple

$(x_1, x_2, ..., x_n)$. Compute $S = \sum\limits_{i=1}^{i=n} p_i x_i$. Algorithm B returns the answer 'yes' if $S \geq K$, and it returns the answer 'no', otherwise. Similarly, the clique decision problem reduces to the clique optimization problem.

Two problems L_1 and L_2 are polynomially equivalent iff $L_1 \leq L_2$ and $L_2 \leq L_1$. This polynomial equivalence is used to find other members of different complexity classes. We now introduce two important complexity classes: *NP*-hard and *NP*-complete.

NP-hard

A problem L is *NP*-hard if and only if *satisfiability* reduces to L or any other *NP*-hard problem reduces to L. If we could solve L in polynomial time, then all problems in *NP* are solvable in polynomial time.

NP-complete

A problem L is *NP*-complete if L is *NP*-hard and $L \in NP$. Karp defined: A decision problem D is *NP*-complete if $D \in NP$ and for every $D' \in NP$, $D' \leq D$. Cook defined: A problem $D \in NP$ is *NP*-complete if for every problem $D' \in NP$, there exists a polynomial algorithm in which questions of the type: "what is the answer to the instance with respect to D?" can be asked, and the answer be used. He calls such a question-answering device an *oracle*, and its use is like a subroutine. Clearly, if there is a polynomial algorithm for some problem D that is *NP*-complete (according to this definition), then $P = NP$. For, if each of the calls to the oracle takes a polynomial time to answer, and there can be only polynomial number of such calls, then the whole process is polynomially bounded. Aho, Hopcroft and Ullman defined: A problem D is *NP*-complete if $D \in NP$ and the existence of a polynomial algorithm for it implies a polynomial algorithm for every $D' \in NP$. Clearly, $NPC_{Karp} \subseteq NPC_{Cook} \subseteq NPC_{Aho}$. None of these inclusions is known to be strict, but equality has not been demonstrated either.

An *NP*-complete problem is strongly *NP*-complete iff it remains *NP*-complete when integers are coded in unary. Examples are *SAT*, 3-dimensional matching, clique, vertex cover, directed Hamiltonian circuit problem, etc. There are *NP*-hard problems that are not *NP*-complete. A diagrammatic representation of the relationship of the complexity classes P, NP, *NP*-hard and *NP*-complete problems could be as shown in Figure 6.5.

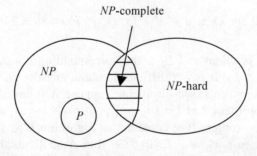

FIGURE 6.5 *P, NP, NP*-complete and *NP*-hard problems.

How do we prove a problem is *NP*-complete? Given a problem *U*, the steps involved in proving that it is *NP*-complete are the following:

Step 1: Show that *U* is in *NP*.
Step 2: Select a known *NP*-complete problem, *V*.
Step 3: Construct a reduction from *V* to *U*.
Step 4: Show that the reduction requires polynomial time.

We have already mentioned that the satisfiability problem is *NP*-complete. This means that if we can find a polynomial time algorithm for satisfiability, then all other problems in *NP* can be solved in polynomial time. To prove that all other problems reduce to the given problem, that is, a candidate problem to be tested for *NP*-completeness, is an involved process. An alternative is to show that some other known *NP*-complete problem reduces to the new problem to be characterized. The other *NP*-complete problems that are quite handy to prove *NP*-completeness of many other problems include 3-*SAT*, 3-dimensional matching, vertex-cover, clique, Hamiltonian circuit, partition, etc. When constructing a polynomial time reduction from 3-*SAT* to a problem, we look for structures in the problem that can simulate the variables and clauses in Boolean formulae. Such structures are called *gadgets*. As an example, in the reduction of a 3-*SAT* to a clique problem (Section 6.6), individual nodes simulate variables and triples of nodes simulate clauses.

When we have to cope with *NP*-complete problems, we generally adopt the following methods:

(a) Use dynamic programming, backtracking or branch-and-bound technique to reduce the computational cost. This might work only if the problem size is not too big.
(b) Find sub-problems of the original problem that have polynomial-time solutions.
(c) Use approximation algorithms to find approximate solution in polynomial time.
(d) Use randomized algorithms to find solution in affordable time with a high probability of correctness of the solution.
(e) Use heuristics like greedy method, simulated annealing or genetic algorithms, etc. However, the solutions produced cannot be guaranteed to be within a certain distance from the optimal solution. Rigorous analysis of heuristic algorithms is generally difficult.

We give a short list of *NP*-complete problems. Later, we will show how some of these problems are used for *NP*-completeness proofs.

6.2 A BRIEF LIST OF *NP*-COMPLETE PROBLEMS[4]

Given below is a brief list of *NP*-completeness problems. Some of these problems remain *NP*-complete even when their domains are substantially restricted.

3SAT: Given a finite collection of clauses on a finite set of Boolean variables such

---

[4] A long list of *NP-complete* problems is available in M.R. Garey and D.S. Johnson, *Computers and Intractability: A Guide to the Theory of NP-Completeness*, W.H. Freeman, 1979.

that each clause contains 3 literals, is there a truth assignment for the Boolean variables such that all the clauses are satisfied simultaneously?

3-dimensional Matching: Given a set $M \subseteq U \times V \times W$, where U, V, and W are disjoint sets having the same number (n) of elements, is there a subset $M' \subseteq M$ such that M' has n elements and no two elements of M' agree in any coordinate?

Vertex-Cover: Given a graph $G = (V, E)$ and a positive integer $k \leq |V|$, is there a subset $X \subseteq V$ such that $|X| \leq k$ and for each edge $(u, v) \in E$, at least one of u and v belongs to X?

Clique: Given a graph $G = (V, E)$ and a positive integer $k \leq |V|$, is there a subset $X \subseteq V$ such that $|X| \geq k$ and every two vertices in X are joined by an edge in E? Clique is a completely connected sub-graph.

Hamiltonian Circuit: Given a graph $G = (V, E)$, does G contain a Hamiltonian circuit? Hamiltonian circuit is a permutation of the vertex set such that every two consecutive nodes in the permutation and also the first and the last nodes of the permutation are adjacent in V.

Partition: Given a finite set U and a size function s from U to the positive integers, is there a subset $V \subseteq U$ such that the following is satisfied?

$$\sum_{a \in V} s(a) = \sum_{b \in U - V} s(b)$$

Graph k-colorability (Chromatic Number): Given a graph $G = (V, E)$ and a positive integer $k \leq |V|$, is G k-colorable? That is, does there exist a function $f: V \to \{1, 2, \ldots, k\}$ such that $f(u) \neq f(v)$ wherever $(u, v) \in E$?

Feedback Vertex Set: Given a directed graph $G = (V, E)$ and a positive integer $k \leq |V|$, is there a subset $V' \subseteq V$ with $|V'| \leq k$ such that V' contains at least one vertex from every directed cycle in G?

Partition into Triangles: Given a graph $G = (V, E)$ with $|V| = 3q$ for some integer q, can the vertices of G be partitioned into q disjoint sets $V_1, V_2, \ldots, V_q$, each containing exactly three vertices, such that for each $V_i = \{u_i, v_i, w_i\}$, all three of the edges (u_i, v_i), (u_i, w_i), (v_i, w_i) are present?

Independent Set: Given a graph $G = (V, E)$ and a positive integer $k \leq |V|$, does G contain an independent set of size k or more, that is, a subset $V' \subseteq V$ such that $|V'| \geq k$ and no two vertices in V' are joined by an edge?

Planar Sub-graph: Given a graph $G = (V, E)$ and a positive integer $k \leq |E|$, is there a subset $E' \subseteq E$ with $|E'| \geq k$ such that $G' = (V, E')$ is planar?

Hamiltonian Completion: Given a graph $G = (V, E)$ and a positive integer $k \leq |V|$, is there a superset E' containing E such that $|E' - E| \leq k$ and the graph $G' = (V, E')$ has a Hamiltonian circuit?

Sub-graph Isomorphism: Given two graphs $G = (V_1, E_1)$, $H = (V_2, E_2)$, does G contain a sub-graph isomorphic to H, that is, a subset $V \subseteq V_1$ and a subset $E \subseteq E_1$ such that

$|V| = |V_2|$, $|E| = |E_2|$, and there exists a one-to-one function f: $V_2 \rightarrow V$ satisfying $(u, v) \in E_2$ if and only if $(f(u), f(v)) \in E$?

Degree Constrained Spanning Tree: Given a graph $G = (V, E)$ and a positive integer $k < |V|$, is there a spanning tree for G in which no vertex has degree greater than k?

Longest Circuit: Given a graph $G = (V, E)$ and length function $l(e) \in Z^+$ for each $e \in E$ and a positive integer k, is there a simple circuit in G of length k or more?

Set Packing: Given a collection C of finite sets and a positive integer $k \leq |C|$, does C contain at least k mutually disjoint sets?

Bin Packing: Given a finite set U of items and a size $s(u) \in Z^+$ for each $u \in U$, a positive integer bin capacity B, and a positive integer k, is there a partition of U into disjoint sets $U_1, U_2, ..., U_k$ such that the sum of the sizes of the items in each U_i is B or less?

String-to-string Correction: Given a finite alphabet Σ, two strings $x, y \in \Sigma^*$(closure of Σ), a positive integer k, is there a way to derive the string y from the string x by a sequence of k or fewer operations of single symbol deletion or adjacent symbol interchange?

Integer Knapsack: Given a finite set U, for each $u \in U$ a size $s(u) \in Z^+$, and a value $v(u) \in Z^+$, and positive integers B and k, is there an assignment of non-negative integers $c(u)$ to each $u \in U$ such that $\sum_{u \in U} c(u)s(u) \leq B$ and $\sum_{u \in U} c(u)v(u) \geq k$?

Quadratic Congruences: Given positive integers a, b and c, is there a positive $x < c$ such that $x^2 \equiv a(mod\ b)$?

Quadratic Diophantine Equations: Given positive integers a, b and c, are there positive integers x and y such that $ax^2 + by = c$?

Non-Tautology: Given a Boolean expression E over a set U of variables using the connectives 'not', 'or', 'and', 'implies', is there a truth assignment for U that makes E false?
We will now show how a number of problems are characterized as *NP*-complete.

6.3   THEOREM: *SAT* IN CNF IS *NP*-COMPLETE

Proof:

Step 1:   A non-deterministic algorithm guesses a truth assignment for the variables and checks in polynomial time whether this assignment of variables satisfies all the clauses. So *SAT* is in *NP*.

Step 2:   We show that every language $L \in NP$ is polynomially transformable to *SAT*. Let M be a non-deterministic Turing machine (NTM) of polynomial complexity accepting L. Let x be an input to M. From (M, x), we construct a Boolean expression Φ such that Φ is satisfiable if and only if M accepts x. The formula is the conjunction of several formulae. It includes general properties of Turing machine, specification of input string on the tape, specification of an accepting computation and specification of the transition function of the Turing machine. Without loss of generality, we assume that the NTM has a single one-side infinite tape. Let the states of M be $\{q_0, q_1, q_2, ..., q_k\}$, the tape-symbols be $\{x_0, x_1, x_2, ..., x_m\}$,

x_0 being blank, $|x| = n$ and the complexity of M be the polynomial $p(n)$. If M accepts x, there is at least one sequence of state transitions $q_0 \rightarrow q_1 \rightarrow q_2 \rightarrow \cdots \rightarrow q_a$ such that q_0 is an initial state and q_a is an accepting state.

The idea behind the reduction is to simulate the action of M on the input x. The Boolean expression Φ will take the value *true* if and only if the assignment to the variables represents a sequence of transitions $q_0 \rightarrow q_1 \rightarrow q_2 \rightarrow \cdots \rightarrow q_a$ of M leading to the acceptance of the input. For constructing Φ, we define the following propositional variables:

- *Cell*(i, j, t) is *true* if and only if the ith cell on the input tape contains the symbol x_j at time t, where $1 \leq i \leq p(n)$, $1 \leq j \leq m$, and $0 \leq t \leq p(n)$.

- *State*(i, t) is *true* if and only if M is in state q_i at time t, where $0 \leq i \leq k$ and $0 \leq t \leq p(n)$.

- *Head*(i, t) is *true* if and only if the tape head is scanning tape cell i at time t, where $1 \leq i \leq p(n)$ and $0 \leq t \leq p(n)$.

The total number of propositional variables introduced is polynomially bounded from the above $(O(p^2(n)))$. Let us also introduce the predicate $Pred(y_1, y_2, ..., y_l)$[5] that has value *true* when exactly one of the arguments $y_1, y_2, ..., y_l$ has value *true*. *Pred* has length $O(l^2)$. We use the following assertions about the Turing machine.

1. Tape head is scanning exactly one cell at a time. Let A_t assert that at time t, M is scanning exactly one cell. Then $\Phi_1 = A_0 A_1 \ldots A_{p(n)}$, where $A_t = Pred(Head(1, t)$, $Head(2, t), ..., Head(p(n), t))$. Φ_1 has length $O(p^3(n))$, as each *Pred* has a length of $O(p^2(n))$.

2. Each tape cell has exactly one symbol at each unit of time. Let B_{i_t} represent the assertion that the ith tape cell contains exactly one symbol at time t. Then, $\Phi_2 = B_{i_0} B_{i_1} \ldots B_{i_{p(n)}}$, where $B_{i_t} = Pred(Cell(i, 1, t), Cell(i, 2, t), ..., Cell(i, m, t))$. The length of Φ_2 is $O(p^2(n))$ as m is fixed for a Turing machine.

3. At time t, M is in one and only one state. This is captured as

$$\Phi_3 = \prod_{0 \leq t \leq p(n)} Pred(State(1, t), State(2, t), ..., State(k, t)).$$

Since k is a constant for a given M, Φ_3 is of length $O(p(n))$.

4. At most one tape cell can be changed at any time t. This is captured through

$$\Phi_4 = \prod_{i,j,t} [(Cell(i,j,t)\,Cell(i,j,t+1) + \overline{Cell(i,j,t)}\ \overline{Cell(i,j,t+1)}) + Head(i,t)].$$

This asserts that either the tape head is scanning cell i at time t or the jth symbol is in cell i at time $t + 1$ if and only if it were there at time t. Length of Φ_4 is bounded by $O(p^2(n))$.

---

[5] As an example $Pred(y_1, y_2, y_3) = (y_1 + y_2 + y_3)\ (\overline{y}_1 + \overline{y}_2)(\overline{y}_2 + \overline{y}_3)(\overline{y}_1 + \overline{y}_3)$.

5. The change in state, head position, and cell contents are as defined by the transition function of M. This is captured through

  (i) The ith cell does not contain symbol j at time t, or
  (ii) The read-write head is not scanning cell i at time t, or
  (iii) M is not in state v at time t, or
  (iv) The next configuration of M is obtained from the previous as prescribed by the transition function of M.

This is captured as $\Phi_5 = \prod_{i,j,v,t} R_{ijvt}$

where

$$R_{ijvt} = \overline{Cell(i,j,t)} + \overline{Head(i,t)} + \overline{State(v,t)}$$

$$+ \sum Cell(i,j_r,t+1)\, State(v_r,t+1)\, Head(i_r, t+1).$$

Here, the summation is over r and it ranges over all possible moves[6] of M when scanning symbol x_j in state q_v. The length of Φ_5 is $O(p^2(n))$.

6. The initial condition is captured through

$$\Phi_6 = State(0,0)Head(1,0) \prod_{1 \le i \le n} Cell(i,j_i,0) \prod_{n < i \le p(n)} Cell(i,0,0)$$

The initial condition states that at time $t = 0$, M is in q_0, M is scanning the leftmost tape cell, the first n tape cells, cells 1 through n initially contain the input string x, the remaining tape cells contain blank. Clearly, the length of Φ_6 is $O(p(n))$.

7. M eventually enters the final state, q_a. So, we have $\Phi_7 = State(a, p(n))$.

The Boolean expression Φ is the product $\prod_{i=1}^{i=7} \Phi_i$. Since each of Φ_i, $1 \le i \le 7$ requires at most $O(p^3(n))$ symbols, Φ has $O(p^3(n))$ symbols assuming one symbol per variable. Thus the length of Φ is a polynomial function of the length of x.

Given an accepting sequence of computation of M, we can find an assignment of *true* and *false* values to the prepositional variables *Cell*, *State* and *Head* that will make Φ *true*. Conversely, given an assignment of values to the variables of Φ making Φ *true*, we can easily find an accepting sequence of computation. Thus, Φ is satisfiable if and only if M accepts x. Since we did not put any restriction on the language accepted by M, any language in *NP* is polynomially transformable to the satisfiability problem for Boolean expressions.

The expressions Φ_1, Φ_2, ..., Φ_7 defined above are either already in conjunctive normal form (CNF) or can be expressed in CNF through the use of the laws of Boolean algebra with at most a constant factor increase in length. Φ_1, Φ_2, Φ_3 are already in CNF. Φ_4 can be

expressed as $\Phi_4 = \prod_{i,j,t} [(Cell(i,j,t) + \overline{Cell(i,j,t+1)} + Head(i,t))(\overline{Cell(i,j,t)} + Cell(i,j, t+1)$

$+ Head(i, t))]$ from the Boolean identity: $(x + \bar{y} + z)(\bar{x} + y + z) = \bar{x}\,\bar{y} + xy + z$.

---

[6] Because of non-determinism, there may be more than one move but the number of moves is finite.

The expression Φ_5 can be expressed in a conjunctive normal form whose length is independent of n. Converting Φ_5 to conjunctive normal form increases the length of Φ_5 by at most a constant factor. Φ_6, Φ_7 are already in CNF since they are product of single literals. So Φ can be put in CNF without increasing the length by more than a constant factor.

Step 3:   The above reduction can be carried out in polynomial time. Hence, *SAT* in CNF is *NP*-complete.

6.4   THEOREM: 3-*SAT* IS *NP*-COMPLETE

Proof:
   Step 1:   We show that 3-*SAT* $\in$ *NP*.
   For, if the set of clauses is satisfiable, all we need to do is to use a satisfying truth assignment as the guess and verify that this assignment is indeed consistent and satisfying. This can be done in polynomial time in the number of clauses.
   Step 2:   We select *SAT* as a suitable *NP*-complete problem for reduction to the 3-*SAT* problem.
   Step 3:   We show that *SAT* problem does reduce to the 3-*SAT* problem. A clause containing one variable x_1 can be replaced by

$$(x_1 + y_1 + y_2)(x_1 + \overline{y}_1 + y_2)(x_1 + y_1 + \overline{y}_2)(x_1 + \overline{y}_1 + \overline{y}_2)$$

where y_1 and y_2 are two new variables. A clause containing two variables x_1, x_2 can be replaced by the product,

$$(x_1 + x_2 + y_1)(x_1 + x_2 + \overline{y}_1)$$

where y_1 is a new variable. By introducing $k - 3$ new variables $\{y_1, y_2, ..., y_{k-3}\}$ a clause of length $k > 3$ can be replaced by $k - 2$ clauses of length 3, without changing the satisfiability of the set of clauses. This can be done as follows:
   The clause $\{x_1, x_2, ..., x_k\}$ is replaced by *AND* of the following clauses:

$$\{x_1, x_2, y_1\}, \{\overline{y}_1, x_3, y_2\}, \quad ..., \{\overline{y}_i, x_{i+2}, y_{i+1}\}, ..., \{\overline{y}_{k-3}, x_{k-1}, x_k\}.$$

If a truth assignment for x_1, x_2, ..., x_k contains at least one 'true' literal, then the long clause $\{x_1, x_2, ..., x_k\}$ is satisfied. Further, the y variables can be assigned truth values to satisfy all the clauses of length three that are not satisfied by one of the x values. If x_1 or x_2 is true, we assign $y_1 = y_2 = ... y_{k-3} =$ '*false*'. If x_{k-1} or x_k is true, we assign $y_1 = y_2 = ... y_{k-3} =$ '*true*'. If some $x_r =$ '*true*' for $2 < r < k - 1$, we assign $y_1 = y_2 = ... y_{r-2} =$ '*true*' and $y_{r-1} = y_r = ... y_{k-3} =$ '*false*'. At least one of these cases is applicable. If a truth assignment for x_1, x_2, ..., x_k makes them all 'false', then the long clause is not satisfied and no choice of truth values for the y variables will satisfy all the $k - 2$ short clauses. Proving in the reverse direction is quite obvious.
   Step 4:   The replacement of long clauses by short ones can be done in time that is bounded by a polynomial in the length of the input that describes the original set of clauses.

The number of clauses in the transformed set of 3-literal clauses is $\sum\limits_{k_i \geq 3} (k_i - 2) + 2 \sum\limits_{k_i = 2} 1 + 4 \sum\limits_{k_i = 1} 1$,

where k_i is the number of literals in the ith original clause. Obviously, the transformation can be carried out in polynomial time. Hence 3-SAT[7] is NP-complete.

6.5   THEOREM: (0, 1) INTEGER PROGRAMMING (IP) IS NP-COMPLETE

The (0, 1) pure-integer programming problem is defined as maximize $\{Px: Ax \leq d, x \in \{0, 1\}*\}$, where P is an n-component cost-vector, A is a $m \times n$ coefficient matrix, d is an m-component resource vector, x is an n-component (0, 1)-vector, n is the number of variables and m is the number of constraints.

Proof:

   Step 1:   We show that IP $\in$ NP. We guess a solution vector $v = \{v_1, v_2, ..., v_n\}$ non-deterministically and check that $Av \leq d$, where A is the coefficient matrix of the constraints and d is the given vector of constraints. The decision version of integer programming asks existence of a (0, 1)-vector satifying all the constraints; there is no objective function.

   Step 2:   We select SAT as a suitable NP-complete problem for reduction to the IP problem. We can write SAT problems as (0, 1)-integer programming problems. For example, the Boolean formula $E = x_1 + x_2 + x_3$ is satisfied if and only if $-x_1 - x_2 - x_3 < 0$, $x_1, x_2, x_3 \in \{0, 1\}$.

   Step 3:   We show that SAT problem does reduce to IP problem. Let $E = C_1 \wedge C_2 \wedge ... C_k$ be a Boolean expression in conjunctive normal form (CNF) and let $x_1, x_2, ..., x_n$ be the variables occurring in E. A and d are defined as

   $A = (a_{ij})$, where $1 \leq i \leq k$, $1 \leq j \leq n$ and

   $d = (d_i)$, where $1 \leq i \leq k$.

a_{ij} is -1 if x_j occurs in C_i, it is 1 if $\overline{x}_j$ occurs in C_i and it is 0 otherwise. $d_i = 1 -$ (number of variables x_j occurring in C_i). E is satisfiable iff there is a (0, 1)-vector v such that $Av \leq d$. First, we establish our claim in the forward direction. Suppose E is satisfiable with assignment θ of the variables, that is $\theta(E)$ is 'true'. We define $v_j = \theta(x_j)$ for all j.

Then $(Av)_i = \sum\limits_{j=1}^{j=n} a_{ij} v_j = - \sum\limits_{x_j \in C_i} \theta(x_j) + \sum\limits_{\overline{x}_j \in C_i} \theta(x_j) \leq 1 - \sum\limits_{x_j \in C_i} 1 = d_i$ since there is either

$\overline{x}_j \in C_i$ with $\theta(\overline{x}_j) = 1$ or $x_j \in C_i$ with $\theta(x_j) = 0$.

   We now prove the reverse. Let v be a (0, 1) vector with $Av \leq d$. Let us define truth assignment θ by $\theta(x_j) = v_j$. We claim that $\theta(E) = 1$. Let us prove by contradiction. We assume that $\theta(E) \neq 1$. Then there must be an i such that $\theta(C_i) = 0$. In particular, $\theta(x_j) = v_j = 0$ if $x_j \in C_i$ and $\theta(x_j) = v_j = 1$ if $\overline{x}_j \in C_i$.

   Hence, $d_i \geq (Av)_i = - \sum\limits_{x_j \in C_i} v_j + \sum\limits_{\overline{x}_j \in C_i} v_j = \sum\limits_{\overline{x}_j \in C_i} 1 > d_i$, a contradiction. So $\theta(E) = 1$.

---

[7] 2-SAT has deterministic polynomial time algorithm.

Step 4:   The transformation from *SAT* to IP can be carried out in polynomial time. Hence, IP is *NP*-complete.

6.6   THEOREM: THE CLIQUE PROBLEM IS *NP*-COMPLETE

Proof:

Step 1:   We show that the clique problem belongs to *NP*.

We guess a subset X of the vertices V of the graph. Checking whether X is a clique can be accomplished in polynomial time by checking whether for every pair of vertices $u, v \in X$, the edge (u, v) belongs to E and counting that the number of vertices in X is at least k.

Step 2:   We select 3-*SAT* as a suitable *NP*-complete problem for reduction to the clique problem.

Step 3:   We show that 3-*SAT* problem does reduce to the clique problem (refer Figures 6.6 and 6.7).

Let $\Psi = C_1 \wedge C_2 \wedge C_3 \wedge C_4 \cdots \wedge C_k$ be a Boolean formula in conjunctive normal form with k clauses where each clause C_i has exactly three distinct literals x_1^i, x_2^i, x_3^i. We construct a graph $G = (V, E)$ such that Ψ is satisfiable if and only if G has a clique of size k.

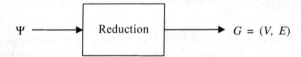

FIGURE 6.6   Reduction of 3-*SAT* problem to clique problem.

For each clause $C_i = (x_1^i \vee x_2^i \vee x_3^i)$ in Ψ, we create vertices v_1^i, v_2^i and v_3^i. Collection of all such vertices for all the clauses in Ψ defines V. The edges in E are drawn as:

Edges connect vertices corresponding to literals from different clauses provided these literals are consistent, that is, these literals are not the true and complemented form of the same variable. Edges are not present between different literals from the same clause. This forms the gadget for this proof. For example, let us consider $\Psi = (x_1 \vee \overline{x}_2 \vee x_3) \wedge (\overline{x}_1 \vee x_2 \vee x_3)$. The graph G will be as shown in Figure 6.7.

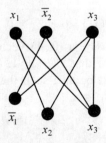

FIGURE 6.7   Example reduction of 3-*SAT* to clique.

The above construction of G can easily be done in polynomial time. We now prove that this transformation is a reduction.

We assume first that Ψ has a satisfying assignment. Then each clause C_i contains at least one literal that is assigned value *true* and each such literal has a corresponding vertex in G. We pick one such *true* literal from each clause yielding a set of vertices X with k elements. It is claimed that X is a clique. For any two vertices $v_m^i, v_n^j \in X$, where $i \neq j$, both the corresponding literals x_m^i and x_n^j are mapped to *true* by the given satisfying assignment, and so the literals cannot be complements. Thus, by the construction of G, the edge $(v_m^i, v_n^j) \in E$.

Conversely, suppose G has a clique X of size k. No edges in G connect vertices corresponding to the same clause. So, X contains exactly one vertex per clause. We can assign *true* to each literal x_m^i such that $v_m^i \in X$ without the problem of assigning *true* to both a literal and its complement. Each clause is satisfied, and so Ψ is satisfied. Variables corresponding to the vertices not in the clique are set arbitrarily.

Step 4:   The transformation in Step 3 can be carried out in polynomial time. So, the clique problem is *NP*-complete.

6.7   THEOREM: THE INDEPENDENT SET PROBLEM IS *NP*-COMPLETE

Proof:

Step 1:   We show that independent set problem belongs to the *NP* class. Given an independent set V' of a graph $G = (V, E)$, it is easy to verify that there is no edge $(u, v) \in E$ whenever $u, v \in V'$.

Step 2:   We select the clique problem as a suitable *NP*-complete problem for reduction to the independent set problem. This is shown in Figure 6.8.

Step 3:   We show that the clique problem does reduce to the independent set problem. If the input I of the clique problem consists of $G = (V, E)$ and k, let $f(I)$ consist of CG and k, where CG is the graph complementary to G, that is $CG = (V, E')$, where $(u, v) \in E'$ if and only if $(u, v) \notin E$. A subset of vertices of $V' \subseteq V$ is a clique in G if and only if V' is an independent set in CG.

Suppose $V' \subseteq V$ is a clique of size k in G. All the nodes in V' are connected to each other through edges and $|V'| = k$. Since all the nodes in V' are connected to each other in G, there will not be any edge amongst this group of nodes in CG and so they form an independent set of size k in CG.

Conversely, suppose V' forms an independent set of size k in CG. Since G is complementary to CG, there will be edges between all pairs of nodes in V' in G and so V' forms a clique of size k in G.

Thus the answer to I with respect to clique is 'yes' if and only if the answer to $f(I)$ is 'yes' with respect to the independent set.

Step 4:   Obviously, the reduction can be carried out in polynomial time. Hence independent set problem is *NP*-complete.

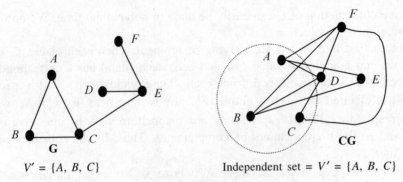

V' = {A, B, C}   Independent set = V' = {A, B, C}

FIGURE 6.8   Reduction of clique to independent set.

6.8   THEOREM: THE VERTEX-COVER PROBLEM IS *NP*-COMPLETE

Proof:

Step 1:   We prove that this problem belongs to the *NP* class of problems. Suppose that we are given a graph $G = (V, E)$ and an integer k. We choose the vertex-cover $X \subseteq V$ non-deterministically. The verification algorithm checks (i) whether $|X| \le k$, (ii) for each edge $(u, v) \in E$, whether $u \in X$ or $v \in X$. These can obviously be done in polynomial time.

Step 2:   We select *clique* as the *NP*-complete problem to be reduced to the vertex-cover problem.

Step 3:   This is the reduction step (see Figures 6.9 and 6.10). Given an undirected graph $G = (V, E)$, we define the complement of G as $CG = (V, E1)$, where $E1 = \{(u, v)| (u, v) \notin E\}$. The reduction algorithm takes an instance $\langle G, k \rangle$ of the clique problem as input and computes CG. The output of the reduction algorithm is $\langle CG, |V| - k \rangle$ of the vertex-cover problem.

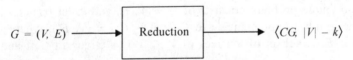

$G = (V, E)$ ⟶ Reduction ⟶ $\langle CG, |V| - k \rangle$

FIGURE 6.9   Reduction of clique to vertex-cover.

We have to prove that this transformation is a reduction indeed. This means that we have to prove that $G = (V, E)$ has a clique of size k if and only if the graph CG has a vertex-cover of size $|V| - k$.

First, suppose G has a clique X of size k. It is claimed that $V - X$ is a vertex-cover in CG. If $(u, v) \in E1$, then $(u, v) \notin E$ and this implies that at least one of u or v does not belong to X, since every pair of vertices in X is connected by an edge of E. At least one of u or v is in $V - X$, and this means that the edge (u, v) is covered by $V - X$. Since (u, v) is chosen arbitrarily from $E1$, every edge of $E1$ is covered by a vertex in $V - X$. Hence, the set $V - X$ having size $|V| - k$ forms a vertex-cover for CG.

We now prove in the reverse direction. Suppose CG has a vertex-cover $VC \subseteq V$, where $|VC| = |V| - k$. For all $u, v \in V$, if $(u, v) \in E1$, then $u \in VC$ or $v \in VC$ or both. The contra-

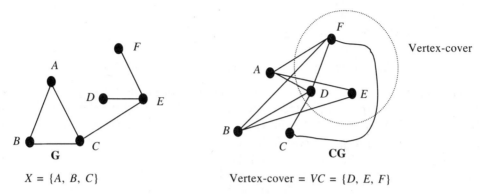

FIGURE 6.10 Example reduction of clique to vertex-cover.

positive[8] of this is that for all $u, v \in V$, if $u \notin VC$ and $v \notin VC$, then $(u, v) \in E$. In other words, $V - VC$ is a clique, and it has size $|V| - |VC| = k$.

Step 4:   The above reduction can be carried out in polynomial time. Hence, the vertex-cover problem is *NP*-complete.

6.9   THEOREM: THE DIRECTED HAMILTONIAN PATH PROBLEM (DHP) IS *NP*-COMPLETE

Proof:

Step 1:   A non-deterministic algorithm guesses an ordering of the vertices and checks in polynomial time that all the required edges belong to the edge set of the given graph.

Step 2:   We select *vertex-cover* as the *NP*-complete problem to be reduced to the directed Hamiltonian path problem.

Step 3:   This is the reduction step. Given a graph $G = (V, E)$ and an integer k, we construct a directed graph $G' = (V', E')$ such that G' has a directed Hamiltonian path if and only if a set of k vertices of V covers the edges of G. Suppose $V = \{v_1, v_2, \ldots, v_n\}$. Introducing k new vertices $u_1, u_2, \ldots, u_k$, we define the vertices of G' as

$V' = \{u_1, u_2, \ldots, u_k\} \cup \{[v_i, (v_i, v_j), 0], [v_i, (v_i, v_j), 1], [v_j, (v_i, v_j), 0], [v_j, (v_i, v_j), 1] \mid v_i,$ $v_j \in V$ and $(v_i, v_j) \in E\}$. G' consists of $k + 4|E|$ nodes. For the graph in Figure 6.11, the edge lists are:

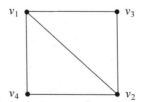

FIGURE 6.11 Example graph.

---

[8] Contra-positive means "*P implies Q*" is equivalent to "*Not Q implies Not P*".

(1) for v_1, (v_1, v_2), (v_1, v_3), (v_1, v_4),
(2) for v_2, (v_1, v_2), (v_2, v_3), (v_2, v_4),
(3) for v_3, (v_1, v_3), (v_2, v_3),
(4) for v_4, (v_1, v_4), (v_2, v_4).

The graph has a vertex-cover of size 2 consisting of the nodes v_1 and v_2. The node set of the graph G' corresponding to the graph shown in Figure 6.11 consists of $V' = \{u_1, u_2\}$ $\cup$ $\{[v_1, (v_1, v_2), 0], [v_1, (v_1, v_2), 1], [v_2, (v_1, v_2), 0], [v_2, (v_1, v_2), 1], [v_1, (v_1, v_3), 0], [v_1, (v_1, v_3), 1], [v_3, (v_1, v_3), 0], [v_3, (v_1, v_3), 1], [v_1, (v_1, v_4), 0], [v_1, (v_1, v_4), 1], [v_4, (v_1, v_4), 0], [v_4, (v_1, v_4), 1], [v_2, (v_2, v_3), 0], [v_2, (v_2, v_3), 1], [v_3, (v_2, v_3), 0], [v_3, (v_2, v_3), 1], [v_2, (v_2, v_4), 0], [v_2, (v_2, v_4), 1], [v_4, (v_2, v_4), 0], [v_4, (v_2, v_4), 1]\}$

The edge-set E' of G' is defined as:

(1) each u_j, $1 \le j \le k$ has an edge to the vertices $[v_i, (v_i, v_l), 0]$ such that the edge (v_i, v_l) is the first edge on the list for v_i,
(2) there is an edge from $[v_i, (v_i, v_l), 1]$ to each u_j if (v_i, v_l) is the last edge on the list for v_i,
(3) there is an edge from $[v_i, (v_i, v_l), 1]$ to $[v_i, (v_i, v_m), 0]$ if edge (v_i, v_m) immediately follows edge (v_i, v_l) on the list for v_i,
(4) there is an edge from $[v_i, (v_i, v_j), 0]$ to $[v_i, (v_i, v_j), 1]$,
(5) there is an edge from $[v_i, (v_i, v_j), 0]$ to $[v_j, (v_i, v_j), 0]$ and $[v_j, (v_i, v_j), 0]$ to $[v_i, (v_i, v_j), 0]$,
(6) there is an edge from $[v_i, (v_i, v_j), 1]$ to $[v_j, (v_i, v_j), 1]$ and $[v_j, (v_i, v_j), 1]$ to $[v_i, (v_i, v_j), 1]$.

Number of edges belonging to type 1 is $k|V|$, to type 2 is $k|V|$, to type 3 and type 4 together is $\sum_{v_i \in V} (2|List(v_i)| - 1)$, to type 5 is $2|E|$ and to type 6 is $2|E|$. For the example in Figure 6.11, E' will consist of 8 edges of type 1, 8 edges of type 2, 16 edges of type 3 and type 4 together, 10 edges of type 5 and 10 edges of type 6; in all 52 edges. Figure 6.12 shows the relevant edges for a typical node v_i.

We now show that G' has a directed Hamiltonian path (DHP) if and only if G has a set of k vertices covering all its edges. Let us assume that $v_1, v_2, ..., v_k$ cover all the edges of G. Let $L_{i1}, L_{i2}, ..., L_{il}$ be the list of edges incident on v_i, $1 \le i \le k$. Consider the cycle:

u_1, $[v_1, L_{11}, 0]$, $[v_1, L_{11}, 1]$, $[v_1, L_{12}, 0]$, $[v_1, L_{12}, 1]$, ..., $[v_1, L_{1i_1}, 0]$, $[v_1, L_{1i_1}, 1]$, u_2, $[v_2, L_{21}, 0]$, $[v_2, L_{21}, 1]$ ... and so on through the edge lists of $v_3, v_4, ..., v_k$, then finally back to u_1.

This cycle passes through every vertex of G' except those vertices in the edge lists of the vertices other than $v_1, v_2, ..., v_k$. For each pair of vertices $[v_j, (v_p, v_j), 0]$, $[v_j, (v_p, v_j), 1]$, $p \le k$, $j > k$ of G', the cycle can be extended, since (v_p, v_j) is incident upon some v_p, $1 \le p \le k$. We replace the edge from $[v_i, (v_i, v_j), 0]$ to $[v_i, (v_i, v_j), 1]$ in the cycle by the

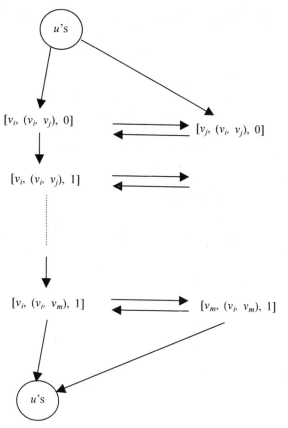

FIGURE 6.12 Edges for v_i.

path $[v_i, (v_i, v_j), 0]$ $[v_j, (v_i, v_j), 0]$ $[v_j, (v_i, v_j), 1]$ $[v_i, (v_i, v_j), 1]$. The cycle so revised for each v_j and (v_i, v_j) contains every vertex of G' and hence is a Hamiltonian circuit and so has a Hamiltonian path.

Conversely, suppose G' has a Hamiltonian path. This path can be broken into k paths. Each path starts at a vertex u_i and ends at a vertex u_j excepting the last path that ends at a vertex $[v, (v, w), 1]$. There exists a vertex v such that each vertex on the path from u_i to u_j is of the form $[v, (v, w), 0]$ or $[v, (v, w), 1]$, where $(v, w) \in E$, or is of the form $[w, (v, w), 0]$ or $[w, (v, w), 1]$. The first component of each vertex on the path from u_i to u_j is either the vertex v or its neighbour. We may associate some specific vertex v with each of the k paths. For every vertex $[v_i, (v_i, v_j), 0]$ or $[v_i, (v_i, v_j), 1]$ of G', (v_i, v_j) is incident upon one of the k vertices of G associated with a path. The k vertices thus form a vertex-cover of G. We conclude that G' has a DHP if and only if there exist k vertices in G such that every edge of G is incident upon one of these k vertices.

Step 4: The above reduction can be carried out in polynomial time. Hence, the directed Hamiltonian path problem is *NP*-complete.

6.10 THEOREM: THE HAMILTONIAN PATH (HP) PROBLEM IS *NP*-COMPLETE

Proof:

Step 1: Given a graph $G = (V, E)$ and two distinguished vertices s and t, the problem of finding a simple path in G with end points s and t, that passes through all other vertices is the Hamiltonian path problem. We prove that this problem belongs to the *NP* class of problems. Given a path, we verify whether the path begins at s and ends at t and all other vertices of V appear only once on the path. This can obviously be verified in polynomial time.

Step 2: We select the DHP problem as the *NP*-complete problem to be reduced to the HP problem. This is shown in Figure 6.13.

Step 3: This is the reduction step. Let the input I of DHP consist of the digraph $G = (V, E)$ and the two vertices s and t. We define an instance $f(I)$ as:

$$G' = (V', E')$$

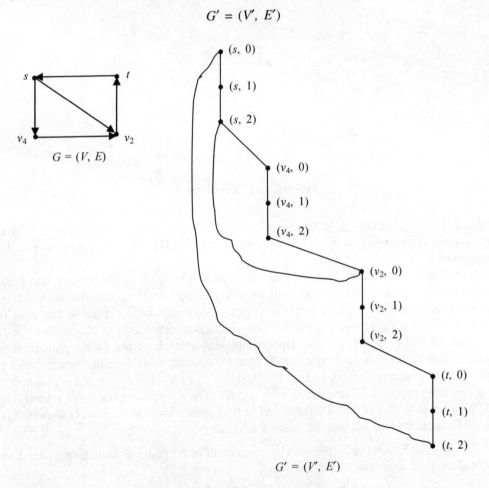

$$G' = (V', E')$$

FIGURE 6.13 Reduction of DHP to HP.

where

$V' = \{(v, 0), (v, 1), (v, 2) \mid v \in V\}$ and
$E' = \{((v, 0), (v, 1)), ((v, 1), (v, 2)) \mid v \in V\} \cup \{((u, 2), (v, 0)) \mid (u, v) \in E\}$

The two end points are $(s, 0)$ and $(t, 2)$.

It is easy to see that if there is a directed Hamiltonian path P from s to t in G, then there is a Hamiltonian path P' in G' with endpoints $(s, 0)$ and $(t, 2)$. P' consists of all the edges in the first part of the definition of E', and if (u, v) is in P, then $((u, 2), (v, 0))$ is included in P'.

Now assume that P' is a solution to the HP problem specified by $f(I)$. Clearly, all the edges of the first part of the definition of E' appear in P' or there would not be any way to pass through some $(v, 1)$. We can now scan P' from $(s, 0)$ to $(t, 2)$. Clearly, P' starts with $((s, 0), (s, 1)), ((s, 1), (s, 2))$ and ends with $((t, 0), (t, 1)), ((t, 1), (t, 2))$. Whenever $((u, 2), (v, 0))$ is used in P', we can use (u, v) in G. Thus, the resulting directed path is simple, starts at s and ends at t and passes through all other vertices of G.

Step 4: The above reduction can be carried out in polynomial time. Hence, the Hamiltonian path problem is *NP*-complete.

6.11 THEOREM: THE HAMILTONIAN CYCLE (HC) PROBLEM IS *NP*-COMPLETE

This can be proved by reducing HP to HC. Add a new vertex p and two new edges (p, s) and (t, p).

6.12 THEOREM: THE TRAVELING SALESPERSON PROBLEM (TSP) IS *NP*-COMPLETE

A salesperson must visit n cities where every city is connected to all other cities. There is a positive cost involved in visiting a city from another. The salesperson must visit each city exactly once and return to the city of start. The problem is to determine whether there is a tour of length at most k.

Proof:

Step 1: We show that TSP $\in$ *NP*. Given the sequence of n cities in the tour, we check that this sequence contains each vertex exactly once and sum up the costs of the edges and check whether the sum is at most k. This can be carried out in polynomial time.

Step 2: We select the Hamiltonian cycle problem as the known *NP*-complete problem to be reduced to TSP.

Step 3: This is the reduction step. Let $G = (V, E)$ be an instance of the Hamiltonian-cycle problem. We construct an instance of TSP (shown in Figure 6.14) as follows:

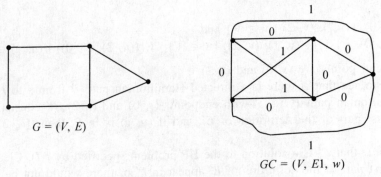

FIGURE 6.14 Reduction of HC to TSP.

We form a weighted complete graph $GC = (V, E1, w)$, where $E1 = \{(i, j)|\ i, j \in V\}$, and define the edge cost function w by

$$w(i, j) = \begin{cases} 0, (i, j) \in E \\ 1, (i, j) \notin E \end{cases}$$

The instance of TSP is then $<GC, 0>$. We show that the graph G has a Hamiltonian-cycle if and only if the graph GC has a tour of cost at most 0.

First, suppose that G has a Hamiltonian-cycle C. Each edge in C belongs to E and thus has cost 0 in GC. Thus, C is a tour in GC with cost 0.

Conversely, suppose that the graph GC has a tour $C1$ of cost at most 0. Since, the costs of the edges in $E1$ are 0 and 1, the cost of the tour $C1$ is exactly 0. Therefore, $C1$ contains only edges belonging to E. We conclude that $C1$ is a Hamiltonian-cycle in the graph G.

Step 4: The above reduction can be carried out in polynomial time. Hence, TSP is *NP*-complete.

SUMMARY

There are many fundamental problems for which we have no efficient algorithm. In fact, there is a large class of simple problems for which there is (probably) no efficient algorithm. This chapter gives an introduction to non-deterministic algorithms that are later used in problem classification. The notions of *P, NP, NP*-hard and *NP*-complete problems are defined. How to prove a problem to be *NP*-complete through polynomial reduction from an already known *NP*-complete problem has been illustrated through a number of examples. A short list of well known *NP*-complete problems is provided for general awareness. The theory of *NP*-completeness gives a technique for separating tractable from (probably) intractable problems. If a polynomial time algorithm can be found for any problem that is *NP*-complete, then by a chain of polynomial time reductions, all the *NP*-complete problems can be solved in polynomial time. $P \neq NP$ remains a famous unproven conjecture for more than three decades.

EXERCISES

6.1 Give a polynomial time algorithm for the 2-*SAT* problem in the conjunctive normal form.

6.2 Show that *SAT* reduces to the 3-*SAT* problem.

6.3 Distinguish between decision, counting and optimization problems and give examples. What are the steps involved in proving a problem *NP*-complete? Specify six problems already proved to be *NP*-complete.

6.4 Show that the subset-sum problem is in *P* if the target value is expressed in unary.

6.5 Construct an instance of vertex-cover by reduction from the 3-*SAT* instance,

$$(x_1 + x_2 + \overline{x}_3)(x_4 + x_5 + x_6)(x_1 + \overline{x}_2 + x_5)(x_1 + \overline{x}_4 + \overline{x}_6)$$

6.6 Show that the knapsack problem is solvable in polynomial time if the input is given in unary coding.

6.7 Develop a non-deterministic algorithm of complexity $O(n)$ to determine whether there is a subset of the n numbers x_i, $1 \le i \le n$ that sums to W.

6.8 Show that the set partition problem reduces to the 0/1 knapsack decision problem.

6.9 Show that polynomial reduction is transitive.

6.10 Show that the vertex-cover problem for trees is in *P*.

6.11 Show that the bin packing problem can be solved in polynomial time if the bin packing decision problem can be solved in polynomial time.

6.12 Prove that if a problem $A \in NP$ and problem B reduces to A, then $B \in NP$.

6.13 Given that the Hamiltonian cycle problem is *NP*-complete for undirected graph, prove that:
   (i) Hamiltonian cycle problem for directed graphs is *NP*-complete,
   (ii) Unweighted simple longest-path problem for directed graphs is *NP*-complete.

6.14 Justify that $P \subseteq NP$.

6.15 Is the following Boolean formula satisfiable?

$$(x + y)(x + \overline{y})(\overline{x} + y)(\overline{x} + \overline{y})(x + y + z)$$

6.16 Examine closure of the classes *P*, *NP* under union and concatenation.

6.17 Prove that presence of 3-clique in a graph can be decided in polynomial time.

6.18 Show that *NP* is closed under star operation. ($NP^* = \{x_1, x_2, x_3, ..., x_n| n \ge 0$ and each $x_i \in NP\}$).

6.19 Prove that satisfiability of Boolean formulae given in disjunctive normal forms is solvable in polynomial time.

6.20 Reduce the clause $\left(x_2 x_3 + \left(\overline{x_3 + x_5}\right)\right) x_2$ to a set of 3-*SAT* clauses.

6.21 Given a Boolean formula in n literals, find an upper bound on the size of the associated 3-*SAT* formula.

6.22 Show the different Hamiltonian cycles present in K_5.

APPROXIMATION ALGORITHMS

7.0 INTRODUCTION

An *approximation algorithm* for a problem P is an algorithm that generates approximate solutions for P. A feasible solution with value close to the value of an optimal solution is called an approximate solution. Why do we need *approximation algorithm*? Sometimes, approximate solutions close to the exact solution may be what we are interested. For example, the TSP travels 19,000 km or 19,200 km does not make much difference in practice. For *NP*-hard problems, an approximate solution may be all that one can expect to find within a reasonable amount of computing time.

How do we characterize approximation algorithms? This is decided based on the deviation of the result found by the approximation algorithm from the optimal solution. The deviation could be absolute or relative. Let A be an algorithm that generates a feasible solution to every instance I of a problem P. Let $FO(I)$ be the value of an optimal solution to I and let $FA(I)$ be the value of the feasible solution generated by A. We can characterize a number of approximation algorithms as described below.

Absolute approximation

A is an absolute approximation algorithm for problem P if and only if for every instance I of P,

$$|FO(I) - FA(I)| \leq k \text{ for some constant } k.$$

$f(n)$-approximation

A is an $f(n)$-approximation algorithm if and only if for every instance I of size n,

$$|FO(I) - FA(I)|/FO(I) \leq f(n)$$

assuming that $FO(I) > 0$.

ε-approximation

A is an ε-approximation algorithm if and only if for every instance I of size n,

$$|FO(I) - FA(I)|/FO(I) \leq \varepsilon,$$

for some constant ε. $FO(I)$ is assumed to be greater than zero.

Approximation scheme

$A(\varepsilon)$ is an approximation scheme if and only if for every $\varepsilon > 0$ and problem instance I, $A(\varepsilon)$ generates a feasible solution such that $|FO(I) - FA(I)|/FO(I) \leq \varepsilon$, $FO(I)$ being assumed to be greater than zero.

Polynomial time approximation scheme (PTAS)

An approximation scheme is a polynomial time approximation scheme if and only if for every fixed $\varepsilon > 0$, it has a computing time that is polynomial in the problem size.

Fully polynomial time approximation scheme (FPTAS)

An approximation scheme whose computing time is a polynomial both in the problem size and in $1/\varepsilon$ is a fully polynomial time approximation scheme.

Every *NP*-complete problem can be transformed into any other *NP*-complete problem. Suppose we have two *NP*-complete problems X_1 and X_2. If there is an algorithm A to find optimal solution to X_1, then we can reduce an instance of X_2 to an instance of X_1 and use A to find an optimal solution to X_2. If we have an approximation algorithm A_{approx} for solving X_1, can we use A_{approx}, to find an approximate solution of the same quality to the instance of X_2? Unfortunately, the answer is 'no'. A good approximation of the optimum in one problem can lead to a very bad solution in another problem.

We now describe a number of approximation algorithms. Only a few *NP*-hard problems have polynomial time approximation algorithms.

7.1 PLANAR GRAPH COLOURING

The problem is to determine the minimum number of colours needed to colour a planar graph, $G = (V, E)$. It is known that every planar graph is four-colourable. One may easily determine if a graph is 0-, 1- or 2-colourable. A graph is 0-colourable if the vertex set is empty. It is one-colourable if the edge set is empty. It is two-colourable if it is a bipartite graph. A graph is bipartite if V can be partitioned into $V1$ and $V2$ such that $E = \{(u, v)|$ $u \in V1$ and $v \in V2\}$. Determining whether a planar graph is 3 colourable is *NP*-hard. However, as already mentioned, all planar graphs are four-colourable. An approximation algorithm for the planar graph colouring may be written as:

```
Procedure Graph_colour (G = (V, E))
   Case
        V = φ : Return(0);
        E = φ : Return(1);
```

```
        G Bipartite: Return(2);
        Default: Return(4);
    Endcase
End Graph_colour
```

The above is an absolute approximation algorithm with $|FO(I) - FA(I)| \leq 1$. It finds exact answer in all the cases except the 'default case'. The error in the default case can be at most 1. What is the complexity of the above approximation algorithm? It is dependent on the complexity of determining whether a planar graph is bipartite or not. This can be accomplished in $O(|V| + |E|)$ time and hence, the complexity of the above approximation algorithm is $O(|V| + |E|)$.

7.2 JOB SCHEDULING

We have n jobs to be processed on m processors without preemption, that is, an assigned job cannot be withdrawn from a processor before completion. The processors are identical. Obtaining minimum finish time schedules on m, $m \geq 2$ processors is *NP*-hard. We have an approximation algorithm that generates schedules with a finish time close to that of an optimal schedule.

An instance I of the job scheduling problem is described by a set of n jobs with completion times t_i, $1 \leq i \leq n$, and m, the number of processors. We describe an approximation algorithm called LPT (longest processing time) algorithm. Whenever a processor becomes free, the longest time job from the set of still unassigned jobs is assigned to the processor that just became free. Ties are broken in an arbitrary manner.

EXAMPLE 7.1 Consider an instance of this problem as described below:

Processing times (t_i) of 6 jobs are 10, 9, 8, 7, 6 and 5 respectively. Also, $m = 3$, $n = 6$. Gnatt chart for LPT scheduling is shown in Figure 7.1.

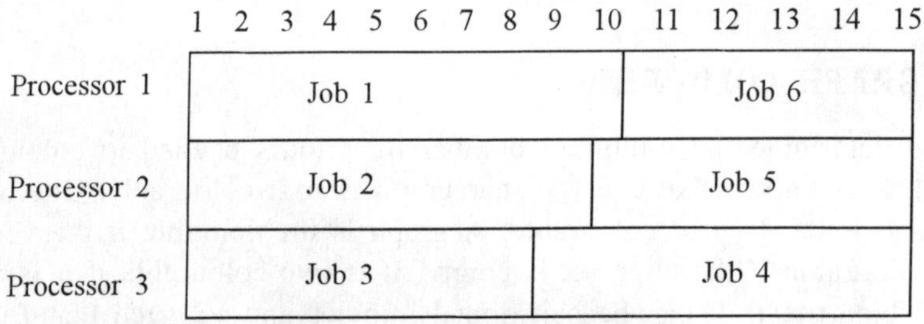

FIGURE 7.1 Gnatt chart for LPT schedule.

The finish time is 15 under the LPT schedule. The optimal schedule must require at least $(\Sigma t_i)/3 = 45/3 = 15$ units of time. Hence in this instance, the LPT schedule provides optimal solution though the situation is not so good always. Let us see an instance where LPT schedule requires more time than the optimal schedule.

EXAMPLE 7.2   In this case $m = 3$, $n = 7$ and the job processing times are 8, 8, 7, 7, 6, 6 and 3. We draw the Gnatt charts for both the optimal and the LPT schedules as in Figures 7.2(a) and 7.2(b).

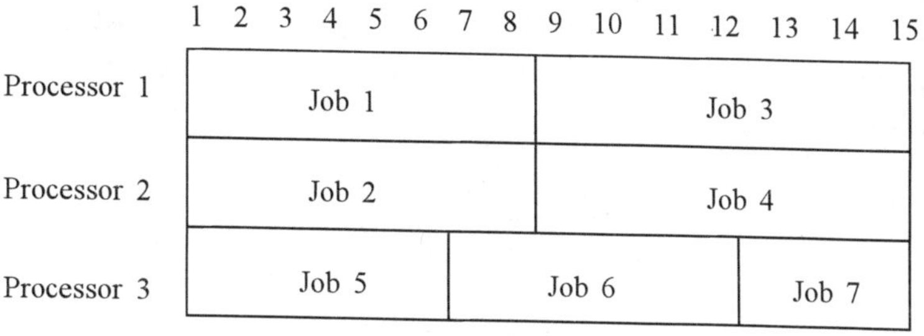

FIGURE 7.2(a)   Optimal schedule.

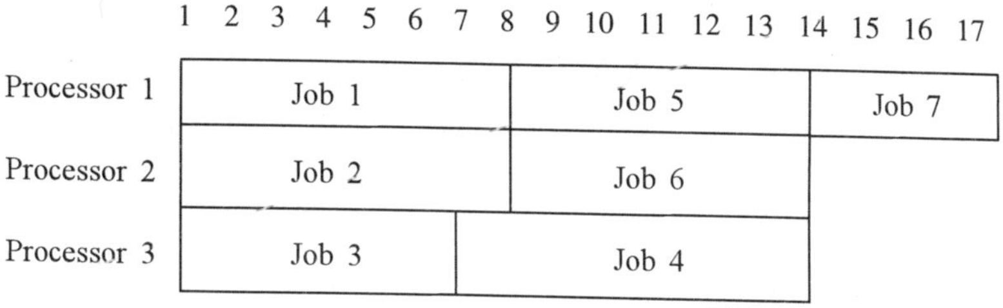

FIGURE 7.2(b)   LPT schedule.

The optimal schedule would require 15 units of time while the LPT schedule would require 17 units of time.

Theorem 7.1   Let $FO(I)$ be the finish time of an optimal m processor schedule for instance I of an n-job scheduling problem and $FA(I)$ be the finish time of LPT schedule for the same instance, then:

$$\frac{|FO(I) - FA(I)|}{FO(I)} \leq \frac{1}{3} - \frac{1}{3m}$$

Proof:
For $m = 1$, the theorem is trivially true. Let us assume that for some $m > 1$, there exists a set of jobs for which the theorem is not true. Let $(t_1, t_2, t_3, ..., t_n)$ be an instance I with the least number of jobs for which the theorem is violated. Let us relabel the jobs in such a way that $t_1 \geq t_2 \geq t_3 \geq ... \geq t_n$ and an LPT schedule is obtained by assigning jobs in the order 1, 2, 3, ..., n. Let $FA(I)$ be the finish time of the LPT schedule. Let k be the index of the job with the latest completion time. The claim is that k has to be n.

Suppose it is otherwise, that is, $k < n$. The finish time fA of the LPT schedule for the jobs 1, 2, ..., k is also $FA(I)$. The finish time, fO of an optimal schedule for the k jobs is no more than $FO(I)$.

Hence $|fO - fA|/fO \geq |FO(I) - FA(I)|/FO(I) > 1/3 - 1/(3m)$. The latter inequality follows from our assumption that the instance I violates the theorem.

So, $|fO - fA|/fO > 1/3 - 1/(3m)$. This contradicts our assumption that I is the smallest m processor instance for which the theorem is violated. Hence $k = n$.

The second part of the proof is concerned with showing that in no optimal schedule for I can more than two jobs be assigned to any processor. Hence, $n \leq 2m$. Since job n has the latest completion time in the LPT schedule for I, it follows that this task is started at time $FA(I) - t_n$ in this schedule. No processor can be idle until this time.

Hence, we write:

$$FA(I) - t_n \leq \frac{1}{m} \sum_{i=1}^{i=n-1} t_i$$

Therefore,

$$FA(I) \leq \frac{1}{m} \sum_{i=1}^{i=n} t_i + \frac{m-1}{m} t_n$$

Since, $FO(I) \geq \dfrac{1}{m} \displaystyle\sum_{i=1}^{i=n} t_i$, we conclude that $FA(I) - FO(I) \leq \dfrac{m-1}{m} t_n$

Hence,

$$\frac{|FO(I) - FA(I)|}{FO(I)} \leq \frac{m-1}{m} \times \frac{t_n}{FO(I)}$$

But from the assumption on the instance I, that is, $\dfrac{|FO(I) - FA(I)|}{FO(I)} > \dfrac{1}{3} - \dfrac{1}{3m}$

We have,

$$\frac{1}{3} - \frac{1}{3m} < \frac{m-1}{m} \times \frac{t_n}{FO(I)}$$

$$m - 1 < \frac{3(m-1)t_n}{FO(I)} \Rightarrow FO(I) < 3t_n$$

Hence, no more than two jobs can be assigned to any processor in an optimal schedule. When the optimal schedule requires at most two jobs on any processor, then it may be shown that the LPT schedule is also optimal. Hence, for this case $\dfrac{|FO(I) - FA(I)|}{FO(I)} = 0$. This contradicts the assumption on I. So, there can be no instance I that violates the theorem.

7.3 BIN PACKING

We are given n objects of different capacities to be placed in bins each of capacity C. The problem is to pack bins with these objects so that the total number of bins required is minimum. No object can be broken and partly filled in one bin and the other part(s) in other bin(s). This is also a NP-hard problem. No polynomial time algorithm is available for this problem. We assume that the n objects have capacities $c_1, c_2, c_3, ..., c_n$ respectively. There are many other problems which are basically bin packing problems but with different descriptions. One such problem is finding the minimum number of tapes each of fixed length required to store a number of programs of different lengths where no program can be split and stored on more than one tape.

EXAMPLE 7.3   Suppose $C = 15$, $n = 5$ and $(c_1, c_2, c_3, c_4, c_5) = (8, 11, 10, 4, 7)$.

For this problem, we need three bins but the third bin is partly empty (see Figure 7.3). This is an optimal solution since $\lceil$(total capacity of the objects)/bin capacity$\rceil = \lceil 40/15 \rceil = 3$.

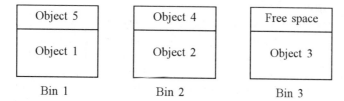

FIGURE 7.3 Bin packing example.

There are a number of simple heuristics for solving this problem. Most common among them are next-fit, first-fit, best-fit, first-fit decreasing and best-fit decreasing. The first three are online heuristics while the latter two are off-line heuristics. All the online heuristics have the initial condition that the first object is already packed in a bin.

Next-fit

It packs the next object into an active bin if it fits in the bin; otherwise the heuristic uses a new bin for the object, which is marked as the active bin.

First-fit (FT)

Objects are considered in the order 1, 2, 3, ..., n for packing into the bins. To pack object i, we find the least index bin that has still unutilized capacity to accommodate this object. If no such bin exists, we take one new bin for packing.

Best-fit (BT)

Objects are considered in the same order 1, 2, 3, ..., n for packing into the bins but we select the bin that will be left with minimum free space after this object is fitted. In the case of a tie, the bin with the minimum index is selected. If no existing bin can accommodate this object, we take a new bin for packing this object.

First-fit decreasing (FFD)

The objects are first sorted into a list of non-increasing capacities. The sorted objects are then considered with the highest capacity object first and the least capacity object last for packing into bins according to the first-fit heuristics.

Best-fit decreasing (BFD)

The objects are first sorted into a list of non-increasing capacities. The sorted objects are then considered with the highest capacity object first and the least capacity object last for packing into bins according to the best-fit heuristics.

The time complexity of next-fit is $O(n)$ for n objects while those of first-fit and best-fit are $O(n \log n)$. Next-fit, first-fit and best-fit are called on-line because objects are packed as they arrive. The off-line algorithms require that all the objects be available before the packing starts. The time complexities of first-fit decreasing and best-fit decreasing are $O(n \log n)$ for n objects.

Let us consider the following example for illustration of the above five heuristics: $C = 15$, $n = 7$ and $(c_1, c_2, c_3, c_4, c_5, c_6, c_7) = (8, 11, 10, 4, 7, 9, 3)$.

For the above problem, next-fit and first-fit require 5 bins each while the best-fit, first-fit decreasing, and best-fit decreasing require 4 bins each. The optimal solution requires 4 bins. Hence for this problem instance, the best-fit, first-fit decreasing, and best-fit decreasing find the optimal solution. What is the quality of solutions generated by these approximation algorithms in general? It can be shown theoretically that the packing generated by either the first-fit or the best-fit algorithm will require no more than 1.7 times the number of bins required in the optimal solution plus 2. The packing generated by either the first-fit decreasing or the best-fit decreasing will require no more than 11/9 times the number of bins required in the optimal solution plus 4. Next fit produces a worst packing of 2 times the optimal value.

Figure 7.4(a) shows bin packing using different heuristics.

Better-fit

We introduce a heuristic for one-dimensional bin packing called better-fit[1]. The heuristic packs a *left-out* object in the first bin that it can fill better than any of the existing objects in the bin for better packing. The replaced object becomes a candidate for packing with better-fit heuristic, starting with the first bin. The process continues till a replaced object cannot be better-fitted in any way. The last replaced object is then packed with the best-fit heuristic.

While fitting the ith object using better-fit, it can replace at most m objects in the bins, where m is the number of distinct object sizes in the list of objects. Summing over all possible values of i, gives the total maximum number of replacements as $mn(n-1)/2$. Hence, better-fit requires $O(n^2 m)$ time.

With the objects arranged in decreasing order of sizes, no object can replace other objects and the performance of better-fit is equivalent to that of best-fit-decreasing. When the objects are arranged in increasing order of sizes, better-fit fills the initial bins with small objects that cannot be replaced by larger objects. Thus the larger objects require separate bins and it provides poor result. Better-fit provides the best performance in the average case when the object sizes are independent, identically distributed random variables.

---

[1] A.K. Bhatia and S.K. Basu, "Packing Bins using Multi-chromosomal Genetic Representation and Better-fit Heuristic", in *Proc. of the 11th International Conference on Neural Information Processing* (*ICONIP* 2004), Calcutta, India, LNCS 3316, N.R. Pal et. al., (Ed.), pp. 181–186, 2004.

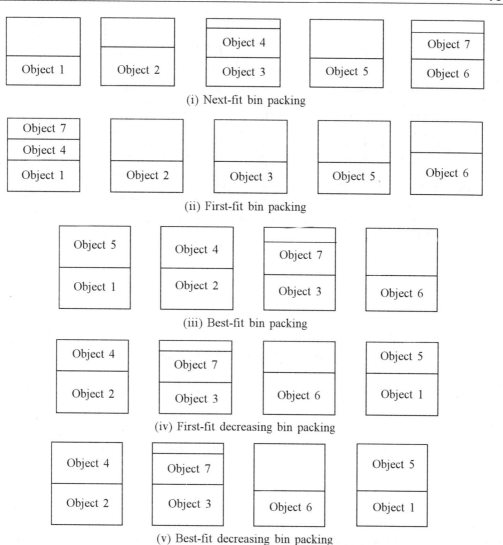

(i) Next-fit bin packing

(ii) First-fit bin packing

(iii) Best-fit bin packing

(iv) First-fit decreasing bin packing

(v) Best-fit decreasing bin packing

FIGURE 7.4(a) Bin packing using different heuristics.

To illustrate the working of better-fit, consider an instance of bin packing problem where 10 objects are to be packed in bins of capacity 10. The objects have the following sizes:

Object	1	2	3	4	5	6	7	8	9	10
Size	8	3	5	2	1	6	3	5	4	7

With the initial distribution of objects as shown in Figure 7.4b(i), object 10 is left out. We pack object 10 in the first bin displacing object 6 [Figure 7.4b(ii)]. Capacity of bin 1 is fully utilized by doing this. Now we have to pack object 6. Since there is no room in the first bin, we try to pack object 6 in bin 2 [Figure 7.4b(iii)] displacing object 8. Since bins 1 and 2 do not have adequate room left to pack object 8, we pack it in bin 3 displacing

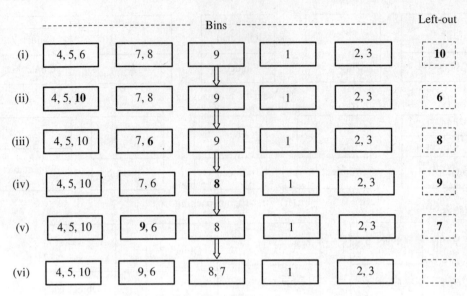

FIGURE 7.4(b)   **Bin packing using better-fit.**

object 9 [Figure 7.4b(iv)]. Now object 9 can be better fitted in bin 2, displacing object 7 [Figure 7.4b(v)]. Object 7 can now be fitted in bin 3 without displacing any existing object and no more object is left out [Figure 7.4b(vi)]. The heuristics algorithm is now terminated.

      Better-fit creates a ripple effect that continues till the last object cannot do a better-fit in any of the bins.

7.4   APPROXIMATION ALGORITHM FOR VERTEX-COVER

The problem is to find a vertex-cover of minimum size in a given undirected graph. The problem is *NP*-Hard. It is not very difficult to find an approximation algorithm for the vertex-cover problem that returns a solution that is near optimal. The size of the vertex-cover returned by the approximation algorithm is guaranteed to be no more than twice the size of an optimal vertex-cover. Let the graph be denoted by $G = (V, E)$ and the cover by C. The pseudocode for the algorithm may be written as:

```
Procedure Avc(G = (V,E))
  C = φ; /* Empty set */
  E1 = E;
  Repeat {
    If (u, v) ∈ E1 Then {
    C = C ∪ {u, v};
    E1 = E1 - {(x, y) | x, y ∈ V, one of x and y is either u or v};
    }
    Endif
  Until E1 = φ;
  Return(C);
End Avc
```

The running time of this algorithm is $O(|E|)$ using an appropriate data structure for representation of $E1$. What is the quality of the solution generated by the above approximation algorithm? It is no more than twice the value of the optimal solution. Let X be the subset of edges chosen by the above approximation algorithm. The algorithm ensures that no two edges in X share a common vertex. This is because of the fact that once an edge is chosen, all other edges in $E1$ incident on its end points are deleted from $E1$. One pass through the loop adds two new nodes to C and hence $|C| = 2*|X|$.

The optimal vertex-cover must include at least one end point of each edge in X. Since no two edges in X share a vertex, no vertex in the cover is incident on more than one edge in X. So $|X| \leq |CO|$, where CO is the optimal cover, that is the cover having the minimum number of vertices. Hence:

$|C| = 2*|X| \leq 2*|CO|.$

$|FO(I) - FA(I)|/FO(I) \leq 1$

So the above algorithm is a 1-approximation algorithm.
We apply the above algorithm to the graph of Figure 7.5.

$C = \phi$
$E1 = \{(1, 2), (1, 3), (2, 4), (3, 4), (3, 6), (4, 5), (4, 6), (5, 7), (6, 7)\}$
$C = \{1, 2\}$
$E1 = \{(3, 4), (3, 6), (4, 5), (4, 6), (5, 7), (6, 7)\}$
$C = \{1, 2, 3, 4\}$
$E1 = \{(5, 7), (6, 7)\}$
$C = \{1, 2, 3, 4, 5, 7\}$
$E1 = \phi$

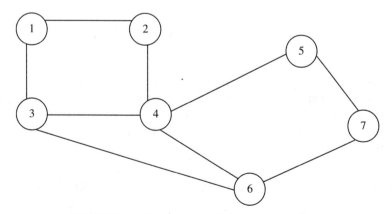

FIGURE 7.5 Example graph for vertex-cover.

The optimal cover CO is $\{2, 3, 5, 6\}$.

$$\frac{|FO(I) - FA(I)|}{FO(I)} = \frac{|4 - 6|}{4} = \frac{1}{2}$$

7.5 APPROXIMATION ALGORITHM FOR SET COVER

The problem is: given a universe U of n elements, a collection of subsets, $S = \{S_1, S_2, ..., S_k\}$ of U, and a cost function, $Cost: S \to Q^+$, we have to find a minimum cost sub-collection of the elements of S that covers all elements of U. We define frequency (f) of an element as the number of sets it is in. The vertex-cover problem is a special case of set cover with $f = 2$. We use the greedy method for this. The approach we adopt is: we iteratively pick up the most cost-effective set and remove the covered elements until all the elements are covered. Let C be the set of elements already covered at the beginning of an iteration. During this iteration, the cost-effectiveness of a set S is defined as the average cost at which it covers new elements, that is, $Cost\ (S)/|S - C|$. The price of an element is defined to be the average cost at which it is covered. When a set S is picked, we can think of its cost being distributed equally among the elements covered. We give pseudocode for the approximation algorithm below.

```
Procedure Set_cover
   C = ϕ;
   While C ≠ U Do
      Find the most cost-effective set(A) in the current iteration;
      CE = Cost(A)/|A - C|;
      For each element(e) ∈ A - C, price(e) = CE;
      C = C ∪ A;
      S = S - {A};
   Endwhile
   Output the picked sets;
End Set_cover
```

Let us number the elements of U in the order in which they were covered by the algorithm, resolving ties arbitrarily. Let $e_1, e_2, e_3, ..., e_n$ be this numbering. We claim that for each $i \in \{1, 2, ..., n\}$, $price(e_i) \leq OPT/(n - i + 1)$. For proof, we argue as follows. In any iteration, the leftover sets of the optimal solution can cover the remaining elements at a cost of at most OPT. Therefore, among these sets, there must be one having cost-effectiveness of at most $OPT/|U - C|$. In the iteration in which element e_i was covered, $U - C$ contained at least $n - i + 1$ elements. Since e_i was covered by the most cost-effective set in this iteration, it follows that $price(e_i) \leq OPT/|U - C| \leq OPT/(n - i + 1)$. The greedy algorithm is an H_n factor approximation algorithm for the minimum set cover problem, where $H_n = 1 + (1/2) + (1/3) + \cdots + (1/n)$. Since the cost of each set picked is distributed among the new elements covered, the total cost of the picked set cover is equal to $\sum_{i=1}^{i=n} price(e_i)$. But this is at most $1 + (1/2) + (1/3) + \cdots + (1/n)$ times OPT.

Let us illustrate the working of the above algorithm for the following instance where $U = \{1, 2, 3, 4, 5, 6, 7, 8, 9\}$, $S = \{\{1, 5, 6\}, \{1, 2, 5, 7\}, \{1, 2, 4\}, \{3, 5, 6, 9\}, \{1, 5, 7, 8, 9\}, \{2, 4, 6, 8\}, \{1, 3, 7\}\}$, $k = 7$. $Cost$ of a set is the sum of the squares of the elements in it. $Cost(S_1) = 62$, $Cost(S_2) = 79$, $Cost(S_3) = 21$, $Cost(S_4) = 151$, $Cost(S_5) = 220$, $Cost(S_6) = 120$, $Cost(S_7) = 59$.

$$C = \phi$$

$$CE(S_1) = \frac{62}{3} = 20.66$$

$$CE(S_2) = \frac{79}{4} = 19.75$$

$$CE(S_3) = \frac{21}{3} = 7.00$$

$$CE(S_4) = \frac{151}{4} = 37.75$$

$$CE(S_5) = \frac{220}{5} = 44.00$$

$$CE(S_6) = \frac{120}{4} = 30.00$$

$$CE(S_7) = \frac{59}{3} = 19.66$$

S_3 is the most cost-effective set at this stage.

$S_3 - C = \{1, 2, 4\}$, $Price(1) = 7$, $Price(2) = 7$, $Price(4) = 7$ and C is now $\{1, 2, 4\}$.

$$CE(S_1) = \frac{62}{2} = 31$$

$$CE(S_2) = \frac{79}{2} = 39.5$$

$$CE(S_4) = \frac{151}{4} = 37.75$$

$$CE(S_5) = \frac{220}{4} = 55$$

$$CE(S_6) = \frac{120}{2} = 60.00$$

$$CE(S_7) = \frac{59}{2} = 29.5$$

S_7 is the most cost-effective set at this stage.

$Price(3) = 29.5$, $Price(7) = 29.5$, and C is now $\{1, 2, 4, 3, 7\}$.

$S = \{\{1, 5, 6\}, \{1, 2, 5, 7\}, \{3, 5, 6, 9\}, \{1, 5, 7, 8, 9\}, \{2, 4, 6, 8\}\}$

$$CE(S_1) = \frac{62}{2} = 31$$

$$CE(S_2) = \frac{79}{1} = 79$$

$$CE(S_4) = \frac{151}{3} = 50.33$$

$$CE(S_5) = \frac{220}{3} = 73.33$$

$$CE(S_6) = \frac{120}{2} = 60.00$$

S_1 is the most cost-effective set at this stage.

$Price(5) = 31$, $Price(6) = 31$, and C is now $\{1, 2, 4, 3, 7, 5, 6\}$.

$S = \{\{1, 2, 5, 7\}, \{3, 5, 6, 9\}, \{1, 5, 7, 8, 9\}, \{2, 4, 6, 8\}$

$$CE(S_2) = \frac{79}{0} = \infty$$

$$CE(S_4) = \frac{151}{1} = 151$$

$$CE(S_5) = \frac{220}{2} = 110$$

$$CE(S_6) = \frac{120}{1} = 120$$

S_5 is the most cost-effective set at this stage.

$Price(8) = 110$, $Price(9) = 110$, and C is now $\{1, 2, 4, 3, 7, 5, 6, 8, 9\}$.

$S = \{\{1, 2, 5, 7\}, \{3, 5, 6, 9\}, \{2, 4, 6, 8\}$

The total cost of set cover = $3 \times 7 + 2 \times 29.5 + 2 \times 31 + 2 \times 110 = 21 + 59 + 62 + 220 = 362$.

7.6 APPROXIMATION ALGORITHM FOR MINIMUM DEGREE SPANNING TREE

Given a graph, the problem is to find a spanning tree whose degree is minimum. The degree of a node is the number of edges incident on the node. The degree of a graph is the maximum of the degrees of its nodes. Minimizing the degree of a spanning tree is finding a smallest integer k for which there exists a spanning tree in which each vertex has at most k incident edges.

A Hamiltonian path in a graph is a degree two spanning tree. If we have a procedure for finding a minimum-degree spanning tree in a graph, we can use the procedure to find a Hamiltonian path in any graph that has one. Deciding whether a graph has a Hamiltonian path is *NP*-hard. Determining whether a minimum-degree spanning tree has degree two is presumed to be computationally difficult. So we look for an approximation algorithm for solving the minimum-degree spanning tree. We describe below an approximation algorithm for the problem.

We start with any spanning tree T of the graph G. Let d be the degree of T. Let S be the set of vertices having degree d or $d - 1$ in the current spanning tree. Let T_1, T_2, ..., T_r be the sub-trees resulting from removal of the nodes in S from T. If there are no edges between these sub-trees, the number r of trees T_i is at least $|S|(d - 1) - 2(|S| - 1)$ and the algorithm terminates. On the other hand, if there is an edge between two distinct sub-trees T_i and T_j, inserting this edge in T and removing another edge from T results in a spanning tree with no more vertices having degree at least $d - 1$. We repeat this process on the new spanning tree. The algorithm terminates after a relatively small number of improvements. It can be proved that the number of iterations is $O(n \log n)$, where n is the number of vertices in G.

For an input graph with n nodes and m edges, the algorithm requires time slightly more than the product of n and m. As for the quality of the solution, it finds a spanning tree whose degree is guaranteed to be at most one more than the minimum degree. For a graph having Hamiltonian path, the spanning tree found using the algorithm is either a Hamiltonian path or a spanning tree of degree three. The algorithm also finds a witness, set S of vertices proving that T's degree is nearly optimal.

Let d denote the degree of T and V_i denote the set of vertices comprising sub-tree T_i, $1 \leq i \leq r$. Any spanning tree T' must connect up the sets V_1, V_2, ..., V_r and the vertices x_1, x_2, ..., $x_{|S|} \in S$, and must use at least $r + |S| - 1$ edges to do so. Since no edge goes between distinct sets V_i, all these edges must be incident on the vertices of S. Therefore,

$$\sum \{ \text{degree}_{T'}(x) \big| x \in S \} \geq r + |S| - 1 \geq |S|(d - 1) - 2(|S| - 1) + |S| - 1$$

$$= |S|(d - 1) - (|S| - 1),$$

where $\text{degree}_{T'}(x)$ denotes the degree of x in the tree T'. Thus the average of the degrees of vertices in S is at least $\dfrac{|S|(d - 1) - (|S| - 1)}{|S|}$, which is strictly greater than $d - 2$. Since the average of the degrees of vertices in S is greater than $d - 2$, it follows that at least one vertex has degree at least $d - 1$. Hence the minimum degree is at least $d - 1$.

A spanning tree of the graph in Figure 7.6(a) is shown in Figure 7.6(b).

The degree of the spanning tree, d is 4. We remove all the nodes from the tree having degree either 4 or 3. This results in a number of trees as shown in Figure 7.6(c).

Adding the edge between the trees T_2 and T_4 and removing the edge (4, 7) from the spanning tree, results in a new spanning tree with degree at least 3 as shown in Figure 7.6(d).

The degree of the spanning tree, d is 3. We remove all the nodes from the tree having degree either 3 or 2. This results in a number of trees as shown in Figure 7.6(e).

Adding an edge between T_1 and T_2 and deleting an edge (4, 5) from the spanning tree, we get the spanning tree shown in Figure 7.6(f).

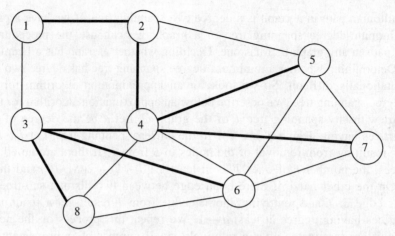

FIGURE 7.6(a)   Example graph for minimum degree spanning tree.

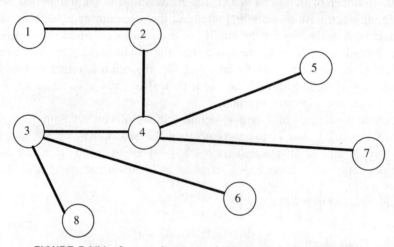

FIGURE 7.6(b)   A spanning tree of the graph in Figure 7.6(a).

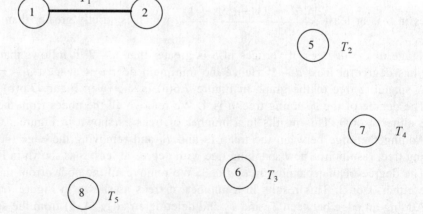

FIGURE 7.6(c)   Trees resulting from the removal of nodes with degree 3 or 4.

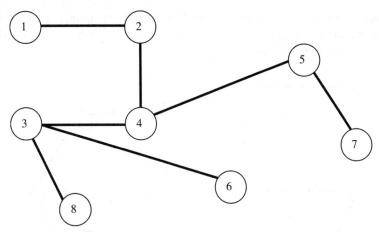

FIGURE 7.6(d) A spanning tree of the graph in Figure 7.6(a).

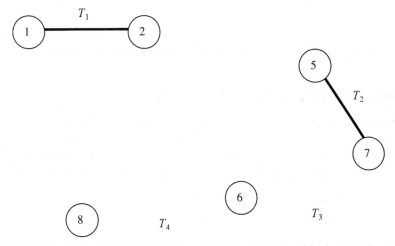

FIGURE 7.6(e) Trees resulting from the removal of nodes with degrees 3 or 2.

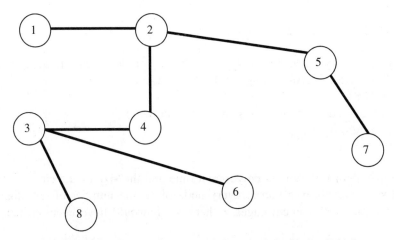

FIGURE 7.6(f) A spanning tree of the graph in Figure 7.6(a).

Continuing this way, we can get smaller degree spanning trees. An instance of approximately minimum degree spanning tree is shown in Figure 7.6(g) which has one degree more than the optimal solution.

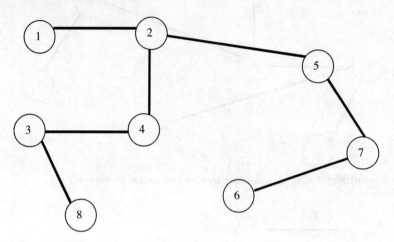

FIGURE 7.6(g)   An approximately minimum degree spanning tree of the graph in Figure 7.6(a).

7.7   APPROXIMATION ALGORITHM FOR MAX-CUT

A cut in an undirected graph $G = (V, E)$ is a partition of the set V into V_1, V_2 and a cut-edge is an edge that connects a node in V_1 to a node in V_2. The size of a cut is the number of cut-edges. The max-cut problem demands a cut of the input graph with the maximum number of cut-edges. The problem is *NP*-complete. The following pseudocode is an approximation algorithm for the max-cut problem.

```
Procedure Max-cut(G = (V,E))
   K = 0; /* Cut size */
   V₁ = ϕ;
   V₂ = V;
   Repeat
   {
      If moving node from V₁ to V₂ or V₂ to V₁ increases the cut size,
      Then make the move and update K;
      Endif
   } Until cut size does not increase;
   Write(V₁,V₂,K);
End Max-cut
```

The above algorithm runs in polynomial time and the size of the cut is at least half the optimal cut size. We observe that at every node of *G*, the number of cut edges is at least as large as the number of uncut edges. Otherwise, it would have been shifted. Adding the number of cut-edges at every node, we note that the total number of cut-edges is at least equal to the total number of uncut-edges. So G has at least as many cut-edges as the number of uncut edges. Therefore, the cut contains at least half of the edges of G.

Let us illustrate working of the above algorithm for the graph of Figure 7.7. The steps are shown below:

$$V_1 = \phi$$
$$V_2 = \{1, 2, 3, 4, 5, 6\}$$
$$V_1 = \{1\}$$
$$V_2 = \{2, 3, 4, 5, 6\}$$
$$K = 3$$
$$V_1 = \{1, 2\}$$
$$V_2 = \{3, 4, 5, 6\}$$
$$K = 5$$
$$V_1 = \{1, 2, 4\}$$
$$V_2 = \{3, 5, 6\}$$
$$K = 6$$
$$V_1 = \{2, 4\}$$
$$V_2 = \{1, 3, 5, 6\}$$
$$K = 7$$
$$V_1 = \{2, 4, 5\}$$
$$V_2 = \{1, 3, 6\}$$
$$K = 8$$

No further improvement takes place. Optimal solution is found indeed.

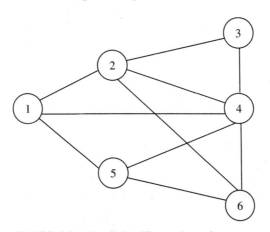

FIGURE 7.7 Graph for illustration of max-cut.

7.8 APPROXIMATION ALGORITHM FOR TRAVELING SALESPERSON (TSP)

The traveling salesperson problem is in general, very complicated. We do not know any polynomial time algorithm to solve this problem. The time complexity of this problem for a tour of n cities is $O(n^2 2^n)$ using dynamic programming. This is a famous *NP*-hard problem. For a special case of the problem, we can find a polynomial time approximation algorithm. We assume that the edges have non-negative weights and the distance (d) matrix satisfies the triangle inequality, that is, for any three cities i, j, k, the distances satisfy: $d(i, j) \leq d(i, k) + d(k, j)$. This property will hold if the cities are on Euclidean plane and the distances are straightline distances.

Let $G = (V, E)$ be a complete undirected graph on $n(>2)$ nodes. This graph will definitely be Hamiltonian. Consider any Hamiltonian cycle H in it. Let us assume that this cycle has length L. H will consist of n edges. If we remove any edge from H, the remaining $n - 1$ edges form a path (called Hamiltonian path) that touches each node of G exactly once, but it does not return to the starting node. The length of the resulting Hamiltonian path is at most L, since the edges are assumed to have non-negative weights. Since the Hamiltonian path touches each node, it is a spanning tree over n nodes of G. If the length of the minimum spanning tree of G is L_{min}, then the Hamiltonian path must have length greater than or equal to L_{min} and hence $L \geq L_{min}$.

Let us choose one vertex in the minimum spanning tree as the root of the minimum spanning tree. We now start from this root and visit all the branches of the tree by traversing the edges of the tree and return to the root. This is similar to drawing a free hand line enclosing the spanning tree. We draw a free hand line on both sides of each edge of the minimum spanning tree. The length of the closed free hand line will be at least $2 * L_{min}$. When the free hand line is as close as possible to the edges of the tree, the length of the closed line will be exactly $2 * L_{min}$. We are certain to visit each node at least once. In fact, some nodes are visited more than once in the process. Now, we remove such duplicate nodes one by one. If a segment of the closed curve is ..., $i, j, k, i, l, ...$, we replace this segment by ..., $i, j, k, l, ...$ This means that instead of drawing along the edge (k, i) and (i, l) we draw directly from k to l. This edge does not exist in the tree but is present in the graph and by drawing directly from k to l, we are bound to get a shorter length because of the triangle inequality holding amongst any three nodes of the graph. In this way, we get rid of repetition of the nodes one by one in the tour (except for the root node). Successive removal of duplication of nodes leads to smaller and smaller tour lengths. Ultimately, we get a sequence of nodes where each node (except the root node) appears only once and this defines tour of TSP with length guaranteed to be less than equal to $2 * L_{min}$. The length of the tour found by this approximation algorithm is therefore no more than twice the length of the optimal tour. Christofides' approximation algorithm for the Euclidean traveling salesperson problem gives length of the tour less than or equal to $1.5 * L_{min}$.

Let us consider a TSP problem defined by the following distance matrix:

$$
\begin{array}{c c c c c c}
 & A & B & C & D & E \\
A & \begin{bmatrix} 0 \\ 5 \\ 7 \\ 9 \\ 3 \end{bmatrix} & \begin{matrix} 5 \\ 0 \\ 4 \\ 12 \\ 6 \end{matrix} & \begin{matrix} 7 \\ 4 \\ 0 \\ 10 \\ 3 \end{matrix} & \begin{matrix} 9 \\ 12 \\ 10 \\ 0 \\ 8 \end{matrix} & \begin{matrix} 3 \\ 6 \\ 3 \\ 8 \\ 0 \end{matrix}
\end{array}
$$

Let us first draw a minimum spanning tree using either the Kruskal's algorithm or the Prim's algorithm. A minimum spanning tree for the graph defined by the above distance matrix will be as in Figure 7.8 (shown in thick lines) and the minimum spanning tree has length 18.

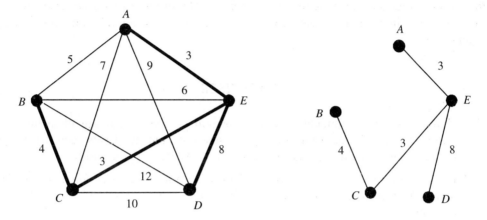

FIGURE 7.8   Minimum spanning tree.

In tracing from the root as explained above, we get the sequence *AECBCEDEA*. Length of this tour is less than or equal to $2 * L_{min}$. By removing the repetition of *C*, we get the following sequence of nodes *AECBEDEA*. The length of the sequence is less than that of the previous sequence because of the assumption of triangle inequality. We now remove the first repetition of *E* and get *AECBDEA*. Length of this sequence is further reduced. We now remove the second repetition of *E* and get the sequence *AECBDA*. This sequence represents a shortest tour for the TSP approximately. The shortest tour is: $A \rightarrow E \rightarrow C \rightarrow B \rightarrow D \rightarrow A$ having length $3 + 3 + 4 + 12 + 9 = 31$ as shown in Figure 7.9.

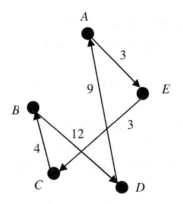

FIGURE 7.9   Tour of TSP.

SUMMARY

In this chapter, we have introduced the notion of approximation algorithms. Approximation algorithms that run in polynomial time and provide solutions within the bounded proximity of the optimal solutions are quite useful in practice. The problems we have discussed in this chapter include bin packing, vertex-cover, max-cut, set cover, minimum-degree spanning tree, and TSP.

EXERCISES

7.1 Given a set S of elements and a collection of sets containing elements from S, outline a heuristic algorithm to find the smallest number of sets such that the union of these sets contains all the elements of S. Analyze the algorithm.

7.2 Find approximate solutions to the following bin packing problem using first-fit and best-fit decreasing heuristics. $N = 5$, $P = (10, 5, 2, 9, 6)$, $W = (12, 11, 6, 7, 9)$, $C = 30$.

7.3 Consider the following algorithm:

```
Procedure Cover(G = (V, E))
    X = φ;
    Repeat
        v = a vertex of maximum degree in V;
        X = X ∪ {v};
        V = V - {v};
        E = E - {(u, w) | u = v or w = v};
    Until E = φ;
    Return(X);
End Cover
```

Does this algorithm always generate a minimum node cover?

7.4 Develop an efficient algorithm to determine whether a graph can be painted with just two colours.

7.5 Explain how to implement first-fit and best-fit heuristics for bin packing in $O(N \log N)$ time.

7.6 Study empirically the efficacy of the different heuristics for the bin packing problem. Using random numbers, generate different problem instances.

7.7 Solve the following bin packing problem using first-fit, best-fit, first-fit decreasing, and best-fit decreasing heuristics:

Capacity = 20, Number of objects = 8, Size of the objects are 12, 5, 13, 7, 4, 9, 10 and 4.

7.8 Give an example on which first-fit does at least as bad as 5/3 times the optimal.

7.9 Give a factor 2 tight example for the next-fit.

7.10 Show that the approach of sorting the objects by decreasing ratio of profit to weight, and then greedily picking the objects in this order can be made to perform arbitrarily badly for 0/1 knapsack problem.

7.11 A subset of vertices V' of a graph $G = (V, E)$ is said to be independent if and only if no two vertices in V' are adjacent in G. The following is a greedy approach to construct a maximum independent set:

```
Procedure Independent(G = (V,E))
  V' = φ;
  While there is a v ∈ V - V' and v not adjacent to any vertex in
V'
      V' = V' ∪ {v};
  Endwhile
  Return(V')
End Independent
```

Give an example graph where the above algorithm shows its worst behaviour.

7.12 Use the approximation algorithm of Section 7.4 for finding the vertex-cover of the following graph. How does the approximate solution differ from the optimal solution?

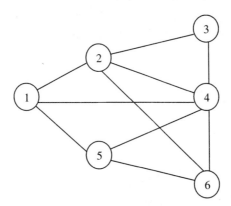

7.13 Consider the following set cover problem. $U = \{a, b, c, d, e, f\}$, $S = \{\{a, b, c\}, \{b, c, f\}, \{b, c, d, e\}, \{d, e, f\}, \{a, c, d, e\}, \{a, c, d, e, f\}\}$. Costs of the elements of S are 12, 7, 19, 18, 20, 35 respectively. Find an approximately minimum set cover.

7.14 Find an approximately minimum-degree spanning tree for the following graph. How does the degree of this spanning tree differ from that of the optimal solution?

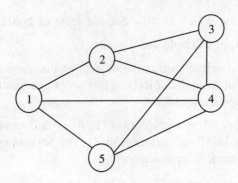

7.15 Give an approximate solution for a TSP having the following distance matrix.

$$\begin{bmatrix} 0 & 3 & 5 & 9 \\ 3 & 0 & 6 & 7 \\ 5 & 6 & 0 & 9 \\ 9 & 7 & 9 & 0 \end{bmatrix}$$

7.16 Write pseudocode for first-fit heuristic.

7.17 Apply the better-fit heuristic to the solutions of Exercise 7.7 and see whether one can get a better packing of the bins.

7.18 Consider a bin packing problem with bins of capacity C and objects of sizes S_i, where $1 \leq i \leq n$. Show that, if the S_i's are constrained to follow $S_i > C/3$, then the bin packing problem can be formulated as a graph matching problem (refer Section 9.8).

RANDOMIZED ALGORITHMS

8.0 INTRODUCTION

Algorithms where some of the actions are dependent on chance are generally termed as *probabilistic algorithms* or *randomized algorithms*. There are mainly two advantages. For many problems, randomized algorithms run faster than the known best deterministic algorithms. Moreover, these algorithms are simpler to describe and implement than the deterministic algorithms of comparable performance. The results of randomized algorithms may not always be hundred per cent correct. Correctness of the output of these algorithms is characterized by some probability. By running the algorithms for a longer time, the probability of correctness of the result may be increased. Probabilistic algorithms react differently for the same input at different times. The execution time, and the result may be different from one use to the next. The behaviour of probabilistic algorithms is so because of their dependence on the use of random variables.

Though, probabilistic algorithms are described by many authors as "Monte-Carlo Techniques", four major subdivisions of these algorithms can be made. These are: Numerical, Monte-Carlo, Las Vegas, and Sherwood.

Numerical probabilistic algorithms

For many real-life problems, it is not possible to arrive at closed form solutions, or to find an exact solution because of the uncertainties involved in the data or because of the limitation of a digital computer in representing irrationals. For some other problems, finding the exact solution requires a long time. Randomness can be used to find an approximate numerical solution of such problems. It is difficult to find the average length of a queue in closed form in a complex system. But an approximate value of the average queue length can be estimated through simulation using randomness and this result will improve, the more times we run the simulation. All these algorithms are called numerical probabilistic algorithms. These algorithms produce approximate results and the quality of the solution can be improved if we run the algorithm for a longer time.

Monte-Carlo algorithms

There are some problems for which we need to find the exact answer. An approximate answer is meaningless for such problems. In decision problems, the answer is either '*yes*' or '*no*'. There is no scope for an approximate answer for these problems. Another example is finding the factors of an integer. The notion of an 'approximate factor' is meaningless. The probabilistic algorithms that are used to solve these kinds of problems are called Monte-Carlo algorithms. A Monte-Carlo algorithm always gives an answer but the answer is not necessarily correct. By running the algorithm for a longer time, the probability of correctness of the result can be increased. There is always a certain doubt associated with the correctness of the result of Monte-Carlo algorithms. Monte-Carlo algorithms for the decision problems are characterized as having: one-sided error and two-sided errors. A Monte-Carlo algorithm is said to have one-sided error if the probability that its output is wrong for at least one of the possible outputs (*yes/no*) that it produces. A Monte-Carlo algorithm is said to have two-sided errors if there is non-zero probability that it errs when it outputs either '*yes*' or '*no*'.

Las Vegas algorithms

Las Vegas algorithms may or may not find an answer but whenever it finds an answer, the answer is correct. The probability of finding an answer increases if the algorithm is repeated enough number of times on the given instance.

Sherwood algorithms

These algorithms always give an answer and the answer is correct. These algorithms are used when we have a deterministic algorithm that shows different performances for the worst case and the average case. Quick-sort algorithm shows this differential behaviour for the average and the worst cases. It runs in $O(n \log n)$ time on the average for sorting n elements. But for the same size of data, it has quadratic time performance in the worst case. By introducing an element of randomness, the behaviour of the algorithm may be made insensitive to the input data. The randomness reduces and sometimes obliterates the difference between time requirement for the good instances and the bad instances. The Sherwood algorithms not only reduce the gap in the time performance of the worst-case behaviour and the average case behaviour of the algorithm but the randomness in the algorithm may deprive us of the expected behaviour of the best case. Randomness tends to make the best case's behaviour look like that of the average case behaviour.

8.1 SOME COMPLEXITY CLASSES

RP (Randomized polynomial time)

This consists of all the languages L that have a randomized algorithm A running in worst-case polynomial time such that for any input x in Σ^* (set of all strings over the alphabet Σ),

$x \in L \Rightarrow Prob[A \; accepts \; x] \geq 0.5$, and

$x \notin L \Rightarrow Prob[A \; accepts \; x] = 0.$

The choice of the bound 0.5 on the error probability is arbitrary. *RP* algorithm is a Monte-Carlo algorithm that can err only when $x \in L$. This is referred to as one-sided error. The class *co-RP* consists of languages that have polynomial-time randomized algorithms erring only in the case when $x \notin L$. Problems belonging to *RP* and *co-RP* classes can be solved by randomized algorithm with zero-sided error, that is, a Las Vegas algorithm.

ZPP (Zero error probabilistic polynomial time)

This is the class of languages that has Las Vegas algorithms running in expected polynomial time.

PP (Probabilistic polynomial time)

It consists of all languages *L* that have a randomized algorithm *A* running in worst-case polynomial time such that for any input *x* in Σ^*,

$x \in L \Rightarrow Prob[A \ accepts \ x] > 0.5$, and

$x \notin L \Rightarrow Prob[A \ accepts \ x] < 0.5$.

BPP (Bounded error probabilistic polynomial time)

This consists of all languages *L* that have a randomized algorithm *A* running in worst-case polynomial time such that for any input *x* in Σ^*,

$x \in L \Rightarrow Prob[A \ accepts \ x] \geq 0.75$, and

$x \notin L \Rightarrow Prob[A \ accepts \ x] \leq 0.25$.

8.2 COMPUTING π

Suppose we are throwing darts at a target consisting of a square inscribed with a circle as shown in Figure 8.1. The probability of any point inside the square being hit is the same for all the points. If the side of the square is $2r$, its area is $4r^2$ and the area of the circle is πr^2. The darts thrown are made to fall inside the square; some of them will fall inside the circle too. If we throw *n* darts and count the number, say *k*, of darts falling inside the circle, the ratio *n/k* will be approaching the ratio of the area of the square and the area of the circle when *n* is sufficiently large. In the limiting case, $n/k = (4r^2/\pi r^2)$, that is $\pi = 4k/n$. This gives a basis for estimating a value of π. The larger the *n* becomes, that is, the more the number of times we go on throwing darts, the more accurate the value of π will be. This is an example of numerical probabilistic algorithm. We write below the pseudocode for this algorithm. *UNIFORM*(0, 1) is a function returning uniformly random number between 0 and 1.

```
Procedure Pi
  k =0;
  For j = 1 to n Do
    x = UNIFORM(0, 1);
    /* UNIFORM(0, 1) returns a uniformly random number between
    0 and 1 */
```

```
        y = UNIFORM(0, 1);
        If (x² + y² ≤ 1) Then k = k + 1;
     Endfor
     Print("Value of π =", 4k/n);
  End Pi
```

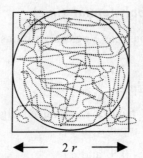

← — 2 r — →

FIGURE 8.1   Calculation of π.

8.3   NUMERICAL INTEGRATION

This is another example of numerical probabilistic algorithm. Here, we discuss how randomness can be used to find integral of a continuous function. Look at Figure 8.2(a). Let f be a continuous function from [0, 1] to [0, 1]. The size of the area bounded by the curve,

$y = f(x)$, the x-axis, the y-axis and the line $x = 1$ is given by $\int_0^1 f(x)\,dx$.

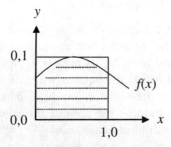

FIGURE 8.2(a)   Integration.

To estimate the value of the integral, we could throw sufficiently large number of darts (n) at the unit square; each point in the unit square being equally likely to be hit by the darts. We then count how many of the darts (k) hit the square below the curve $f(x)$. The ratio k/n of the darts hitting the square below the curve and the total number of darts thrown gives the value of the integral when n is sufficiently large. We give a pseudocode for this randomized algorithm.

```
Procedure Integrate1(f(x), 0, 1)
  k = 0;
  For j = 1 to n Do
    x = UNIFORM(0, 1);
    y = UNIFORM(0, 1);
    If (y ≤ f(x)) Then k = k + 1;
  Endfor
  Print("Value of the Integral =", k/n);
End Integrate1
```

Suppose f is a continuous function from $[a, b]$ to $[c, d]$ as shown in Figure 8.2(b),

where a, b, c, and d are real numbers and $a \leq b$ and $c \leq d$, then the integral $\int_a^b f(x)\, dx$ can

be evaluated by the randomized algorithm given below.

```
Procedure Integrate2(f(x), a, b, c, d)
  k = 0;
  For j = 1 to n Do
    x = UNIFORM(a, b);
    y = UNIFORM(c, d);
    If (y ≤ f(x)) Then k = k + 1;
  Endfor
  Result = (b - a){c + (d - c)k/n};
  Print("Value of the Integral =", Result);
End Integrate2
```

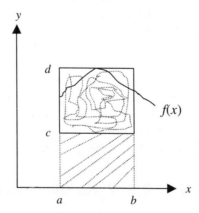

FIGURE 8.2(b) Another integration.

8.4 PRIMALITY TESTING

The problem is to test whether a given number N is prime. A randomized algorithm looks for certain kinds of certificates for compositeness of the given number (N). If such a certificate is found, the algorithm stops and outputs that the number is not a prime. If no such certificate is found with a number of attempts, the algorithm stops and declares that N is prime with a very small chance of being wrong.

```
    Procedure Ptesting(N, k)
      /* k is the number of attempts to test N for primality */
        i = 1;
    L:  r = UNIFORM(1, N - 1);
        Remainder = MOD(N, r);
        /* MOD(N, r) returns the residue of N divided by r */
        If (Remainder = 0) Goto Out;
        i = i + 1;
        If(i ≤ k) Then Goto L;
        Print("N is Prime");
        Stop;
    Out:Print("N is Composite");
        Stop;
    End Ptesting
```

Let us now see the behaviour of the above Monte-Carlo algorithm for testing primality of a given number. The parameter (k) controls the number of repetitions. By increasing the value of k, the probability of the error that the number is composite but is declared as prime by the algorithm may be reduced. When the number N is indeed a prime, the above algorithm will assert it with zero chances of error. But when the number is composite, the algorithm may sometimes wrongly output that the number is prime.

If we choose one r at random, and say that N is prime if r is found not to be a certificate for N's compositeness, we have a chance of less than 0.5 to be wrong; as at least half of the r's would have caused us to say no if the answer is no. If we choose two such r at random, and say N is prime if neither of them is found to be a witness to N's compositeness, the probability that we are wrong is less than 0.25. If we choose three such r, the probability of error reduces to 0.125, and so on. By repeating sufficient number of times, we can have confidence in the algorithm to our desired level of expectation. For k times repetition, the probability of error, that is, the number is declared prime but is actually composite will be less than $1/2^k$. Whenever the algorithm is tested for a number which is prime, the answer will be '*yes*' with hundred per cent certainty. But when it is applied on a composite number, it may give a wrong answer with a small probability ($< 1/2^k$).

8.5 RANDOMIZED ALGORITHM FOR MAJORITY ELEMENT

This is another example of Monte-Carlo algorithm. An array has a majority element if there is one element that is occurring in more than half of the array locations. A deterministic algorithm will require quadratic time because we would have to potentially compare every element to every other element until we find one that occurs in more than half of the array locations. The following pseudocode gives a randomized algorithm for detection of majority element.

```
Procedure  Main
  Array A(N);
  Counter = 0;
  For i = 1 to k Do
    Call Majority (A,N,R,E);
    If R = 'True' Then Counter = Counter + 1; Endif
    If Counter > 0 Then Goto Label; Endif
  Endfor
  Label: If Counter > 0 Then
        Print("Majority Element =", E);
      Else
        Print("No Majority Element");
    Endif
End Main

Procedure Majority(A,N,R,E)
  Array A(N);
  R = 'False';
  Choice = UNIFORM(1,N);
  Count = 0;
  For i = 1 to N Do
    If A(i) = A(Choice) Then Count = Count + 1; Endif
  Endfor
  If (Count > N/2) Then
    R = 'True';
    E = A(Choice);
  Endif
End Majority
```

If the procedure Majority( ) makes R = 'True', it means that the array has a majority element. The answer is correct. But if the procedure makes R = 'False', we are not sure whether the array has got a majority element or not. We might have picked up the wrong element for checking the presence of a majority element in the array. If there is a majority element, the probability of picking a minority element is less than 0.5. If we go on calling the procedure Majority ( ), the chance of missing the majority element goes on reducing geometrically. If we use Majority ( ) ten times, the probability of missing the majority element if there is a majority element is less than $(0.5)^{10} = 0.00097$.

The complexity of the algorithm is $O(Nk)$, where k is the number of times procedure Majority ( ) is invoked.

8.6 RANDOMIZED MIN-CUT

Let $G = (V, E)$ be a connected, undirected loop-free multi-graph on n vertices. In a multi-graph, there may be more than one edge between any pair of vertices. A cut in a multi-graph is a partition of the vertex set V into two disjoint non-empty subsets V_1, V_2 such that

$V_1 \cap V_2 = \phi$ and $V_1 \cup V_2 = V$. The size of a cut is the number of edges crossing the cut. Our objective is to obtain a minimum size cut in a given multi-graph using randomization. To find a min-cut, we contract the input graph randomly a number of times. Contracting a graph means that we merge the two end vertices of a picked up edge. If as a result, there are several edges between some pairs of vertices, we retain them all. Edges between vertices that are merged are removed so that there are never any self-loop. We give below pseudocode of a Monte-Carlo algorithm for finding min-cut.

```
Procedure Min-cut(G = (V,E))
   While |V| > 2 Do
      Select an edge (x,y) belonging to E uniformly at random;
      Contract the edge (x,y);
   Endwhile
   Return(|E|);
End Min-cut
```

Edge contraction does not change the min-cut size. The cut determined by the above algorithm contains precisely the edges that have not been contracted. Counting the edges between the remaining two vertices yields an estimate of the size of a minimum cut of G. The algorithm does not always produce the correct size of the minimum cut. Repeating the algorithm a number of times and choosing the smallest value returned by the runs yields the correct size of a minimum cut with high probability. We illustrate working of the algorithm on the graph shown in Figure 8.3. The min-cut value found is 4 while the correct value is 2. The number beside an edge in the figure represents multiplicity of edges between the nodes.

Suppose the min-cut size of the graph is d. Let us consider a particular min-cut *cut* with d edges. G then has at least $dn/2$ edges where n is the number of nodes in the graph. This is so because of the fact that had the graph had a vertex of degree less than d, then its incident edges would be a minimum cut of size less than d. The probability of picking an edge belonging to the cut in the first step is at most $d/(dn/2) = 2/n$. So the probability of not picking an edge belonging to the *cut* in the first step is at least $1 - (2/n)$. Assuming that in the first step we did not pick up an edge belonging to the *cut*, the probability of picking an edge belonging to the *cut* is at most $2/(n - 1)$ as there are at least $d(n - 1)/2$ edges. So the probability of not picking an edge belonging to the *cut* in the first and second steps is at least $[1 - (2/n)][1 - 2/(n - 1)]$. The probability of not picking an edge belonging to the cut in the first i steps is at least,

$$\left(1 - \frac{2}{n}\right)\left(1 - \frac{2}{n-1}\right) \cdots \left(1 - \frac{2}{n-i+1}\right)$$

So the probability of not picking an edge belonging to the cut in the $n - 2$ steps of the algorithm is at least,

$$\left(1 - \frac{2}{n}\right)\left(1 - \frac{2}{n-1}\right) \cdots \left(1 - \frac{2}{n-(n-2)+1}\right) = \frac{2}{n(n-1)}$$

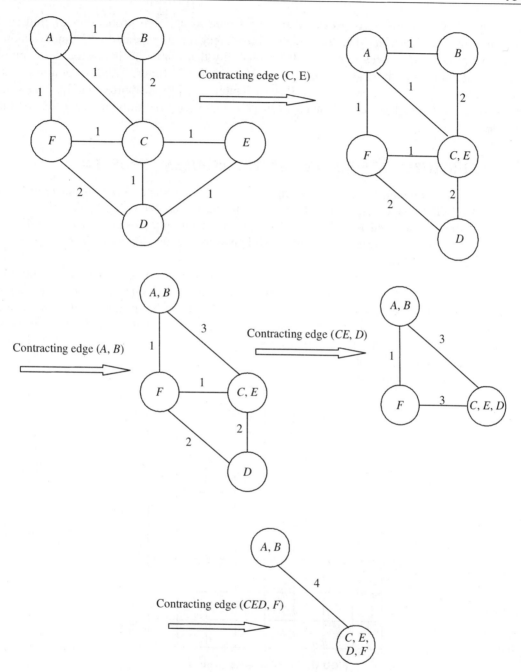

FIGURE 8.3   Min-cut.

The above expression is greater than $2/n^2$ which means, the probability of finding a particular min-cut is greater than $2/n^2$. If the above algorithm is repeated $n^2/2$ times, making independent random choices each time, the probability that a min-cut is not found in any of the $n^2/2$ attempts is at most $[1 - (2/n^2)]$ $[1 - (2/n^2)]$ ... $[n^2/2]$ times. This expression is less than $1/e$, where $e = 1 + 1 + 1/2! + 1/3! + \cdots$ which is 2.71828 approximately. Thus, the probability of failure has been reduced from $[1 - (2/n^2)]$ to $1/e$ through repetition of the process.

8.7 RANDOMIZED ALGORITHM FOR THE n-QUEENS PROBLEM

Las Vegas algorithms never return a wrong answer but sometimes they will not return any answer at all. The longer these algorithms are run, the higher their probability of success. The basic strategy adopted is: a Las Vegas algorithm randomly makes decisions and then checks to see if they have resulted in a successful answer. We develop a Las Vegas algorithm for the n-queens problem.

Suppose we have n queens to be placed on an $n \times n$ chessboard so that no two queens attack each other. A queen attacks another queen if it is on the same row or on the same column or on the same diagonal (major or minor). We place the queens on the board one after another so that each new queen is placed randomly in one of the cells on the next row that are not attacked. When the Las Vegas algorithm cannot place a queen on a row, it just gives up and signals a failure.

One possible solution to the 8-queens problem is shown in Figure 8.4.

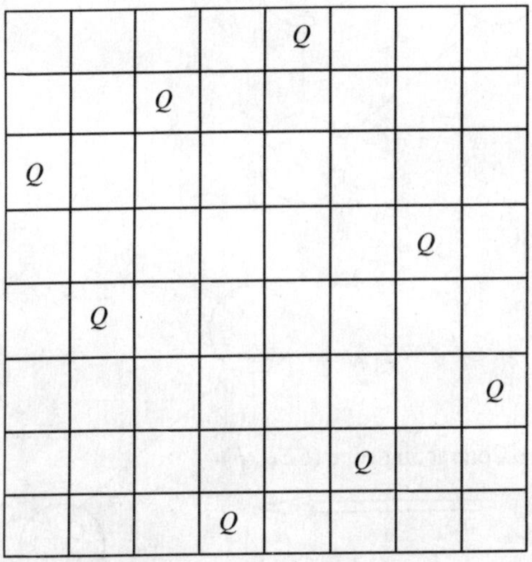

FIGURE 8.4 8-queens problem.

The following is a randomized algorithm for the n-queens problem.

```
Procedure Lvnqueens
  Array Loc(n, n), Avail(n), Result(n)
  Row = 1;
  Repeat
    Possible = 0;
    For i = 1 to n Do
      If Loc(Row, i) is not attacked Then
      Possible = Possible + 1;
      /* Possible indicates the number of non-attacked positions
      in the current row */
      Avail(Possible) = i;
      Endif
    Endfor
    If Possible = 0 Then
      Return ("Failure");
      /* The current queen cannot be safely placed */
    Endif
    r = UNIFORM(1, Possible);
    k = Avail(r);
    /* One of the non-attacked positions is randomly selected */
    Result(Row) = k;
    Row = Row + 1;
  until Row > n;
  Return("Success", Result);
End Lvnqueens
```

8.8 RANDOMIZED SELECTION

Let us consider the problem of selection of the kth smallest element in a set S of n elements. The elements are from a totally ordered universe. We assume that the elements of S are distinct. Let $r_s(t)$ denote the rank of element t in S and $S_{(i)}$ the ith smallest element of S. Adopting this notation, our objective is to select $S_{(k)}$. We give below the randomized algorithm developed by Floyd and Rivest:

Step 1: Pick $n^{3/4}$ elements independently and uniformly at random from S with replacement. This may be a multi-set because of replacement. Let us call this M. (Note: In a multi-set the elements may not be distinct.)

Step 2: Sort M in $O(n^{3/4} \log n)$ time using an efficient deterministic sorting technique like quick-sort.

Step 3: By comparing a and b to every element of S, we determine the ranks of a and b [$r_s(a)$ and $r_s(b)$ respectively], a is the lth smallest element of M and b is the hth smallest element of M, l is the maximum of $\{\lfloor kn^{-1/4} - n^{1/2} \rfloor, 1\}$ and h is the minimum of $\{\lceil kn^{-1/4} + n^{1/2} \rceil, n^{3/4}\}$.

Step 4:   If $k < n^{1/4}$ Then {
$\quad P = \{y \in S \mid y \leq b\};$
$\quad r = k;$
$\quad$ }
$\quad$ Else {
$\quad\quad$ If $k > n - n^{1/4}$ Then {
$\quad\quad\quad P = \{y \in S \mid y \geq a\};$
$\quad\quad\quad r = k - r_s(a) + 1;$
$\quad\quad$ }
$\quad\quad$ Else {
$\quad\quad\quad$ If $k \in [n^{1/4}, n - n^{1/4}]$ Then
$\quad\quad\quad$ {
$\quad\quad\quad\quad P = \{y \in S \mid a \leq y \leq b\};$
$\quad\quad\quad\quad r = k - r_s(a) + 1;$
$\quad\quad\quad$ }
$\quad\quad$ }

If NOT $(S_{(k)} \in P$ AND $|P| \leq 4n^{3/4} + 2)$ Repeat Steps 1 through 3.

Step 5:   Sort P in $O(|P| \log |P|)$ steps.

Step 6:   Print($P_{(r)}$); /* $P_{(r)}$ is $S_{(k)}$ */

The basic idea of this algorithm is to identify two elements a and b in S such that both of the following statements hold with high probability.

1. The element $S_{(k)}$ that we seek is in P, the set of elements between a and b.
2. The set P of elements is not very large, so that we can sort P without much cost.

Let us illustrate the above algorithm with a numerical example. Let S be the set $\{2, 5, 9, 16, 12, 8, 7, 33, 17, 20, 11, 19, 45, 10, 22, 25\}$. Suppose we are interested in finding the 5th smallest element of the set. In this instance $n = 16$, $k = 5$. We pick up $n^{3/4} = 8$ elements independently and uniformly at random from S with replacement. Suppose we have picked up $M = \{2, 7, 20, 11, 22, 9, 16, 9\}$. After sorting, we get $M = \{2, 7, 9, 9, 11, 16, 20, 22\}$. Also,

$$l = \text{maximum} \left(\left\lfloor \frac{k}{n^{1/4}} - n^{1/2} \right\rfloor, 1 \right) = \text{maximum} \left(\left\lfloor \frac{5}{2} - 4 \right\rfloor, 1 \right) = 1$$

$$h = \text{minimum} \left(\left\lceil \frac{k}{n^{1/4}} + n^{1/2} \right\rceil, n^{3/4} \right) = \text{minimum} \left(\left\lceil \frac{5}{2} + 4 \right\rceil, 8 \right) = 7$$

$a = 2$, $b = 20$, $r_S(2) = 1$, $r_S(20) = 12$, $k \in [2, 14]$

$P = \{2, 5, 9, 16, 12, 8, 7, 17, 20, 11, 19, 10\}$

$r = 5 - 1 + 1 = 5$

Sorted $P = \{2, 5, 7, 8, 9, 10, 11, 12, 16, 17, 19, 20\}$

Thus, the 5th smallest element in S is 9.

8.9 RANDOMIZED QUICK-SORT

This is an example of Sherwood type randomized algorithm. It has the property (like any other Sherwood algorithm) that the difference between the worst (best) case behaviour and the average case behaviour is reduced because of the use of randomness. However, this does not affect the correctness of the output. This random algorithm does badly if the randomness is simulated using a bad random number generator. With a good random number generator, the randomized quick-sort becomes insensitive to the input data as far as the worst-case input is concerned.

We select the partitioning element at each step randomly so that each element in the array is equally likely to be picked up as the partitioning element. With a uniform random number generator, we expect that the input data array partitioning will be well balanced on the average. We give below pseudocode for randomized quick-sort. We assume that the input is available in the one-dimensional array A with the lower subscript L and the higher subscript H.

```
Procedure Rquicksort (A, L, H)
   Array A(n)
   If L < H Then
      i = UNIFORM(L, H);
      X = A(L);
      A(L) = A(i);
      A(i) = X;
      Q = Partition(A, L, H);
      Q1 = Q + 1;
      Rquicksort(A, L, Q);
      Rquicksort(A, Q1, H);
      For j = L to Q Do
         Print(A(j));
      Endfor
      For j = Q1 to H Do
         Print(A(j));
      Endfor
   Endif
End Rquicksort

Procedure Partition(A, L, H)
   Array A(n)
   X = A(L);
   i = L - 1;
   j = H + 1;
   While (True)
      Repeat j = j - 1 Until A(j) ≤ X Or j ≤ L;
      /* Looking for elements smaller than or equal to the pivot
      element */
      Repeat i = i + 1 Until A(i) > X Or i ≥ H;
         /* Looking for elements greater than the pivot element */
```

```
   If i < j Then
       TEMP = A(i);
       A(i) = A(j);
       A(j) = TEMP;
     Else
         Return(j);
     Endif
   Endwhile
 End Partition
```

The expected number of comparisons for the randomized quick-sort is $O(nH_n)$, where

H_n is the nth harmonic number, defined as $H_n = \sum_{k=1}^{k=n} \dfrac{1}{k}$. Since, $H_n \sim \ln n + \Theta(1)$, the expected

running time of the randomized quick-sort is $O(n \log n)$.

SUMMARY

In this chapter, we have introduced randomized algorithms that solve problems using random numbers. These algorithms are simpler to describe and implement. The different flavours of randomized algorithms are numerical probabilistic algorithms, Monte-Carlo algorithms, Las Vegas algorithms and Sherwood algorithms. Complexity classes for randomized algorithms were discussed in this chapter. For the sake of illustration, we have given algorithms for computation of π, numerical integration, primality testing, majority element selection, n-queens problem, selection, and quick-sort. These examples cover all the different flavours of randomized algorithms.

EXERCISES

8.1 Develop a probabilistic algorithm to find the value of the integral:

$$\int_{0}^{2} \sqrt{4 - x^2}\, dx$$

8.2 Give a Monte-Carlo algorithm for finding the majority element in an array.

8.3 Give a Sherwood-type sorting algorithm.

8.4 Make empirical study of probabilistic primality testing algorithm on your machine.

8.5 Demonstrate empirically how accuracy changes with repetition for probabilistic numerical integration. Take a few standard numerical integrals whose closed-form results are known for comparison.

8.6 Demonstrate empirically how randomized quick-sort compares with the deterministic quick-sort.

8.7 Find the fifth smallest element from the set {2, 7, 20, 6, 5, 4, 3, 28, 19, 15, 11, 90, 17, 65, 11, 67} using randomized selection.

8.8 An element is called a minority element if it is not a majority element. Modify the algorithm of section 8.5 to find a minority element.

8.9 Demonstrate the working of randomized quick-sort for the following list of numbers: 200, 7, 20, 62, 15, 44, 3, 28, 19, 15, 11, 90, 17, 65, 18, 77.

8.10 Devise a randomized min-cut algorithm where two vertices are randomly selected and coalesced.

8.11 Analyze the algorithm developed for the Problem 8.10.

8.12 Prove that the randomized min-cut algorithm of Section 8.6 can be implemented in $O(n^2)$ time for any multi-graph with n vertices.

8.13 Find a randomized algorithm for two-dimensional convex-hull problem.

8.14 Analyze the average-case complexity of the algorithm of Problem 8.13.

8.15 Prove that edge contraction does not alter the min-cut size in a multi-graph.

9
GRAPH ALGORITHMS

9.0 INTRODUCTION

Graph theory plays a very important role in computer science. Many problems arising in computing can be modeled in an abstract setting by means of graph. From our knowledge of graph theory, it becomes easier to comprehend the problem and find solution of the same. Graph theory has applications in physics, chemistry, computer science, ecology, economics, electrical engineering, game theory, genetics, operations research, etc. Algorithmic graph theory is an important research area among computer scientists and mathematicians. In this chapter, we discuss a few representative graph algorithms such as breadth-first search, depth-first search, topological sorting, finding strongly-connected components, and articulation points of a graph, etc.

9.1 GRAPH-THEORETIC TERMINOLOGY

The theory of graphs and digraphs work as mathematical models for a wide variety of problems, both practical as well as theoretical. In this section, we introduce some of the common graph-theoretic terms and some important characterizations of a few graph objects.

Graph

It is an ordered pair (V, E), where V is the non-empty set of nodes (points or vertices) and E is a subset of $V \times V$, called edges (lines or arcs). Two vertices u, v of a graph G are said to be adjacent if there is an edge (u, v) belonging to E. A weighted graph is a pair (G, W), where G is a graph (V, E) and W is a real valued function, $W: E \rightarrow R^+$. A graph is directed if all its edges have directions. An example graph is shown in Figure 9.1(a).

Sub-graph

A graph $H = (V_1, E_1)$ is a sub-graph of $G = (V, E)$ if V_1 is a subset of V and E_1 is a subset of E. G is called a super-graph of H. Figure 9.1(b) shows a subgraph of the graph of Figure 9.1(a).

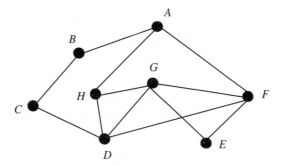

FIGURE 9.1(a) Example graph.

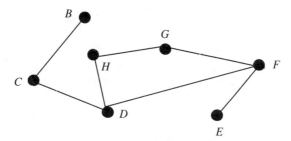

FIGURE 9.1(b) Sub-graph of Figure 9.1(a).

Degree of a node

The degree of a node is the number of edges incident on the node. If the degrees of the nodes of a graph are the same, then it is called a regular graph. A degree 3 regular graph on 4 vertices is shown in Figure 9.1(c).

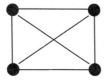

FIGURE 9.1(c) Degree 3 regular graph on 4 vertices.

Eccentricity

Eccentricity of a node is defined as the maximum of its distances from all other nodes.

Diameter

Diameter of a graph is the maximum of the eccentricities of its nodes.

Centre

A node with minimum eccentricity is called a center of the graph.

Radius

Radius of a graph is the eccentricity of its center.

Complete graph

A graph $G = (V, E)$ is called complete if for every pair of nodes v_i, $v_j \in V$, where $i \neq j$, $(v_i, v_j) \in E$. Each node in a complete graph on n nodes has degree $n - 1$. Figure 9.1(d) shows a complete graph on 4 nodes.

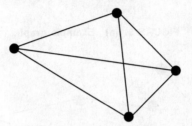

FIGURE 9.1(d)   Complete graph on 4 nodes.

Bipartite graph

A graph $G = (V, E)$ is called bipartite if V can be partitioned into V_1 and V_2 such that for all e belonging to E, one end of e is in V_1 and the other end is in V_2. Figure 9.1(e) shows a bipartite graph.

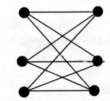

FIGURE 9.1(e)   Bipartite graph.

Walk

A walk is defined as a finite alternating sequence of vertices and edges beginning and ending with vertices, such that each edge is incident on the vertices preceding and following it. Vertices with which a walk begins and ends are called its terminal vertices. It is possible for a walk to begin and end at the same vertex. Such a walk is called a closed walk. A walk that is not closed is called an open walk.

Trail

A walk is termed a trail if all of its edges are distinct.

Path

An open trail in which no vertex appears more than once (and necessarily all edges are distinct) is called a path.

Circuit

A closed walk in which no vertex appears more than once is called a circuit. A circuit is also called a cycle or a loop. A circuit having even number of edges is called an even circuit and a circuit having odd number of edges is called an odd circuit.

Acyclic graph

A graph having no cycle is called an acyclic graph.

Connected graph

A graph G is connected if there is at least one path between every pair of vertices in G. Intuitively, a graph is connected if we can reach any vertex from any other vertex by traveling along the edges. A disconnected graph contains two or more connected maximal sub-graphs. Each of these maximally connected sub-graphs is called a component of the graph G. The graph in Figure 9.1(f) is a disconnected graph and contains two maximally connected sub-graphs H_1 and H_2 that are the components of G.

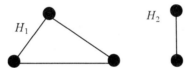

FIGURE 9.1(f) Disconnected graph.

Tree

A tree is a connected graph without cycle. There are other equivalent definitions of a tree. A graph G with n vertices is called a tree if G is connected and has $n - 1$ edges or G is circuitless and has $n - 1$ edges or there is exactly one path between every pair of vertices in G or G is a minimally connected graph. A tree is shown in Figure 9.1(g).

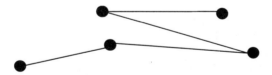

FIGURE 9.1(g) Tree.

Forest

It is a collection of trees. A forest is shown in Figure 9.1(h).

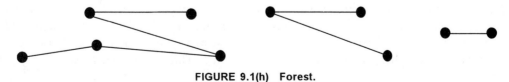

FIGURE 9.1(h) Forest.

Spanning tree

A tree T is said to be a spanning tree of a connected graph G if T is a sub-graph of G and T contains all vertices of G. A spanning tree with the smallest weight in a weighted graph is called minimal spanning tree of the graph. Figure 9.1(i) shows a spanning tree of the graph of Figure 9.1(a).

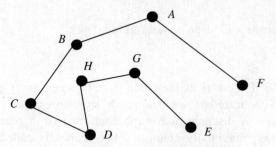

FIGURE 9.1(i)   Spanning tree of example graph of Figure 9.1(a).

Transitive closure

Transitive closure of a graph $G = (V, E)$ is the graph $G^* = (V, E')$, where $E' = \{(u, v) \mid$ there is a path between u and v in $G\}$. G^* is the transitive closure of G in Figure 9.1(j).

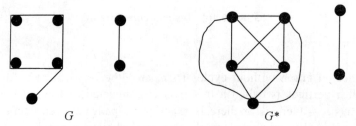

FIGURE 9.1(j)   Transitive closure.

9.2   BREADTH-FIRST SEARCH

Given a graph $G = (V, E)$ and a source vertex X, breadth-first search systematically visits the nodes of G that are reachable from X. It computes the distance from X of all the vertices reachable from X. The search produces as output the breadth-first tree with X as the root node. For any vertex v reachable from X, the path in the breadth-first-tree from X to v represents a shortest path from X to v in G.

The search expands the frontier of discovery of nodes in a systematic way. It visits nodes at a distance d from X before visiting nodes at a distance $d + 1$. To keep track of the nodes regarding their discovery, we use three colours (green, blue and red) to colour the nodes of the graph. Initially, all nodes are coloured green and later these are coloured blue and finally red. A node first discovered during the search is made non-green. If $(u, v) \in E$ and vertex u is red, then vertex v is either blue or red. This means that all nodes adjacent to red nodes have been discovered. Blue nodes may have some adjacent green nodes. We assume that the adjacency information is supplied in the form of adjacency lists.

Initially, the breadth-first search constructs a breadth-first tree with only one node which is node X. Whenever a green node v is discovered in the course of scanning the adjacency list of an already discovered node u, the node v and the edge (u, v) are added to the tree and u is called the parent of v. Since a node is discovered at most once, it has at most one parent.

The colour of node i is kept in the variable $colour(i)$, the parent of node i in the variable $P(i)$, and the distance of node i from X in the variable $d(i)$. We use a first-in first-out queue (Q) as the data structure to control the order in which the nodes are visited. Pseudocode for breadth-first search may be written as shown below where we assume that $HEAD(Q)$ supplies a copy of the element from the front of the queue Q without removing it from the queue, $[Q, v]$ denotes that the element v is added to the rear of the queue, $Dequeue(Q)$ removes the front element of the queue.

```
Procedure Bfs(G,X)  /* G = (V,E), X ∈ V */
   For each u ∈ V - {X} DO
     Colour(u) = Green;
     d(u) = ∞;
     P(u) = NIL; /* Parent of u is none */
   Endfor
   Colour(X) = Blue;
   d(X) = 0;
   P(X) = NIL;
   Q = [X];
   While Q ≠ NULL DO
     u = HEAD(Q);
     /* u gets a copy of the element at
     the front of the queue */
     For each v adjacent to u DO
       If Colour(v) = Green Then
         Colour(v) = Blue;
         d(v) = d(u) + 1;
         P(v) = u; /* Parent of v is u */
         Q = [Q,v];
         /* v is inserted at the rear
         end of the queue */
       Endif
     Endfor
     Dequeue(Q);
     /* u is removed from the queue */
     Colour(u) = Red;
   Endwhile
End Bfs
```

Let us consider the graph in Figure 9.2 with seven vertices *A, B, C, D, E, F, G* with the adjacency lists {*B, D*}, {*A, C, E*}, {*B, E, G*}, {*A, E, F*}, {*B, C, D*}, {*D, G*}, and {*C, F*} respectively. We start the breadth-first search from the node A.

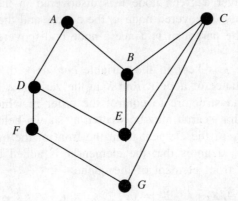

FIGURE 9.2 Example graph for breadth-first search.

Initially, *Colour(B), Colour(C), Colour(D), Colour(E), Colour(F)* and *Colour(G)* are all made green. Thereafter, *Colour(A)* = *blue*, *d(A)* = 0, *P(A)* = NIL, and *Q* contains *A* only. *A* is now expanded, *u* = *A*. *Colour(B)* = *blue*, *d(B)* = *d(A)* + 1 = 1, *P(B)* = *A*, *B* is inserted at the end of the queue. *Colour(D)* = *blue*, *d(D)* = *d(A)* + 1 = 1, *P(D)* = *A*, *D* is inserted at the end of the queue. Colour of *A* is made *red*, that is *A* becomes a dead node. *A* is removed from the queue. Queue now contains *B* and *D*; *B* is at the front of the queue.

B is now the expanding node. Working of the algorithm on the graph of Figure 9.2 is illustrated below. When the algorithm terminates, all the nodes are coloured red and the queue becomes empty.

(A)	(B)	(C)	(D)	(E)	(F)	(G)	d(v)	P(v)	Q
	Green	Green	Green	Green	Green	Green			
Blue	Green	Green	Green	Green	Green	Green	d(A)=0	P(A)=NIL	[A]
Blue	Blue	Green	Green	Green	Green	Green	d(B)=1	P(B)=A	[A,B]
Blue	Blue	Green	Blue	Green	Green	Green	d(D)=1	P(D)=A	[A,B,D]
Red	Blue	Blue	Blue	Green	Green	Green	d(C)=2	P(C)=B	[B,D,C]
Red	Blue	Blue	Blue	Blue	Green	Green	d(E)=2	P(E)=B	[B,D,C,E]
Red	Red	Blue	Blue	Blue	Blue	Green	d(F)=2	P(F)=D	[D,C,E,F]
Red	Red	Blue	Red	Blue	Blue	Blue	d(G)=3	P(G)=C	[C,E,F,G]
Red	Red	Red	Red	Blue	Blue	Blue			[E,F,G]
Red	Red	Red	Red	Red	Blue	Blue			[F,G]
Red	Red	Red	Red	Red	Red	Blue			[G]
Red	Red	Red	Red	Red	Red	Red			[ ]

The breadth-first search tree for the graph of Figure 9.2 is shown in Figure 9.3. The tree shows that the nodes B and D are at a distance 1 from the node A. The nodes C, E, F are at a distance 2 from the node A and the node G is at a distance 3 from the node A. We have discovered nodes B and D before discovering nodes C, E, F and node G has been discovered at the last.

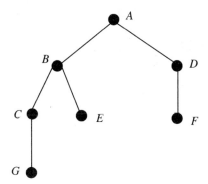

FIGURE 9.3   Breadth-first tree of the graph of Figure 9.2.

After initialization, no node is ever coloured green. Each node is put into the queue at most once. Assuming that the operations of putting in a queue and removing from the queue each requires constant time, the total time required for queue operations is $O(|V|)$. Adjacency list of each node is examined at most once and the sum of the lengths of all the adjacency lists is $2|E|$, at most $O(|E|)$ time is required in scanning the adjacency lists. The time required for initialization is $O(|V|)$. So, the total time for breadth-first search is $O(|V|+|E|)$.

9.3   DEPTH-FIRST SEARCH

Depth-first search explores deeper and deeper in the graph following the edges first. It explores deeper from the most recently explored node to which another unexplored node is connected by an edge. This continues till all the reachable nodes are covered. If some more nodes are still left, the search continues from one such node in the depth-first manner. This means that if we have reached node v from node u, and no other node is adjacent to v, the search will look for whether any other node w can be reached from u, if so it continues, otherwise, it will look for any node that can be reached from the node from which we reached u. This continues till no node can be reached from any ancestor of u. We use adjacency lists for the depth-first search.

Whenever a node v is discovered during a scan of the adjacency list of a previously discovered vertex u, depth-first search records this by setting v's predecessor, $P(v)$ to u. We colour the vertices as in the breadth-first search case with three colours green, blue and red to record the state of the nodes as far as the search is concerned. Nodes are initially coloured green, they are then coloured blue during discovery and are made red when the nodes' adjacency lists are examined completely.

The search produces a depth-first tree for a connected graph and a depth-first forest for a disconnected graph. In addition, for each node (u) we record when the node is first discovered, that is coloured blue, through $t1(u)$ and when the search finishes examining u's adjacency list, that is, when it is coloured red through $t2(u)$. Obviously, $t1(u) < t2(u)$. Vertex u is green before $t1(u)$, it is blue between $t1(u)$ and $t2(u)$ and is red afterwards.

```
Procedure Main_Dfs(G = (V, E))
  For each vertex u ∈ V Do
    Colour(u) = Green;
    P(u) = NIL;
  Endfor
  T = 0; /* Time counter is initialized */
  For each vertex u ∈ V Do
    If Colour(u) = Green Then Call Dfs(u, T);
    Endfor
End Main_Dfs

Procedure Dfs(u, T)
  Colour(u) = Blue;
  T = T + 1;
  t1(u) = T;
  For each v ∈ Adjacency List(u) Do
    If Colour(v) = Green Then
      P(v) = u;  /* Predecessor of v is u */
      Call Dfs(v, T);
    Endif
  Endfor
  Colour(u) = Red;
  T = T + 1;
  t2(u) = T;
End Dfs
```

The initialization loop in Main_Dfs routine requires time proportional to $|V|$. The Dfs routine is called at most $|V|$ times. During the execution of the Dfs(v), the loop inside Dfs is repeated at most $|Adjacency List(v)|$ times. For all Dfs calls together, the time is proportional to $|E|$, because the total number of entries in all the adjacency lists together is $2|E|$. So, the total running time of Dfs is $O(|V| + |E|)$.

Consider the graph in Figure 9.4 which has seven vertices: $A, B, C, D, E, F,$ and G with adjacency lists $\{B, D\}, \{A, C, E\}, \{B, E, G\}, \{A, E, F\}, \{B, C, D\}, \{D\},$ and $\{C\}$ respectively.

Initially, $Colour(A), Colour(B), Colour(C), Colour(D), Colour(E), Colour(F),$ and $Colour(G)$ are all made green and P of all the nodes are set NIL. T is set to 0. Dfs(A) is called. Thereafter, $Colour(A) = blue, T = 1, t1(A) = 1, P(A) = $ NIL. A is now expanded, $u = A$. Progress of the algorithm is as shown below.

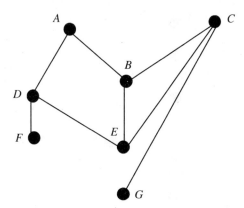

FIGURE 9.4 Example graph for depth-first search.

(A)	(B)	(C)	(D)	(E)	(F)	(G)	$t1(v)$	$t2(v)$	$P(v)$
Green	Green	Green	Green	Green	Green	Green			
Blue	Green	Green	Green	Green	Green	Green	$t1(A)=1$		$P(A)=NIL$
Blue	Blue	Green	Green	Green	Green	Green	$t1(B)=2$		$P(B)=A$
Blue	Blue	Blue	Green	Green	Green	Green	$t1(C)=3$		$P(C)=B$
Blue	Blue	Blue	Green	Blue	Green	Green	$t1(E)=4$		$P(E)=C$
Blue	Blue	Blue	Blue	Blue	Green	Green	$t1(D)=5$		$P(D)=E$
Blue	Blue	Blue	Blue	Blue	Blue	Green	$t1(F)=6$		$P(F)=D$
Blue	Blue	Blue	Blue	Blue	Red	Green		$t2(F)=7$	
Blue	Blue	Blue	Red	Blue	Red	Green		$t2(D)=8$	
Blue	Blue	Blue	Red	Red	Red	Green		$t2(E)=9$	
Blue	Blue	Blue	Red	Red	Red	Blue	$t1(G)=10$		$P(G)=C$
Blue	Blue	Blue	Red	Red	Red	Red		$t2(G)=11$	
Blue	Blue	Red	Red	Red	Red	Red		$t2(C)=12$	
Blue	Red	Red	Red	Red	Red	Red		$t2(B)=13$	
Red	Red	Red	Red	Red	Red	Red		$t2(A)=14$	

A depth-first search tree of the graph in Figure 9.4 is shown in Figure 9.5.

9.4 TOPOLOGICAL SORTING

A topological sorting of a directed acyclic graph $G = (V, E)$ is a linear ordering of its nodes such that if G contains an edge (u, v), then u appears before v in the ordering. If the graph contains directed cycle, then no topological sorting of the nodes is possible. After topological sorting of the directed graph, if the nodes are placed on a line, all the edges of G will be directed left to right. There can be no edge directed in the opposite direction. There are many

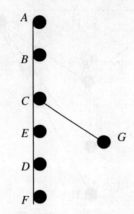

FIGURE 9.5 Depth-first tree.

applications where topological sorting is required. For example, suppose a number of tasks are to be executed one after the other but there are certain precedence constraints, that is, some tasks are to be finished before other tasks can be done. How to proceed about it? We have to first find a linear ordering of these tasks observing the dependency constraints. This can be done through topological sorting of the graph representing the tasks and their dependencies.

A pseudocode for the topological sorting is given below:

```
Procedure Topological_sort(G = (V,E))
   Call Main_Dfs(G) to compute the finishing times t2(v)
for each node of V;
   Output the vertices (v) in decreasing order of t2(v);
End Topological_sort
```

The depth-first search requires $O(|V| + |E|)$ time. Creation of the linked-list requires $O(|V|)$ time. Hence topological sorting requires $O(|V| + |E|)$ time. Let us now illustrate topological sorting for the acyclic graph of Figure 9.6(a). The topologically sorted order is shown in Figure 9.6(b).

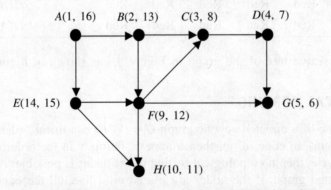

FIGURE 9.6(a) Example graph for topological sorting.

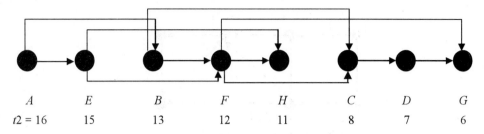

A	E	B	F	H	C	D	G
$t2 = 16$	15	13	12	11	8	7	6

FIGURE 9.6(b)   Topologically sorted order.

9.5   STRONGLY-CONNECTED COMPONENT

Strongly-connected component of a directed graph $G = (V, E)$ is a maximal sub-set of nodes, $U \subseteq V$ such that for every pair of vertices u and v in U, we can reach v from u and u from v by following the directed edges. From G, we define $G' = (V, E')$, where $E' = \{(u, v)|$ $(v, u) \in E\}$. That is, E' consists of the edges of G with their directions reversed. We claim that G and G' have the same strongly-connected components. This is so, because if there is a path from u to v and v to u in G, then there will be paths from v to u and u to v in G'. We give the following pseudocode for finding the strongly-connected components of a directed graph:

```
Procedure Strongly_connected_component(G = (V,E))
    Call Main_Dfs(G) to compute the finishing times t2(v) for each
node of V;
    Find out G';
    Call Main_Dfs(G') with the restriction that u is considered
before v if t2(u) > t2(v) as found in Call Main_Dfs(G);
    Output the vertices of each tree in the depth-first forest
generated through Call Main_Dfs(G') as a separate strongly connected
component;
    End Strongly_connected_component
```

Each call to Main_Dfs requires $O(|V| + |E|)$ time. Given an adjacency list representation, generation of G' from G requires $O(|V| + |E|)$ time. Generation of strongly-connected components from the depth-first trees of G' requires $O(|V|)$ time. Hence the overall complexity of this algorithm is $O(|V| + |E|)$.

The strongly-connected components of the graph of Figure 9.7(a) are $\{A\}$, $\{B\}$, $\{E\}$, $\{F\}$, $\{H\}$, and $\{C, I, D\}$ as shown in Figure 9.7(c). Figure 9.7(b) shows depth-first search of G'.

9.6   ARTICULATION POINTS OF A GRAPH

An articulation point of a graph $G = (V, E)$ is a node $v \in V$ whose removal disconnects G. An alternative way of defining articulation point is that for distinct nodes x, u and $v \in V$, if every path between the nodes u and v passes through x, then x is an articulation point. A bridge

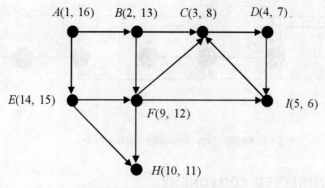

FIGURE 9.7(a)   Computing finishing time.

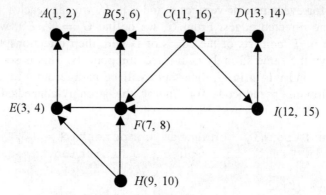

FIGURE 9.7(b)   Depth-first search of *G'*.

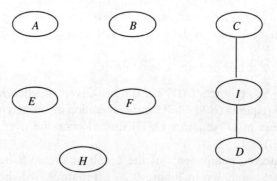

FIGURE 9.7(c)   Depth-first forest: each tree represents a strongly-connected component.

is an edge of G whose removal disconnects G. Articulation points of a graph can be found by making a depth-first search of the graph. Let $G_T = (V, E_T)$ be the depth-first tree of the graph G. The set of edges $E - E_T$ are called the back edges. These are the edges of G that are not included in the depth-first tree. The root of G_T is an articulation point of G if it has at least two children. Since there is no edge between one branch of the tree and the other branch (presence of this would have created a cycle), removing the root will create at least two components. A non-root node v is an articulation point of G if and only if there is no back edge (u, w) such that u is a descendant of v (including itself) and w is a proper ancestor of v. w is a proper ancestor of v in G_T if the path from the root to v passes through w. The two situations could be represented as in Figure 9.8(a).

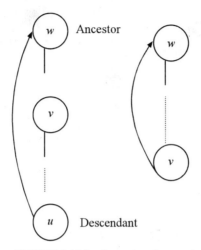

FIGURE 9.8(a)   Ancestor-descendant.

If there is no back edge, removal of v will make the nodes in G_T that are down the tree after v disconnected from other nodes of the graph. To decide whether a non-root node v is an articulation point or not, we introduce the following function:

$Low(v) =$ Minimum$\{t1(v), t1(w)\}$, where $t1$ is the discovery time as found in the depth-first search and (u, w) is a back edge for some descendant u of v or itself to an ancestor w of v. Pseudocode for the algorithm may be written as follows:

```
Procedure Articulation_point(G = (V,E))
  Call Main_Dfs(G);
  Find out Low(v) for each node v ∈ V;
  Determine the articulation points as follows:
  {
    If the root has more than one child then it is an articulation
    point;
    Check for all other nodes v whether it has a child x such
    that Low(x) ≥ t1(v) then v is an articulation point;
  }
End Articulation_point
```

Depth-first search of G requires $O(|V| + |E|)$ time. Finding $Low(v)$ for all $v \in V$ requires $O(|E|)$ time. Determining the articulation points at the last stage of the algorithm requires $O(|E|)$ time. Hence the overall complexity of the algorithm is $O(|V| + |E|)$. Let us find the articulation points of the graph in Figure 9.8(b).

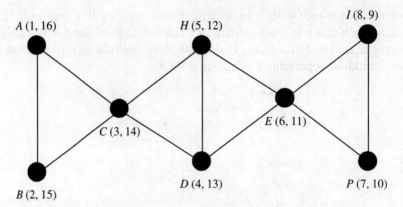

FIGURE 9.8(b)   Depth-first search of an example graph.

Figure 9.8(c) shows the depth-first tree of the above graph augmented with back edges (indicated through discontinuous lines).

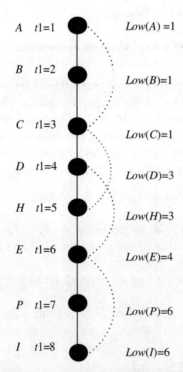

FIGURE 9.8(c)   Depth-first tree augmented with back edges.

The root has only one child, so it cannot be an articulation point. Amongst the other nodes C has a child D having $Low(D) \geq t1(C)$ and E has a child P having $Low(P) \geq t1(E)$. So C and E are the only articulation points of G.

9.7 TRANSITIVE CLOSURE OF A GRAPH

For a given graph $G = (V, E)$, we are sometimes interested in knowing whether there is a path of length one or more between any two nodes of the graph. If there is an edge between two nodes i and j, we say that there is a path of length one between i and j. If there is no edge between i and j but there are edges between i and k, and between k and j where $i \neq k \neq j$, then we say that there is a path of length two between i and j. In this way, there may be paths of length 3, 4 or more between i and j. The maximum possible path length may be $n - 1$ for a graph having n nodes. We may use Floyd's algorithm to find solution to this problem but the algorithm that finds the existence of paths of length 1 or more between any two nodes in a directed graph predates Floyd's algorithm.

Let $C(i, j)$ be 1 if there is a directed edge from node i to node j, 0 otherwise. We plan to compute path matrix $PL(i, j)$ for the directed graph such that $PL(i, j) = 1$ if there is a path of length one or more from node i to node j, otherwise, $PL(i, j) = 0$. The matrix PL is called the transitive closure of the adjacency matrix C.

We give below pseudocode for finding transitive closure of the adjacency matrix.

```
Procedure Warshall(C(n,n))
  Array P(n,n), PP(n,n), PL(n,n);
    For i = 1 to n Do
    For j = 1 to n Do
      P(i,j) = C(i,j);
      PL(i,j) = C(i,j);
    Endfor
    Endfor
  For pl = 1 to n Do
    For i = 1 to n Do
    For j = 1 to n Do
      PP(i,j) = 0
    For k = 1 to n Do
      PP(i,j) = PP(i,j) + P(i,k) * C(k,j);
    Endfor
    Endfor
    Endfor
    For i = 1 to n Do
    For j = 1 to n Do
      P(i,j) = PP(i,j);
      PL(i,j) = PL(i,j) + P(i,j);
    Endfor
    Endfor
  Endfor
  Return (PL);
End Warshall
```

The above algorithm obviously requires $O(n^4)$ time because of 4 nested 'Do loops', each ranging 1 through n. We show below the snapshots of the algorithm to find the transitive closure of the directed graph of Figure 9.9.

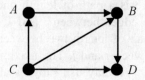

FIGURE 9.9   Input graph for transitive closure.

$$
C = \begin{array}{c} \\ A \\ B \\ C \\ D \end{array}
\begin{array}{cccc} A & B & C & D \\ \end{array}
\left[\begin{array}{cccc}
0 & 1 & 0 & 0 \\
0 & 0 & 0 & 1 \\
1 & 1 & 0 & 1 \\
0 & 0 & 0 & 0
\end{array} \right]
\qquad
P^1 = \begin{array}{c} \\ A \\ B \\ C \\ D \end{array}
\begin{array}{cccc} A & B & C & D \\ \end{array}
\left[\begin{array}{cccc}
0 & 1 & 0 & 0 \\
0 & 0 & 0 & 1 \\
1 & 1 & 0 & 1 \\
0 & 0 & 0 & 0
\end{array} \right]
$$

P^1 indicates that there are paths of length 1 from A to B, B to D, C to A, C to B and C to D.

$$
P^2 = \begin{array}{c} \\ A \\ B \\ C \\ D \end{array}
\begin{array}{cccc} A & B & C & D \\ \end{array}
\left[\begin{array}{cccc}
0 & 0 & 0 & 1 \\
0 & 0 & 0 & 0 \\
0 & 1 & 0 & 1 \\
0 & 0 & 0 & 0
\end{array} \right]
$$

P^2 indicates that there are paths of length 2 from A to D, from C to B and from C to D.

$$
P^3 = \begin{array}{c} \\ A \\ B \\ C \\ D \end{array}
\begin{array}{cccc} A & B & C & D \\ \end{array}
\left[\begin{array}{cccc}
0 & 0 & 0 & 0 \\
0 & 0 & 0 & 0 \\
0 & 0 & 0 & 1 \\
0 & 0 & 0 & 0
\end{array} \right]
$$

P^3 indicates that there is a path of length 3 from C to D.

$$
P^4 = \begin{array}{c} \\ A \\ B \\ C \\ D \end{array}
\begin{array}{cccc} A & B & C & D \\ \end{array}
\left[\begin{array}{cccc}
0 & 0 & 0 & 0 \\
0 & 0 & 0 & 0 \\
0 & 0 & 0 & 0 \\
0 & 0 & 0 & 0
\end{array} \right]
$$

P^4 indicates that there is no path of length 4 between any pair of nodes.

$$PL = P^1 + P^2 + P^3 + P^4 = \begin{array}{c} \\ A \\ B \\ C \\ D \end{array} \overset{\begin{array}{cccc} A & B & C & D \end{array}}{\begin{bmatrix} 0 & 1 & 0 & 1 \\ 0 & 0 & 0 & 1 \\ 1 & 2 & 0 & 3 \\ 0 & 0 & 0 & 0 \end{bmatrix}}$$

PL indicates that there are unique paths from A to B, from A to D, from B to D, from C to A, two paths from C to B, and three paths from C to D.

9.8 GRAPH MATCHING

Matching of a graph $G = (V, E)$ is M where $M \subseteq E$, such that no two members of M are incident on the same vertex. Consider the graph in Figure 9.10(a). The subset of edges M_1 = {(B, C), (D, E), (F, G)} as shown by thickened edges in Figure 9.10(b) is a matching. Given a graph G, finding a maximum matching M of G is the graph matching problem. When $|M| = \lfloor |V|/2 \rfloor$, the largest possible in the graph with $|V|$ nodes, it is called *complete* or *perfect matching*. Consider the graph given in Figure 9.10(a). This graph has 8 vertices, so a maximal (perfect) matching M_2 should have cardinality 4. $M = \{(A, B), (C, D), (G, H)\}$ is not complete or perfect. But the matching $M_2 = \{(A, B), (C, D), (E, F), (G, H)\}$ shown in Figure 9.10(c) by thickened edges is complete or perfect.

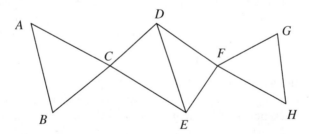

FIGURE 9.10(a) Example graph G for matching.

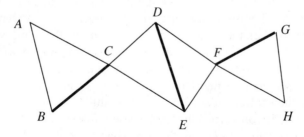

FIGURE 9.10(b) Example matching (M_1).

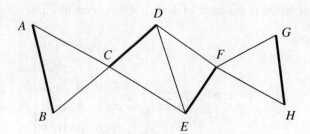

FIGURE 9.10(c)   Complete matching M_2.

A typical matching problem involves pairing off compatible boys and girls in a dancing event. Assigning workers to jobs for which they have skills is also a matching problem. These problems are basically matching problem in bipartite graphs. We need to understand some terms like *matched edges*, *free edges*, *matched node*, *exposed node*, *alternating path*, and *augmenting path* for further exposition. Let us consider a matching M of a graph G.

An edge belonging to M is called a *matched edge*; an edge not belonging to M is called a *free edge*. Nodes that are the end points of matched edges are called *matched nodes*; other nodes are called *exposed nodes*. A path in G is a sequence of edges $\{(v_1, v_2), (v_2, v_3), \ldots (v_{k-1}, v_k)\}$. If the first, third, fifth, … edges in this path are free and the second, fourth, sixth, … edges are matched, then this path is termed an alternating path of free and matched edges. In Figure 9.10(b) $\{(B, C), (C, D), (D, E), (E, F)\}$ is an alternating path. An alternating path $\{(v_1, v_2), (v_2, v_3), \ldots (v_{k-1}, v_k)\}$ is an augmenting path if the nodes v_1, v_k are exposed nodes. The alternating path $\{(B, C), (C, D), (D, E), (E, F)\}$ in Figure 9.10(b) is not an augmenting path as the nodes B and F are not exposed nodes. The alternating path $\{(A, B), (B, C), (C, D), (D, E), (E, F), (F, G), (G, H)\}$ in Figure 9.10(b) is an augmenting path as the nodes A and H are exposed nodes. Before we proceed further, we need to understand two results in this connection.

Result 1:   Let P be the set of edges on an augmenting path $\{v_1, v_2, \ldots, v_{2k}\}$ in a graph G with respect to the matching M_1. Then $M_2 = M_1 \oplus P$ is a matching of size $|M_1| + 1$, where $\oplus$ is the symmetric difference of M_1 and P.

Proof: First we show that M_2 is a matching. Suppose it has two edges e_i, e_j that are incident on the same vertex in G. We have to consider three cases: (i) e_i, $e_j \in M_1 - P$, (ii) e_i, $e_j \in P - M_1$, (iii) $e_i \in M_1 - P$ and $e_j \in P - M_1$. In the case (i), we have two edges in M_1 sharing a vertex, which is a contradiction. In the case (ii), the edges in $P - M_1$ are edges of the form (v_{2l-1}, v_{2l}), and hence, two of them cannot be incident upon the same vertex. For the case (iii), suppose an edge $e_j = (v_{2l-1}, v_{2l})$ in $P - M_1$ has a node in common with another edge $e_i \in P - M_1$. Without losing generality, we assume that this vertex is v_{2l}. But v_{2l} is a node of the edge $e_r = (v_{2l}, v_{2l+1}) \in M_1$. Hence, the two edges e_i and e_r of M_1 have a common vertex. This is a contradiction. It then follows that M_2 is a matching.

P contains $2k - 1$ edges of which k are free. These k free edges are $\{(v_1, v_2), \ldots, (v_{2k-1}, v_k)\}$. The remaining $k-1$ edges belong to M_1. M_2 has one edge more than M_1. Hence $M_2 = M_1 \oplus P$.

Result 2:   A matching M_1 in a graph G is maximum if and only if there is no augmenting path in G with respect to M_1.

Proof: From the previous result, we can easily prove that if M_1 is maximum, then there is no augmenting path in G with respect to M_1. Otherwise, the augmenting path could be used to increase the cardinality of matching. For the other direction of proof, let us assume that there is no augmenting path in G with respect to M_1 and M_1 is not the maximum. Since M_1 is not maximum, there is a matching M_2 where $|M_2| > |M_1|$.

Consider the edges in $(M_2 - M_1) \cup (M_1 - M_2)$, which form a sub-graph (not necessarily connected) of G. In the subgraph $G' = (V, M_1 \oplus M_2)$, all the vertices have degree two or less. If the degree is two, one of the edges is in M_1 and the other in M_2. Thus, all the connected components of G' will be either paths or cycles of even length. In all the cycles, we have the same number of edges in M_1 and M_2. But we assumed that $|M_2| > |M_1|$, it must be the case that in one of the paths we have more edges from M_2 than from M_1. This path is then an augmenting path, which contradicts our assumption.

This result can be used to find maximum matching in a graph. Start with an arbitrary matching and then go on discovering augmenting paths. We now discuss matching in a bipartite graph shown in Figure 9.10(d).

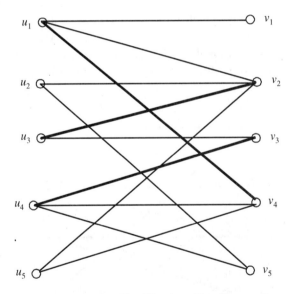

FIGURE 9.10(d)   Matching in a bipartite graph.

We start with the matching $M_1 = \{(u_1, v_4), (u_3, v_2), (u_4, v_3)\}$, which is not complete as shown in Figure 9.10(d). The augmenting path starts with an exposed vertex (let it be u_2) with respect to this matching. Let the augmenting path be $P_1 = \{u_2, v_2, u_3, v_3, u_4, v_5\}$. $M_2 = M_1 \oplus P_1 = \{(u_1, v_4), (u_2, v_2), (u_4, v_3), (u_4, v_5)\}$ has cardinality 4, one more than M_1.

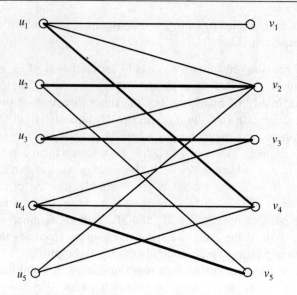

FIGURE 9.10(e)   Matching M_2 in a bipartite graph.

We now find an augmenting path with respect to M_2 starting with the free vertex u_5 [Figure 9.10(e)]. Let this path be $P_2 = \{u_5, v_4, u_1, v_1\}$. $M_3 = M_2 \oplus P_2 = \{(u_2, v_2), (u_3, v_3), (u_4, v_5), (u_5, v_4), (u_1, v_1)\}$ has cardinality 5. We cannot find any augmenting path with respect to M_3 and so the matching is perfect or complete [Figure 9.10(f)]. Moreover, there is no exposed node after this matching.

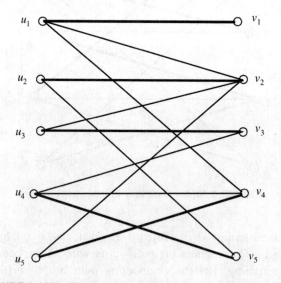

FIGURE 9.10(f)   Maximum matching M_3 in a bipartite graph.

SUMMARY

In this chapter, we have given a few graph-theoretic definitions and introduced the two widely used graph algorithms: depth-first search and breadth-first search. These two algorithms are quite useful for finding algorithmically other properties of graphs. We have shown how depth-first search is used for topological sorting of the nodes of a directed graph, finding the strongly-connected components of a graph, and finding the articulation points of a graph. We have also given algorithms for finding transitive closure and matching in bipartite graphs.

EXERCISES

9.1 Show how the depth-first search progresses through the following graph if the search starts from node 3 and the neighbours of a given node are examined: (a) in increasing numerical order, (b) in decreasing numerical order.

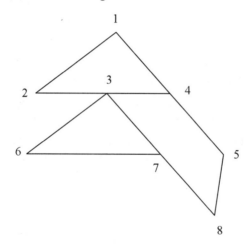

9.2 Analyze the running time of depth-first search if the input is given in the form of adjacency matrix.

9.3 Make a breadth-first search of $K_{3,3}$ and depth-first search of K_5.

9.4 From a given adjacency list representation of a directed graph, how do you find the in-degree and out-degree of the vertices? Analyze the algorithm.

9.5 The reverse of a directed graph $G = (V, E)$ is the graph $G^R = (V, E^R)$, where $E^R = \{(u, v) \mid (v, u) \in E\}$. Describe an algorithm to find G^R from G. Analyze the complexity of the algorithm.

9.6 Give an efficient algorithm to compute the diameter of a tree and analyze the running time of your algorithm.

9.7 Draw a Hamiltonian graph with 10 vertices and 20 edges. Construct a non-Hamiltonian graph with the same number of vertices and edges.

9.8 Test whether a given directed graph is acyclic using depth-first search.

9.9 Give an algorithm to find Euler circuit in a graph, provided one exists. (A connected, undirected graph has an Euler circuit if and only if every vertex is of even degree. Euler circuit is a path that starts and ends at the same vertex and includes each edge exactly once.)

9.10 Prove or disprove 'An undirected graph $G = (V, E)$ is bi-connected if and only if for each pair of distinct vertices u and v, there are two distinct paths from u to v that have no vertex in common except u and v'.

9.11 Find a topological ordering of the following graph:

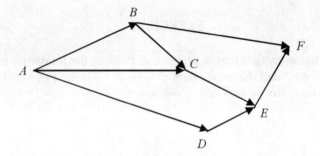

9.12 Give an algorithm to find a maximum spanning tree. Analyze its complexity.

9.13 Give an algorithm to find the minimum number of edges that need to be deleted from an undirected graph so that the resulting graph is acyclic.

9.14 Topological sorting on a directed acyclic graph may be carried out by removing nodes with in-degree zero one by one. Develop an algorithm for this and analyze its complexity for both the adjacency matrix and adjacency list representations.

9.15 What are strongly-connected components? Find algorithmically the strongly-connected components of the following graph:

9.16 Enumerate paths of all lengths in the graph of Problem 9.15.

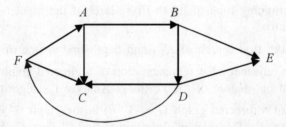

9.17 Find the articulation points of the following graph using the algorithm of Section 9.6.

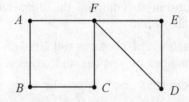

9.18 Find matching for the following graph:

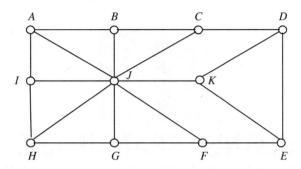

9.19 Find the minimum cost matching for the following weighted graph:

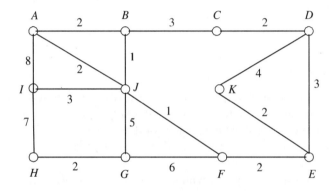

9.20 Let D be the maximum degree in a bipartite graph BG. Show that BG has a matching of size at least $|E|/D$.

9.21 Find the number of perfect matchings for the following graph with $2N$ nodes:

10

BACKTRACKING, BRANCH AND BOUND

10.0 INTRODUCTION

A *backtracking*[1] algorithm is a method of building up feasible solutions of a combinatorial optimization problem through enumeration. A backtracking algorithm is an exhaustive search; that is, all feasible solutions are considered and so it will always find the optimal solution. Pruning methods can be used to avoid considering some feasible solutions that are not optimal.

The solutions to the problems for which backtracking is useful are in the form of a vector, $X = (X_1, X_2, X_3, ..., X_N)$. The vector component, X_k is to be selected from a finite set S_k. There is a criterion function F of the feasible solution. The method calls for either maximization or minimization of $F(X)$. Suppose $m_k = |S_k|$. There are $m = m_1 m_2 m_3 m_4 ... m_N$ possibilities from which the solution(s) are to be found based on the criterion function. Backtracking algorithm finds the same answer as would be found by the brute force approach but it finds the solution with far fewer than m trials.

The solution vector is built component by component. We start with fixing the value of X_1 from the possible m_1 values. We then try to fix the value of X_2 from the possible m_2 values and so on. If at any stage, it is found that the partial vector generated so far $(X_1, X_2, X_3, ..., X_k)$ is not going to be part of the optimal solution ultimately, we look for an alternative to X_k. If for all possible values of X_k, there is no chance of ultimate success, we remove X_K from the partial solution and pay attention to fixing X_{k-1} again. If this time also, the chance of success is nil, we go to find an alternative value for X_{k-2}. This continues till we find a partial vector that has the chance of leading us to the ultimate solution. The major advantage of this method is that if at any stage of the search, it is found that the partial vector $(X_1, X_2, X_3, ..., X_k)$ can in no way lead to an optimal solution, then m_{k+1} $m_{k+2}, ..., m_N$ possible vectors may be ignored entirely.

---

[1] The name was coined by D.H. Lehmer.

10.1 4-QUEENS PROBLEM

Let us illustrate the method of backtracking with the 4-queens problem. We are given 4 queens to be placed on a 4 × 4 chessboard so that no two queens are on the same row, column or diagonals (both major and minor). A solution to the problem is a 4-tuple where queens are placed with the above constraints. We place each queen on a separate row so that the first constraint is satisfied. Queen Q_i, $1 \le i \le 4$ is placed on the ith row. Let us start with placing the first queen in the first column. Having placed the first queen in the first column, we cannot place the second queen in the first or the second column. We can place the second queen in the third column. Having placed the first and the second queens as above, we cannot place the third queen anywhere. So, we have to seek alternative placement for the queen two. We now place the second queen in the fourth column. Having placed the queen one in the column one, the queen two in the column four, we can place the queen three in the column two only. Having placed the queen one in the column one, the queen two in the column four and the queen three in the column two, we are not left with any room for placement of the

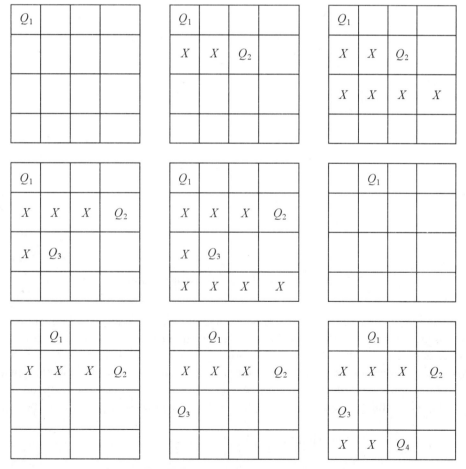

FIGURE 10.1 4-queens problem.

queen four. We now have to make backtracking and see whether there is any alternative cell for placement of the queen one that will eventually lead to a solution. We now start with placement of the queen one in the column two. Having placed the queen one in the column two, we can place the queen two in the column four only. We can then place the queen three in the column one. Having placed the queen one in the column two, the queen two in the column four and the queen three in the column one, we can place the queen four in the column three. So the vector (2, 4, 1, 3) represents a solution to the 4-queens problem as shown in Figure 10.1.

A search tree for the above problem is shown in Figure 10.2. The solution is generated by outputting the numbers appearing on the path from the root to the oval with darkened boundary. This search tree contains 16 nodes while the tree generated by brute force will contain 65 (= 1 + 4 + 12 + 24 + 24) nodes.

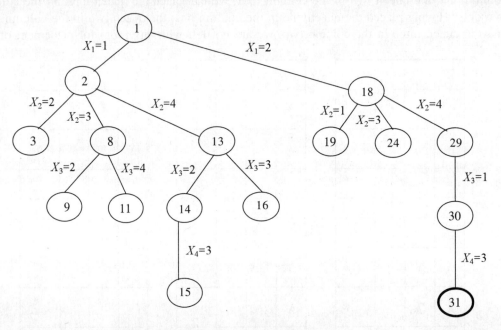

FIGURE 10.2 Search tree for 4-queens problem.

The above problem of 4-queens can be extended to the 8-queens problem. Here we have to place 8-queens on an 8×8 chess board with the same set of restrictions as in the case of the 4-queens problem. One solution to the 8-queens problem is (4, 6, 8, 2, 7, 1, 3, 5) where the first queen is placed on the row one, column number four, the second queen is placed on the row two, column six and so on. The general problem is to place n queens on an $n \times n$ chess board. The solution space for the n-queen's problem consists of n out of n^2 possibilities,

that is, $^{n^2}C_n = \dfrac{(n^2)!}{n!(n^2-n)!}$ possibilities.

10.2 SORTING

Let us see how backtracking can be used for sorting of numbers. We have a number of good sorting methods like quick-sort, merge-sort, etc. and so backtracking is not generally used for sorting. This example is just for the sake of illustrating the backtracking method. Let us assume that we have to sort a list of four numbers 15, 5, 55, 25 in ascending order. The solution is a 4-tuple whose first component is the least element of the given list, the second component is the second least element of the given list, and so on. The general problem of sorting n numbers in ascending (descending) order can be cast as an n-queens problem where the n queens having specific weights are to be placed on a line such that a heavier (lighter) queen cannot be on the left of a lighter (heavier) queen.

The search tree for this problem of sorting 4 numbers is shown in Figure 10.3. The sorted sequence is generated by outputting the numbers appearing on the path from the root to the oval with darkened boundary.

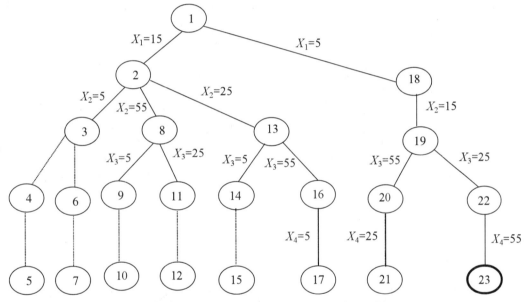

FIGURE 10.3 Search tree for sorting 4 numbers.

We have explored 16 nodes out of total 65 nodes. Let us now give a number of definitions connected with search tree nodes. Nodes are classified as: *Live, E-node* and *Dead nodes*. A node which has been generated and all of whose children have not yet been generated is called a *Live node*. *E-node* is a live node whose children are currently being generated. A *Dead node* is a generated node that is either not to be expanded further or one for which all of its children have been generated.

10.3 SUM OF SUBSETS PROBLEM

Given a set (S) of N objects with weights $(w_1, w_2, ..., w_N)$ and a value M, we have to find subsets of objects of S whose total weight equals M. As an example, let N be 4, M be 25 and the weight vector (w_1, w_2, w_3, w_4) be $(10, 25, 5, 10)$. The solutions may be represented in the form of fixed length 0/1 tuples or in the form of variable length tuples where the components of the tuples are the indices of the objects included in the solution. For the above example, fixed length solution tuples are $(0, 1, 0, 0)$ and $(1, 0, 1, 1)$. The above solutions in variable length tuples are (2) and $(1, 3, 4)$. Depending on the way of representation of the solutions, we will have different search trees.

Let us first discuss about the search tree for the fixed tuple case. We start at node 1. We then expand node 1 creating node 2 making $x_1 = 1$, meaning that object 1 is included in the subset. We then expand node 2 creating node 4 making $x_2 = 1$. These two objects make the sum 35 violating the problem constraint. We do not expand node 4 because no solution is possible in the sub-tree whose root is node 4. We then backtrack and explore the alternative branch from node 2 reaching node 5 with $x_2 = 0$. From node 5 we reach node 10 making $x_3 = 1$ and finally at the solution state represented by node 20 with $x_4 = 1$. So we reach the solution $(1, 0, 1, 1)$. For other solutions, there is no point in exploring further from node 10. We backtrack to node 5 and try the alternative. We explore node 11 and node 22. Since there is no solution on this branch, there is no point in exploring the other branch from node 11. No further exploration is possible from node 2. We look for the alternatives originating from node 1. We have an alternative path taking us to node 3 making $x_1 = 0$. We expand further from node 3 reaching node 6, making $x_2 = 1$. This is a solution state and no solution can then lie beyond node 6. So no further exploration in the sub-tree with node 6 as the root is made. If we are interested in further solutions, we explore the alternative branch originating from node 3. We explore nodes 7, 14 and 28 and find that this does not lead to any solution. We then explore the alternative path originating from node 7 and explore nodes 15 and 30 and discover no further solutions in these explorations. In the search tree shown in Figure 10.4, the solution states are shown by ovals with darkened boundary. We have explored 15 nodes while 23 $(= 1 + 2 + 4 + 8 + 8)$ nodes are possible in all.

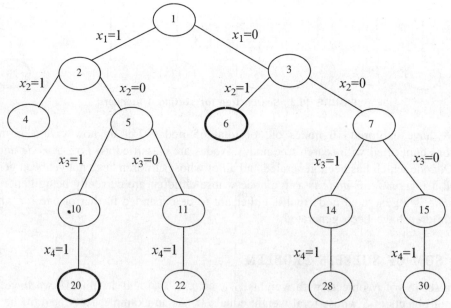

FIGURE 10.4   Search tree for sum of subsets problem (fixed tuple length).

We now describe the search tree for the variable length tuple representation case. We expand node 1 into nodes 2, 3, 4 and 5 making x_1 equal to 1, 2, 3, 4 respectively. We then expand node 2 into nodes 6, 7 and 8 making x_2 equal to 2, 3 and 4 respectively. Node 6 violates the constraint of the problem and therefore becomes dead. We then expand node 7 to node 10 and reach the solution (1, 3, 4). Node 8 becomes dead because no further choice for expansion is available. Node 3 is a solution state and no further expansion is possible. From node 4 we can reach node 9 only and no new solution is generated. From node 5, we have no hope left to find a solution. So, we have only two solutions and they are (1, 3, 4) and (2) in the variable tuple representation. The solution states are shown by ovals with thickened boundary in Figure 10.5.

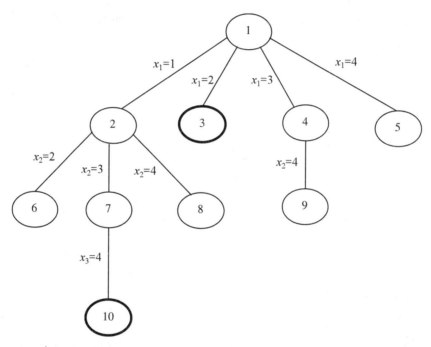

FIGURE 10.5   Search tree for sum of subsets problem (variable tuple length).

10.4   KNAPSACK PROBLEM

A problem instance of knapsack consists of a profit vector $P = (p_1, p_2, ..., p_n)$, a weight vector $W = (w_1, w_2, ..., w_n)$, a capacity C of the knapsack. It is required to find the maximum value of $\sum p_i x_i$ subject to $\sum w_i x_i \leq C$ and $x_i \in \{0, 1\}$ for all i. An n-tuple $(x_1, x_2, ..., x_n)$ of 0s and 1s is a feasible solution if $\sum w_i x_i \leq C$. One way of solving this problem is to try all 2^n possible n-tuples of 0s and 1s. We can build up an n-tuple, one candidate at a time by first choosing a value for x_1, then choosing a value for x_2, and so on. Backtracking provides a simple method for generating all the possible n-tuples. After each n-tuple is generated, it is checked for feasibility. If it is feasible, then its profit is compared to the current best solution found upto that point. The current best solution is updated whenever a better feasible solution is found.

Let CP be the current profit and CW be the current sum of the weights of the objects included in the partial solution. The above method generates 2^n binary n-tuples. This approach is impractical. Not all n-tuples of 0s and 1s are feasible. For the knapsack problem, one simple method of pruning is to observe that we must have $\sum_{i=1}^{i=k} w_i x_i \le C$ for any partial solution $(x_1, x_2, ..., x_k)$. In other words, we can check the partial solutions to see if the feasibility condition is satisfied. Consequently, if $k \le n$ we set current weight, $CW = \sum_{i=1}^{i=k} w_i x_i$ and then we have to consider x_k from $\{0, 1\}$ if $CW + w_k \le C$, otherwise from $\{0\}$.

Let us consider the knapsack problem instance: $n = 4$, $P = (2, 1, 4, 3)$, $W = (5, 3, 7, 6)$, $C = 11$. The search tree for the fixed length tuple approach is shown in Figure 10.6(a).

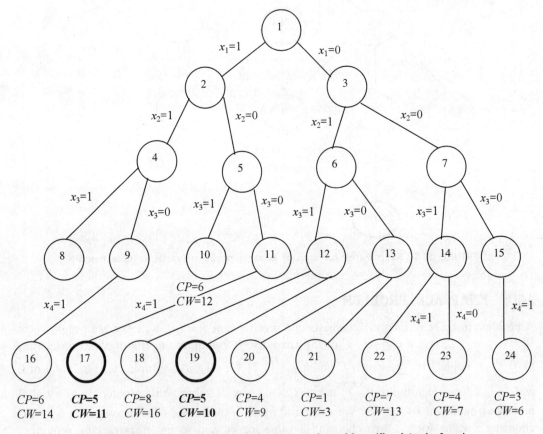

FIGURE 10.6(a)   State space tree for knapsack problem (fixed tuple form).

The solution states are 17 and 19 representing the solutions (1, 0, 0, 1) and (0, 1, 1, 0) respectively with the same profit 5. The search tree for the variable length tuple approach is shown in Figure 10.6(b).

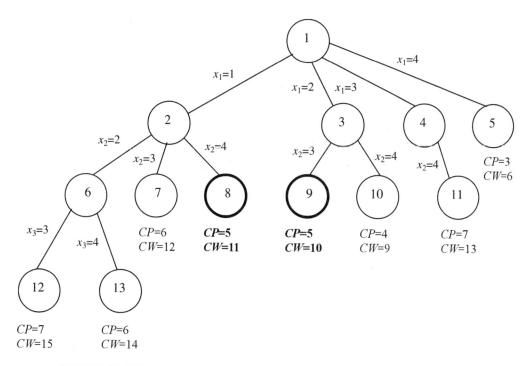

FIGURE 10.6(b)   State space tree for knapsack problem (variable tuple form).

The solution states are 8 and 9 representing the solutions (1, 4) and (2, 3) respectively with the same profit 5.

10.5   GENERATION OF ALL CLIQUES OF A GRAPH

To generate all the cliques of a graph $G = (V, E)$, we define k-*tuple* $(x_1, x_2, ..., x_k)$ of vertices a partial solution if and only if $(x_1, x_2, ..., x_k)$ is a clique. We denote $S_0 = \{\}$, $S_{k-1} = \{x_1, x_2, ..., x_{k-1}\}$, $S_k = \{x_k\} \cup S_{k-1}$. To avoid duplication, we impose a total ordering $<$ on the vertices V, and use them according to this ordering. That is, we think of V as an ordered list, $V = (v_1, v_2, ..., v_n)$ where $v_1 < v_2 < \cdots < v_n$. We define the choice set as $C_k = \{v \in V - S_{k-1} | (v, x) \in E$ for $x \in S_{k-1}$ and $v > x\}$, $C_0 = V$.

For the sake of illustration, we find out all the cliques in the graph of Figure 10.7. The state space tree is shown in Figure 10.8. The graph has a clique of size 4, 5 cliques of size 3, 8 cliques of size 2, and 5 cliques of size 1 as shown in the search tree.

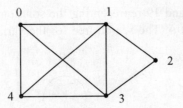

FIGURE 10.7 Example graph for all cliques problem.

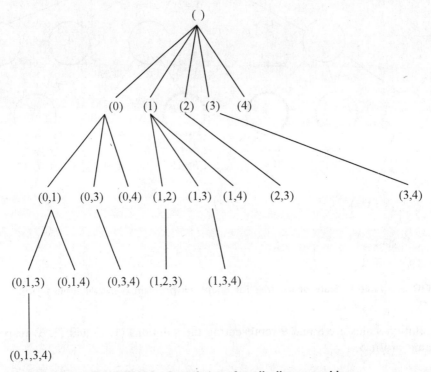

FIGURE 10.8 Search tree for all cliques problem.

10.6 BRANCH-AND-BOUND TECHNIQUE

Branch-and-bound is a technique for exploring an implicit directed acyclic graph like the backtracking method. Optimal solutions to some problems like assignment of tasks to workers, etc. can be found using the technique of branch-and-bound. At each node of the directed acyclic graph, we calculate a bound on the possible value of any solution that might lie further on in the graph. If the bound shows that any such solution must necessarily be worse than the best solution found so far, then we need not go on exploring this part of the graph. The difficulty with good bounding functions is that as they are implemented at each step, they may require more time than is saved by pruning the search tree. So, a decision is to be made whether it is more efficient to use better bounding functions and generate less nodes, or to use less effective bounding functions that take less time to calculate, but then we have to build up larger sub-trees.

There are a few important differences between backtracking and branch-and-bound algorithms. A backtracking algorithm does a pre-order depth-first search of the state space tree. A branch-and-bound algorithm is not restricted to a depth-first search of the state space tree; it may use a depth-first search if it needs so. Branch-and-bound technique generates nodes according to several rules; the most natural one is the best-first rule wherein the most promising node at the present moment is expanded first. A branch-and-bound technique must completely search the state space tree for an optimal value.

10.6.1 Assignment Problem

Let us first discuss about the assignment problem. We are given N tasks and N workers. All the workers can accomplish all these tasks but at different costs. We are given an $N \times N$ cost matrix whose $(i, j)^{th}$ entry indicates the cost of accomplishing the jth task by the ith worker. The problem is to make an assignment of these tasks to the workers, one task per worker so that all the tasks are accomplished with minimum cost. We solve this problem using branch and bound.

Let us consider the following cost matrix.

		Tasks →			
		1	2	3	4
Workers	A	90	12	50	51
↓	B	70	10	58	80
	C	16	85	8	70
	D	11	37	80	21

We can find an upper bound of the cost by making the assignments: task 1 to A, task 2 to B, task 3 to C and task 4 to D. The cost is $90 + 10 + 8 + 21 = 129$. We find a lower bound by picking up the minimum cost from each column and adding these: $11 + 10 + 8 + 21 = 50$. So the cost of any assignment should be in the range 50–129. The lower bound guides us in our decision for expanding the search tree nodes. At the first step in the searching for solution, we have the option of assigning worker A any of the tasks 1, 2, 3 and 4 with costs 90, 12, 50 and 51 respectively.

The option of assigning task 2 to worker A appears to be the best at this stage with the lowest cost. So we decide to explore further from this node. This is shown in Figure 10.9(a).

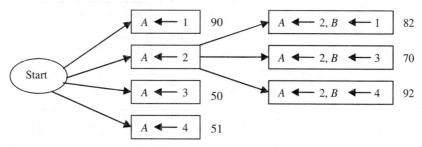

FIGURE 10.9(a) Exploration of search tree with worker A assigned task 2.

At this stage, the node for assignment of task 3 to worker A with cost 50 appears to be more promising and so we expand this node. Assignment costing more than the upper bound is shown with an asterisk. This is shown in Figure 10.9(b).

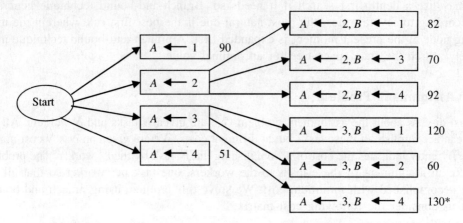

FIGURE 10.9(b)   **Exploration of search tree with worker A assigned task 3.**

We now find that the node where we have assigned task 4 to worker A is the most promising and so decide to explore starting from this node and the search tree will be as shown in Figure 10.9(c).

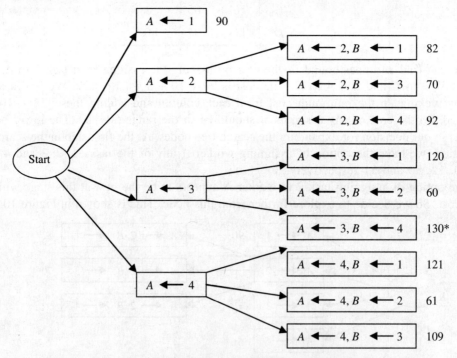

FIGURE 10.9(c)   **Exploration of search tree with worker A assigned task 4.**

At this stage the most promising node is the one with task 3 assigned to worker *A* and task 2 assigned to worker *B* with cost 60 and therefore, we expand this node for exploration. This is shown in Figure 10.9(d).

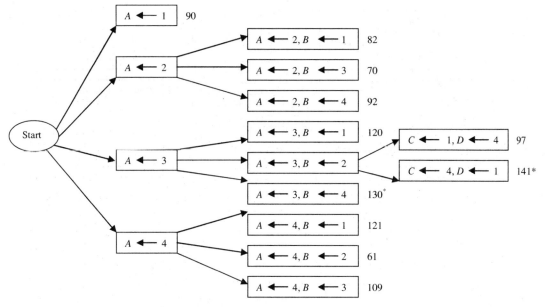

FIGURE 10.9(d) Exploration of search tree with worker *A* assigned task 3 and worker *B* assigned task 2.

At this stage the most promising node is the one with task 4 assigned to worker *A* and task 2 assigned to worker *B* with cost 61 and this node may be expanded for exploration. This is shown in Figure 10.9(e).

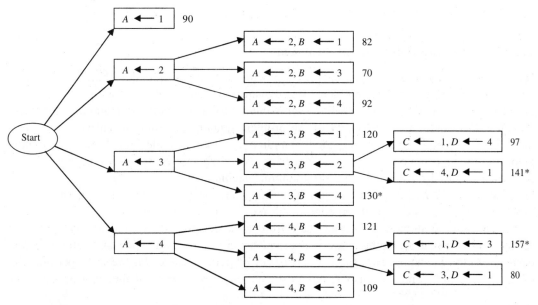

FIGURE 10.9(e) Exploration of search tree with worker *A* assigned task 4 and worker *B* assigned task 2.

At this stage the most promising node is the one with task 2 assigned to worker A and task 3 assigned to worker B with cost 70 and therefore this node may be expanded for exploration. This is shown in Figure 10.9(f).

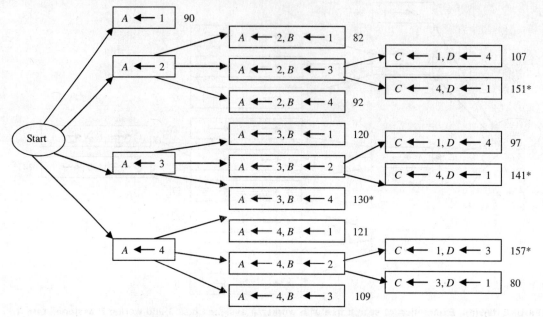

FIGURE 10.9(f) Search tree for assignment problem.

At this stage we have reached the optimal solution with task 4 assigned to the worker A, task 2 to worker B, task 3 to worker C, and task 1 assigned to worker D with a total cost 80. The Hungarian method solves this problem in polynomial time.

10.6.2 Traveling Salesperson Problem

We solve the traveling salesperson problem with branch-and-bound technique. We have already shown how to solve this problem using dynamic programming. The worst-case complexity of this problem was shown to be $O(N^2 2^N)$ for N-city tour with dynamic programming approach. Although the worst-case complexity of the problem remains the same when we use branch-and-bound technique, the use of good bounding functions enables the branch-and-bound algorithm to solve some problem instances of the traveling salesperson problem in much less time than required by the dynamic programming technique.

Let $G = (V, E)$ be a directed graph defining an instance of the traveling salesperson problem. Let m_{ij} be the cost of the edge (i, j). We assume $m_{ii} = \infty$ and $|V| = N$. Without loss of generality, we assume that the tour starts from some designated city (called city 1) and the salesperson visits all the other cities once and no city is visited twice and returns to the designated city. So the solution space S consists of $|P|$ points, where P is the set of permutation of $(2, 3, 4, \ldots, N)$. The size of S is obviously $(N - 1)!$. We represent the solution space by a state space tree. We define three cost functions c, l, and u, where $l(i) \leq c(i) \leq u(i)$ for all nodes i of the state space tree. The cost c is such that the solution node with the least value of c corresponds to a shortest tour in G. One possible choice for c is

$$c(i) = \begin{cases} \text{Length of tour defined by the path from the root to } i, \text{ if } i \text{ is a leaf.} \\ \text{Cost of a minimum cost leaf in the subtree } i, \text{ if } i \text{ is not a leaf.} \end{cases}$$

$l(i) = $ The length of the path defined at node i.

A better value of l can be obtained by using the reduced cost matrix corresponding to G. A row (column) is said to be reduced if it contains at least one zero and all the remaining entries are non-negative. A matrix is reduced if every row and every column is reduced. Let us consider the graph of Figure 10.10 and its cost matrix.

$$
\begin{array}{c c c c c}
 & A & B & C & D \\
A & \infty & 12 & 5 & 7 \\
B & 11 & \infty & 13 & 6 \\
C & 4 & 9 & \infty & 18 \\
D & 10 & 3 & 2 & \infty
\end{array}
$$

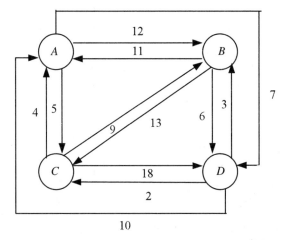

FIGURE 10.10   Example graph for the TSP problem.

Since every tour on this graph includes exactly one edge (i, j) with $i = k$, $1 \leq k \leq 4$, and exactly one edge (i, j) with $j = k$, $1 \leq k \leq 4$, subtracting a constant θ from every entry in a column or row of the cost matrix reduces the length of every tour by exactly θ. A minimum cost tour remains a minimum cost tour following the reduction. If θ is chosen to be the minimum entry in row i (column j), then subtracting it from all the entries in row i (column j) introduces a zero into row i (column j). Repeating this as often as needed, the cost matrix can be reduced. The total amount subtracted from the columns and rows is a lower bound on the length of a minimum-cost tour and can be used as the l-value for the root of the state space tree.

We associate a reduced cost matrix with every node in the traveling salesperson state space tree. Let M be the reduced cost matrix for node A and let B be a child of A such that the tree edge (A, B) corresponds to inclusion of edge (i, j) in the tour. If B is not a leaf, then the reduced cost matrix for B may be obtained as:

   (i) Change all the entries in row i, column j of M to ∞. This excludes use of any more edges leaving vertex i or entering vertex j.
  (ii) Set $M(j, 1)$ to ∞. This excludes use of the edge $(j, 1)$.
 (iii) Reduce all the rows and columns in the resulting matrix except for rows and columns containing only ∞.

If T is the total amount subtracted in step (iii), then $l(B) = l(A) + M(i, j) + T$. For leaf nodes, $l = c$ is easily computed as each leaf defines a unique tour. For the upper bound u, we assume $u(i) = \infty$ for all nodes i.

The search tree for the graph of Figure 10.10 is shown in Figure 10.11.

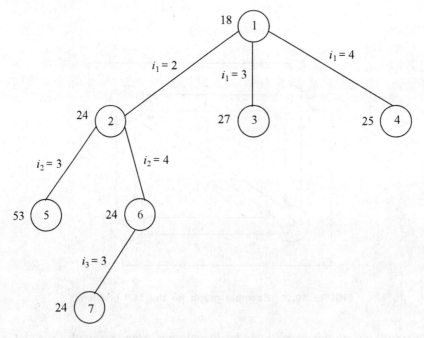

FIGURE 10.11 Search tree for the TSP problem.

The root of the search tree (node A) of the graph has the minimum cost 18. This is found by reducing the cost matrix M by subtracting 5 from row 1, 6 from row 2, 4 from row 3, 2 from row 4, and subtracting 1 from column 2. The total amount subtracted is 18. The minimum cost of the tour is at least 18 and the reduced cost matrix is:

$$
\begin{array}{c c c c c}
 & A & B & C & D \\
A & \begin{bmatrix} \infty & 6 & 0 & 2 \\ B & 5 & \infty & 7 & 0 \\ C & 0 & 4 & \infty & 14 \\ D & 8 & 0 & 0 & \infty \end{bmatrix}
\end{array}
$$

The reduced cost matrix at node 2 of the search tree following path (A, B) is:

$$
\begin{array}{c c c c c}
 & A & B & C & D \\
A & \begin{bmatrix} \infty & \infty & \infty & \infty \\ B & \infty & \infty & 7 & 0 \\ C & 0 & \infty & \infty & 14 \\ D & 8 & \infty & 0 & \infty \end{bmatrix}
\end{array}
$$

The minimum cost $l(2) = l(1) + M(1, 2) + T = 18 + 6 + 0 = 24$. The reduced cost matrix at node 3 of the search tree following the path (A, C) is:

$$
\begin{array}{c c c c c}
 & A & B & C & D \\
A & \begin{bmatrix} \infty & \infty & \infty & \infty \\ B & 0 & \infty & \infty & 0 \\ C & \infty & 0 & \infty & 10 \\ D & 3 & 0 & \infty & \infty \end{bmatrix}
\end{array}
$$

The minimum cost $l(3) = l(1) + M(1, 3) + T = 18 + 0 + 9 = 27$. The reduced cost matrix at node 4 in the search tree following the path (A, D) is:

$$
\begin{array}{c c c c c}
 & A & B & C & D \\
A & \begin{bmatrix} \infty & \infty & \infty & \infty \\ B & 0 & \infty & 2 & \infty \\ C & 0 & 4 & \infty & \infty \\ D & \infty & 0 & 0 & \infty \end{bmatrix}
\end{array}
$$

The minimum cost $l(4) = l(1) + M(1, 4) + T = 18 + 2 + 5 = 25$. At this stage, we find that the path (A, B) is the most promising with the minimum cost 24 and so we expand the node 2.

The node 5 is generated following the path (A, B, C). The reduced cost matrix at node 5 is:

$$
\begin{array}{c}
\begin{array}{cccc} A & B & C & D \end{array} \\
\begin{array}{c} A \\ B \\ C \\ D \end{array}
\begin{bmatrix}
\infty & \infty & \infty & \infty \\
\infty & \infty & \infty & \infty \\
\infty & \infty & \infty & 0 \\
0 & \infty & \infty & \infty
\end{bmatrix}
\end{array}
$$

The minimum cost $l(5) = l(2) + M(2, 3) + T = 24 + 7 + 22 = 53$. The reduced cost matrix at node 6 in the search tree following the path (A, B, D) is:

$$
\begin{array}{c}
\begin{array}{cccc} A & B & C & D \end{array} \\
\begin{array}{c} A \\ B \\ C \\ D \end{array}
\begin{bmatrix}
\infty & \infty & \infty & \infty \\
\infty & \infty & \infty & \infty \\
0 & \infty & \infty & \infty \\
\infty & \infty & 0 & \infty
\end{bmatrix}
\end{array}
$$

The minimum cost $l(6) = l(2) + M(2, 4) + T = 24 + 0 + 0 = 24$. The most promising node to expand now is node 6 and we generate node 7 following the path (A, B, D, C). The reduced cost matrix at node 7 is:

$$
\begin{array}{c}
\begin{array}{cccc} A & B & C & D \end{array} \\
\begin{array}{c} A \\ B \\ C \\ D \end{array}
\begin{bmatrix}
\infty & \infty & \infty & \infty \\
\infty & \infty & \infty & \infty \\
0 & \infty & \infty & \infty \\
\infty & \infty & \infty & \infty
\end{bmatrix}
\end{array}
$$

The minimum cost $l(7) = l(8) + M(4, 3) + T = 24 + 0 + 0 = 24$. So the optimal tour of the traveling salesperson will be A to B, B to D, D to C and C to A costing 24 as shown in Figure 10.12.

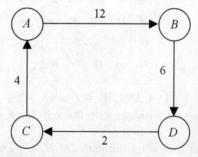

FIGURE 10.12 Optimal tour of the TSP.

SUMMARY

In this chapter we showed how backtracking is used in solving many search problems. The problems we have solved using this technique include 4-queens, knapsack, sorting, generation of all cliques of a graph, sum of subsets problem. The branch and bound technique helps to cut down futile search in those branches of search tree that does not appear promising. We have used branch-and-bound technique to solve worker assignment and TSP problems for illustration. Backtracking and branch-and-bound both traverse a 'state space tree'. Backtracking uses depth-first search while the branch-and-bound technique may traverse the tree in any manner. Branch-and-bound technique is used only to solve optimization problems. These two techniques are most often used on problems having potentially exponential or factorial time complexity.

EXERCISES

10.1 Solve the TSP problem having the following cost-matrix using branch-and-bound technique.

$$
\begin{array}{c c c c c}
 & A & B & C & D \\
A & \infty & 5 & 2 & 3 \\
B & 4 & \infty & 1 & 5 \\
C & 4 & 2 & \infty & 3 \\
D & 7 & 6 & 8 & \infty
\end{array}
$$

10.2 Make a comparative study on your machine of the backtracking and the Las Vegas algorithms for n-queens problems. Take $n = 4, 8, 16, 32, 64$.

10.3 Make comparative empirical study of the dynamic programming, branch-and-bound, greedy approaches to the 0/1 integer and knapsack problems.

10.4 Design computer experiments to study the effectiveness of branch-and-bound, and backtracking techniques for TSP.

10.5 Solve the following 0/1 knapsack problem using branch-and-bound technique: $P = (11, 21, 31, 33)$, $W = (2, 11, 22, 15)$, $C = 40$, $n = 4$.

10.6 Find a Hamiltonian circuit in the following graph using backtracking.

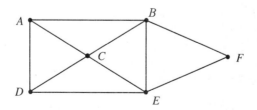

10.7 Generate all permutations of $\{a, b, c, d\}$ using backtracking.

10.8 Solve the TSP problem for the following graph using branch-and-bound technique.

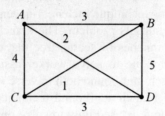

10.9 Solve the 5-queens problem using backtracking.

10.10 Generate all the cliques of the graph of Problem 10.6 using the algorithm of Section 10.5.

10.11 Which formulation of backtracking requires less time: fixed length or the variable length tuple approach? Demonstrate empirically on your computer.

10.12 Draw the search tree to colour the graph with the three colours: red, blue, green.

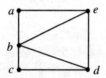

10.13 The sum of subsets problem is to find all combinations of the n given distinct numbers whose sum is M. Draw the state space tree for the problem with the numbers 7, 5, 12, 18, 20, 8 and $M = 25$.

10.14 Design a backtracking algorithm to find all the Hamiltonian cycles in a Hamiltonian graph. What is the worst-case time complexity of the algorithm?

10.15 Write a pseudocode for the assignment problem.

11

LOWER BOUND TECHNIQUES

11.0 INTRODUCTION

Lower bound denotes the minimum resources required to solve a computational problem. The resources include time and space. The objective of finding lower bound is to understand what minimum resources are required to solve a problem using any algorithm. Lower bound indicates the inherent computational complexity of the given problem. We shall be discussing about time complexity only in this chapter.

No algorithm takes time less than the lower bound. Finding lower bound is often difficult. However, in many cases we can trivially find the lower bound. For example, finding the maximum element from a given array of N unordered elements has a lower bound $\Omega(N)$, because every element must be examined. Multiplication of two $N \times N$ matrices has a lower bound of $\Omega(N^2)$ because N^2 elements of the product matrix must be computed. Any algorithm for generating all the permutations of N distinct elements has a lower bound $\Omega(N!)$ since the size of the output is $N!$. The problem of evaluating a polynomial of degree N at a given point has a lower bound $\Omega(N)$ since all the coefficients have to be processed by any algorithm for polynomial evaluation.

Why do we need to find lower bounds? Knowledge of the lower bound for a problem helps us decide whether a given algorithm for the problem is optimal or not. We do not have to compare the given algorithm with all possible algorithms (known and unknown) to decide the optimality. If the given algorithm's time complexity is higher than that of the lower bound, then there is the possibility of improvement. If the given algorithm's time complexity matches with the lower bound, it indicates that the performance of the algorithm cannot be improved in the asymptotic sense; however, improvement may be made through finding a smaller multiplicative constant.

The important methods available for proving lower bounds are: comparison tree, adversary argument, reduction techniques, input/output argument, etc. In this chapter, we shall be discussing comparison tree, adversary argument and reduction method. Input/output arguments are simple but in many cases they lead to trivial lower bounds. For the N-city TSP, the input-output argument gives the lower bound $\Omega(N^2)$ as there are $N(N-1)/2$ intercity distances. This bound is of no use as there is no known polynomial time algorithm for TSP.

11.1 COMPARISON (DECISION) TREE

Comparison (decision) tree is used for representing comparison-based algorithms like sorting, searching, etc. No arithmetic involving the elements is done but elements can be compared and exchanged. To sort three distinct elements $A(1)$, $A(2)$ and $A(3)$ the comparisons to be made can conveniently be represented by a tree having $3! = 6$ leaves as shown in Figure 11.1. In the interior nodes of the tree, we have labels like $A(i)?A(j)$ representing that we are comparing $A(i)$ and $A(j)$ at this node. The input could be any possible permutation. There is one leaf in the tree corresponding to each permutation.

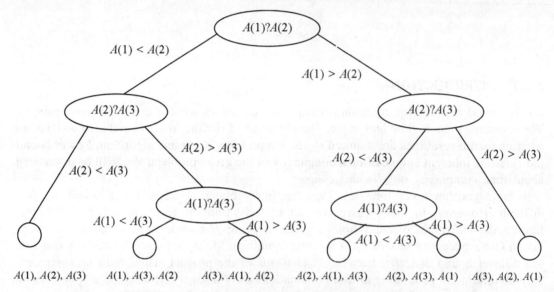

FIGURE 11.1 Comparison tree for sorting three elements.

11.1.1 Sorting

Let us use the comparison tree to find the lower bound for sorting. Let $T(N)$ be the minimum number of comparisons that are sufficient to sort N elements in the worst case. If all the internal nodes are at levels less than K, then there are at most 2^K leaf nodes, one more than the number of internal nodes. Therefore, if we let $K = T(N)$, then $N! \leq 2^{T(N)}$. Since, $T(N)$ is an integer, we get the lower bound $T(N) \geq \lceil \log(N!) \rceil$.

However, from Stirling's approximation for the logarithm of factorial, we have

$$\lceil \log(N!) \rceil = N \log N - N/(ln\ 2) + 0.5 \log N + O(1).$$

Hence, $T(N)$ is bounded from bottom by $N \log N$. So any comparison based sorting algorithm needs $\Omega(N \log N)$ time.

11.1.2 Searching

Suppose we have to search for an element from an ordered array A so that $A(1) < A(2) < \cdots < A(N)$. Let $T(N)$ be the minimum number of comparisons needed in the worst case to decide whether a given element $x \in A$. Let us consider all possible comparison trees for the searching problem. The value of $T(N)$ is greater than or equal to the longest path from the root to a leaf in such a tree. There must be N internal nodes in all these comparison trees corresponding to the N possible positions of occurrence of x in the array A. If all the internal nodes of a binary tree are at levels less than or equal to K, then there are at most $2^K - 1$ internal nodes. Then, $N \le 2^K - 1$ or $K \ge \log(N + 1)$. Hence, $T(N) = K \ge \lceil \log(N + 1) \rceil$.

11.2 REDUCTION METHOD

A problem $\Pi 1$ reduces to another problem $\Pi 2$ in time $T(N)$ if an instance of $\Pi 1$ can be converted to an instance of $\Pi 2$ and a solution for $\Pi 1$ can be found from a solution of $\Pi 2$ in time less than or equal to $T(N)$. To show that the problem $\Pi 2$ is at least as hard as another problem $\Pi 1$ with a known lower bound, we need to reduce $\Pi 1$ to $\Pi 2$. For an example, consider the problem $\Pi 1$ to be the selection problem and $\Pi 2$ to be the sorting problem. If we have to select the ith smallest element from a given array A of N elements, we first sort the array in ascending order and then pick up the element $A(i)$. So the selection problem reduces to the sorting problem.

The technique may be used to find the lower bound of one problem $\Pi 1$ or $\Pi 2$ while we have lower bound information for the other of the problems $\Pi 1$ and $\Pi 2$. Let us consider two sets S_1 and S_2, each with N elements. The problem $\Pi 1$ is to check whether the two sets are disjoint or not, that is whether $S_1 \wedge S_2 = \Phi$. We select $\Pi 2$ as the sorting problem. We show that $\Pi 1$ reduces to $\Pi 2$ in $O(N)$ time as described below. Let,

$$S_1 = \{k_1, k_2, ..., k_N\} \quad \text{and} \quad S_2 = \{r_1, r_2, ..., r_N\}.$$

We create an instance X of $\Pi 2$ of size $2N$ as

$$X = (k_1, 1), (k_2, 1), ..., (k_N, 1), (r_1, 2), (r_2, 2), ..., (r_N, 2).$$

We sort X in lexicographic order creating X'. Construction of X from S_1 and S_2 requires $O(N)$ time. Once we have the sorted sequence X', we can scan the elements of X' from the left to the right and check whether there are two successive elements $(l, 1)$ and $(m, 2)$ such that $l = m$. If there is no such element in X', then S_1 and S_2 are disjoint. Checking this in X' requires $O(N)$ time.

So, we conclude that checking disjointedness of two sets, each having N elements, has the lower bound $\Omega(N \log N) - O(N) = \Omega(N \log N)$ at most.

We take the problem of convex hull to further illustrate the reduction technique for finding the lower bound. Given N points in the plane, the problem is to identify the vertices of the hull in some order. This problem also requires $\Omega(N \log N)$ time. We use $\Pi 1$ as the sorting problem and $\Pi 2$ as the convex hull problem.

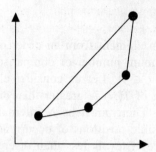

FIGURE 11.2   Reduction of sorting to convex hull problem.

Let $\Pi 1$ be the problem of sorting the numbers $X = x_1, x_2, ..., x_N$. We create an instance of $\Pi 2$ as the collection of N points on the plane (shown in Figure 11.2) as:

$$(x_1, x_1^2), (x_2, x_2^2), ..., (x_N, x_N^2).$$

Generation of these N points require $O(N)$ time. The convex hull of these N points will have these N points as the vertices ordered according to the x-coordinate values. If $H = (k_1, k_1^2), (k_2, k_2^2), ..., (k_N, k_N^2)$ is the output (in counterclockwise order) for $\Pi 2$, we can identify the point of H with the least x-coordinate in $O(N)$ time. If (k', k'^2) is this point, the sorted order of X is the x-coordinate of points in H starting with k' and moving counterclockwise. Thus finding the output for $\Pi 1$ from the solution of $\Pi 2$ requires $O(N)$ time. Therefore, computing the convex hull of N given points on a plane requires $\Omega(N \log N)$ time.

Let us consider the Euclidean minimum spanning tree problem. Given N points on the Cartesian plane, we have to construct a tree of minimum total length whose vertices are the given points. Let us use the element uniqueness problem ($\Pi 1$) as a problem with a known lower bound ($N \log N$). We transform any set $x_1, x_2, ..., x_N$ of N real numbers into a set of N points in the Cantesian plane as $(x_1, 0), (x_2, 0), ..., (x_N, 0)$ in $O(N)$ time. Let T be a minimum spanning tree for this set of points. Verifying whether T contains a zero-length edge will answer the question about uniqueness of the given numbers. This verification requires $O(N)$ time. This reduction implies that $\Omega(N \log N)$ is a lower bound for the Euclidean minimum spanning tree problem too.

11.3   ADVERSARY ARGUMENT

To use adversary arguments for proving lower bound of any algorithm solving a problem, the adversary gives an input at each point in the algorithm where a decision is made such that the algorithm is made to work more to provide the result. The adversary gradually constructs a bad input instance for the algorithm while it answers the questions. The adversary's answers are internally consistent, that is, all the answers taken together are consistent. It is some valid input but the most difficult input for the algorithm. If the adversary can manage to force the algorithm to perform $T(N)$ steps, then $T(N)$ is a lower bound for the number of steps needed in the worst case. To arrive at a good lower bound, the adversary should be as clever as possible to make the algorithm work harder. A lower bound is obtained by measuring the amount of work needed to shrink a set of potential inputs to a single input along the most time-consuming path.

11.3.1 Selection

Selection is an important problem in data processing. Selection problem involves finding the maximum, minimum, k^{th} maximum, k^{th} minimum elements from a collection of elements. The decision tree model provides the worst-case lower bound of $\lceil \log(N + 1) \rceil$ for the search problem. This is the number of comparisons required for the binary search. This lower bound is good for the binary search but the decision tree model does not give good lower bound for the selection problem. A decision tree for the selection problem must have at least N leaves because any one of the N keys in the collection may be the output, that is, it could be the k-th smallest element. Thus, we may infer that the height of the tree (and the number of comparisons done in the worst case) is at least $\lceil \log N \rceil$. This is not at all a good lower bound as finding the largest key requires $N - 1$ comparisons.

Let us now see how adversary arguments are used to establish a better lower bound for the problem of finding the maximum and the minimum elements. We assume that all the keys are distinct. For a key k_1 to be the maximum, it should not have lost any comparison. Similarly, for a key k_2 to be the minimum, it should not have won any comparison. If we count each win as one unit of information, and each loss as one unit of information, an algorithm to decide the minimum and the maximum elements correctly must collect at least $(N - 1) + (N - 1) = 2N - 2$ units of information. The adversary adopts a strategy to give as minimum units of new information as possible to the algorithm with each comparison. We describe the state of a key as 'V' meaning that the key has won at least one comparison and never lost a comparison, 'D' meaning the key has lost at least one comparison and never won a comparison, 'VD' meaning the key has won and lost at least one comparison, 'E' meaning the key has not yet faced any comparison. Every time a key enters the 'V' state or the 'D' state, the algorithm gains one unit of information. A state of 'E' does not convey any information. Table 11.1 elaborates how the algorithm gains information from key comparisons.

TABLE 11.1 Key comparisons in adversary arguments for finding maximum and minimum elements

Status of keys (k_1, k_2) involved in comparison	Adversary responds	New states of keys (k_1, k_2)	Units of new information generated
(E, E)	$k_1 > k_2$	(V, D)	2
(V, E) or (VD, E)	$k_1 > k_2$	(V, D) or (VD, D)	1
(D, E)	$k_1 < k_2$	(D, V)	1
(V, V)	$k_1 > k_2$	(V, VD)	1
(D, D)	$k_1 > k_2$	(VD, D)	1
(V, D) or (VD, D) or (V, VD)	$k_1 > k_2$	No change	0
(VD, VD)	Consistent reply	No change	0

The adversary passes on at most 1 unit of new information to the algorithm through his/her reply except in the case where both the keys have never participated in any comparison.

In the latter case, the adversary passes two units of new information. The algorithm can get 2 units of information from one comparison where the two keys have not been involved in any previous comparison. An algorithm can exploit at most $N/2$ such comparisons so that it can get at most N units of information. From the other comparisons, the algorithm can get at most 1 unit of new information. The algorithm needs at least $N - 2$ units of additional information. The algorithm must do at least $N - 2$ more comparisons. Thus to get $2N - 2$ units of information, the algorithm must do $(N/2) + N - 2 = (3N/2) - 2$ comparisons in total.

This lower bound is better than that provided by the decision tree model. We reach this bound by pairing up the elements into $N/2$ groups and making comparison in each group to find $N/2$ winners and $N/2$ losers. This requires $N/2$ comparisons. Next, the maximum of the winners is found through $(N/2) - 1$ comparisons. Similarly, the minimum of the losers is found through $(N/2) - 1$ comparisons. So the total number of comparisons required is $(3N/2) - 2$. $\Omega(N)$ is a lower bound of this problem.

11.3.2 Median Finding

We now use adversary arguments to find the lower bound to the median finding problem. Without loss of generality, we assume that the keys are all distinct. To find the median, an algorithm must know the relation of every other key to the median. For any key k, the algorithm must know that k is either greater than the median or is less than the median. We brand a comparison as essential or non-essential. A comparison is called essential if it is the first comparison for k_1, where, $k_1 > k_2$ for some $k_2 >$ median or $k_1 < k_2$ for some $k_2 <$ median. Other comparisons are termed non-essential. The essential comparison fixes the relation of k_1 to the median. An adversary forces an algorithm to make more non-essential comparisons. The adversary chooses some value for the median and assigns a value to a key when the algorithm uses that key in a comparison. So long as he/she can do so, the adversary will assign values to the new keys involved in a comparison so as to put the keys on opposite sides of the median. The adversary may not assign values larger than the median to more than $(N - 1)/2$ keys, nor values smaller than the median to more than $(N - 1)/2$ keys. The adversary keeps track of the assignment to the keys to ensure non-violation of these restrictions. Let us denote the status of a key by 'Sup', 'Inf', 'E'. 'Sup' represents that the key has been assigned a value larger than the median, 'Inf' represents that the key has been assigned a value less than the median, 'E' represents that the key has not been involved in comparison. The adversary's action for these states of the key are as shown in Table 11.2.

TABLE 11.2   Key comparisons in adversary arguments for finding median (non-essential)

States of keys (k_1, k_2)	Adversary's action
(E, E)	Makes $k_1 > k_2$
(Sup, E) or (E, Sup)	Assigns a value smaller than median to the key with status E
(Inf, E) or (E, Inf)	Assigns a value larger than median to the key with status E

Each of the above comparisons is non-essential. These create at most one 'Sup' key and at most one 'Inf' key. In all the cases, if there are already $(N - 1)/2$ keys with status

'Sup' or 'Inf', the adversary ignores the above rules and assigns values greater (or smaller) than the median to the new keys. When only one key without a value remains, the adversary assigns the value median to that key. Whenever the algorithm compares two keys with status (Sup, Sup) or (Inf, Inf) or (Sup, Inf), the adversary simply gives the correct response based on the values he/she has already assigned to the keys.

Since the adversary is free to make the indicated assignments until there are $(N - 1)/2$ 'Sup' keys or $(N - 1)/2$ 'Inf' keys, he/she can force any algorithm to do at least $(N - 1)/2$ non-essential comparisons. The total number of comparisons consists of $(N - 1)$ essential comparisons and $(N - 1)/2$ non-essential comparisons. So any algorithm to find the median of N keys must do at least $3(N - 1)/2$ comparisons in the worst case. Median finding problem has a lower bound $\Omega(N)$.

SUMMARY

Proving lower bound for an arbitrary problem is in general very difficult. However, we have some simple techniques to prove lower bounds for some selected problems. In this chapter, we have given a brief introduction to some of these techniques for proving lower bounds. The techniques we have used are decision tree for proving lower bounds for sorting and searching, reduction method for convex hull and Euclidean minimum spanning tree, adversary argument for selection and median finding problems. We have not attempted to discuss lower bounds for algebraic problems that are usually found in other texts. Proving tight lower bounds for many interesting problems are challenging.

EXERCISES

11.1 Prove that any comparison-based sorting technique needs $\Omega(N \log N)$ time for sorting N elements.

11.2 What is the minimum number of comparisons required to find the median of the following list of elements? 2, –3, 12, 5, 40, 7, 11.

11.3 Show that the median of five distinct values can be found with no more than six comparisons.

11.4 Draw the comparison tree for sorting 4 elements.

11.5 Show that any computation for evaluating the following expressions requires at least four multiplications: $ac + bd, bc + ad, ac - bd, bc - ad$.

11.6 Draw the decision tree for quick-sorting 4 elements.

11.7 Develop an algorithm to sort five keys with only seven comparisons in the worst case.

11.8 Prove the lower bound for searching for a key in an ordered array using adversary argument.

11.9 How many arithmetic operations are required by a fast algorithm to evaluate

$$P(x) = \sum_{k=0}^{k=n} {}^{n}C_k x^k \text{ , where } {}^{n}C_k \text{ are the binomial coefficients.}$$

11.10 Show how to multiply two complex numbers $x = a + ib$ and $y = c + id$ using only three scalar multiplications.

11.11 What is the lower bound of time complexity of any algorithm finding the 5th largest key from n distinct keys?

11.12 The partitioning operation in quick-sort on an array of n elements requires $\theta(n)$ time. Prove it.

11.13 Show that the lower bound of the time required for heap-sort of n elements is $n \log n$.

GENETIC ALGORITHMS

12.0 INTRODUCTION

John Holland[1] founded the field of genetic algorithms (GAs) in the early seventies. The philosophy behind the use of genetic algorithms is based on the principle of natural selection in evolutionary processes. In nature, each species faces challenges for survival because of the harsh environment. The species adapt themselves to the environment for survival. Those species that are fitter for the environment survive and those with lesser fitness disappear. Genetic algorithms are search methods based on 'survival of the fittest' and natural genetics. These algorithms use randomness in the selection, reproduction, mutation and such other operators inspired by the natural genetics.

Just as simulated annealing, a stochastic search technique derived from statistical mechanics and inspired by the annealing process in physical sciences is used to find globally near optimal solutions to hard problems, genetic algorithms have found a large number of applications in optimization, automatic programming, machine learning, economics, ecology, VLSI design and many other areas. The major difference between genetic algorithm and simulated annealing is that simulated annealing deals with a single potential solution at a time whereas genetic algorithm deals with a collection of potential solutions at a time.

12.1 HOW TO USE GENETIC ALGORITHMS?

Genetic algorithms work with a population of the potential solutions of the candidate problem represented in the form of chromosomes. Each chromosome is composed of variables called genes. Each chromosome (*genotype*) maps to a fitness value (*phenotype*) on the basis of the objective function of the candidate problem.

---

[1] Holland, J.H, *Adaptation in Natural and Artificial Systems,* University of Michigan Press, 1975.

To use a genetic algorithm for a particular problem, we must first decide on:

  (i) how to represent potential solutions of a problem in the form of chromosomes,

  (ii) a way to create an initial population of potential solutions,

 (iii) the evaluation function for rating the potential solutions in terms of fitness,

 (iv) selection of individuals from the current population for applying genetic operators like cross-over, mutation, etc.,

  (v) the values of the parameters like initial population size, cross-over probability, mutation probability, etc., and

 (vi) when to terminate the algorithm?

12.2 HOW DOES A GENETIC ALGORITHM WORK?

A genetic algorithm is generally started with a randomly generated population of individuals[2]. These individuals are potential solutions of the problem under study. Three genetic operators, namely, *selection*, *crossover* and *mutation* work on these individuals. A selection method is used to select the individuals according to their fitness values. The selected individuals reproduce to create the next generation. The crossover operator recombines the individuals selected for reproduction with a pre-specified probability of crossover. The mutation operator induces changes in the chromosomes by complementing each bit of an individual with a pre-specified probability of mutation. The following pseudocode outlines the working of a simple genetic algorithm:

```
Procedure GA
  Generation = 0;
  Generate Initial Population P(0);
  Find Fitness of the Individuals in P(0);
  While (Termination Condition Not Satisfied) Do
    Generation = Generation + 1;
    Select P(Generation) from P(Generation - 1) based on fitness;
    Change Individuals in P(Generation) through Genetic Operators;
    Find Fitness of the Individuals in P(Generation);
  Endwhile
End GA
```

Binary representation is common in genetic algorithms. The potential solutions are represented in the form of binary strings. Suppose there are 10 objects in a knapsack problem and we pick up the objects 2, 5, 7 to be put in the knapsack, the solution may be represented as 0100101000. Real values in numerical functions may also be represented using bit vector. The length of the vector depends on the required precision. Suppose we want to represent a variable x in the range $[-1, 2]$ and the precision should be 6 places after the decimal point. This will require 22 bits as a binary vector (chromosome) since $2^{21} < 3000000 \leq 2^{22}$.

---

[2] Individual, chromosome and string mean the same thing in this chapter.

The mapping from a binary string into a real number x in the range $[-1, 2]$ is straightforward. The binary string is converted to decimal string x' and the real number x is found as $x = -1.0 + 3x'/(2^{22} - 1)$. The above two representations may not be suitable for certain other problems like traveling salesperson problem. If we adopt binary representation of N-city TSP problem, each city should be coded as a string of $\lceil \log_2 N \rceil$ bits and a chromosome (solution) will be of $N \lceil \log_2 N \rceil$ bits. A mutation can result in a sequence of cities, which is not a tour; we may get the same city twice in a sequence.

The binary string representation of potential solutions may not be suitable for all applications. We have to look for alternative representations depending on the problem. We may use real-value representation for problems like numerical function optimization. The permutation coding is commonly used for the TSP.

To apply the above algorithm, we need to clearly spell out how the initial population is formed. This is usually generated through random mechanism. Each individual in the initial population is randomly generated.

The evaluation function can take different forms depending on the problem. For the 0/1 knapsack problem, the evaluation function could be the total profit earned. For the 1-dimensional bin packing problem, it could be the average of the square of the occupancy ratio of the bins. For the TSP problem, it could be the cost of the tour. For most of the applications, formulation of the fitness function is obvious from the problem statement. However, for some problems formulation of a useful fitness function is nontrivial.

There are many choices of selection methods. The notable among them are *proportionate selection*, *rank selection*, *tournament selection*, etc. In the case of proportionate selection, individuals are selected for reproduction based on their fitness values. The higher the fitness value, the higher is its probability of reproduction. In this scheme, the highly fit individuals get more chances of propagating their genetic materials to the next generation while individuals with very low fitness values are likely to be deprived of the chance to propagate their genetic materials to the next generation.

After the selection probabilities have been assigned to an individual with a selection scheme, the individuals may be selected for reproduction with the 'roulette-wheel' sampling that works as:

1. Let C = sum of the expected values of selection of the individuals in the population.
2. Repeat step 3 twice to select the two parents for mating.
3. Generate a uniform random integer r between 1 and C. Loop through the population, summing the expected values of the individuals, and select the individual where the sum is greater than r.
4. Repeat step 2 till the number of individuals generated is equal to the population size.

Controlling predominance of individuals with higher values of fitness taking lion's share in reproduction, rank selection is used. In rank selection, individual with rank i (in terms of fitness values) gets a chance for reproduction proportional to $2i/(n(n + 1))$, where n is the number of individuals in the population.

Tournament selection is similar to rank selection in terms of selection pressure, but it is computationally more efficient and more amenable to parallel implementation. It proceeds as follows. Two individuals are chosen from the present population at random. A random number r is then generated between 0 and 1. If $r < k$ (where k is a given parameter, a typical value is 0.75), the fitter of the two individuals is selected to be a parent; otherwise the less fit individual is selected. The two are then returned to the original population and can be selected again.

Steady state genetic algorithms select a few (say 2) individuals that are subjected to the genetic operators. If the offsprings thus produced are better than the worst individuals in the population, they replace the worst individuals. The steady state GA stagnates and it keeps making more trials on the existing population for a very large number of generations. This method is used in rule-based systems.

Elitism can be part of any selection method. It ensures that the best individual is passed on unperturbed to the subsequent population. It is difficult to rebuild a highly fit chromosome due to the disruptive effect of genetic operators. Elitism retains such chromosomes to guide the search towards the global optimum.

The two important genetic operators used in GA are crossover and mutation. The operators help to exploit and explore the search space. Crossover operator helps in the exploration of the potential solutions available at the present population and the mutation operator brings diversity in the population of potential solutions. The crossover could be 1-point or multipoint. Through crossover, progeny shares the genetic material of its parents. We illustrate below 1-point crossover using binary representation.

$$
\begin{array}{lll}
1\ 0\ 0\ \big|\ 1\ 1\ 0\ 1 & \text{Crossover} & 1\ 0\ 0\ 0\ 1\ 0\ 1 \\
0\ 1\ 1\ \big|\ 0\ 1\ 0\ 1 & \Longrightarrow & 0\ 1\ 1\ 1\ 1\ 0\ 1 \\
\text{Parents} & & \text{Offspring}
\end{array}
$$

The crossover point is selected randomly. The crossover operation is based on probability. We generally assign p_c, the probability of crossover a value in the range 0.6 to 0.8. We select two parents from the current population and generate a random number in the range 0 to 1. If the value of the random number is less than or equal to p_c, we do apply crossover to the selected parents, otherwise we do not apply the crossover operator to the selected parents.

Mutation is a bit-wise operator. We assign a small value to the probability of mutation, p_m. A typical value is 0.01. For each bit, we generate a random number between 0 and 1. If the value of the random number is less than or equal to p_m, we mutate the bit.

$$
1\ 0\ 1\ 0\ 1 \quad \longrightarrow \quad 1\ 0\ 1\ 1\ 1
$$
$$
4^{\text{th}}\ \text{bit mutated}
$$

There is no general guideline for the size of the population. For typical problems it is of the size of a few tens or less. The number of generations is decided based on the proximity of the solution to the optimal value and the amount of time one can afford.

Constrained functions require special treatment. Because of the effect of the genetic operators, some of the individuals in the population may become infeasible. We may add *penalty* terms to the evaluation function to reduce the probability of these individuals getting selected for reproduction. The penalty terms could take the form of linear, quadratic, logarithmic or any other form in the order of deviation of these individuals from feasibility. The alternative is to *repair* these infeasible solutions to make it feasible. These repair algorithms could be random, greedy or any other heuristic-based algorithm. A repair mechanism requires additional computation time.

12.3 WHY GA WORKS

The theoretical foundation of genetic algorithm is based on the notion of *schema*—a template allowing exploration of similarities among chromosomes. A schema consists of a number of fixed positions with specified values of 0 and 1 and '*' (don't care symbol). A schema represents all strings (a hyperplane, or a subset of the discrete search space), which match it on all positions other than '*'. 101*101*1 is a schema and 101010101, 101010111, 101110101, 101110111 are the four instances of the schema. Considering binary strings of length m, there are 3^m possible schemata in total. In a population of size n, between 2^m and $n2^m$ different schemata may be represented.

The two important properties of a schema are 'schema order' and 'defining length'. The order of a schema is the number of fixed positions, that is, the number of positions where '*' does not occur; either 0 or 1 occurs. The defining length of a schema is the distance between the first and the last fixed positions in the schema. For the schema 101*101*1, the order is 7 and the defining length is 8.

Schemata and their properties are interesting notational devices for rigorously discussing and classifying string similarities. They provide the basic means for analyzing the net effect of reproduction and genetic operators on the building blocks contained within the population.

Suppose there are $m(H, t)$ instances of a particular schema H contained within the population at generation t. During reproduction, a string is copied according to its fitness. We expect to have $m(H, t + 1)$ representatives of the schema in the generation $t + 1$ as given by the equation:

$$m(H, t + 1) = m(H, t) \cdot f(H) / \bar{f}$$

where $f(H)$ is the average fitness of the schema H and $\bar{f}$ is the average fitness of the population.

This means that a particular schema grows as the ratio of the average fitness of the schema to the average fitness of the population.

Crossover has a disruptive effect on the schema. A schema survives when the crossover site falls outside the defining length. The survival probability under simple crossover is $1 - \delta(H)/(l - 1)$, where $\delta(H)$ is the defining length of the schema and l is the length of the string. This is because a schema is likely to be disrupted whenever a site within the defining length is selected from the $l - 1$ possible sites. If crossover is performed by random choice, say with probability p_c at a particular mating, the survival probability may be given by the expression:

$$p_s \geq 1 - p_c \frac{\delta(H)}{l - 1}$$

The combined effect of reproduction and crossover may now be considered. Assuming independence of the reproduction and crossover operations, we obtain:

$$m(H, t + 1) \geq m(H, t) \frac{f(H)}{\bar{f}} \left[1 - p_c \frac{\delta(H)}{l - 1} \right]$$

Let us now consider the effect of mutation. For a schema H to survive, all of the specified positions must themselves survive. Let p_m be the probability of mutation. An allele (gene/a bit in the chromosome) survives with probability $(1 - p_m)$. A particular schema survives when each of the fixed positions in the schema survives. Let $O(H)$ denote the order of a schema. The probability of survival of a schema under mutation can be expressed as $(1 - p_m)^{O(H)}$. For small values of p_m, the schema survival probability may be expressed as $1 - O(H)p_m$.

Combining the effects of reproduction, crossover and mutation, we may write:

$$m(H, t + 1) \geq m(H, t) \frac{f(H)}{\bar{f}} \left[1 - p_c \frac{\delta(H)}{l - 1} - O(H)p_m \right]$$

The significance of this expression is that *short, low-order, above-average schemata receive exponentially increasing trials in subsequent generations*. This is referred as the *schema theorem* or the *fundamental theorem* of GA.

Schema theorem and Markov chain analysis are the two prominent theories of genetic algorithms. Other GA theories include statistical mechanics based analysis, and analysis based on quantitative genetics, used in plant and animal breeding experiments.

12.4 SOME GA IMPLEMENTATIONS

Genetic algorithms have been used to solve hard optimization problems. For the sake of illustration, we have chosen four problems to be solved using GA. They are numerical function optimization, 0/1 knapsack, bin-packing and traveling salesperson problem.

12.4.1 Numerical Function Optimization

One constrained and one unconstrained function have been taken as examples to demonstrate the use of genetic algorithms to optimize numerical functions.

Unconstrained function

Minimize $F(X) = \sum_{i=1}^{n-1} (1 - x_i)^2 + 100(x_{i+1} - x_i^2)^2$ with $-5.12 \leq x_i \leq 5.12$, $i = 1, n$.

The global optimum value of the function $F(X^*) = 0$ is located at $X^* = [1.0, 1.0, ...]$. The number of variables taken in this study is equal to 10.

Constrained function

We take a polynomial constrained function with seven variables and four constraints.

$$\text{Minimize } F(X) = (x_1 - 10)^2 + 5(x_2 - 12)^2 + x_3^4 + 3(x_4 - 11)^2$$

$$+ \ 10x_5^6 + 7x_6^2 + x_7^4 - 4x_6 x_7 - 10x_6 - 8x_7$$

with $-10 \leq x_i \leq 10$, $i = 1,7$ and subject to the following constraints:

$$127 - 2x_1^2 - 3x_2^4 - x_3 - 4x_4^2 - 5x_5 \geq 0$$

$$282 - 7x_1 - 3x_2 - 10x_3^2 - x_4 + x_5 \geq 0$$

$$196 - 23x_1 - x_2^2 - 6x_6^2 + 8x_7 \geq 0$$

$$-4x_1^2 - x_2^2 + 3x_1 x_2 - 2x_3^2 - 5x_6 + 11x_7 \geq 0$$

The function has a global optimum $F(X^*) = 680.6300573$ located at

$X^* = (2.330499, 1.951372, -0.4775414, 4.365726, -0.6244870, 1.038131, 1.594227)$.

The original problem of optimizing the constrained function is transformed into optimization of the function:

$$f(X) = F(X) + \varepsilon\delta \sum_{j=1}^{p} \phi_j$$

where p is the total number of constraints, δ is penalty coefficient, $\varepsilon = -1$ for maximization and $+1$ for minimization, and ϕ_j is penalty related to the jth constraint. We take $\delta = 1$ and ϕ_j equal to absolute deviation of the jth constraint from the feasible region.

We use binary coding with 16 bits for each variable, thus having chromosome length equal to the number of variables multiplied by 16. A maximization fitness function of the form $1/(1 + f(x))$ has been used where $f(X)$ is the minimization objective function for a test example.

The experiments have been conducted with single-point crossover and random mutation. The parameter values in our experiments are taken as: population size = 100, probability of crossover = 0.6, probability of mutation = $1/l$, where l is the chromosome length. The GA is run for 1000 generations for each experiment. A total of 10 experiments have been conducted on both the test functions.

Table 12.1 shows the results obtained with the genetic algorithm. Real value genetic coding has also been used for numerical function optimization, which provides better results compared with the binary coding.

Since many functions arising in practice contain multiple optima, traditional methods like steepest descent alone may not be adequate to solve such problems. Moreover, gradient-based methods require derivative information of the function to guide the search process and

TABLE 12.1   Results of the GA run on the two functions (10 experiments)

Results	Unconstrained function	Constrained function
Best result	8.2850	680.9125
Worst result	318.9971	711.7839
Average	67.6310	691.4164
Std. deviation	96.5502	11.5709

may be trapped in a local optimum in the search space if the objective function is multi-modal[3].

12.4.2   0/1 Knapsack Problem

Given a profit vector p_i, a weight vector w_i, and knapsack capacity C, the problem is to

maximize $\sum_{i=1}^{i=n} p_i x_i$ subject to $\sum_{i=1}^{i=n} w_i x_i \leq C$, where $x_i \in \{0, 1\}$, $1 \leq i \leq n$ and n is the number of objects.

Genetic coding for 0/1 knapsack problem is a straightforward string of bits. A bit is 1 if the corresponding decision variable (gene) is part of the solution. We use two types of initial populations—randomly generated chromosomes of bits (random multi-gene) and chromosomes with single '1' bit (single-gene). For chromosomes of length 7, examples of these two types of individuals are 1010001 and 0010000 respectively. We use two types of mutations—traditional mutation where a '0' bit is made '1' with some predefined probability and heuristic mutation where a desired gene is identified using greedy heuristic and mutated. The heuristic mutation works by taking a sample of five percent of knapsack items and selecting one with the highest (p_i/w_i) value among the sampled items.

The effects of recombination/crossover and mutation can make an individual infeasible. Such individuals are replaced with the respective type of chromosome, that is, random multi-gene chromosome is replaced by random multi-gene chromosome and single-gene chromosome is replaced by single gene chromosome.

We use rank selection, double-point crossover, crossover probability 0.6, mutation probability $1/n$ where n is the number of items, and population size 50. Each of the experiments is run for 2000 generations. $\sum p_i x_i$ is taken as the evaluation function. We use data sets with different knapsack capacities.

Data set is generated as:

w_i = uniformly random between 1 and 100
p_i = uniformly random between 1 and 100

---

[3] Functions containing multiple optimal solutions.

We consider three knapsack capacities as $C_1 = 200$, $C_2 = 0.5 \Sigma w_i$ and $C_3 = 0.8 \Sigma w_i$. The results are shown in Table 12.2.

TABLE 12.2   Results of knapsack problem

Problem size	Knapsack capacity	Optimum value	Single-gene chromosomes		Multi-gene chromosomes	
			Random mutation	Heuristic mutation	Random mutation	Heuristic mutation
100	C_1	1360	829	1255	⊗	⊗
	C_2	4345	4010	4213	4014	3972
	C_3	5020	4808	4978	4794	4858
250	C_1	1828	776	1728	⊗	⊗
	C_2	10484	9410	10098	9462	8981
	C_3	12696	11839	12518	11856	11892
500	C_1	2930	852	2770	⊗	⊗
	C_2	20602	18252	19791	18228	16509
	C_3	24190	22559	23945	22509	22900

Note: The symbol ⊗ indicates that the combination could not find solution due to cent percent infeasibility of chromosomes.

The scheme with initial population of multi-gene random chromosomes cannot solve the problem instances with C_1 capacity, because all the chromosomes remain infeasible during the GA run. The scheme with single-gene chromosomes combines the genes (bits) one by one and can solve all the problem instances. Further, the scheme with heuristic mutation provides much better results than those obtained with the random mutation.

12.4.3   Bin Packing Problem

Various single-chromosome genetic representations can be used for the bin packing problem. These include binary, object membership, object permutation and grouping representation. Here, a multi-chromosomal genetic representation, which captures the problem structure is implemented for the bin packing problem. The coding divides object permutation in groups satisfying the constraint. We term objects as genes and bins as chromosomes.

A gene is the index number of an object, thus having its unique identification. Each chromosome consists of a subset of genes, which can be accommodated in it on the basis of problem constraints. An individual is a set of such chromosomes. Individual construction from different object indices provides different individuals and a collection of such individuals forms the population.

Figure 12.1 shows two individuals (IndivI and IndivII) constructed with the *next-fit* heuristic (described in Chapter 7, Section 7.3) for the bin packing example problem instance with 10 objects and a bin size equal to 10 as given below.

Object index (o_i):	1	2	3	4	5	6	7	8	9	10
Object size (s_i):	8	3	5	2	1	6	3	5	4	7

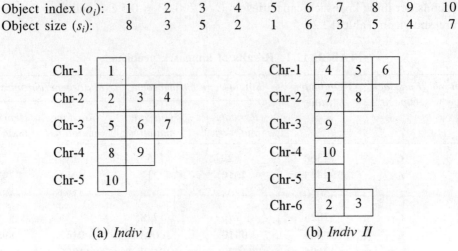

(a) *Indiv I*   (b) *Indiv II*

FIGURE 12.1   Two individuals with the multi-chromosome coding.

IndivI starts from index '1' and IndivII from index '4'. Each individual contains chromosomes that are shown by 'chr-j' in Figure 12.1. Genetic operators are designed in a way so as not to induce infeasibility of the individuals.

Crossover

Application of the crossover operator involves five steps.

1. Randomly extract one chromosome from each of the two individuals (*IndivI* and *IndivII*) selected for reproduction. Let chromosome $A \in IndivI$ and chromosome $B \in IndivII$.
2. Define three sets: $(A - B)$, $(B - A)$ and $(A \cup B)$.
3. Remove the objects in set $(B - A)$ from *IndivI* and those in set $(A - B)$ from *IndivII*.
4. Insert objects of the set $(A \cup B)$ into the chromosomes belonging to *IndivI* as well as *IndivII* with a problem related heuristic while honouring the constraints.
5. Build new chromosomes from the remaining objects (which do not fit in any of the chromosomes in an individual) and append them to the respective individual.

Mutation

The mutation operator for multi-chromosome representation works at the chromosome level of an individual. It involves three steps:

1. Remove a chromosome from the individual with a pre-specified probability of mutation.
2. Insert the genes of the removed chromosome into the remaining chromosomes in the individual with a problem related heuristic, honouring the constraints.
3. Build a new chromosome from the remaining genes and append it to the individual.

We hybridize the multi-chromosome representation with the appropriate heuristics such as best-fit (see Chapter 7, section 7.3). The heuristic is used to fit the left-out genes after the action of genetic operators. The genetic parameters such as population size is taken in the range 4 to 10 and the probabilities of mutation and crossover are fixed after a number of trials on the basis of object sizes.

The objective function used in the bin-packing problem takes care of the number of bins/chromosomes in an individual and the level to which the bins are filled. The function is one of maximization and determines the fitness of an individual as:

$$F(Indiv.) = \sum_{j=1}^{j=z} (f_j/C)^2/z$$

where $F(Indiv.)$ is the fitness of an individual, f_j is the sum of the object sizes in the jth chromosome, C is the bin capacity and z is the number of chromosomes in an individual.

The above genetic algorithm has been implemented on the test data available on the Internet. The first type of data sets, called 'uniform' consists of integer object sizes uniformly random in the interval [20,100] with a bin capacity equal to 150. Twenty instances are available for each of the problem sizes 120, 250, 500 and 1000. The second type of data sets, called 'triplets', consists of real object sizes in the interval [25.0, 50.0] and a bin capacity equal to 100. The objects are generated in a way so as to fill the bins exactly with three objects. The 'triplets' also have twenty problem instances for each of size 60, 120, 249 and 501.

Table 12.3 shows the results in 10 experiments for each of the twenty instances of a problem type and size. It provided results, which are 4.35 percent above the theoretical optimum in the uniform problem instances and 7.5 percent above the theoretical optimum in the triplet instances, which require the objects to fit exactly in all the bins. The theoretical optimum is obtained by dividing the sum of object sizes by the bin size, which is a lower bound for the bin-packing problem.

TABLE 12.3   Overall average and worst performances (in percentages)

Problem type	Problem size	Average (% above optimum)	Worst (% above optimum)
Uniform	120	1.43	4.35
	250	1.75	3.96
	500	2.05	4.08
	1000	2.00	3.79
Triplets	60	5.00	5.00
	120	3.64	7.50
	249	3.74	6.02
	501	4.51	6.59

The results can be improved further by using a heuristic better than the best-fit. This improvement will be both in terms of the quality of the solution and the computational time.

The multi-chromosomal representation and set-based genetic operators can be used for solving other grouping problems[4] like graph colouring, etc.

12.4.4 Traveling Salesperson Problem

The traveling salesperson problem is one of the earliest problems attempted by the GA community. Several genetic representations and operators have been proposed for the problem over the years. Binary representation cannot be used for this problem as the standard genetic operators such as crossover and mutation result in invalid chromosomes. There are duplicate cities in the chromosomes and some of the cities are missing. It also results in lengthy chromosomes when the number of cities is large. Adjacency representation, ordinal representation, path representation and matrix representation are the other prominent representations used for the problem. The path representation is the natural and the most widely used coding. In this representation, a tour is coded as a permutation of city indices. Two chromosomes for a 9 city problems with the coding are:

$$1\ 2\ 6\ 3\ 7\ 5\ 9\ 4\ 8 \quad \text{and} \quad 1\ 9\ 2\ 6\ 8\ 7\ 4\ 3\ 5.$$

Classical crossover operators such as single-point crossover produce invalid chromosomes with this coding as well. Therefore, special crossover operators[5] such as partially mapped crossover (PMX), order crossover (OX) and cycle crossover (CX) have been used.

A genetic algorithm with path representation is implemented here with circular linked list as the data structure. It utilizes the genetic operators similar to those used for the bin-packing problem. A problem-related heuristic, which is a variant of greedy heuristic, has been used for the generation of initial population and the working of the genetic operators. With this heuristic, a city is inserted into the partial tour at a location where it causes minimum increase in the partial tour length.

The crossover operator used is a small range double-point crossover that makes a double point cut of size equal to five percent of the number of cities/nodes, thus preserving major portion of the evolved chromosomes. Working of the genetic operators is explained below.

Crossover

The operator works as:

1. Perform crossover on the two parents (say *I* and *II*) with a pre-specified probability of crossover.
2. Mark one crossover point randomly in the range $[1, n]$ and select another crossover site by adding $0.05 * n$ to the previously marked crossover point, where n is the number of cities.
3. Extract the sub-strings between the two crossover points from both the chromosomes. Let the sub-string $A \in I$ and $B \in II$.

---

[4] Grouping problems demand partitioning of a list of objects into optimum number of groups.

[5] References (Goldberg, 1989) and (Michalewicz, 1994) discuss these operators.

4. Define three sets: $(A \cup B)$, $(A - B)$, $(B - A)$.
5. Remove the nodes in $(B - A)$ from the chromosome-*I* and those in $(A - B)$ from the chromosome-*II*.
6. Insert the nodes in $(A \cup B)$ into the chromosomes *I* and *II* with a problem-related heuristic.

Mutation

The mutation operator works as:

1. Remove a gene undergoing mutation from the chromosome with a pre-specified probability of mutation.
2. Insert the gene into the chromosome with a problem-related heuristic.

The genetic algorithm has been implemented with the following genetic parameters: population size = 20, crossover probability = 0.5, mutation probability = $0.7 * (1/n)$, and total number of generations = 1000.

Tournament selection with tournament size of two and probability of selection of the better chromosome equal to 0.8 have been used.

The objective function is the length of the tour represented by a chromosome.

The genetic algorithm has been run on TSP instances of size 14 to 783 taken from the TSPLIB[6], available on the Internet. It can reach the optimum tour length up to the problem instance of 105 cities. Table 12.4 displays the average and worst tour lengths obtained in 10 experiments.

TABLE 12.4   Performance of the genetic algorithm on TSP instances (10 experiments)

Problem Instance	Number of cities	Optimum	Average results (% above optimum)	Worst results (% above optimum)
Burma14	14	3323	0.0	0.0
Gr24	24	1272	0.0	0.0
Att48	48	10628	0.1	0.2
Lin105	105	14379	3.3	6.8
D198	198	15780	2.9	11.3
Lin318	318	42029	5.3	7.8
Att532	532	27686	4.4	5.8
Rat783	783	8806	7.1	8.1

Several representations and operators may be used in genetic algorithms to solve the traveling salesperson problem. Some of these may be useful for small problem instances. For larger problem instances, some of these representations may be unmanageably large. Some representations lead to invalid tours after the application of the genetic operators. Schemata

---

[6] TSPLIB is available at various locations on the Internet and is a library of sample instances for the TSP (and related problems) from various sources and of various types.

analysis for most of the operators is quite difficult. To get better results, one has to power genetic algorithms with good local search heuristic. There is still good scope to find out GA which would include 'the best' representation and genetic operators and a good local improvement operator for the TSP.

12.4.5 Function Optimization, Neighbourhood Annealing and Implicit Elitism

Non-linear, multi-modal and tightly constrained optimization problems are difficult to solve. We use a real-coded genetic algorithm (RCGA) augmented with a heuristic mutation operator based on annealing neighbourhood to solve these problems. We also use a notion of *implicit elitism*[7], in which some of the high-fitness chromosomes are transferred unperturbed to the population in the subsequent generations. A combination of implicit elitism and traditional explicit elitism provides the best results in most of the test functions.

A numerical optimization problem over continuous parameter space is defined as:

Minimize $F(X)$, $X = (x_1, x_2, ..., x_n)$, $x_i \in R$, $1 \leq i \leq n$

subject to $g_j(X) \leq 0$, $j = 1, ..., p$ and $h_k(X) = 0$, $k = p+1, ..., m$

where $L_i \leq x_i \leq U_i$, $i = 1, ..., n$ are the decision variables, p is the number of inequality constraints, $(m - p)$ is the number of equality constraints, L_i and U_i are the lower and upper bounds on the variables, respectively.

If $m = 0$, we have an unconstained problem and $m > 0$ provides us with a constraint problem.

The class of problems overwhelms human quest for finding the global optimum due to large dimensions, poorly understood function landscapes, non-linearity and multi-modality. There are no deterministic methods available to solve these problems. Conventional methods are categorized into two groups: direct search methods, and gradient-based methods. Direct search methods start the search from an initial point and are guided by the objective function values. Gradient-based methods start the search from an initial point and use the derivative information to proceed further in the search space. They fail when the derivative information of the objective function and/or that of the constraints are not available. The conventional methods get trapped in local optima.

RCGAs have been used for these problems, which have proved superior to binary-coded genetic algorithms in terms of both the quality of solution and the computational time spent.

Various constraint handling methods have been used with genetic algorithms for the constrained problems. Penalty methods are the most commonly used constraint handling technique, where a *penalty term* is incorporated into the objective function to calculate the fitness value of infeasible individuals. All the previous evolutionary approaches perturb the whole chromosome by using recombination and mutation operators. Evolutionary strategies perturb the chromosomes with the mutation operator. The crossover operators used for

---

[7] A.K. Bhatia and S.K. Basu, "Implicit Elitism in Genetic Search", LNCS 4234, Springer-Verlag, pp. 781–788, 2006.

RCGAs perturb the chromosomes in pursuit of effective schemata processing. Random perturbation of the whole chromosome leads to suboptimal solution. Genetic algorithm (GA) with appropriate dosage of both the operators is successful in reaching the global optimum. Problem-related heuristics make GAs more effective in marching towards the global optimum.

In this section, we use simple RCGA with decreasing neighbourhood search as a heuristic for solving numerical optimization problems. We also use *implicit elitism* derived from the mutation operator. We study the efficacy of RCGA using neighbourhood annealing and implicit elitism on both constrained and unconstrained numerical test functions considered as important benchmarks in the literature.

Neighbourhood annealing

We use a neighbourhood annealing mutation operator for RCGA that searches in the neighbourhood of the gene undergoing mutation from the beginning of GA run. The neighbourhood gets reduced with increasing generation number. In the neighbourhood set-up, the variable x_i undergoing mutation with a pre-specified probability of mutation at the generation $t+1$ is updated as:

$$x_i^{t+1} = x_i^t + d * s_i^t$$

If $x_i^{t+1} < L_i, x_i^{t+1} = L_i$ and if $x_i^{t+1} > U_i$, then

$$s_i^t = e^{-a*t/T} * b(U_i - L_i) * \text{uniform } [0,1],$$

and $\qquad d = +1$ if $r \le 0.5$, $d = -1$ if $r > 0.5$, $r = $ uniform $[0, 1]$

where T is the maximum number of generations and uniform $[0, 1]$ denotes a uniform random number in the range $[0, 1]$. We tune and fix value of the parameter b at 0.2. Value of the parameter a is fixed at 15 so that the term $e^{-a*t/T}$ approaches the floating point precision of the machine, approximately, at generation T.

The variable x_i is updated in the range $[x_i - 0.2(U_i - L_i), x_i + 0.2(U_i - L_i)]$ initially. The selection operator selects the individual with values of x_i near the global optimum x_i^* at the next generation. The variable starts marching towards x_i^* from the beginning of genetic search and there is less chance of its being stuck at the suboptimal point (Figure 12.2).

Implicit elitism

Genetic algorithms start with a population of randomly generated strings, which are perturbed by genetic operators over generations. Function value of a randomly generated string has the tendency to be around the centre of the search space (Central Limit Theorem). Likewise, random perturbations in the strings caused by crossover and mutation operators try to push the strings towards the mean function value in the search space. On the other hand, the selection operator in GAs pulls the strings towards the optimum. When an equilibrium is reached between the two opposite forces, the GA gets converged to a suboptimal value. Elitism has been used in GAs to obtain near optimal results, which makes sure that the individual having the best function value in a population is retained in the next generation.

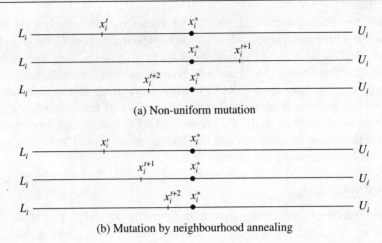

(a) Non-uniform mutation

(b) Mutation by neighbourhood annealing

FIGURE 12.2 **Search process of the GA with (a) non-uniform mutation and (b) mutation by neighbourhood annealing between the lower limit (L_i) and the upper limit (U_i) of a real variable x in three generations.**

We call this traditional form of elitism as *explicit elitism*. The elitist GA has theoretically been shown to converge to the global optimum.

Mutation operator is applied to every gene in a chromosome with a prespecified probability of mutation. Mutation with probability of mutation $p_m = 1/l$, where l denotes the chromosome length, which indicates that on the average one gene will be changed in a string of length l. Mutation with $p_m \geq 1/l$ is likely to perturb gene(s) in each chromosome, thus perturbing all the chromosomes in the population. With $p_m \geq 1/l$, even the elite copied to the new population with explicit elitism is subjected to perturbation by the mutation operator and has a tendency to move towards the mean function value. Thus, a GA with or without explicit elitism is likely to lose its strength to move towards the global optimal after a few generations with $p_m \geq 1/l$.

The mutation operator can be used to induce implicit elitism in GAs. With a value of $p_m < 1/l$, there is non-zero probability of all the genes in a string remaining unperturbed. Thus, the mutation operator leaves a few strings unperturbed in the population with this value of the p_m. The crossover operator with a probability of crossover $p_c < 1$, also leaves a few of the strings unperturbed. A few strings pass on unperturbed to the new population with the above values of the p_m and the p_c. Further, the selection operator is fitness biased and selects the high fitness strings with higher probability. The population at the next generation is a mixture of the perturbed chromosomes and the chromosomes passed on unperturbed from the previous generation. If the perturbed chromosomes have higher fitness than the unperturbed chromosomes, they get selected to form the population at the subsequent generation. Otherwise, the unperturbed chromosomes are passed on to the population at the subsequent generation. Thus, there is non-zero probability of transfer of a few high fitness strings without any change to the new population. We call the process *implicit elitism*.

With implicit elitism, the elite retained through explicit elitism also has non-zero probability to pass on unperturbed to the subsequent population. Thus, the GA with implicit elitism maintains its strength till it reaches the global optimum because either it is at the same level of fitness or it is moving ahead towards the optimum.

Let $p_m = h*1/l$, where h is a scalar factor. Value of $h < 1$ makes the $p_m < 1/l$. The crossover operator is applied after selection of parents for reproduction. The selected chromosomes undergo crossover with a prespecified value of p_c. After selection and crossover, all the chromosomes in the population are subjected to mutation operation which acts at the gene-level. Values of $h < 1$ and $p_c < 1$ imply occurrence of implicit elitism in GAs.

An algorithmic description of the simple RCGA used for numerical function optimization is as follows:

```
Procedure RCGA
    Decide the values of h and p_c;
    p_m = h*(1/l);
    Explicit_Elitism = {true, false};
    /*Explicit elitism is same as the traditional form of elitism
in GAs */
    Mutation_Type ={Non-uniform, Neighbourhood Annealing};
    Decide the value of T; /* Maximum number of generations*/
    t = 0;
    Initialize P(t);
    /* P(t) is the population at generation t */
    Evaluate P(t);/* The evaluation function includes penalty term
in the constrained functions. */
    While (t < T) Do
    t = t + 1;
      If (Explicit_Elitism) Then
        Elite = The best individual in P(t - 1);
      Endif
    While (P(t) is not complete) Do
      Select two parents from P(t - 1); /*with replacement */
      Apply crossover operator with probability p_c, generating two
      offsprings;
    Endwhile
    Mutate each gene in P(t) with probability p_m, using Mutation_Type;
    If (Explicit_Elitism) Then
      Replace an individual at a random position in P(t) with Elite;
      Evaluate P(t);
    Endif
    Endwhile
End RCGA
```

Test functions

We study effectiveness of the RCGA on five unconstrained (UC-1 through UC-5) and five constrained test functions (C-1 through C-5). These functions are given in the appendix.

Unconstrained test functions

The UC-1 is generalized Rosenbrock's function. It is a continuous function. The optimum is located in a parabolic valley with a flat bottom, which makes it a difficult landscape to search. We take the number of variables (n) equal to 30 and 100 for the test function.

UC-2 is the generalized Rastrigin's function. The function is made from the sphere model by adding a modulating term. It is a continuous and multi-modal function. The number of local minima in the function landscape increases exponentially with the increase in problem dimension. We take $n = 30$ in this test case.

UC-3 is Schwefel's function. It is a continuous and unimodal function with a narrow valley, making it a difficult landscape to search. We take $n = 30$ for this function.

UC-4 is Griewank's function. The function is continuous and multi-modal. It is difficult to optimize, because it is non-separable and contains unreachable hills and valleys in the function landscape. The number of variables taken for the function is equal to 30.

UC-5 is Michalewicz's function. The function is multi-modal, having $n!$ local optima. We take 100 variables for this function.

Constrained test functions

C-1 is quadratic with nine linear inequality constraints, six of which are active at the optimum. It has 0.0111% feasible search space.

C-2 consists of a linear objective function with three linear and three non-linear inequality constraints. All the constraints are active at the optimum. The function has 0.0010% feasible search space.

C-3 is a polynomial with four non-linear inequality constraints. Two constraints are active at the optimum. It has 0.5121% feasible search space.

C-4 is a non-linear objective function with three non-linear equality constraints. All the constraints are active at the optimum. The function has less than 0.0001% feasible search space.

C-5 is a quadratic function having three linear and five non-linear inequality constraints, six of which are active at the optimum. The feasible search space is 0.0003%.

Genetic operators and parameters

We adopt real number coding in our experiments. The individuals for the real coding are generated as:

$$x_i = \text{uniform } [0, 1] \times (U_i - L_i), \quad i = 1, ..., n$$

We take the probability of mutation $p_m = h \times 1/l$ with three options for the value of h: 0.7, 1.0, and 1.5. Each real-coded gene is mutated with probability p_m. The experiments have been conducted with the options of non-uniform mutation and mutation with neighbourhood annealing. We execute GA with and without using the explicit elitism. A single-point crossover operator with crossover probability equal to 0.5 is taken for all the experiments. We adopt linear rank selection method with the value 1.5 assigned to the best individual, so as to create a moderate selection pressure. The population size is fixed at 60 through parameter tuning.

We adopt the penalty method for the constrained test problems. The fitness of a feasible string is based on the function value of the individual. If the individual is infeasible, a penalty term $P(X)$ is added to the function value as:

$$f(X) = F(X) + P(X)$$

Various forms of penalty functions such as static penalties, dynamic penalties, annealing penalties, adaptive penalties, etc. are reported in the literature. We use the dynamic/non-stationary penalty function. The infeasible individuals are penalized increasingly in this method as they reach near the feasible region in the search space. It makes the penalty term effective throughout the GA run. It is easy to implement and it offers a parameter that we have used to tune the penalty term for the constrained test functions.

The penalty term in this method is calculated as:

$$P(X) = (c \times t) \sum_{j=1}^{j=m} |d_j(X)|$$

where $d_j(X)$ is the measure of violation of the jth constraint, t is the current generation number, c is a constant and its values are tuned and fixed at 0.01, 100, 0.001, 0.0001, and 0.01 for the test functions C-1, C-2, C-3, C-4, and C-5, respectively.

We adopt the fitness function $1/[1 + f(X)]$ except in the test functions UC-5 and C-1 where the fitness function used is $[-f(X)]$, $f(X)$ being the objective function to be minimized.

Search progress of the RCGA

This subsection demonstrates the progress of search process of the RCGA using the two types of mutation operators: the non-uniform and the neighbourhood annealing. In these experiments, we use $p_m = 1/l$ and T is fixed at 5000 generations. The RCGA has been run with the explicit elitism. Other genetic operators and parameters are the same as described previously. Figures 12.3 and 12.4 show the progress of RCGA in a single run on each of the test functions using the two mutation operators on unconstrained and constrained functions respectively.

The figures depict the best function value reached at a generation. It is observed from the results that the RCGA with neighbourhood annealing starts moving towards the optimum from the beginning of the search process while the RCGA with non-uniform mutation has slower progress initially due to higher level of randomness in the search process, as shown in Figure 12.2. However, the neighbourhood annealing cannot always escape the local optimum in the unconstrained test functions with the value of T equal to 5000 generations.

In the constrained test functions (Figure 12.4), the vertical line indicates start of feasibility. Feasibility usually starts earlier with the neighbourhood annealing mutation. The RCGA with non-uniform mutation reaches the feasible part of the search space much later and the search progress remains inferior to the neighbourhood annealing throughout the RCGA run.

This happens due to sensitivity of the constrained spaces to randomness. A highly random perturbation of genes in the non-uniform mutation induces infeasibility and the search process becomes directionless because of the penalty term in the evaluation function.

Performance of the RCGA

We run the RCGA for a large number of generations with the three objectives: (i) to observe whether it can reach the global optimum or not, (ii) to reveal the differences in the search process of the non-uniform mutation and the mutation with neighbourhood annealing, and (iii) to highlight the effect of implicit elitism in the continuous search spaces.

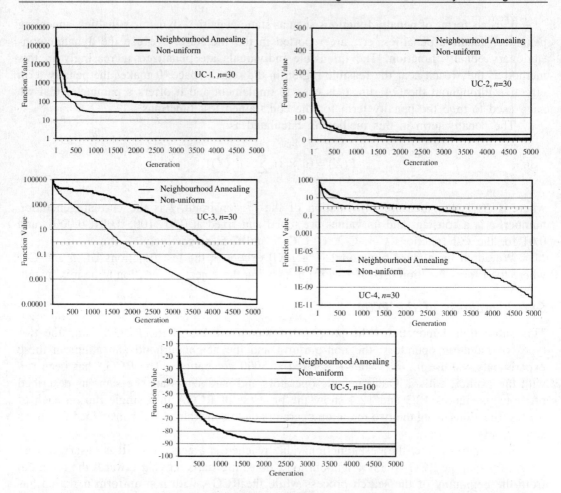

FIGURE 12.3   **Search progress of the RCGA with neighbourhood annealing and non-uniform mutation on the unconstrained test functions.**

The RCGA has been executed for all the unconstrained and constrained test functions mentioned earlier. The maximum number of generations (T) has been fixed at 100 thousands for all the functions. The RCGA could not reach the global optimum in the case of the test function UC-1 with mutation factor $h = 0.7$, explicit elitism and neighbourhood annealing mutation. Therefore, we have tuned the parameter T for this function and fixed it at 300 thousands for $n = 30$ and 2000 thousands for $n = 100$.

Tables 12.5, 12.6, 12.7, and 12.8 show the experimental results[8]. In these tables, B is used for best, W for worst, A for average, SD for standard deviation, and F for per cent experiments providing feasible solution. The best results for the categories 'best' and 'average'

---

[8] A. K. Bhatia, Studying the Effectiveness of Genetic Algorithms in Solving Certain Classes of Problems, Ph.D. Thesis, Department of Computer Science, Banaras Hindu University, 2003.

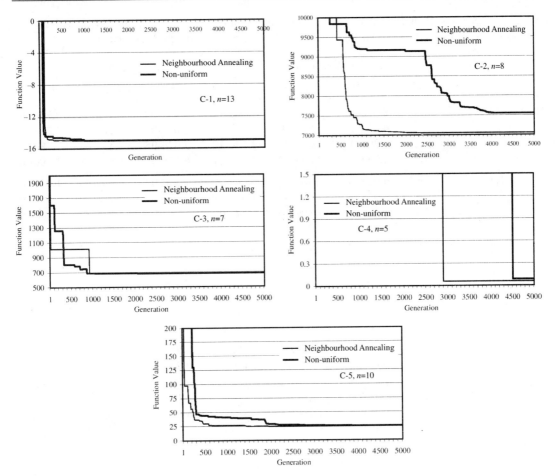

FIGURE 12.4   Search progress of the RCGA with neighbourhood annealing and non-uniform mutation on the constrained test functions.

are highlighted. Explicit elitism is the same as the traditional form of elitism in genetic algorithms. Implicit elitism occurs when $h < 1$ (and $p_c < 1$). Tables 12.5 and 12.6 show the results of the RCGA run on the unconstrained functions, using neighbourhood annealing mutation and the non-uniform mutation respectively. Tables 12.7 and 12.8 show the results for the constrained functions using the two mutation operators. All the results are summary of 10 experiments, except the results for the function UC-1 ($n = 100$) which are summary of 5 experiments.

The RCGA with both the mutation operators can reach near the global optimum in the unconstrained test functions. The non-uniform mutation provides better results than the neighbourhood annealing, except in the case of the function UC-1. The better performance of the non-uniform mutation is because of better fine-tuning abilities of the operator. The results obtained with the non-uniform mutation in the case of UC-4 are even better than the global optimum equal to -99.2784 reported in the literature.

TABLE 12.5   Result of RCGA execution with neighbourhood annealing on unconstrained test functions in 10 experiments except those for UC-1 ($n = 100$) are in 5 experiments

F-id	n	F(X*)		Without explicit elitism			With explicit elitism		
				h = 0.7	h = 1.0	h = 1.5	h = 0.7	h = 1.0	h = 1.5
UC-1	30	0	B	8.72e-08	1.66e-10	2.98e-10	4.05e-09	7.52e-09	2.29e-08
			W	8.16e-07	6.20e-09	5.18e-10	2.04e-04	2.28e-07	4.28e-07
			A	2.39e-07	2.57e-09	**3.77e-10**	2.04e-05	3.13e-08	7.18e-08
			SD	2.05e-07	2.26e-09	7.21e-11	6.12e-05	6.57e-08	1.19e-07
	100	0	B	6.6337	7.48e-10	1.44e-09	1.60e-09	3.68e-09	1.02e-08
			W	9.0485	1.22e-09	1.51e-09	1.83e-09	4.78e-09	1.33e-08
			A	7.8282	**9.80e-10**	1.47e-09	1.76e-09	4.26e-09	1.18e-08
			SD	0.9859	1.95e-10	2.42e-11	9.29e-11	3.93e-10	1.18e-09
UC-2	30	0	B	18.9042	19.8991	26.8638	0	2.13e-14	6.65e-14
			W	32.8336	42.7832	43.7781	5.33e-14	0.9949	0.9949
			A	27.06286	30.4457	33.6295	**2.43e-14**	0.0994	0.3980
			SD	3.8739	6.3271	5.5361	1.61e-14	0.2984	0.4874
UC-3	30	0	B	5.32e-10	8.27e-10	1.35e-09	3.13e-11	6.16e-11	1.38e-10
			W	8.39e-10	1.25e-09	2.48e-09	1.07e-10	1.88e-10	2.47e-10
			A	7.11e-10	1.01e-09	1.88e-09	**5.90e-11**	1.26e-10	1.81e-10
			SD	9.19e-11	1.49e-10	3.10e-10	2.29e-11	3.24e-11	3.06e-11
UC-4	30	0	B	8.17e-11	2.36e-10	3.86e-10	7.47e-14	2.07e-13	7.32e-13
			W	0.0295	0.0221	0.0073	0.0980	0.0980	0.0517
			A	0.0044	0.0068	**7.39e-04**	0.0385	0.0348	0.0248
			SD	0.0088	0.0068	0.0022	0.0296	0.0321	0.0194
UC-5	100	−99.2784	B	−89.9411	−87.3025	−84.6854	−98.6991	−96.4768	−92.7437
			W	−84.4718	−81.6688	−77.7793	−97.8865	−94.5671	−90.2371
			A	−88.1748	−84.4005	−81.0128	**−98.3604**	−95.4699	−91.4892
			SD	1.4865	1.5858	2.3137	0.2719	0.7662	0.9146

The RCGA with neighbourhood annealing can find near-optimal solution in all the constrained functions. The non-uniform mutation fails to reach near the global optimum in the case of the functions C-2 and C-5. The poor performance of the non-uniform mutation in the constrained functions is due to its sensitivity to randomness inherent in the working of the mutation operator.

The implicit elitism shows its effect in both the unconstrained and the constrained problems, as most of the best results in the categories 'best' and 'average' are obtained with $h = 0.7$. Some of the best results are also obtained with higher values of h, but the results with $h = 0.7$ are just near these function values. In Table 12.7, the best average function value of 7117.27 for C-2 is obtained with $h = 1.0$, while the result obtained with $h = 0.7$ is 7117.32.

Most of the best results are obtained when $h = 0.7$ and the explicit elitism is used. Thus the results demonstrate synergy between the implicit and the explicit elitism in the continuous function landscapes.

TABLE 12.6 Result of RCGA execution with non-uniform mutation on unconstrained test functions in 10 experiments except those for UC-1($n = 100$) are in 5 experiments

F-id	n	F(X*)		Without explicit elitism			With explicit elitism		
				h = 0.7	h = 1.0	h = 1.5	h = 0.7	h = 1.0	h = 1.5
UC-1	30	0	B	7.75e-04	4.24e-04	0.0040	2.01e-04	7.84e-04	0.0017
			W	0.0142	0.0093	0.0119	0.0260	0.0948	0.1187
			A	0.0088	**0.0043**	0.0072	0.0066	0.0220	0.0482
			SD	0.0037	0.0028	0.0023	0.0089	0.0306	0.0427
	100	0	B	0.0125	0.0019	4.5312	1.04e-06	1.24e-05	2.65e-05
			W	15.9962	12.5300	12.3631	2.85e-06	1.76e-05	7.12e-05
			A	10.1920	7.5910	9.9732	**2.21e-06**	1.44e-05	4.98e-05
			SD	6.2721	5.1800	3.2164	6.97e-07	2.01e-06	1.59e-05
UC-2	30	0	B	4.9747	4.9747	2.9848	0	0	0
			W	10.9445	11.9395	10.9445	0	0	0
			A	7.4621	8.8551	7.8601	**0**	0	0
			SD	1.7376	2.4553	2.2001	0	0	0
UC-3	30	0	B	2.91e-12	6.01e-13	3.41e-13	9.16e-15	2.28e-15	1.42e-15
			W	1.10e-10	5.79e-11	3.60e-12	1.17e-13	3.75e-14	1.72e-14
			A	4.33e-11	8.85e-12	1.69e-12	4.65e-14	1.59e-14	**6.32e-15**
			SD	4.13e-11	1.65e-11	1.20e-12	3.19e-14	1.11e-14	4.69e-15
UC-4	30	0	B	2.33e-18	1.51e-18	1.46e-18	1.24e-18	1.40e-18	1.51e-18
			W	0.0516	0.0565	0.0394	0.0612	0.0465	0.0906
			A	0.0275	0.0187	**0.0091**	0.0304	0.0132	0.0270
			SD	0.0174	0.0156	0.0117	0.0206	0.0170	0.0296
UC-5	100	−99.2784	B	−97.7438	−98.3155	−97.9275	−99.5958	−99.4388	−99.1048
			W	−96.3380	−96.8679	−96.0613	−99.5384	−99.2946	−98.7931
			A	−97.1151	−97.6648	−97.1636	**−99.5657**	−99.3804	−98.9574
			SD	0.4769	0.4454	0.6160	0.0187	0.03920	0.0910

Effect of implicit elitism is prominently visible in the case of RCGA with non-uniform mutation, particularly in the constrained functions. All the best values are obtained when $h = 0.7$, as shown in Table 12.8. The results with the other values of h are very poor. In the function C-5, the average value obtained is 26.75 with $h = 0.7$ and 38.18 with $h = 1.5$ when the RCGA is run without explicit elitism. The reason for this wide gap in the results can be attributed to the combined effect of randomness in high value of p_m (because of the high value of h) and the non-uniform mutation.

Non-uniform and neighbourhood annealing are heuristic mutation operators for the continuous search spaces and provide better results when the probability of mutation is high. A higher value of h implies higher probability of mutation. Therefore, some of the best function values are obtained when $h = 1.0$ or $h = 1.5$. However, the implicit elitism is also effective as the results with $h = 0.7$ are just near the best function values reached with higher

TABLE 12.7   Result of the RCGA execution with neighbourhood annealing on constrained test functions in 10 experiments

F-id	F(X*)		Without explicit elitism			With explicit elitism		
			$h = 0.7$	$h = 1.0$	$h = 1.5$	$h = 0.7$	$h = 1.0$	$h = 1.5$
C-1	−15	B	−15	−15	−15	-15	−15	−15
		W	−12.4531	−15	−15	−12.4531	−13	−13
		A	−14.3453	**−15**	−15	−14.5453	−14.6	−14.8
		SD	1.0099	4.74e-08	6.12e-08	0.9175	0.8	0.8
		F%	100	100	100	100	100	100
C-2	7049.3309	B	7067.88	7092.54	7083.21	7145.41	7086.11	7057.91
		W	7178.64	7149.78	7162.06	7560.10	7553.98	7469.04
		A	7117.32	**7117.27**	7120.24	7328.53	7301.11	7246.73
		SD	35.30	19.41	24.88	111.71	142.17	118.74
		F%	100	100	100	100	100	100
C-3	680.630057	B	680.6318	680.6321	680.6308	680.6304	680.6304	680.6302
		W	680.6393	680.6400	680.6416	680.6343	680.6323	680.6328
		A	680.6356	680.6347	680.6354	680.6316	680.6311	**680.6309**
		SD	0.0022	0.0029	0.0033	0.0012	0.0006	0.0006
		F%	100	100	100	100	100	100
C-4	0.0539498	B	0.06395	0.056711	0.064538	0.054073	0.054695	0.054041
		W	1.0	0.442274	0.441924	0.073382	0.445919	0.078122
		A	0.355410	0.295723	0.293799	**0.059939**	0.173418	0.060546
		SD	0.273910	0.177658	0.179504	0.005044	0.177689	0.007342
		F%	100	100	100	100	100	100
C-5	24.306209	B	24.30836	24.30915	24.30953	24.31305	24.34847	24.31784
		W	24.32286	24.32862	24.33020	24.94623	24.72359	24.43386
		A	**24.31355**	24.31906	24.31713	24.48117	24.44028	24.37235
		SD	0.00422	0.00609	0.00649	0.21681	0.10733	0.04047
		F%	100	100	100	100	100	100

values of h. Effect of implicit elitism is more prominent than the effect of non-uniform mutation in the constrained functions, as the best values are always reached with $h = 0.7$ and this mutation operator (Table 12.8). This indicates that the non-uniform mutation is a weaker heuristic compared with the neighbourhood annealing for the constrained function landscapes.

The increase in selection pressure with use of explicit elitism might be obstructive in some function landscapes and beneficial to others. The increased selection pressure is generally beneficial in the unconstrained test functions and the GA with explicit elitism provides better results. In the case of constrained test functions, it is obstructive in the test case C-2. The results with the presence of explicit elitism are inferior to the situation without explicit elitism with both the mutation operators.

This study has been performed with the objectives: to show that the simple RCGA is effective in solving continuous parameter optimization problems and to demonstrate the

TABLE 12.8   Result of the GA execution with non-uniform mutation on constrained test functions in 10 experiments

F-id	F(X*)		Without explicit elitism			With explicit elitism		
			$h = 0.7$	$h = 1.0$	$h = 1.5$	$h = 0.7$	$h = 1.0$	$h = 1.5$
C-1	−15	B	−14.9166	−14.4180	−14.2867	−15	−15	−15
		W	−14.4758	−13.7606	−13.2127	−15	−15	−14.9999
		A	−14.6503	−14.1007	−13.7755	**−15**	−15	−14.9999
		SD	0.1204	0.2342	0.4083	2.43-11	9.37e-08	4.31e-06
		F%	100	100	100	100	100	100
C-2	7049.3309	B	7233.54	7732.57	8326.11	7249.92	7251.89	7254.57
		W	7328.52	7926.34	8579.97	7468.50	7921.17	8282.42
		A	**7294.69**	7846.78	8420.42	7410.14	7468.71	7594.09
		SD	24.35	57.07	84.55	89.33	207.02	336.70
		F%	100	100	100	100	100	100
C-3	680.630057	B	680.6456	680.6433	680.7126	680.6312	680.6314	680.6315
		W	680.6662	680.7152	680.8070	680.6368	680.6423	680.6381
		A	680.6551	680.6716	680.7629	**680.6334**	680.6350	680.6343
		SD	0.0070	0.0221	0.0291	0.0019	0.0033	0.0020
		F%	100	100	100	100	100	100
C-4	0.0539498	B	0.99999	0.99282	0.59339	0.054451	0.056070	0.056816
		W	1.0	1.0	0.94451	0.064004	0.10903	0.097136
		A	0.99999	0.99928	0.69041	**0.057790**	0.074423	0.072046
		SD	1.20e-07	0.00215	0.09185	0.00376	0.01639	0.01088
		F%	100	100	100	100	100	100
C-5	24.306209	B	26.20347	29.34501	37.21265	24.33735	24.41689	24.36372
		W	27.38851	31.61599	39.07534	25.46303	26.74617	27.82069
		A	26.75425	30.59436	38.18900	**24.77746**	25.13121	25.30654
		SD	0.32388	0.64961	0.47901	0.35569	0.79615	0.99605
		F%	100	100	100	100	100	100

effect of implicit elitism on epistatic[9] function landscapes. The RCGA can reach very near the global optimum in all the test functions, although it requires a large number of function evaluations. The RCGA using non-uniform mutation shows poor performance on some of the constrained functions due to its role in introduction of high levels of randomness in the search process.

The results demonstrate synergy between the implicit elitism and the traditional explicit elitism. Role of other factors like selection pressure and the power of heuristic mutation needs to be studied, which might have affected the results of a few test functions. The RCGA provides comparable or even better results for all the test functions compared with those of

---

[9] Epistasis means strong interaction among genes in a chromosome.

a few recent formulations of evolutionary algorithms. The other formulations might fail in some of the function landscapes, while the RCGA with neighbourhood annealing is robust enough to explore both the unconstrained and the constrained landscapes.

SUMMARY

In this chapter, we have introduced the basics of genetic algorithms, which are finding a large number of applications in optimization problems, especially those not satisfactorily handled by the conventional methods. We have discussed about how a GA works and the important operators generally used in a GA implementation. The important steps in GA implementation are: decision about coding, selection method, fixing the values of genetic parameters like population size, cross-over type and probability, mutation probability and the length of GA run. The schema theorem, the most widely referred theoretical basis of GA has been explained. The above has been supplemented through GA implementations of a few problems like numerical function optimization, knapsack, bin packing and traveling salesperson problems. These experiments are to demonstrate how a GA can be used for a real application. The basic differences of GA from most of the traditional optimization methods are that GAs use a coding of variables instead of variables directly, a population of solutions instead of a single solution, and stochastic operators instead of deterministic operators. These attributes make GA-based search robust and applicable to a wide variety of problems. GAs are made more effective in finding optimal or near optimal solutions through the use of problem-related heuristics.

EXERCISES

12.1 Show that any string of length k is an instance of 2^k different schemata.

12.2 A population contains 5 strings as shown below:

Individual	Fitness
010010	17
100011	19
111000	18
001100	14
110001	11

Given the mutation and crossover probabilities as 0.01 and 0.75 respectively, calculate the expected number of schemata of the form 11**** in the next generation.

12.3 Find the defining length and order of the following schemata: *1*1*0*, *11****, 111111*, **1***1.

12.4 How does optimization through GA differ from conventional optimization techniques?

12.5 A population at generation t consists of:

Chromosome	Fitness value	Number of copies
10000	15	5
01100	10	5
10011	20	10
01101	5	5
01110	15	5

Assuming $p_m = 0.01$ and $p_c = 1$, find the expected number of schemata of the form ****1 in the generation $t + 1$.

12.6 A search space consists of 10^6 points. Find the total number of schemata for binary and decimal coded genetic algorithms.

12.7 Minimize the function $F(x_1, x_2, x_3, x_4) = \sum\limits_{i=1}^{i=4} x_i^2$, $-5.12 \le x_i \le 5.12$ using 10-bit coding.

12.8 Discuss how parallelism can be exploited in GA.

12.9 What is the number of schemata of order k in strings of length l bits?

12.10 Plan experiments to compare the performance of GAs using one-point and multi-point crossovers for the 0/1 knapsack problem.

12.11 Consider bit strings of length 7. Calculate the probability of surviving mutation for the following schemata if the probability of mutation, $p_m = 0.1$.

$$**1**11, \ 11***1*, \ 1*1*1**$$

13

PARALLEL ALGORITHMS

13.0 INTRODUCTION

Parallel algorithms have been a topic of research since early 1960s even though there were no parallel computers at that time. Emergence of large-scale parallel computers during the past few decades has made this field one of primary interest to researchers and designers. Work in this field can be broadly categorized under two groups: (i) design of parallel algorithms with unbounded degree of parallelism, (ii) design of parallel algorithms with bounded degree of parallelism. The first group of studies has helped more in understanding complexity related properties of parallel algorithms while the second group has helped in programming for realistic parallel computers rather than for theoretical parallel computational machines.

A parallel algorithm may be thought as a collection of independent task modules executed in parallel and communicating with each other during the execution of the algorithm. Kung has proposed a framework for classifying parallel algorithms. He has identified three important dimensions of parallel algorithms (see Figure 13.1). These three dimensions of the

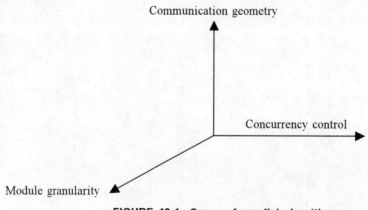

FIGURE 13.1 Space of parallel algorithms.

space of parallel algorithms are orthogonal to one another. These dimensions are: concurrency control, task granularity and communication geometry. While designing parallel algorithms, one has to address the following issues:

(i) How are the concurrent activities controlled?
(ii) What are the granularities of the task modules?
(iii) How do these task modules interact, that is, what is their communication geometry?

There are at least three ways to design a parallel algorithm to solve a problem. These are: (1) one may detect and exploit any inherent parallelism in an existing sequential algorithm, (2) one may invent a new parallel algorithm, (3) one can adapt another parallel algorithm that solves a similar problem. Blind transformation of a sequential algorithm to the parallel form often leads to very poor speedup. Communication plays an important role in parallel algorithms. Sometimes the communication complexity is higher than the computational complexity, that is, more time is spent in routing data among the processors than the time actually required for manipulating the data. A major issue in parallel algorithm design is to minimize this communication overhead.

Flynn[1] classified computer architectures into four groups: SISD (Single Instruction Stream-Single Data Stream), SIMD (Single Instruction Stream-Multiple Data Streams), MISD (Multiple Instruction Streams-Single Data Stream) and MIMD (Multiple Instruction Streams-Multiple Data Streams). Parallel algorithms are executed on SIMD and MIMD machines. The time required to execute the steps of parallel algorithms for SIMD (Single Instruction Multiple Data) computers is predictable because of the lock-step execution mechanism of SIMD algorithms while this is not so for the asynchronous MIMD (Multiple Instructions Multiple Data) machines. The algorithm designer does not have to worry about synchronizing the processors in an SIMD computer—because it is built into the architecture—but for the asynchronous MIMD machines it is not so. The designer has to bring about explicit synchronization in the MIMD algorithms. The time required to execute the steps of a process in parallel algorithms for asynchronous multiprocessors is unpredictable. Based on the measurements done on C.mmp (an MIMD machine), six major sources causing fluctuations in the execution times have been identified. These include variations in the computation time due to different instances of inputs, memory contention, operating system's scheduling policies, variations in the individual processor speeds, etc. The asynchronous behaviour leads to serious issues regarding the correctness and efficiency of an algorithm. The correctness issue arises because, during the execution of an algorithm, operations from different processes may interleave in an unpredictable manner. The efficiency issue arises because any synchronization introduced for correctness reasons takes extra time and also reduces concurrency. Efficiency analysis of algorithms for asynchronous computers is usually difficult; since execution times are random variables rather than constants.

Performance measures

A number of parameters are used to measure the performance of parallel computers. We will briefly discuss speedup and efficiency which are the most widely used parameters.

---

[1] M.J. Flynn, 'Very High Speed Computing Systems', *Proc. IEEE*, Vol. **12**, pp. 1901–1909, 1966.

Speedup: If $T_S(n)$ is the time taken by a uniprocessor to solve a problem of size n using the best sequential algorithm and $T_P(n)$ is the time taken by a parallel system using p processors to solve the same problem, then speedup, $S_P(n)$ is equal to $T_S(n)/T_P(n)$.

Efficiency: Efficiency measures the fraction of time for which a typical processor is usually employed or it is the individual processor's contribution to the speedup. It is defined as the ratio of speedup and the number of processors employed to achieve that speedup, that is, it is the speedup per processor.

About the performance of (parallel) systems, certain (conjectures) predictions are reported in various literature. The most widely referred among these are discussed below.

Grosch's law: It states that the speed of computers is proportional to the square root of its cost. This no longer holds good. It has been made inapplicable by large-scale integration of semiconductor devices.

Minsky's conjecture: The speedup achievable by a parallel computer increases as the logarithm of the number of processors employed, which implies that large-scale parallelism is unproductive.

Amdahl's law

Every programme has some sequential component. Let us suppose that f is the fraction of computation that has to be executed strictly in sequence. Then $(1 - f)$ is the fraction that can be executed in parallel. Let the computation require t_S time for execution on a sequential computer. If a parallel computer containing p processors is used to do the same computation, the time t_P required by this parallel computer would be $t_S * f + t_S * (1 - f)/p$. Hence the speedup achievable is $1/(f + (1 - f)/p)$. This is Amdahl's law for parallel machines. The implication of this law is that a small number of sequential operations can significantly limit the speedup achievable by a parallel computer. This is sometimes termed the sequential bottleneck. For example, if 10 percent of the operations must be performed sequentially, then the maximum speedup achievable is 10, no matter how many processors a parallel computer has.

13.1 PRAM ALGORITHMS

Most of the parallel algorithms are usually described in terms of the PRAM abstraction. This practice is not likely to change in the near future. While developing algorithms in PRAM, one ignores the underlying network architecture of the parallel machine. One never needs to worry about getting the right data to the right place at the right time. In short, the PRAM model abstracts away most of the details associated with the implementation of a parallel algorithm on a parallel machine. There are many variants of PRAM model. What PRAM model to use?

Advocates of the CRCW model point out that they are easier to program than the EREW model and that their algorithms run faster. Critics contend that the hardware to implement concurrent memory operations is slower than the hardware to implement exclusive memory operations. Thus the faster running time of CRCW algorithms is fictitious. Others say that PRAM, either EREW or CRCW, is the wrong model entirely. Processors are connected through a communication network and the communication network should be part of the model. In the following few pages we give PRAM algorithms for a number of representative problems. Before discussing these algorithms, let us introduce some complexity classes for parallel algorithms.

NC class

This class contains well parallelizable problems. Formally, this is the class of problems solvable in poly-logarithmic parallel time using a polynomial number of processors. Problems of size n belonging to this class are solvable in time proportional to $\log^k n$ using polynomial number of processors where $k \geq 0$. For different values of k such as 1, 2, 3, ..., we get the classes NC^1, NC^2, NC^3, ... respectively. Steven Cook coined the name NC for "Nick's Class" because Nick Pippenger was the first person to recognize its importance. Fortunately, the parallel class NC remains the same whether uniform circuit families or shared memory computers are used to define it, although the subclasses NC^k may be different. Examples of problems belonging to this class are: sorting, matrix-multiplication, finding connected components in a graph, planarity testing of a graph, finding minimum weight spanning tree, etc.

RNC class

This is the class of problems solvable by probabilistic circuits with polynomial number of nodes and poly-logarithmic depth. Examples of problems belonging to this class are finding the rank of a matrix over a finite field, finding maximum matching in a graph, testing the singularity of a matrix of polynomials in many variables, abelian permutation group membership problem, etc.

P-complete problems

A problem $L \in P$, the class of problems solvable in polynomial time by deterministic algorithms, is said to be P-complete if every other problem in P can be transformed to L in poly-logarithmic parallel time using a polynomial number of processors. Such a transformation is called Nick's reduction, or NC-reduction in short. The description implies that L is a hardest problem in P from the point of view of finding efficient parallel computations. If it is proved that $L \in NC$ (an unlikely event) then it would follow that $P = NC$. Some of the problems belonging to this class are:

The problem of generability. Let X be a set and $*$ be a binary operation defined on X. T is a subset of X and $x \in X$. Does x belong to the closure of T with respect to $*$?

A Boolean circuit with a specified set of input values is given. Is the output value TRUE?

For a given context-free grammar G, does $L(G)$, the language generated by G contain the empty sentence, ε?

Depth-first search, max-flow in a network, etc. are some of the other P-complete problems.

Figure 13.2 schematically shows how the classes NC, P-complete, and P are positioned with respect to the NP and NP-complete classes.

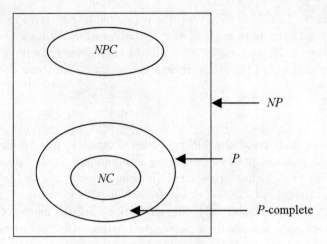

FIGURE 13.2 Problem categories.

We now resume discussion on PRAM algorithms for list ranking, matching, prefix computation, root finding, etc. These problems belong to the *NC* class.

List ranking

We are given a list of n objects. The problem is to compute the distance of each node from the end of the list. To find how far the objects are from the end of the list requires $O(n)$ time for a sequential algorithm. We assume that there are as many processors as the number of list objects and that the ith processor is responsible for the ith object. An efficient parallel solution, requiring only $O(\log n)$ time, is given by the following pseudocode. In the parallel algorithm given below, successor denotes the immediate next neighbour of a node in the list. Figure 13.3 shows working of the algorithm on a list of 5 nodes.

```
Procedure List-Ranking(List)
   For each processor i, Do in parallel
     If successor(i) = NULL Then rank(i) = 0;
                           Else rank(i) = 1;
     Endif
   Enddo
   While there exists a node i such that successor(i) ≠ NULL
     For each processor i, Do in parallel
       If successor(i) ≠ NULL Then
         rank(i) = rank(i) + rank(successor(i));
         successor(i) = successor(successor(i));
       Endif
     Enddo
   Endwhile
End List-Ranking
```

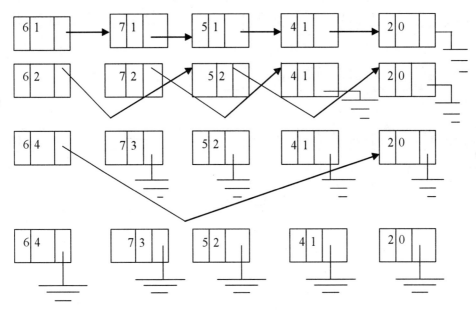

FIGURE 13.3 Snapshots of list ranking.

Since the algorithm terminates only when all the nodes point to NULL and the pointer jumping takes place in geometric progression, the algorithm terminates after $O(\log n)$ jumps for a list of n objects. Hence the complexity of this algorithm is $O(\log n)$. This is an EREW algorithm; since one processor accesses each rank and successor information.

Matching elements of two lists

We are given two linked lists. We have to match the corresponding elements in the two lists. The algorithm assigns to each list node, a pointer to the corresponding node in the other list called its *mate*. The procedure is given below.

```
Procedure Match (Two Lists)
   For all k Do in parallel
     Mate(k) = NULL; /* Indicated as 'N' in the Figure 13.4*/
   Enddo
   mate(1st Node of List 1) = 1st Node of List 2;
   mate(1st Node of List 2) = 1st Node of List 1;
   For all k in parallel Do
     While successor(k) ≠ NULL Do
       If mate(k) ≠ NULL Then
         mate(successor(k)) = successor(mate(k));
       Endif
       successor(k) = successor(successor(k));
     Endwhile
   Endfor
End Match
```

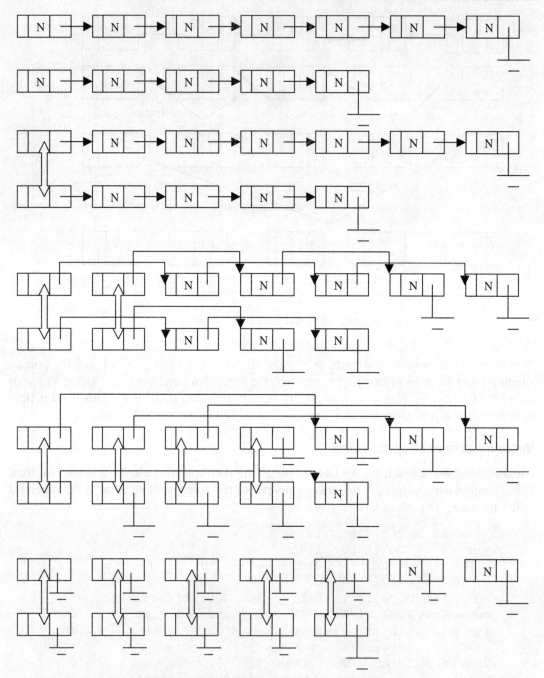

FIGURE 13.4   Matching elements of two lists.

The first line of this pseudocode is for initialization. The component mate is initialized to null in every node. Then the first nodes of the two lists are matched to each other. In the second part, we introduce the pointer jumping technique. A node that has both a successor and a mate will cause its mate's successor to become its successor's mate. This algorithm takes logarithmic time and is of EREW type. Figure 13.4 shows working of the algorithm on an example.

Parallel prefix on a list

A prefix computation is defined in terms of a binary associative operator $\circledR$. The computation takes as input a sequence $<x_1, x_2, ..., x_n>$ and produces as output a sequence $<y_1, y_2, ..., y_n>$ such that $y_1 = x_1$ and $y_k = y_{k-1} \circledR x_k$ for $k = 2, 3, ..., n$. We give an $O(\log n)$ time EREW algorithm for prefix computation using pointer jumping. For convenience, we define the notation $[i, j] = x_i \circledR x_{i+1} \circledR ... \circledR x_j$ for integers i and j in the range $1 \le i \le j \le n$. Then, $[k, k] = x_k$ for $k = 1, 2, ..., n$ and $[i, k] = [i, j] \circledR [j+1, k]$ for $0 \le i \le j < k \le n$. In terms of this notation, the goal of a prefix computation is to compute $y_k = [1, k]$ for $k = 1, 2, ..., n$.

```
Procedure  Prefix(List)
   For  each  processor  i,  Do  in  parallel
     y[i]  =  x[i];
   Enddo
   While there exists a node i such that successor(i) ≠ NULL
      For  each  processor  i,  Do  in  parallel
        If  successor(i)  ≠  NULL  Then
        y[successor(i)]  =  y[i]⊛y[successor(i)];
        successor(i)  =  successor(successor(i));
        Endif
      Enddo
   Endwhile
End  Prefix
```

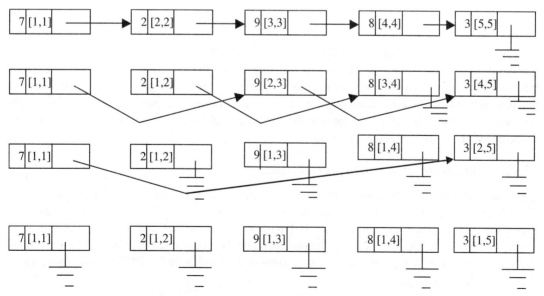

FIGURE 13.5 Snapshots of parallel prefix computation.

This is an exclusive read and exclusive write algorithm and requires an order of log n time for the same reason as explained earlier. The only difference from the list ranking algorithm is that writing by processor i for $y[$ $]$ is done to the successor node. Figure 13.5 shows snapshots of prefix computation on an example.

Finding roots of trees in a forest

A forest is a collection of trees and a tree is a connected graph without cycle. Let us suppose that we are given a forest of binary trees in which each node i has a pointer, parent $[i]$ to its parent and we wish each node to find the identity of the root of its tree. We associate processor i with node i in a forest. After the following pointer-jumping algorithm is executed, the identity of the root of the tree in which node (i) is present will be stored in root (i) of node (i) for all values of i in the forest. Pseudocode for the algorithm is as follows:

```
Procedure Findroots(Forest)
  For each processor i, Do in parallel
    If parent(i) = NULL Then
      root(i) = i;
    Endif
  Enddo

While there exists a node i such that parent(i) ≠ NULL
    For each processor i, Do in parallel
      If parent(i) ≠ NULL Then
        root(i) = root(parent(i));
        parent(i) = parent(parent(i));
      Endif
    Enddo
  Endwhile
End Findroots
```

We claim that Findroots is a CREW algorithm that runs in $O(\log d)$ time, where d is the depth of the maximum-depth tree in the forest. All the writes occurring are exclusive because processor i writes only into node i. Some of the reads are however concurrent, because several nodes may have pointers to the same node. The running time of Findroots is $O(\log d)$ because the length of each path is halved in each iteration. Figure 13.6 illustrates working of the root finding algorithm.

Finding maximum of an array of elements

Here the problem is to find the maximum element in an array of real numbers. We use a CRCW algorithm. We assume that the input array is $A[0, ..., n-1]$. The algorithm uses n^2 processors, each processor comparing $A[i]$ with $A[j]$ for some i and j in the range $0 \leq i$, $j \leq n-1$. In effect, the algorithm performs a matrix of comparisons. We can view each of the n^2 processors as having not only a one-dimensional index in the PRAM, but also a two-dimensional index (i, j).

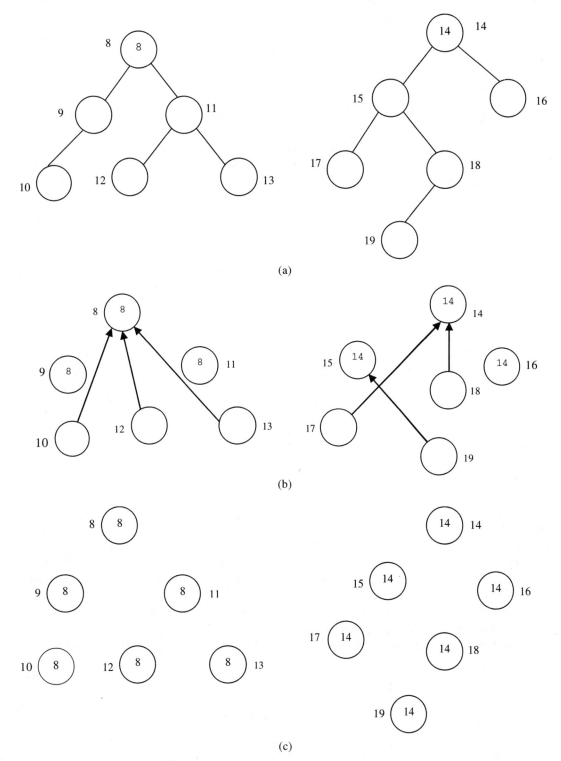

FIGURE 13.6 Snapshots of root finding in a forest.

```
Procedure CRCW_MAX(A)
  Array A(n), m(n)
  n = length(A); /* This gives the number of elements in A*/
  For i = 0 to n - 1, Do in parallel
    m[i] = TRUE;
  Enddo
  For i = 0 to n - 1 and j = 0 to n - 1, Do in parallel
    If A[i] < A[j] Then m[i] = FALSE;
    /* Processors satisfying this condition and having the
  same i-index write the same value 'FALSE' to m[i] */
    Endif
  Enddo
  For i = 0 to n - 1, Do in parallel
    If m[i] = TRUE Then max = A[i]; Endif
  Enddo
  Return(max);
End CRCW_MAX
```

Obviously, in this algorithm many processors are accessing the same location concurrently and multiple processors are writing the same data 'FALSE' into the same location $m[i]$. Hence this is a CRCW algorithm. This CRCW algorithm takes $O(1)$ time. Several processors may write into the same memory location, but if they do, they all write the same value. The EREW model computes the maximum of n elements in Ω (log n) time. Remarkably, the Ω (log n) lower bound for computing the maximum holds even if we permit concurrent reading; that is, it holds for CREW algorithms. Figure 13.7 illustrates operation of the algorithm on the array 7, 3, 2, 9.

Sorting on CRCW

We assume that the concurrent writing into the same memory cell by many processors at the same time is resolved by storing the sum of the integers being written by different processors into the memory cell. Assume that we have N^2 processors available on a CRCW machine and we have to sort N numbers $\{x(1), x(2), ..., x(N)\}$ on this machine. The position of each element $x(i)$ in the sorted sequence is determined by computing $r(i)$, the number of elements smaller than it. If two elements $x(i)$ and $x(j)$ are equal, then $x(i)$ is taken to be the larger of the two if $i > j$; otherwise $x(j)$ is the larger. Once all the $r(i)$ have been computed, $x(i)$ is placed in the position $1 + r(i)$ of the sorted sequence since rank 0 element is placed in the position 1. We assume that the processors are referred by double indices i, j. $P(i, j)$ denotes the processor in row i and column j. The ith row of processors, that is, processors $P(i,*)$ compute $r(i)$, where $*$ denotes don't care situation. Pseudocode for sorting on CRCW PRAM may be written as:

```
Procedure CRCW_Sort(X)
  Array X(N)
  /* X = {x(1),x(2),.......,x(N)} */
  For i = 1 to N, Do in parallel
  For j = 1 to N, Do in parallel
```

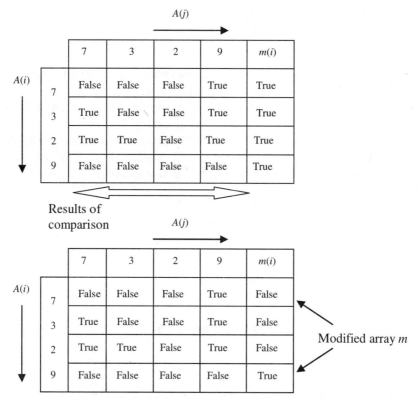

FIGURE 13.7 Finding maximum in O(1) time by CRCW algorithm.

```
If(x(i) > x(j)) or (x(i) = x(j) and i > j)
        Then
    P(i,j) writes 1 in r(i);
        Else
    P(i,j) writes 0 in r(i);
    Endif
  Enddo
  Enddo
End CRCW_Sort
```

Since the *If statement* is executed by all the N^2 processors at the same time, the algorithm requires $O(1)$ time. The main drawback of this algorithm is that we are using a very large number of processors (N^2) to sort N items on a very powerful model of PRAM. The product of time and the number of processors is $O(N^2)$ which is not optimal.

13.2 BOUNDED DEGREE NETWORK ALGORITHMS

In this section we describe a few popular networks and show how some parallel algorithms specific to these networks are designed.

13.2.1 Networks

Ring

Ring network has mostly been used in local area networks. It is a closed chain of processing elements. Each node in the ring has unique predecessor and successor nodes and has degree 2 and so it is a regular network. A ring network with N nodes has diameter $N/2$, that is, $O(N)$ and it can tolerate one fault, that is, communication among the processing elements can be maintained in the event of failure of only one of the processing elements. The symmetrical nature of the ring makes it possible to have a simple routing algorithm. The large diameter of the ring is the major disadvantage of its being used in massive parallel processing. Figure 13.8(a) shows a ring with 5 nodes.

FIGURE 13.8(a) Ring.

Binary tree

The idea of constructing parallel processing architecture when processing elements are connected in the form of a binary tree has been around. The binary tree is a natural way to split up and solve complex 'real world' problems. Some researchers suggest that the binary tree might also be a useful computational structure. Others have observed that the 'divide-and-conquer' paradigm is naturally described by a (usually binary) tree structure and have gone on to design new multiprocessor computers in the form of a binary tree.

In a binary tree machine, each processor or processing element (PE) has three ports to be connected to three other PEs—designated as the parent PE, the left-child PE and the right-child PE respectively—excepting the root PE which does not have connection to parent and the leaf PEs which do not have connections to child PEs. Since the connection is regular and each node has maximum degree three, the structure is suitable for VLSI (Very Large Scale Integration) implementation. The number of nodes (PEs) is $2N - 1$; the number of links is $2N - 2$ and the diameter is $2 \log N$. The line connectivity in a tree structure is one and hence has no inherent fault-tolerance capability. Figure 13.8(b) shows a binary tree with 7 nodes.

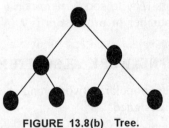

FIGURE 13.8(b) Tree.

Linear array

The simplest interconnection network for parallel processing is linear array. Here, we have N processors numbered $P(1)$, $P(2)$, ..., $P(N)$, each processor $P(i)$ being linked by communication path to processors $P(i-1)$ and $P(i+1)$, where $1 < i < N$ with no other links available and the processors $P(1)$ and $P(N)$ each has only one nearest neighbour. Processor $P(1)$ is connected with $P(2)$ and processor $P(N)$ is connected with $P(N-1)$. Obviously, the number of links is $O(N)$ and the diameter is also $O(N)$. In general, input and output are restricted to the end processors $P(1)$ and $P(N)$, because doing I/O through all the N processors in parallel is not technologically feasible for large values of N as the I/O pads occupy large amount of area on VLSI chips. Linear arrays have been used extensively in the design of systolic[2] algorithms because control and routing of data is simpler in linear array architecture compared to other architectures. Snapping of links between two neighbouring PEs of the linear array leads to two linear arrays with smaller sizes and hence has line connectivity 1. Figure 13.8(c) shows a linear array of 6 processors.

FIGURE 13.8(c)   Linear array.

Mesh array

This is two-dimensional extension of the linear array. Here, N^2 processors are distributed over N linear arrays each containing N processors. These linear arrays are placed side by side in the north to south direction and are connected by north and south links through the PEs on the corresponding positions. If the numbering of the PEs of the linear arrays is made 1 through N in the left to right direction and the linear arrays are numbered successively 1 through N from the north to the south direction, then the kth ($1 \le k \le N$) PE on the linear array number $i(1 < i < N)$ would be connected to the kth PE on the linear array number $(i-1)$ and to the kth PE on the linear array number $(i+1)$. PEs on the 1st linear array do not have north links, similarly PEs on the Nth linear array do not have south links. So each PE in the mesh—excepting the boundary PEs—has 4 connections, 2 to its two neighbours on the same linear array and 2 to the corresponding PEs on the previous and the next linear array. Boundary PEs have either 2 or 3 connections. The 1st and the Nth PEs on the 1st and the Nth linear array have 2 connections each and the other boundary PEs have 3 connections each. The number of links for an $N \times N$ mesh array is $2N^2 - 2N$ which is $O(N^2)$. The diameter is $O(N)$ and the line connectivity is 2. Input and output may be done through the PEs on the periphery of the mesh. In reality, all the peripheral PEs might not be utilized for parallel I/O operations because of the requirement of large I/O pad areas and hence a subset of the peripheral PEs may be utilized for simultaneous I/O operations. Mesh array forms an important model for study of parallel algorithms. Figure 13.8(d) shows a 4×4 mesh.

This architecture may be generalized to higher dimensions in a logically elegant way like a hypercube (described later in this section). The regular pattern of the mesh array

---

[2] A systolic system rhythmically computes and passes data through the system.

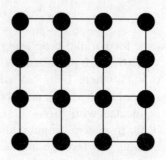

FIGURE 13.8(d) Mesh array.

network makes it suitable for solving many problems from matrix algebra, image processing, etc. and is quite suitable for the divide-and-conquer paradigm. However, its local connectivity nature results in a long communication delay when data have to be moved over a long distance. In an $N \times N$ mesh array, for example, to move data from one PE to another may take as much as $2(N - 1)$ time in the worst case. Thus, a large diameter is the main shortcoming of the mesh array. Therefore, the execution time of the parallel algorithms that need long distance communications is often dominated by the long communication time. To overcome the communication inefficiency, several researchers have augmented the mesh array with various faster mechanisms. One of these augmentations is the use of one or more broadcast buses.

ILLIAC IV

This is an experimental system designed at the University of Illinois at Urbana-Champaign for doing research in parallel processing. The original proposal was to construct a system containing 256 PEs equally distributed over four quadrants, each containing 64 PEs. But only one quadrant was completed. ILLIAC IV connection is an augmented two-dimensional mesh. Each PE in a mesh is connected to its four nearest neighbours in the mesh. The augmentation is done through:

(i) PEs of the same column are joined in the form of rings.
(ii) PEs of all the rows are joined to form a single big ring in the row-major way.

Formally, ILLIAC IV network of size N is characterized by the following four routing functions (R):

$$R_{+1}(i) = (i + 1) \ mod \ N$$
$$R_{-1}(i) = (i - 1) \ mod \ N$$
$$R_{+p}(i) = (i + p) \ mod \ N$$
$$R_{-p}(i) = (i - p) \ mod \ N$$

where $p = N^{0.5}$ and $0 \le i \le N - 1$.

The total number of PEs in an $N \times N$ ILLIAC IV is N^2, the total number of links is $2N^2$ and the diameter is N. Figure 13.8(e) shows an ILLIAC IV with 16 PEs.

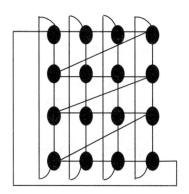

FIGURE 13.8(e)   ILLIAC IV.

Torus

This is also an augmented two-dimensional mesh network where each row of PEs forms a ring and each column of PEs also forms a ring. The total number of PEs is N^2, the total number of links is $2N^2$ and the diameter is N. If the PEs in torus are indexed in row-major way, then the routing functions for an $N \times N$ torus may be written as:

$$Torus_{row+}(i) = (i + 1)\ mod\ N + \lfloor i/N \rfloor * N$$
$$Torus_{row-}(i) = (i - 1)\ mod\ N + \lfloor i/N \rfloor * N$$
$$Torus_{col+}(i) = (i + N)\ mod\ N^2$$
$$Torus_{col-}(i) = (i - N)\ mod\ N^2,\ \text{where}\ 0 \le i \le N^2 - 1.$$

Torus differs from the ILLIAC IV in having separate row rings (as shown in Figure 13.8(f)) instead of single row ring comprising all the PEs.

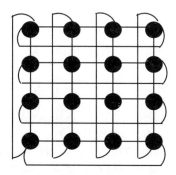

FIGURE 13.8(f)   Torus.

Hypercube

A hypercube is a k-dimensional cube where each node has k-bit address and is connected to k-other nodes. Two nodes in a hypercube are directly connected if their node addresses differ exactly in one bit position. Formally, a k-dimensional hypercube is specified by the following k-routing functions:

$$c_i(a_{k-1}, \ ..., \ a_1 a_0) = a_{k-1} \ ... \ a_{i+1} \ \overline{a}_i \ a_{i-1} \ ..., \ a_0$$

where $0 \leq i \leq k - 1$, $\overline{a}_i$ is the complement of a_i, and 'a's represent the bits in the binary representation of the node address.

There is an elegant recursive definition for a hypercube. An isolated node is a 0-*cube*. Two 0-*cubes* connected by a line is a 1-*cube*. In general, a *k-cube* is defined as the structure resulting from two $(k - 1)$-*cubes* after the corresponding nodes of these two $(k - 1)$-*cubes* are connected by links. The total number of PEs in a *k*-dimensional hypercube is 2^k and the total number of links and diameter are $0.5 \times 2^k k$ and k respectively. There are k edge-disjoint paths between any two PEs, which is a good situation from the fault-tolerance point of view. But the structure is not modularly expandable and the expansion involves changing the number of ports per node. Since several common interconnection topologies such as ring, tree, and mesh can be embedded in a hypercube, the architecture is suitable for both scientific and general-purpose parallel computation. The novelty of this architecture has resulted in several experimental and commercial products such as the Cosmic Cube, Intel iPSC, Ametek System/14, NCUBE/10, Caltech/JPL Mark III, and the Connection Machine. Figure 13.8(g) shows a 4-cube.

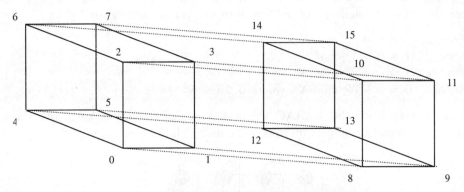

FIGURE 13.8(g)   Hypercube.

Perfect shuffle

In perfect shuffle connection of N PEs, PE(i) is connected to PE(j) where $j = 2i$ for $0 \leq i \leq (N/2) - 1$ and $j = (2i + 1) mod \ N$ for $(N/2) \leq j \leq N - 1$. There is an alternative, but equivalent definition of perfect shuffle. PE(i) is connected by a one-way link to PE(j) if the left cyclic shift of the binary representation of i results in the binary representation of j. A perfect shuffle network of size 8 is shown in Figure 13.8(h).

13.2.2   Network Algorithms

We discuss parallel algorithms for addition, matrix multiplication and sorting on a few networks.

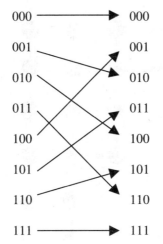

FIGURE 13.8(h) Perfect shuffle.

A look at parallel addition

Suppose we have to add N numbers, where N is an integer power of 2. These N numbers can be added in $N - 1$ addition steps on a sequential processor. However, if multiple processors are available, the N numbers can be added in less than $O(N)$ time by employing the processors simultaneously to carry out the additions. We illustrate below how this is achieved on four very popular interconnection architectures: mesh, tree, hypercube and perfect shuffle network.

Addition on mesh

Suppose, we have to add N numbers using a $\sqrt{N} \times \sqrt{N}$ mesh where each node contains one datum. We can organize the computation as follows. First the nodes on the rightmost ($\sqrt{N}^{th}$) column send their data elements to the corresponding nodes in the $(\sqrt{N} - 1)^{th}$ column. The nodes in this column find the sum of the resident number and that it received from its neighbour on the $\sqrt{N}$-th column. In the next step, the nodes in the $(\sqrt{N} - 1)^{th}$ column send the sum it has calculated to its neighbour in the $(\sqrt{N} - 2)^{th}$ column and the nodes in the $(\sqrt{N} - 2)^{th}$ column add the received data and the resident number. This continues till the 1st column nodes calculate the sum. The above computation requires $(\sqrt{N} - 1)$ send-addition steps. Now we have partial sums in the nodes of the first column. The nodes in the first column add up these partial sums to find the grand total of the numbers in another $(\sqrt{N} - 1)$ steps as illustrated in Figure 13.9. Hence the total time required is $2(\sqrt{N} - 1)$ steps which is $O(\sqrt{N})$, much smaller than $O(N)$ time required for the sequential computation. The speedup in this case is $O(\sqrt{N})$.

Addition on tree

Let us assume that we have a parallel computer where processors are connected in the form of a full binary tree having $N/2$ leaves. The data elements are initially loaded in the leaves of the tree (2 elements per leaf). In step 1, each leaf processor adds the two elements and

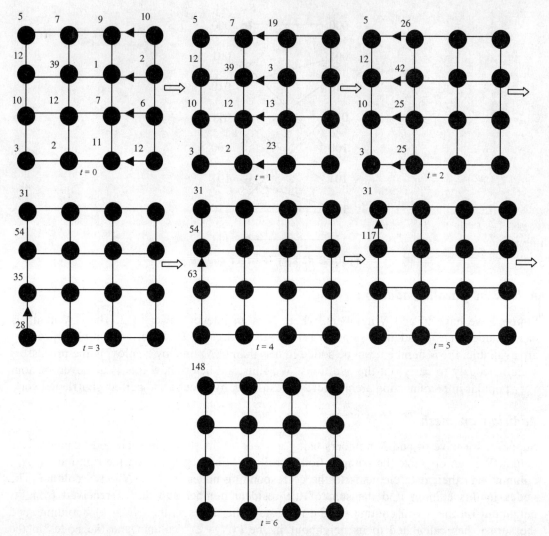

FIGURE 13.9 Addition on mesh.

sends the sum to its parent processor. In the next step, each parent processor adds the two partial sums it received from its children and sends the new sum to its parent. This continues till the lone root of the tree computes the final sum of the N numbers. If there are $N/2$ leaves in the tree, the addition of N numbers will require $\log(N/2)$ addition and send time which is $O(\log N)$; much smaller than the $O(N)$ time required on a sequential machine. Figure 13.10 illustrates how addition is carried out on a tree machine.

Addition on hypercube

Suppose each node of a hypercube with N-nodes has got one datum. A hypercube with N nodes has $\log N$ dimensions. At each time step, a node having a number or a partial sum

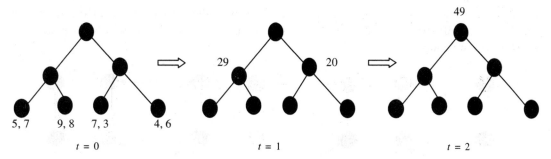

FIGURE 13.10 Addition on tree.

sends it to its neighbour in a particular dimension and the receiving node sums the value it has received from its neighbour and what was available with it. This goes on for all the dimensions of the hypercube one after another. Since there are log N dimensions in a hypercube with N nodes, the sum of N numbers can be computed on a hypercube in $O(\log N)$ send and add steps as illustrated in Figure 13.11. The speedup achieved is $O(N/\log N)$.

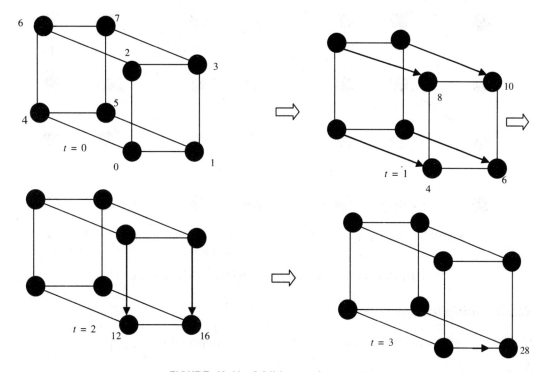

FIGURE 13.11 Addition on hypercube.

Addition on shuffle-exchange network

Addition of N numbers can also be done in $O(\log N)$ time using shuffle-exchange network. For adding N numbers, shuffling of data followed by exchange and addition is carried out log N times. The resulting sum of the N numbers will then be available in the processor number 1 as illustrated in Figure 13.12 for 8 numbers. In this case also we achieve $O(N/\log N)$ speedup.

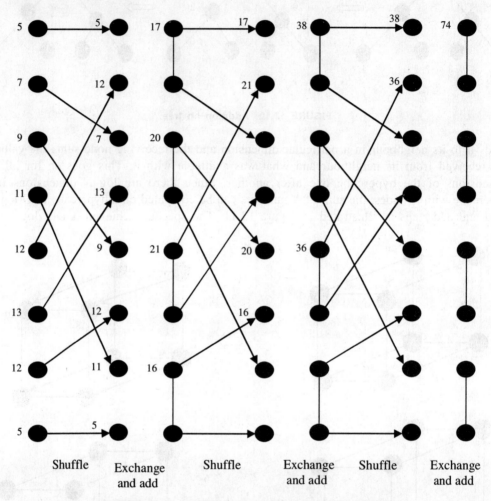

FIGURE 13.12 Addition on shuffle-exchange network.

Matrix multiplication

We discuss matrix multiplication on mesh, torus and hypercube.

On mesh: Let us suppose that we have to multiply two $n \times n$ matrices using an $n \times n$ mesh. Let the input matrices be $A(i, j)$ and $B(i, j)$, $1 \le i, j \le n$. Each processing element PE(i, j) receives one element a_{ij} from matrix A and one element b_{ij} from matrix B for $1 \le i, j \le n$. It is assumed that each PE(i, j) has 4 registers $RA(i, j)$, $RB(i, j)$, $RC(i, j)$ and $RT(i, j)$. Initially $RA(i, j)$ contains a_{ij} and $RB(i, j)$ contains b_{ij}. $RT(i, j)$ is used as temporary storage for matrix elements. $RC(i, j)$ is used to accumulate the elements of the product matrix. Initially only n

PEs have the proper pair of elements from A and B matrices to multiply. By doing some initial shifting of the stored elements of A and B matrices, all the n^2 PEs may be supplied with the proper pair of elements from A and B matrices to do multiplication. This shifting is continued throughout the computation to ensure that every PE is having the proper pair of elements for multiplication. Pseudocode for matrix multiplication on a mesh is given below:

```
Procedure Matrix_Multiplication1(A,B,n)
  Array A(n,n), B(n,n)
  For k = 1 to n - 1 Do
    For all PE(i,1), Do in parallel
      RT(i,1) = RA(i,1);
    /* Makes a copy of register RA */
    Enddo /* 1st Do in parallel loop ending with Enddo*/
    For all PE(i,j) where i > k & j < n, Do in parallel
      RA(i,j) = RA(i,j + 1);
    Enddo /* Data is shifted left along the selected row */
    For all rows, Do in parallel
      For M = 2 to n Do
        /* For all rows in parallel */
      RT(i,M) = RT(i,M - 1);
        /* Sequential transmission along rows */
      Endfor
    Enddo

    For all rows i > k, Do in parallel
      RA(i,n) = RT(i,n); /* For all rows in parallel */
    Enddo
    For all PE(1,j), Do in parallel
      RT(1,j) = RB(1,j);/*Makes a copy of the register RB */
    Enddo
    For all PE(i,j) where j > k & i < n, Do in parallel
      RB(i,j) = RB(i + 1,j);
    Enddo /* Data is shifted south to north along columns */
    For all columns, Do in parallel
      For M = 2 to n Do
        /* For all columns in parallel */
      RT(M,j) = RT(M - 1,j);
      Endfor
    Enddo

    For all columns j > k, Do in parallel
      RB(n,j) = RT(n,j);
    Enddo
  Endfor /* 1st For loop (k) ending with Endfor*/
```

```
       For all PE(i,j), Do in parallel
          RC(i,j) = 0;
       Enddo
   For k = 1 to n Do /*Start of 2nd For loop (k)*/
       For all PE(i,j), Do in parallel
          RC(i,j) = RC(i,j) + RA(i,j)*RB(i,j);
       Enddo
       For all rows, Do in parallel
          RT(i,1) = RA(i,1);
       Enddo
       For all PE(i,j) where j < n, Do in parallel
          RA(i,j) = RA(i,j + 1);
       Enddo
       For all rows, Do in parallel
          For M = 2 to n Do
          RT(i, M) = RT(i,M - 1);
          Endfor
       Enddo
       For all rows, Do in parallel
          RA(i,n) = RT(i,n);
       Enddo
       For all columns, Do in parallel
          RT(1,j) = RB(1,j);
       Enddo
       For all PE(i,j) where i < n, Do in parallel
          RB(i,j) = RB(i + 1,j);
       Enddo
       For all columns, Do in parallel
          For M = 2 to n Do
          RT(M,j) = RT(M - 1,j);
          Endfor
       Enddo
          For all columns, Do in parallel
          RB(n,j) = RT(n,j);
       Enddo
   Endfor /* 2nd For loop (k) ending with Endfor */
   End Matrix_Multiplication
```

The first k-loop is repeated $n - 1$ times. Making copy of the register $RA(i, 1)$ requires constant time. Simultaneous shifting of relevant elements of matrix A along the rows also require constant time. Sequential transmission of saved value of $RA(i,1)$ from PE$(i,1)$ to PE(i, n) require time proportional to $n - 1$. Similarly, saving the value of $RB(1, j)$ takes constant time. Simultaneous shifting of relevant elements of matrix B along the columns requires constant time. Sequential transmission of saved value of $RB(1, j)$ to $RB(n, j)$ requires time proportional to $n - 1$. Hence the first k-loop can be completed in time proportional to $(n - 1)^2$. Initialization of RC registers requires constant time. The second k-loop is repeated n times. The computational steps within this loop can be done in time proportional to $n - 1$. The total time taken for the second k-loop is then proportional to $n(n-1)$. Hence this algorithm requires time proportional to $(n - 1)^2 + n(n - 1) = (n - 1)(2n - 1)$ which is $O(n^2)$.

On torus: Complexity of the above algorithm can be reduced if we augment the mesh with wrap around connections for all the rows and columns, that is, if we use a torus in place of a mesh architecture. When there are wrap around connections, the sequential transmission of $RA(i, 1)$ to $RA(i, n)$ and $RB(1, j)$ to $RB(n, j)$ for all rows and columns in both the k-loops can be dispensed with because these are achieved in constant time through the corresponding wrap around connections. Pseudocode for the matrix multiplication algorithm on a torus may then be given as:

```
Procedure Matrix_Multiplication2(A,B,n)
   Array A(n,n), B(n,n)
   For k = 1 to n - 1 Do
      For all PE(i,j) where i > k, Do in parallel
      RA(i,j) = RA(i,j + 1mod n);
      Enddo /* Data is shifted left along the selected row */
      For all PE(i,j) where j > k, Do in parallel
      RB(i,j) = RB(i + 1mod n,j);
      Enddo /*Data is shifted south to north along columns*/
   Endfor
   For all PE(i,j), Do in parallel
      RC(i,j) = 0;
   Enddo
   For k = 1 to n Do
      For all PE(i,j), Do in parallel
      RC(i,j) = RC(i,j) + RA(i,j)*RB(i,j);
      Enddo
      For all PE(i,j), Do in parallel
      RA(i,j) = RA(i,j + 1mod n);
      Enddo
      For all PE(i,j), Do in parallel
      RB(i,j) = RB(i + 1mod n,j);
      Enddo
   Endfor
   End Matrix_Multiplication2
```

The first k-loop is repeated $n - 1$ times and all the computational steps within the loop are completed in constant time. Initialization of RC registers requires constant time. The second k-loop is repeated n times and the computational steps in this loop can be completed in constant time. Hence the total computation can be completed in time proportional to $2n - 1$ which is $O(n)$. So the additional wrap around connections of a torus over a mesh help us to reduce the computational complexity of matrix multiplication. Figure 13.13 shows the snapshots of matrix multiplications of two 3×3 matrices on a 3×3 torus.

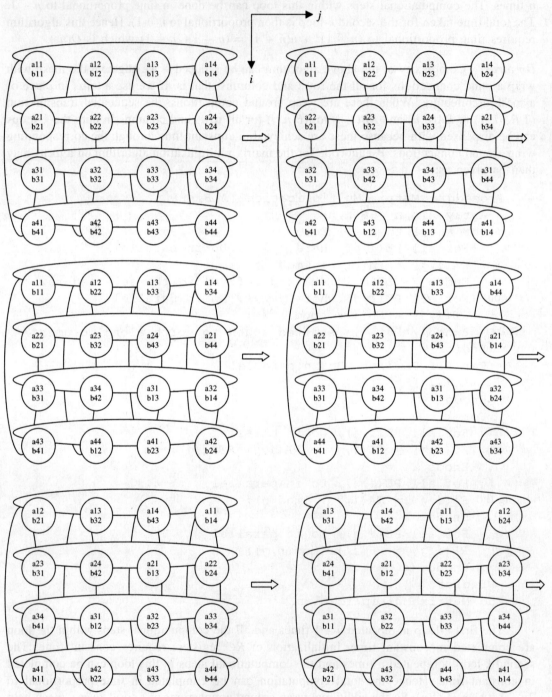

FIGURE 13.13 Contd.

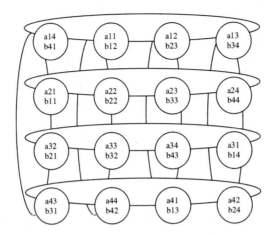

FIGURE 13.13   Matrix multiplication on torus.

On hypercube: We multiply two $n \times n$ matrices using n^3 processing elements connected in the form of a hypercube. In a hypercube of n^3 nodes, each PE is referred by a binary address of 3 log n bits. We map these addresses to the set of integers $\{0, 1, 2, ..., n^3 - 1\}$ for ease of writing the pseudocode. In the rest of this section, we refer log n by q. Initially, the input matrix elements a_{ij} and b_{ij} are loaded into the registers RA and RB of the PE($2^q i + j$) for $0 \le i, j \le n - 1$. Each processing element PE(i) is assumed to have five local registers referred as $RA(i)$, $RB(i)$, $RC(i)$, $RS(i)$ and $RT(i)$ for $0 \le i \le (2^q)^3 - 1$. We use the convention that $RA(i)$, $RB(i)$, $RC(i)$, $RS(i)$ and $RT(i)$ mean the registers RA, RB, RC, RS and RT respectively of the PE(i). At the end of the computation, elements of the product matrix c_{ij}, $0 \le i, j \le n - 1$ will be available in $RC(2^q i + j)$. The parallel algorithm described below makes use of two functions named as *BOOLEAN*( ) and *HYPERCUBELINK*( ). *BOOLEAN* takes two arguments x, y and returns the yth bit in the binary representation of x. *HYPERCUBELINK* takes two arguments x, y and returns an integer formed by complementing the yth bit in the binary representation of x, that is, it gives the address of a hypercube node which is adjacent to the node x along the y axis. Pseudocode for the computation is described below. During the first phase of the execution, elements of the input matrices are distributed among the n^3 PEs of the hypercube. After this *for* loop, a_{ij} will be available in n PE($2^{2q}k + 2^q i + j$)'s in their RA registers, similarly b_{ij} will be available in the registers RB, where $0 \le k \le n - 1$. After the second *for loop* is executed, $RA(2^{2q}k + 2^q i + j)$ will contain a_{ik} for $0 \le j \le n - 1$. After the third *for loop* is executed, $RB(2^{2q}k + 2^q i + j)$ will contain b_{kj} for $0 \le i \le n - 1$.

```
Procedure Matrix_Multiplication3(A,B,n)
   Array A(n,n), B(n,n)
   For y = 3q - 1 down to 2q Do
   For all PE(x) where BOOLEAN(x,y) = 1, Do in parallel
      RT(x) = HYPERCUBELINK(x,y); /* Bits are numbered 0 through
                              3q - 1 */
```

```
        RA(RT(x)) = RA(x);
        RB(RT(x)) = RB(x);
    Enddo
    Endfor
    For y = q - 1 down to 0 Do
    For all PE(x) where BOOLEAN(x,y) ≠ BOOLEAN(x,2q + y),
            Do in parallel
        RT(x) = HYPERCUBELINK(x,y);
        RA(x) = RA(RT(x));
    Enddo
    Endfor
    For y = 2q - 1 down to q Do
    For all PE(x) where BOOLEAN(x,y) ≠ BOOLEAN(x, q + y),
            Do in parallel
        RT(x) = HYPERCUBELINK(x,y);
        RB(x) = RB(RT(x));
    Enddo
    Endfor
    For all PE(x) in parallel Do
        RC(x) = RA(x)*RB(x);
    Enddo
    For y = 2q to 3q - 1 Do
    For all PE(x) where BOOLEAN(x,y) = 0, Do in parallel
        RS(x) = HYPERCUBELINK(x,y);
        RT(x) = RC(RS(x));
        RC(x) = RC(x) + RT(x);
    Enddo
    Endfor
End Matrix_Multiplication3
```

To calculate the time complexity of this algorithm, we note that the first, second and third *for* loops each takes time proportional to q. The total time taken for these three loops is proportional to q. The fourth *for* loop takes constant time. The fifth *for* loop takes time proportional to q. Since these *for* loops are executed one after the other, the total time required for this algorithm is proportional to $q = \log n$. Hence, this algorithm has time complexity $O(\log n)$ and uses n^3 processing elements to multiply two $n \times n$ matrices. Figure 13.14 gives the snapshots for the multiplication of two 2×2 matrices using a 3-*cube*.

Sorting

We discuss parallel sorting on linear array, bitonic merging network, tree and mesh.

Odd-even transposition sort on linear array: In this section we discuss odd–even transposition sort on linear array. Let us assume that we have N processors referred as $P(1)$, $P(2)$, ..., $P(N)$. Processor $P(i)$ is linked to processors $P(i - 1)$ and $P(i + 1)$ for $2 \le i \le N - 1$, $P(1)$ is connected to $P(2)$ only and $P(N)$ is connected to $P(N - 1)$ only. Let the input sequence to

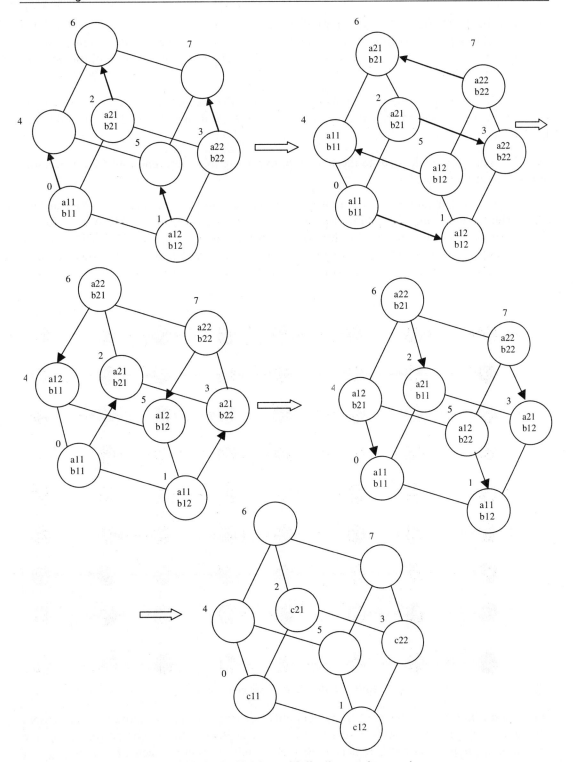

FIGURE 13.14 Matrix multiplication on hypercube.

be sorted be $\{x(1), x(2), ..., x(N)\}$. Initially, each processor contains one item of the input sequence. During the execution of the algorithm, let $y(i)$ denote the data item held by processor $P(i)$ for $1 \leq i \leq N$. Initially, $y(i) = x(i)$. This algorithm repeats the following steps one after the other:

Step 1: In this step all the odd-numbered processors $P(i)$ become active and obtain a copy of $y(i + 1)$ from $P(i + 1)$. If $y(i)$ is greater than $y(i + 1)$, then $P(i)$ and $P(i + 1)$ exchange their data.

Step 2: This step is identical to the first step, excepting that the even-numbered processors are activated this time.

After $\lceil N/2 \rceil$ iterations of the above two steps, no further exchange of data can take place. Hence, when the algorithm terminates $y(i) < y(i + 1)$ for all $1 \leq i \leq N - 1$. Let us illustrate this algorithm on a linear array of length 8 as shown in Figure 13.15. Each of the steps 1 and 2 performs one comparison and two transfers and thus require constant time. Since these two steps are repeated $\lceil N/2 \rceil$ times in the worst case, the time complexity of this algorithm is $O(N)$.

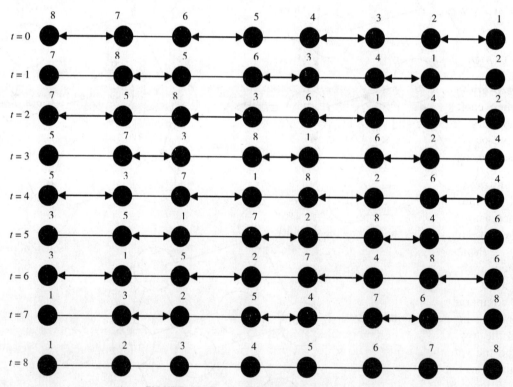

FIGURE 13.15 Sorting on linear array.

Merge-splitting sort: If the number of data items N is larger than p, the number of processors available, each processor holds a subsequence of data items and the comparison-exchange operation of step 1 above is replaced by merge-split operation. Each processor holds a subsequence of length N/p. We assume that N is divisible by p. If N is not divisible by p, we add dummy data to make it divisible. Let $US(i)$ denote the subsequence held by $P(i)$, where $1 \le i \le p$. Initially, each $US(i)$ is random. Each processor sorts its associated subsequence $US(i)$ locally by using a sequential sorting algorithm producing $S(i)$. Then the following two steps are repeatedly done for $\lceil p/2 \rceil$ times.

Step 1:   Each odd-numbered processor $P(i)$ merges the two sorted subsequences $S(i)$ and $S(i + 1)$. It then retains the first half of the merged subsequence and transfers the second half to its neighbour $P(i + 1)$.

Step 2:   This is identical to Step 1 excepting that this time even-numbered processors are activated.

After $\lceil p/2 \rceil$ repetitions of the above two steps in succession, no further exchange of data can take place between two processors. Hence, the sequence $S(1), S(2), ..., S(p)$ is sorted when the algorithm terminates. Local sorting by p processors during the preprocessing stage requires $O((N/p)\log(N/p))$ time by a serial sorting method like merge-sort or quick-sort. Transfer of $S(i + 1)$ into $P(i)$ requires $O(N/p)$ time. Merger of $S(i)$ and $S(i + 1)$ requires at most $2N/p$ steps. Transfer of the second half of the merged sequence into $P(i + 1)$ requires $O(N/p)$ time. Thus, each of the steps 1 and 2 would require $O(N/p)$ time. Since both the steps are repeated at most $\lceil p/2 \rceil$ times, the total running time of this algorithm is $O((N/p)\log(N/p))$ $+ O(p)O(N/p) = O((N/p)\log(N/p) + N)$.

Zero-one principle: The zero-one principle states that if a sorting network works correctly when each input is drawn from the set $\{0,1\}$, then it works correctly on arbitrary input numbers. These numbers could be any set of values from any linearly ordered set. Once we have constructed a sorting network and proved that it can sort all zero-one sequences, we use the zero-one principle to show that it properly sorts sequences of arbitrary values.

Lemma 13.1   If a comparison network transforms the input sequence $X = <x(1), x(2), ..., x(N)>$ into the output sequence $Y = <y(1), y(2), ..., y(N)>$, then for any monotonically increasing function f, the network transforms the input sequence $f(X) = <f(x(1)), f(x(2)), ..., f(x(N))>$ into the output sequence $f(Y) = <f(y(1)), f(y(2)), ..., f(y(N))>$.

Proof: We shall first prove the claim that if f is a monotonically increasing function, then a single comparator with inputs $f(c)$ and $f(d)$ produces outputs $f(\min(c, d))$ and $f(\max(c, d))$. We shall then use induction to prove the lemma. To prove the claim, consider a comparator whose input values are c, d. The upper output of the comparator is $\min(c, d)$ and the lower output is $\max(c, d)$. Suppose, we now apply $f(c)$ to the upper input and $f(d)$ to the lower input. The comparator yields the value $\min(f(c), f(d))$ on the upper output line and the value $\max(f(c), f(d))$ on the lower output line. Since f is a monotonically increasing function, $c \le d$ implies that $f(c) \le f(d)$. Consequently, we have the identities $\min(f(c), f(d))$ $= f(\min(c, d))$ and $\max(f(c), f(d)) = f(\max(c, d))$. Thus, the comparator produces the values $f(\min(c, d))$ and $f(\max(c, d))$ when $f(c)$ and $f(d)$ are its inputs, which completes the proof of the claim.

We can use induction on the depth of each wire in a general comparison network to prove a stronger result: if a wire assumes the value $x(i)$ when the input sequence X is applied to the network, then it assumes the value $f(x(i))$ when the input sequence $f(X)$ is applied (refer Figure 13.16). Because, the output wires are included in this statement, it will prove the lemma.

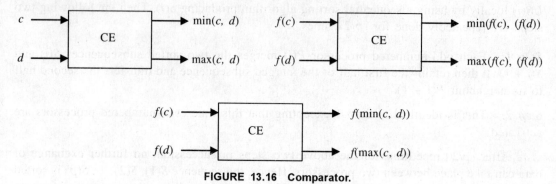

FIGURE 13.16 Comparator.

For the basis, consider a wire at depth 0, that is, an input wire $x(i)$. The result follows trivially: when $f(X)$ is applied to the network, the input wire carries $f(x(i))$. For the inductive step, consider a wire at depth k, where $k \geq 1$. The wire is the output of a comparator at depth k, and the input wires to this comparator are at a depth strictly less than k (refer Figure 13.17). By the inductive hypothesis, therefore, if the input wires to the comparator carry values $x(i)$ and $x(j)$ when the input sequence X is applied, then they carry $f(x(i))$ and $f(x(j))$ when the input sequence $f(X)$ is applied. By our earlier claim, the output wires of this comparator then carry $f(\min(x(i), x(j)))$ and $f(\max(x(i), x(j)))$. Since they carry $\min(x(i), x(j))$ and $\max(x(i), x(j)))$ when the input sequence is X, the lemma is proved.

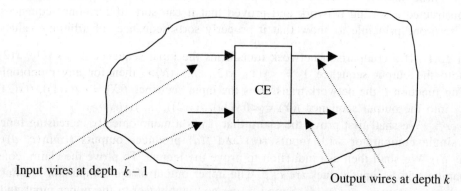

Input wires at depth $k-1$

Output wires at depth k

FIGURE 13.17 Comparison network.

Theorem 13.1 If a comparison network with N inputs sorts all 2^N possible sequences of 0's and 1's correctly, then it sorts all sequences of arbitrary numbers correctly.

Proof: We prove this by contradiction. Suppose that the network sorts all zero-one sequences, but there exists a sequence of arbitrary numbers that the network does not correctly sort. That is, there exists an input sequence $<x(1), x(2), ..., x(N)>$ containing elements $x(i)$ and $x(j)$ such that $x(i) < x(j)$, but the network places $x(j)$ before $x(i)$ in the output sequence. We define a monotonically increasing function f as

$$f(arg) = 0 \text{ if } arg \leq x(i)$$

$$= 1 \text{ if } arg > x(i)$$

Since the network places $x(j)$ before $x(i)$ in the output sequence when $<x(1)$, $x(2)$, ..., $x(N)>$ is input, it follows from the lemma that it places $f(x(j))$ before $f(x(i))$ in the output sequence when $<f(x(1))$, $f(x(2))$, ..., $f(x(N))>$ is input. But since $f(x(j)) = 1$ and $f(x(i)) = 0$, we obtain the contradiction that the network fails to sort the zero-one sequence $<f(x(1))$, $f(x(2))$, ..., $f(x(N))>$.

Batcher's bitonic sorting: This is based on the concept of bitonic sequence. A sequence $<x(1)$, $x(2)$, ..., $x(N)>$ is said to be bitonic if there exists an index i, $1\leq i \leq N$, such that $x(1)$ through $x(i)$ is monotonically increasing (decreasing) and $x(i)$ through $x(N)$ is monotonically decreasing (increasing) or the sequence does not initially satisfy the previous condition but a cyclic shift of the sequence makes it satisfy the condition. For example, $<89, 56, 45, 60, 70, 91, 100>$ is a bitonic sequence. The sequence $<10, 15, 17, 5, 3, 2, 9>$ is also bitonic because a right cyclic shift of the sequence makes it satisfy the conditions.

Theorem 13.2   If $<x(1)$, $x(2)$, ..., $x(2N)>$ is a bitonic sequence and $d(i) = \min(x(i), x(i+N))$, $e(i) = \max(x(i), x(i+N))$ for $1 \leq i \leq N$, then (A) $<d(1)$, $d(2)$, ..., $d(N)>$ and $<e(1)$, $e(2)$, ..., $e(N)>$ are each bitonic, and (B) $\max(<d(1), d(2), ..., d(N)>)$ is less than or equal to $\min(<e(1), e(2), ..., e(N)>)$.

Proof: A cyclic shift of $<x(1)$, $x(2)$, ..., $x(2N)>$ affects $<d(1)$, $d(2)$, ..., $d(N)>$ and $<e(1)$, $e(2)$, ..., $e(N)>$ similarly without affecting the properties (A) and (B). So it is sufficient to prove the theorem for the case where $x(1) \leq x(2) \leq ... \leq x(j - 1) \leq x(j) \geq x(j + 1) \geq ... \geq x(2N)$ for $1 \leq j \leq 2N$. Further, since the reversed sequence $<x(2N)$, $x(2N - 1)$, ..., $x(1)>$ is also bitonic and the properties (A) and (B) are not affected by such reversal, we assume without loss of generality that $N < j \leq 2N$ and prove the theorem for this range. We distinguish between two cases.

Case 1:   If $x(N)$ is less than equal to $x(2N)$, then $x(i) \leq x(i + N)$. Consequently $d(i) = x(i)$ and $e(i) = x(i + N)$ for $1 \leq i \leq N$ and both of (A) and (B) hold.

Case 2:   If $x(N) > x(2N)$, then since $x(j - N) \leq x(j)$ and an index k, $j \leq k < 2N$ can be found such that $x(k - N) \leq x(k)$ and $x(k - N + 1) > x(k + 1)$. It follows that $d(i) = x(i)$, $e(i) = x(N + i)$ for $1 \leq i \leq k - N$ and $d(i) = x(N + i)$, $e(i) = x(i)$ for $k - N < i \leq N$. Hence $d(i) \leq d(i + 1)$ for $1 \leq i \leq k - N$ and $d(i) \geq d(i + 1)$ for $k - N < i < N$, which means that $<d(1)$, $d(2)$, ..., $d(N)>$ is bitonic. Also, $e(i) \leq e(i + 1)$ for $k - N < i < N$, $e(N) \leq e(1)$, $e(i) \leq e(i + 1)$ for $1 \leq i \leq j - N$, $e(i) \geq e(i + 1)$ for $j - N \leq i < k - N$, which means that $<e(1)$, $e(2)$, ..., $e(N)>$ is also bitonic. This completes the proof of (A).

To prove (B), we note that $\max(d(1), d(2), ..., d(N)) = \max(d(k - N), d(k - N + 1)) = \max(x(k - N), x(k + 1))$ and $\min(e(1), e(2), ..., e(N)) = \min(e(k - N), e(k - N + 1)) = \min(x(k), x(k - N + 1))$. Since $x(k) \geq x(k + 1)$, $x(k) \geq x(k - N)$, $x(k - N + 1) \geq x(k - N)$ and $x(k - N + 1) \geq x(k + 1)$, we have $\max(x(k - N), x(k + 1)) \leq \min(x(k), x(k - N + 1))$.

Figure 13.18 gives the diagram of a general bitonic merging network and Figure 13.19 illustrates how a random sequence of 8 elements is sorted using bitonic merging network.

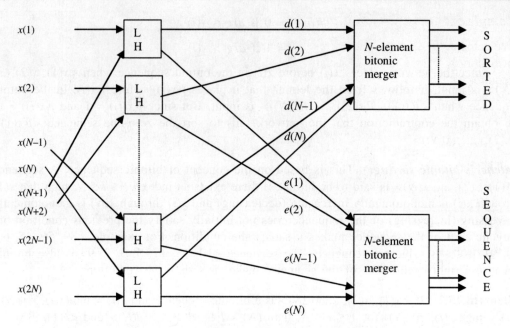

FIGURE 13.18 General bitonic merging network.

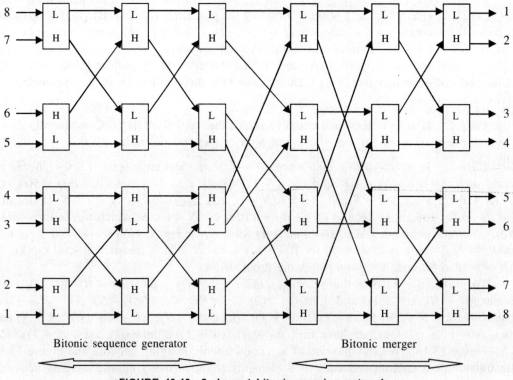

FIGURE 13.19 8-element bitonic merging network.

Complexity analysis for bitonic sorting

We calculate the hardware (in terms of the number of comparators) and time required to sort a random sequence of $N = 2^m$ elements using bitonic sorting. The first stage of the network requires 2^{m-1} bitonic mergers of length 2, each containing one comparator element (CE). The second stage requires 2^{m-2} bitonic mergers of length 4, each containing 4 CEs. The third stage contains 2^{m-3} bitonic mergers of length 8, each containing 12 CEs and so on. Let $C(2^i)$ denote the number of comparators required at the stage i. Then we can write

$$C(2^i) = 1, \ i = 1 \quad \text{and}$$

$$C(2^i) = 2^{i-1} + 2 * C(2^{i-1}) \text{ for } i > 1.$$

The solution for this recurrence relation may be written as $C(2^i) = i2^{i-1}$. Hence the total number of comparators present in the network is:

$$\sum_{i=1}^{i=m} C(2^i) * 2^{m-i} = 0.5 \sum_{i=1}^{i=m} i2^m = N(\log^2 N + \log N)/4 \text{ which is } O(N \log^2 N).$$

To calculate the time complexity, we note that the first stage of the network requires one time step, the second stage requires two time steps, the third stage requires three time steps and so on. In general, stage i requires i time steps. So the total time required for sorting of N random elements may be written as

$$\sum_{i=1}^{i=m} i = \log N(\log N + 1)/2 \text{ which is } O(\log^2 N).$$

Sorting on tree: We assume that the tree has N leaves and the items of the list to be sorted are distributed among the leaves of the tree, one item per leaf. Each data item in the leaves is attached with two fields: position of the data item in the sequence which is the same as the left to right numbering of the leaf PE containing the data item and a flag indicating the next direction of motion of the data through the tree, up indicated by '1' and down indicated by '0'.

Data	Position	Up/down

The computation takes place in pipelined fashion and requires $\log N$ phases. Phase 1 merges $N/2$ bitonic sequences each of length 2 to produce $N/2^2$ bitonic sequences of length 2^2. Phase 2 merges $N/2^2$ bitonic sequences of length 2^2 to produce $N/2^3$ bitonic sequences each of length 2^3. In general, phase i $(1 \leq i < \log N)$ merges $N/2^i$ bitonic sequences of length 2^i to produce $N/2^{i+1}$ bitonic sequences each of length 2^{i+1}. The last phase, that is, phase $\log N$ merges a bitonic sequence of length N to produce a sorted sequence. Merging in phase $i(1 \leq i \leq \log N)$ utilizes $N/2^i$ disjoint sub-trees each of height i in parallel; it then utilizes $N/2^{i-1}$ disjoint sub-trees each of height $i - 1$ in parallel, and so on and ultimately it utilizes $N/2$ disjoint sub-trees each of height 1 in parallel. Disjoint sub-trees are obtained by successively

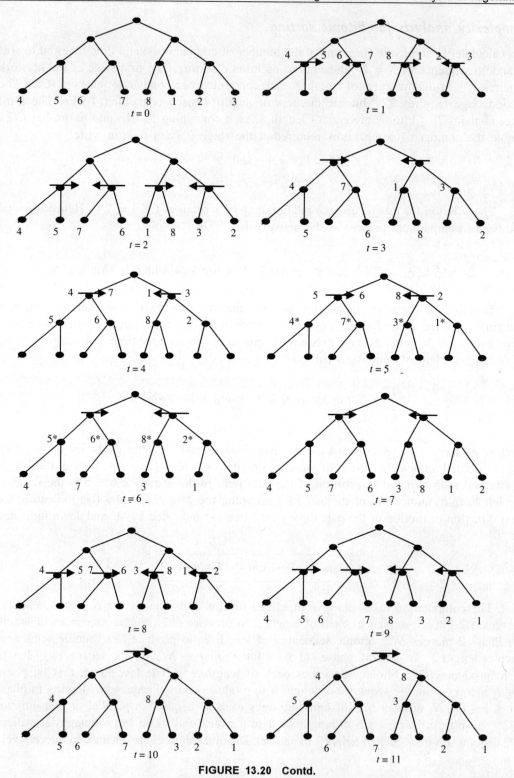

FIGURE 13.20 Contd.

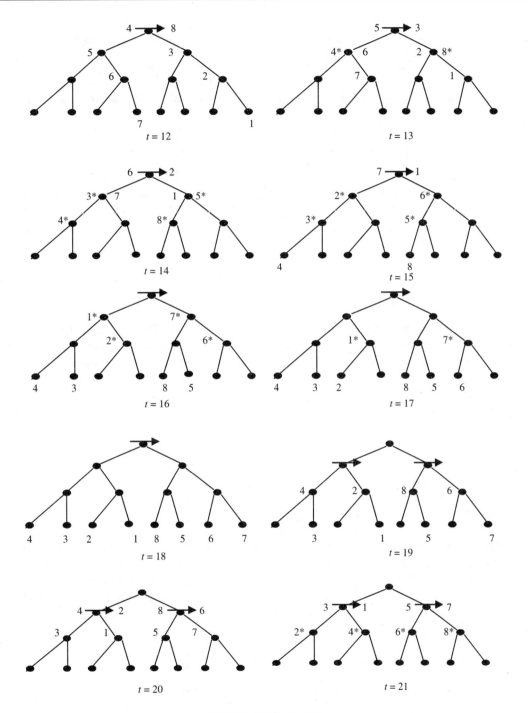

FIGURE 13.20 Contd.

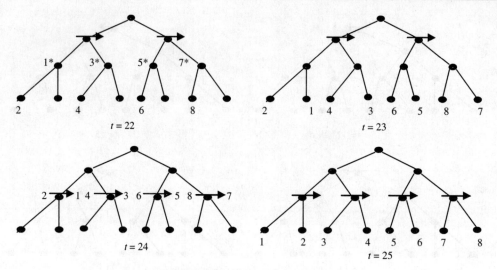

FIGURE 13.20 Sorting on tree.

removing the roots of the previous sub-trees logically. Thus by removing the root of the original tree, we get two disjoint sub-trees of height $\log N - 1$. Then by logically removing the two roots of the two sub-trees of height $\log N - 1$, we get 4 disjoint sub-trees of height $\log N - 2$ and so on. These sub-trees are ordered and are referred by the numbers in the range 1 to $N/2$ in the left to right direction. Roots of the sub-trees behave in two different ways. Either they send the larger of the two data items to the right child and the smaller to the left child or they send the smaller data to the right child and the larger to the left child. These two situations are shown in the attached diagrams (Figure 13.20) by horizontal arrows piercing the roots of the sub-trees. These arrows are directed either left to right representing the situation where the larger datum goes to the right child and the smaller goes to the left child, or right to left representing the reverse situation. We now discuss how to set the arrow directions in the roots of the sub-trees. In any merging phase, say i, the roots of the initial $N/2^i$ disjoint sub-trees, each of height i are programmed to have arrows directed left to right and right to left alternately starting from the leftmost sub-tree. Then we split $N/2^i$ disjoint sub-trees of height i into $N/2^{i-1}$ disjoint sub-trees of height $i-1$. The roots of these $N/2^{i-1}$ sub-trees will have arrow directions the same as it was with their respective parent node in the previous step from which a pair of disjoint sub-trees have been obtained now. This continues till disjoint sub-trees each of height 1 are obtained. The next merging phase starts and the setting of the arrows follows the same pattern. A pseudocode for the algorithm is given below:

```
Procedure Treesort
   For i = 1 to log N Do
      For j = i to 1 Step -1 Do

         For all N/2^j sub-trees of height j, Do in parallel
            Set the position of data among the leaves of sub-trees
            in a left to right numbering;
```

```
             For l = 1 to 2^{j-1} Do
               For Leaf PE(l) and PE(l + 2^{j-1}) Do
                 /*Leaves of disjoint sub-trees are numbered
                 separately by 1,2,3, ... in the left to right
                 direction */
                 Set Direction = '1';
                 Send the record to the respective parents;
                 Set direction = '0' for the data received from the
                 parent;
               Endfor
             Endfor

          For Intermediate PE Do
            The received data from child is sent to its parent PE;
            The received data from the parent PE is transmitted
            to its child PE according to the content of the
            position field;
          Endfor

          For Root PE Do
            Set the direction fields of the two data records from
            its two children to '0';
            Compare the data fields and if the data received from
            the left child is greater than that received from the
            right child and the arrow direction of the root PE is
            left to right or the data received from the right child
            is larger than that received from the left child and
            the arrow direction is right to left, then exchange
            their data fields;
            Send these records to the children according to their
  ·         position fields;
          Endfor
        Enddo
      Endfor
    Endfor
End Treesort
```

A snapshot of the algorithm is shown in Figure 13.20 where the tree has 8 leaves. Data items moving down the tree are shown by putting a star beside it. Data items without star are moving up the tree. In analyzing the algorithm, we note that phase i $(1 \le i \le \log N)$ utilizes $N/2^i$ disjoint sub-trees of height i in parallel, then $N/2^{i-1}$ disjoint sub-trees of height $i - 1$ in parallel, and so on, ultimately utilizing $N/2$ disjoint sub-trees of height 1 each in parallel. Computation for phase i requires:

$$\sum_{j=1}^{j=i} (2i + 2^{i-1} - 1)$$ time steps which is equal to $i^2 + 2^i - 1$. Hence the total time required

for sorting on tree machine is $$\sum_{i=1}^{i=\log N} (i^2 + 2^i - 1) = (1/6)(2 \log^2 N + \log N)(\log N + 1)$$ $+ 2(N - 1) - \log N$, which is $O(N)$.

Sorting on mesh: In this subsection we discuss about sorting on mesh. We have chosen two popular sorting methods on mesh: shear sort and bitonic sort. Before we discuss these, we introduce three important indexing schemes (shown in Figure 13.21) for mesh: row-major indexing, shuffled row-major indexing and snakelike-like row-major indexing. In row-major indexing, the index of the upper leftmost corner PE is the least, the lower rightmost PE has the highest index and on each row, the index value increases from left to right, with every next PE towards right having a value one higher than that of its left neighbour. Shuffled row-major indexing is obtained by shuffling the binary representation of the row-major index. The snake-like row-major indexing can be obtained from the row-major indexing if we reverse the indexing of the PEs of every alternate row of the mesh.

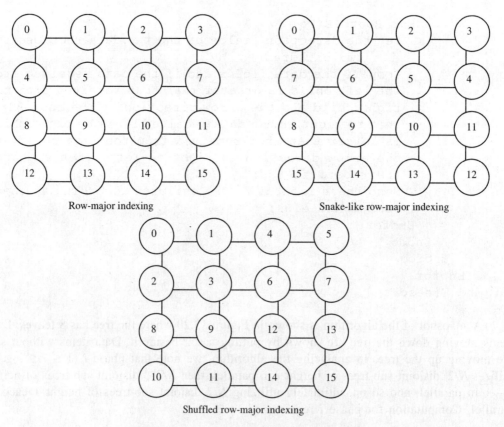

Row-major indexing

Snake-like row-major indexing

Shuffled row-major indexing

FIGURE 13.21 Indexing schemes for mesh.

Shear sort: In this method, we sort N data items distributed over a $\sqrt{N} \times \sqrt{N}$ mesh of processing elements, where each PE contains one datum before and after the sort by alternately sorting the rows and the columns of the mesh. The rows are sorted in the odd phases (1, 3, 5, ...) and the columns are sorted in the even phases (2, 4, 6, ...). The columns are sorted so that the smaller numbers move up in the mesh. The rows are sorted so that the smaller numbers move towards left for the odd numbered rows and towards the right for the even numbered rows; that is, the odd numbered rows (1, 3, 5, ...) are sorted in ascending order and the even numbered rows (2, 4, 6, ...) are sorted in descending order (see Figure 13.22). After $\log N + 1$ phases, the numbers will appear sorted in a snakelike order. By using 0–1 principle, it can be proved that the shear-sort correctly sorts. The main idea in the proof is that at least half of the unsorted rows in the mesh become sorted by applying two phases of the algorithm (a row sort and a column sort). We prove that in any 0–1 matrix, at least half of the rows that are not all 0 or all 1 become all 0 or all 1 simply by sorting the rows and then sorting the columns.

Let us divide the rows of the mesh into three regions: the upper all 0 rows, the lower all 1 rows and the middle dirty rows. Dirty rows contain both 0 and 1. Such division is always possible since we have just finished sorting the columns. Now, we group the dirty rows into consecutive pairs. The effect of sorting rows has six possible outcomes for each pair depending on whether the pair contains more 0s, more 1s, or an equal number of both. Three of these outcomes are shown below and the remaining three outcomes are the reverse of these.

0........01........1	0.........01........1	0........01........1
1....10...........0	1..............10....0	1........10........0
(More 0s)	(More 1s)	(Equal 0s & 1s)

After row sorting, the columns are sorted. Let us assume that the first step in sorting the columns is to compare items in the same column of paired rows, exchanging items if necessary. Once this is done, each pair of rows appears as shown below depending on the number of 0s and 1s in the pair.

0...............0	0...01....10....0	0...............0
1....10..01...1	1..................1	1...............1
(More 0s)	(More 1s)	(Equal 0s and 1s)

Let us move all 0 rows to the upper region and all 1 rows to the lower region as the next step in sorting the columns. The remaining steps required to sort the columns can be carried out arbitrarily. Since at least one row in each pair becomes all 0 or all 1 and is moved out of the middle region after sorting the rows and columns, the middle region decreases in size by at least one-half for each pair of phases. Hence after $2 \log \sqrt{N} = \log N$ phases, the numbers are sorted, except for one row. The algorithm terminates after sorting of this row in the last phase. The columns and the rows can be easily sorted in $\sqrt{N}$ steps using the odd-even transposition sort. Hence the total running time of the algorithm is $\sqrt{N}(\log N + 1)$ steps.

10	12	5	3
2	1	0	6
7	2	11	8
9	6	4	13

Row sort

3	5	10	12
6	2	1	0
2	7	8	11
13	9	6	4

Column sort

2	2	1	0
3	5	6	4
6	7	8	11
13	9	10	12

Row sort

0	1	2	2
6	5	4	3
6	7	8	11
13	12	10	9

Column sort

0	1	2	2
6	5	4	3
6	7	8	9
13	12	10	11

Row sort

0	1	2	2
6	5	4	3
6	7	8	9
13	12	11	10

FIGURE 13.22 Shear sort on a mesh (snakelike row-major indexing).

Bitonic sort on mesh: Nassimi and Sahni have implemented Batcher's bitonic sorting scheme on a mesh-connected computer. Their algorithm requires $14N$ route steps and $2 \log^2 N$ compare-exchange steps (approximately) to sort a two-dimensional array of size $N \times N$ in row-major indexing. The merge algorithm proposed by them requires one of the input sub-files being merged to be sorted in non-decreasing order and the other in non-increasing order. Thompson and Kung have shown that if the shuffled row-major indexing is used, the bitonic sort on mesh-connected computer can also be done in approximately $14N$ route steps and $2 \log^2 N$ compare-exchange steps.

Snapshots of bitonic sort on a 4×4 mesh is shown in Figure 13.23. Arrows indicate the direction of nondecreasing subsequences. Each PE is assumed to have one data item. The steps are:

Step 1: In the first pass, the 4×4 array of input elements is treated as eight 1×2 arrays that are sorted individually.

Step 2: In the second pass, the 4×4 array is treated as four 2×2 arrays and sorted.

Step 3: In the third pass, the 4×4 array is treated as two 2×4 arrays and sorted.

Step 4: In the fourth pass, the 4×4 array is sorted.

13.3 MULTIPROCESSOR ALGORITHMS

Most of the parallel systems operate in SIMD mode. These systems have good performance for certain classes of problems. But they lack in generality, that is, programming these machines for a wide class of problems are sometimes difficult and does not have the desired level of performance. On the other hand, multiprocessors are general purpose in nature and can be used for wide classes of problems. However, unlike SIMD machines, the multiprocessors work mainly in the asynchronous mode. So programmers of these machines have to explicitly take care of synchronization and mutual exclusion problems in the code. A parallel algorithm for a multiprocessor is a set of concurrent processes that may operate simultaneously to perform the required computation. To design an algorithm for a multiprocessor, the workload has to be divided among the processors of the multiprocessors. The division of workload may be done either statically or dynamically. In the static approach, processors are assigned

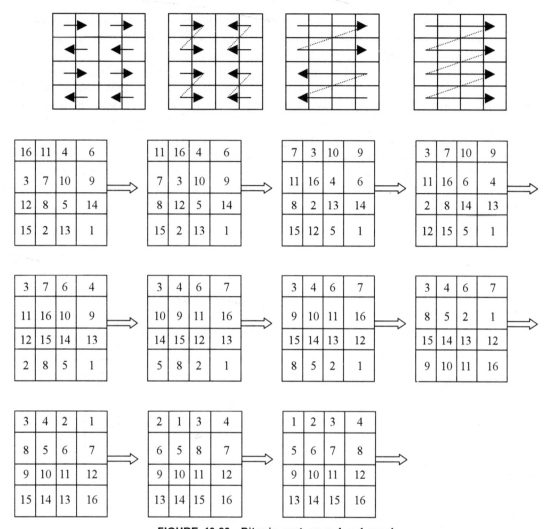

FIGURE 13.23 Bitonic sort on a 4 × 4 mesh.

tasks before the execution of the algorithm begins. In the dynamic approach, processors are assigned tasks as and when individual processors become free. Since multiple processors are working towards a common goal, some form of communication and synchronization is necessary among the processors. The processors may communicate with each other by passing messages through the processor-processor interconnection network or by reading global shared variables.

The two basic techniques used for synchronization are condition synchronization and barrier synchronization. In a set of cooperating processes, it may be the case that the state of a shared data object is such that it is inappropriate for executing a given operation. Any process that attempts such an operation should be delayed until the state of the data object changes to the desired value as the result of other processes operating on it. This type of synchronization is called *condition synchronization. Barrier synchronization* is a method of synchronizing a set of processes by halting at a specified point until all the other processes have also reached that point. This point is known as the barrier point.

Multiprocessing is the cooperative and integrative use of programming, architectural and technological means to execute two or more processes in parallel using multiple processor-based computer systems. A multiprocessor is an integrated computer system with the following characteristics: (i) it involves two or more processors all of roughly the same computational power and each capable of executing processes autonomously, (ii) the processes share a (logically) single, system-wide, memory space, (iii) the processors interact through message passing, (iv) the hardware system as a whole is managed by a single operating system. Multiprocessors are generally classified as tightly coupled and loosely coupled (refer Figure 13.24).

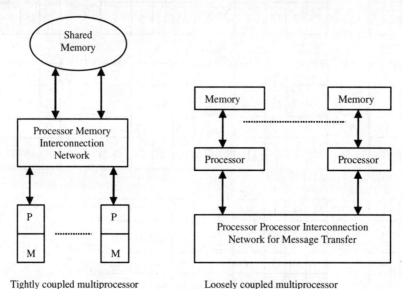

FIGURE 13.24   Architecture of multiprocessors.

Tightly coupled multiprocessor

In this case, processors communicate through a shared main memory. Hence, the rate at which data can be communicated from one processor to the other is on the order of the bandwidth of the memory. A small local memory or high-speed buffer (cache) may exist in each processor. A complete connectivity exists between the processors and the memory. One of the limiting factors to the expansion of a tightly coupled system is the performance degradation due to memory contentions that occur when two or more processors attempt to access the same memory unit concurrently.

Loosely coupled multiprocessor

Loosely coupled multiprocessor systems do not generally encounter the degree of memory conflicts experienced by tightly coupled systems. In such systems, each processor has a number of input/output devices and a large local memory, where it accesses most of the instructions and data. Processes that execute on different computer modules communicate by exchanging messages through the message transfer network. The degree of coupling in such a system is very loose. Loosely coupled systems are usually efficient when the interactions among tasks are minimal. Tightly coupled systems can tolerate higher degree of interactions among tasks without significant deterioration in performance. This type of multiprocessor may also be described as interacting multi-computer system or distributed memory system with message passing protocol. Message transfer network (or system) can take the form of single shared bus or a shared memory system. The latter case can be implemented with a set of memory modules and a processor-memory interconnection network or a multi-ported main memory. Processes can communicate with other processes allocated to the same processor, or with processes allocated to other processors. Communication between tasks allocated to the same processor takes place through the local memory only. Communication between tasks allocated to different processors is through a communication port residing in the communication memory. One communication port is associated with each processor as its input port.

Multiprocessors are more aptly classified as UMA and NUMA. UMA stands for uniform memory access and NUMA stands for non-uniform memory access. As the name implies, in UMA any processor can access any location in the memory with the same time. But in NUMA, all memory locations do not require the same time. In NUMA, accessing local memory locations requires much less time than accessing locations from remote memory. C.mmp is a UMA type multiprocessor and Cm* is a NUMA type multiprocessor.

13.3.1 Summation on Multiprocessor

Let us assume that we have to find the sum of the elements $A(0)$, $A(1)$, ..., $A(N-1)$ available in the shared memory of a tightly coupled multiprocessor containing M processors $P(0)$, $P(1)$, ..., $P(M-1)$. Each processor has some local memory as well. *Total* is a global variable used to store the sum of all the elements. *Sum(i)* is a local variable for the processor $P(i)$ and is used to store the partial sum calculated by the processor(i). Each processor(i) has the local variable L_i to control repetitive execution of codes. *Lock* and *Unlock* statements are used for controlled access to critical sections. Pseudocode for the algorithm is given below:

```
Procedure Multiprocessor_sum
  Array A(N)
  /*1*/ Total = 0;
  /*2*/ For all Processors P(i), 0 ≤ i ≤ M - 1,
                          Do in parallel
                            Sum(i) = 0;
                          Enddo
  /*3*/ For all Processors P(i), 0 ≤ i ≤ M - 1,
                          Do in parallel
  /*3A*/                    For L_i = i to N - 1 Step M Do
  /*3B*/                      Sum(i) = Sum(i) + A(L_i);
                          Endfor
```

```
/*4*/  Lock(Total);
/*5*/  Total = Total + Sum(i);
/*6*/  Unlock(Total);
   Enddo
End Multiprocessor_sum
```

Statement 1 of the above algorithm is executed by a single processor (say, processor(0)) to initialize the global variable *Total*. Statement 2 is executed by all processors in parallel. The loop consisting of statements 3A and 3B is executed by all the processors in parallel. Updation of the shared variable *Total* is done by the processors in sequence and this is achieved by putting the critical section under a pair of *Lock* and *Unlock* statements, which are atomic.

Complexity

We find the worst-case time complexity of this algorithm. If the initial process creates $M - 1$ other processes all by itself, the time complexity of process creation is $\theta(M)$. Assuming that there are as many memory banks as there are processors and there is no memory conflict, the time taken to find the local sums is $\theta(N/M)$. Since *Total* is updated inside a critical-section, processors can access it one after another. Hence, updation of global sum variable will require $\theta(M)$ time. Hence, the complexity of this algorithm is $\theta(M + N/M)$. The minimum of the function $N/M + M$ occurs when $M = \sqrt{N}$. Hence the execution time of this parallel algorithm is minimized when $\theta(\sqrt{N})$ processors are used.

13.3.2   Matrix Multiplication on Multiprocessor

Suppose we have to multiply two matrices $A(n, n)$ and $B(n, n)$ to generate the product matrix $C(n, n)$, using a tightly coupled multiprocessor having p processors. The sequential algorithm may be written as:

```
Procedure Seqmul
   Array A(n,n), B(n,n), C(n,n)
   For i = 1 to n Step 1 Do
     For j = 1 to n Step 1 Do
       Temp = 0;
       For k = 1 to n Step 1 Do
         Temp = Temp + A(i,k) * B(k,j);
       Endfor
       C(i,j) = Temp;
     Endfor
   Endfor
End Seqmul
```

The above multiplication algorithm has cubic complexity on a single processor. There are three loops in the code for sequential machine. The k-loop cannot be made parallel since it contains the data dependent code. Thus either the i or the j loop can be made parallel. If the j-loop is made parallel, the parallel algorithm will execute n synchronizations, one per iteration of the i-loop and the grain size of the parallel code will be $O(n^2/p)$. On the other hand, if the i-loop is made parallel, then the parallel code will execute only one synchronization, that is, at the beginning of the algorithm and the grain size of the parallel code will be $O(n^3/p)$. Grain size is the amount of computation between two synchronizations. Since the main objective of parallelization is to maximize the grain size and minimize the synchronization overhead, we present the i-loop parallelized version of the algorithm.

```
Procedure Mulmatmul
   Global Array A(n,n), B(n,n), C(n,n)
   Global n
   Local i,j, k, t
   For all the processors proc(1), 1 ≤ 1 ≤ p, DO in Parallel
     For i = 1 to n step p DO
        For j = i to n step 1 DO
           Temp = 0;
           For k = 1 to n Step 1 DO
              Temp = Temp + A(i,k) * B(k,j);
           Endfor
           C(i,j) = Temp;
        Endfor
     Endfor
   Enddo
End Mulmatmul
```

Each individual processor calculates n/p rows of the product matrix. Time required for computing one row of the product matrix is $O(n^2)$. Therefore, the computational complexity is $O(n^3/p)$. The synchronization overhead for p processors is $O(p)$, since the processing elements are synchronized only once. The overall complexity of the algorithm is $O(n^3/p + p)$. The above algorithm is suitable for UMA multiprocessors.

13.3.3 Sorting on Shared Memory Multiprocessor

Quinn has presented three parallel sorting algorithms: parallel quick-sort, parallel shell-sort and quick-merge suitable for implementation on tightly coupled multiprocessors. He compared the performance of these algorithms on the Denelcor HEP machine. It is observed that the speedup of parallel quick-sort is constrained, if the partitioning of a sub-list is performed by a single processor. Shell-sort has proven to be amenable to parallelization. But in the final few iterations, the number of independent sub-arrays to be sorted is less than the number of processors available and the higher complexity of sequential shell-sort ($O(N^{3/2})$) wipes out its advantage of more inherent parallelism.

Parallel quick-sort

Quick-sort is a recursive algorithm that partitions an unsorted list into a splitter key and two sub-lists—one containing keys smaller than or equal to the splitter key and the other containing keys larger than the splitter key—and then sorts the sub-lists independently in a recursive manner. A number of processes, one per processor, execute in parallel. The keys to be sorted are stored in a global array. A single global stack stores the indices of sub-arrays that are still unsorted. When a process is free, it checks whether the stack is nonempty and if so, the process locks the stack and pops the indices of an unsorted sub-array off the stack and unlocks the stack. The process partitions the sub-array into two smaller sub-arrays, locks the global stack, pushes the indices of one of the unsorted sub-arrays onto the stack, unlocks the stack, and repeats the partitioning process on the other unsorted sub-array. The parallel quick-sort achieves rather mediocre speedup. The most important reason for this is low amount of parallelism early in the algorithm's execution. In fact, the partitioning of the original unsorted array forms a significant sequential component that puts a ceiling on the maximum speedup achievable, regardless of the number of processors available. Another factor, though less significant is the contention of processes for the shared global stack containing indices of unsorted sub-arrays. Parallel quick-sort has no or low parallelism at the beginning of its execution and high parallelism at the end.

Parallel shell-sort

Execution of the algorithm consists of a number of iterations. For each iteration i, there is an associated distance $d(i)$. Elements whose indices modulo $d(i)$ are equal are sorted using linear insertion sort. The distance is reduced successively with each iteration. The distance in the final iteration is 1. After this iteration, the list is sorted. When the distance is large, the shell-sort is quite amenable to parallelization.

Quick-merge

This is a combination of quick-sort and multi-way merge and has been shown to outperform parallel quick-sort when used to sort a random permutation of the first N integers. It has three phases.

In the first phase, each of the P processors sorts a contiguous set of not more than $\lceil N/P \rceil$ elements using quick-sort. After this phase, all the processors synchronize. In the first sorted list of $\lceil N/P \rceil$ keys, $P - 1$ evenly spaced keys are used as dividers to partition each of the remaining sorted lists into P sub-lists.

The second phase accomplishes the partitioning as follows. Each processor i, $1 \leq i \leq P$, finds for lists 2 through P, the index of the largest key, not larger than the key located at index $\lfloor iN/P \rfloor$ in list 1. After this phase, all the processors synchronize. Each of the sorted sub-lists has now been divided into P sorted sub-lists such that every element in the ith sorted sub-list of every list is greater than any key in any list's $(i - 1)^{th}$ sorted sub-list, for $2 \leq i \leq P$.

In the third phase, each processor i, $1 \leq i \leq P$ performs a P-way merge of the ith sorted sub-lists stored in P different areas. These merges are completely independent of each other. All the processors synchronize after this and the entire list is now sorted.

The worst-case time complexity of sorting N elements using quick-sort is $O(N^2)$. So the first phase of the quick-merge has the worst-case complexity $O((N/P)^2 + P)$, where the $O(P)$ term represents the overhead of synchronization. In the phase two, each processor must perform $P - 1$ binary searches on lists of size not greater than $\lceil N/P \rceil$, hence the worst-case time complexity of phase two is $O(P \log(N/P) + P)$. In phase three, a single processor has to perform a merge sort on $O(N)$ keys in the worst situation. Assuming that a heap with P elements is used to perform a P-way merge in phase three, it then requires $O(P)$ time to initialize the heap and $O(\log P)$ time to perform each of the $O(N)$ merge steps. The complexity of phase three is $O(N \log P + P)$. Hence the worst-case complexity of quick-merge is $O((N/P)^2 + P \log(N/P) + N \log P + P)$. Quinn has observed that parallel quick-sort does better than the parallel shell-sort and the quick-merge algorithm is the clear winner amongst these three parallel algorithms. Quick-merge is only suitable for a small number of processors due to load imbalances caused by the uneven partitioning of the sorted sub-lists. Several modifications to quick-merge have been suggested by different workers.

SUMMARY

In this chapter, we have introduced parallel algorithms. Parallel algorithms help us in solving problems faster using parallel processors. Parallel algorithms are mainly divided into PRAM algorithms and bounded network algorithms. We have discussed a number of PRAM algorithms that are based on pointer jumping technique. These algorithms give us a fair idea about how much parallelism can theoretically be exploited in a problem under different models of computation. We have also introduced a number of common networks used for parallel execution of algorithms. These are ring, tree, mesh, hypercube, etc. We have described three parallel algorithms: addition, matrix multiplication and sorting on some of these networks for the sake of illustration. We have given a brief introduction to multiprocessor algorithms. These algorithms work in asynchronous manner while the bounded network algorithms work in synchronous lock-step manner. A number of references on parallel processing and algorithms are given in the references for further study.

EXERCISES

13.1 Design parallel algorithms to determine the median of a set of numbers using PRAM models.

13.2 Show how the following matrices will be multiplied using Torus

$$\begin{bmatrix} 7 & 9 \\ 2 & 5 \end{bmatrix} \text{ and } \begin{bmatrix} 3 & 2 \\ 6 & 5 \end{bmatrix}$$

13.3 Develop a PRAM algorithm for insertion sort.

13.4 Show how the following expression would be evaluated in parallel

$$a * (b + (c/(d - (e * (f - (g + h))))))$$

13.5 Find the diameter of a k-dimensional mesh containing N^k processing elements.

13.6 Write pseudocode for multiplying two $n \times n$ matrices using a hypercube containing n^2 processing elements. What is its time complexity?

13.7 Find a Hamiltonian cycle in a 4-cube.

13.8 Find the average distance between the nodes in an n-cube.

13.9 Suppose a programme contains 15% code to be executed serially. How do the speedup and the efficiency change if the number of processors is increased from 2 to 4, 4 to 8, and 8 to 16?

13.10 Characterize the following interconnection networks in terms of diameter, regularity, Eulerian, Hamiltonian, edge connectivity, node connectivity, degree-diameter metric: hypercube, mesh.

13.11 Suppose a machine has two multipliers and one adder, all of which can operate simultaneously. Show how the following polynomial can be evaluated on this machine in the minimum number of steps.

$$a_7x^7 + a_6x^6 + a_5x^5 + a_2x^2 + a_0$$

13.12 A programme contains 9% serial code. A parallel processor has 10 CPUs. After every 3 seconds, one new processor fails. Suppose that 50% of the sequential code is to be executed at the beginning and the remaining 50% at the end. The programme runs on a uniprocessor requiring 20 seconds. Each CPU is of equal power. Find out the speedup, if any, achievable in the parallel system and the efficiency of the CPUs.

13.13 Prove that the zero-one principle holds equally well for merging networks, that is, a comparator network merges two sorted sequences of integers iff it merges two sorted sequences of zeros and ones.

13.14 Show how the matrices in Problem 13.2 will be multiplied using a 3-cube.

13.15 Draw a perfect shuffle network containing 16 nodes.

13.16 Does ILLIAC IV network provide advantage in terms of time (asymptotic sense) over mesh network for carrying out bitonic sorting?

13.17 How many necklaces are there in a perfect shuffle network of 16 elements? A necklace in a perfect shuffle network is a group of nodes among which data can be shifted.

13.18 What is the number of comparators required to sort 64 numbers using bitonic sort?

13.19 A two-dimensional mesh is augmented by connecting the PEs on the rows by row buses (one bus for each row) and PEs on the columns by column buses (one bus for each column). If the bus width is 8 bits and the bus transfer time is 10 microseconds, what is the minimum time required to transfer 10 MB of data from the top leftmost PE to the bottom rightmost PE?

13.20 Given a k-dimensional hypercube and a designated source node A, how many nodes are distance t from A, where $0 \leq t \leq k$?

13.21 Given a shuffle exchange network with 2^n nodes, under what circumstances are nodes i and j exactly $2n - 1$ links traversals apart?

13.22 Design a PRAM algorithm to multiply two $n \times n$ matrices, where n is a positive integer power of 2.

13.23 Write a parallel algorithm to add $n^{3/2}$ values on a $\sqrt{n} \times \sqrt{n}$ mesh.

14

BIOINFORMATICS ALGORITHMS

14.0 INTRODUCTION

Bioinformatics is an interdisciplinary field bringing together biology, computer science, mathematics, statistics, and information theory to analyze biological data for interpretation and prediction. Bioinformatics seeks to uncover knowledge from a vast amount of biological data by using computational approaches. Nucleic acids (Deoxyribonucleic acid, Ribonucleic acid) and proteins (macromolecules of amino acids) are the two most important biological molecules of interest in bioinformatics computation. Bioinformatics attempts to answer certain fundamental questions like "which genes are involved in the human immune system?", "chimpanzees or gorillas—who is closer to us genetically?", "which set of genes is responsible for aging process?", "how does a protein fold in 3-dimensional space?", etc.

Cell is universally regarded as the unit of life. All living entities are either composed of a single cell (*prokaryotes*) or multiple cells (*eukaryotes*). Prokaryotes lack nuclear membrane, whereas eukaryotes have their genetic material (DNA) within nuclear membrane. *E.coli* (one kind of bacteria) belongs to the former group, whereas human belongs to the latter category. Adult human body contains 100 trillion cells. Each cell contains different molecules like proteins, lipids, carbohydrates, etc. in its cytoplasm in addition to a copy of the genome (DNA) for that organism in its nucleus. DNA is the same in all the cells of a eukaryotic organism; however the expression could be very different in different cells leading to spectacular specialization during development of an individual organism. Many chemical reactions take place in a cell mainly due to the enzymes (proteins). Cells get supply of nutrients from its surrounding environment.

DNA consists of two long strands coiled in helical form; each strand consists of chemical units called *phosphates, deoxyribose sugars, and nucleotides*: *adenine* (*A*), *guanine* (*G*), *cytosine* (*C*), and *thymine* (*T*). Adenine, guanine, cytosine, and thymine are called the bases of DNA. For the sake of simplicity, a DNA molecule is represented as a string over the alphabet $\Sigma = \{A, T, G, C\}$. These nucleotides (A, T, G, C) bind the two strands (running in antiparallel orientation) in helical form through chemically compatible base pairings (A-T, G-C). These two strands of DNA are complementary in base (nucleotide) sequences. DNA molecules in a cell provide the blueprint for the production of RNA and ultimately for that of proteins. DNA does not build proteins directly; it generates a template in the form of a strand of RNA [uracil (U) is used in place of *thymine* (T) in RNA], which in turn participates in protein production. This flow of information in cells is termed the *central dogma of molecular biology* by Francis Crick (Watson and Crick discovered double helical structure of DNA).

Transfer of genetic information from DNA to protein via RNA takes place according to genetic code. This code varies from organism to organism. The twenty amino acids occurring in proteins are: *alanine, arginine, asparagines, aspartic acid, cysteine, glutamic acid, glutamine, glycine, histidine, isoleucine, leucine, lysine, methionine, phenylalanine, proline, serine, threonine, tryptophan, tyrosine, valine*. Some of these amino acids are small, some medium, and some are large in size. RNA, a sequence of A, U, G, C copied from DNA is exported out of the nucleus to the cytoplasm for translation into a protein primary sequence. RNA is deciphered as a series of three-letter *codons* like *AGU, CUC, GUU, ACU, UCU, UCA, AAU*, where each *codon* corresponds to a particular amino acid. There are some special *codons* like *start codon* to signal the beginning of the transcription process, and *stop codon* to signal end of transcription. A number of codons constitute a gene. A number of genes constitute a chromosome.

The major topics of interest are analysis of protein sequence, DNA sequence, sequence comparison, multiple sequence alignment, prediction of RNA secondary structure, evolutionary relationship using sequences, protein secondary structure prediction, etc. Bioinformatics algorithms use a handful of algorithmic ideas to solve a large number of bioinformatics problems. The objective is to turn a biological problem into a meaningful computational problem. It is hypothesized that nature uses algorithm-like procedures to solve biological problems. But there is a basic difference, which one must understand. In a traditional computer science algorithm, the input is generally precisely known, whereas it is not so in biological algorithms; sometimes the input may be incomplete. Many of the steps in a biological algorithm are not clearly understood also. Out of this uncertainty in input, and inadequate knowledge of the processes involved, we wish to use traditional algorithmic framework to further our understanding about sequences, its contents, evolutionary relationship, etc.

14.1 COMPUTER AND BIOLOGICAL ALGORITHMS

Living organism grows through cell division. Before a cell divides, it must first makes a complete copy of its genetic footprint. DNA replication takes place through a number of phases; each phase requiring elaborate interactions among different types of molecules. The input to the replication process is a pair of complementary strands of DNA, and other necessary biochemical molecules. The output of the replication process is two pairs of complementary strands. Steps of the replication process in bare outline are described below.

Step 1:   A protein complex (DNA helicase) binds to the DNA at certain positions, called replication origins as shown in Figure 14.1(a).

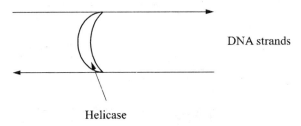

Helicase

FIGURE 14.1(a)   Helicase binding to DNA strands.

Step 2:   Helicase pulls apart the two strands of DNA, creating so-called replication fork as shown in Figure 14.1(b).

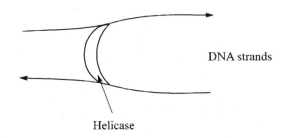

Helicase

FIGURE 14.1(b)   Replication fork.

Two other molecular machines, topoisomerase and single-strand binding proteins bind to the single strands to help relieve the instability of single-stranded DNA macromolecules.

Step 3:   Short single strands of RNA are synthesized [Figure 14.1(c)] by a protein complex called *primerase*. It latches on to specific sites in the newly opened strands.

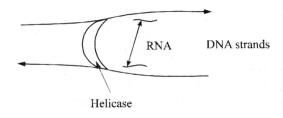

Helicase

FIGURE 14.1(c)   RNA synthesis.

Step 4:   DNA polymerage, another molecular complex binds to each freshly separated template strands of DNA. DNA polymerase attached to the two DNA strands move in the opposite directions [Figure 14.1(d)].

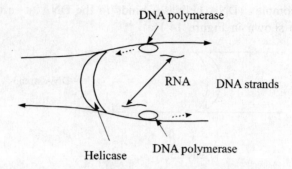

FIGURE 14.1(d)   Attachment of DNA polymerase.

Step 5:   DNA polymerase matches each strand with the complementary base and adds to the growing synthesized chain, [shown as Okazaki fragments in Figure 14.1(e)].

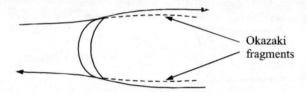

FIGURE 14.1(e)   Okazaki fragments.

Step 6:   Another molecular machine called DNA ligase repairs the gaps in the newly synthesized DNA backbone. This step links together all fragment's (called Okazaki fragments) into a single molecule as shown in Figure 14.1(f). This step also cleans any breaks in the primary strand.

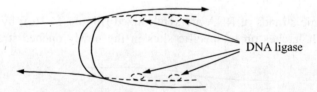

FIGURE 14.1(f)   Linking of Okazaki fragments.

Step 7:   The original strands separate. Two pairs of DNA strands, each pair consisting of one old and one newly synthesized strand, are thus created [Figure 14.1(g)].

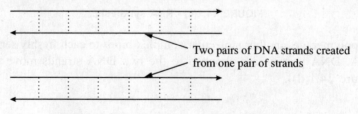

FIGURE 14.1(g)   Two newly created DNA strands.

It is not possible to capture the entire DNA synthesis process in terms of conventional algorithmic language. However, a part of the above biological process may be written in a pseudocode as follows:

```
Procedure DNA_Copy(X, Y)
    Array X(n), Y(n)
    /* X is the original DNA strand, Y is the synthesized strand */
    For i = 1 to n Do
      Case on X(i)
         Case 'A': Y(i) = 'T';
         Case 'T': Y(i) = 'A';.
         Case 'G': Y(i) = 'C';
         Case 'C': Y(i) = 'G';
         Default: Print('Error'); Exit;
         Endcase
      Endfor
      Print(Y);
    End DNA_Copy
```

14.2 MATCHING ALGORITHMS

Matching of strings is an important topic in text processing, bioinformatics, web search, etc. Inexact matching of biological sequences has become a hot topic in bioinformatics computation. The nature of the biological problems, and the omnipresence of random perturbations, dictate that exact matches are never interesting. Furthermore, string searching problems are rarely a goal in themselves in bioinformatics. Usually they are one of the many building blocks for other real problems like classification, structure prediction, multiple sequence alignments or forming phylogenetic trees, etc.

In the following sections, we will first describe the standard exact string matching algorithms like brute force, Knuth-Morris-Pratt, Rabin-Karp, Boyer-Moore and then approximate string matching. The latter part discusses matching of biological sequences using scoring functions.

14.2.1 Exact String Matching Algorithms

Given a pattern string P (= $P(1)P(2)$ ... $P(m)$) of length m and a text string T (= $T(1)T(2)$ ... $T(n)$) of length n over the same alphabet Σ, where $m \leq n$, the string matching problem is to find out whether P occurs anywhere in T, and if it does occur, then at what position(s) in the text T.

Brute force algorithm

The simplest but inefficient way of finding occurrence of P in T is to search for P as a substring of T using the brute force method. This can be modified to find all occurrences of

P in *T*. We simply try to match the first character of the pattern with the first character of the text. If this test succeeds, we try to match the second character, and so on. If there is a mismatch at some position, we slide the pattern one character to the right over the text and repeat the process. When we find at any time that the pattern characters are matching with the characters of the text as poised against the pattern, we declare that the pattern is a substring of the text occurring at the position. A simple algorithmic description is as follows:

```
Procedure Brute_Matching (P, T)
    Array P(m), T(n) /* P pattern array, T text array*/
    For i = 0 to n - m Do
        j = 1;
      While (j ≤ m and T(i + j) = P(j))Do
        j = j +1;
      Endwhile
      If (j > m) Return(i + 1);
    Endfor
    Print("No Match");
End Brute_Matching
```

The *i* loop is repeated $n - m + 1$ times, and for each iteration of the *i*-loop the while loop is repeated at most *m* times. So this naïve algorithm takes $O((n - m + 1) \times m) \approx O(nm)$ for $n \gg m$ time in the worst case to find a match, if it exists in the text. Regarding space requirement, brute force algorithm has $O(m)$ space complexity.

We illustrate working of the algorithm in Figure 14.2, where *P = act,* and *T = gctta actg*. We slide *P* from the left end of *T*, aligning first the leftmost characters of *P* and *T* [Figure 14.2(a)]. We find that there is a mismatch in the first character itself. We shift *P* one character to the right [Figure 14.2(b)]. Here also we find mismatch in the first position. We shift *P* one character to the right [Figure 14.2(c)]. We find mismatch in all the positions. We shift *P* one character to the right [Figure 14.2(d)]. This time also mismatch in all the positions. We shift *P* one character to the right [Figure 14.2(e)]. This time we find mismatch with the second position of *P*. We shift *P* one character to the right [Figure 14.2(f)]. Here we find matching of the corresponding characters in all the positions. The programme returns the current value of $i + 1 = 6$, indicating the presence of *P* in *T* as a substring starting at this position. To see whether *P* occurs at multiple places in *T* as substrings, we have to continue execution of the *i*-loop [Figure 14.2(g)].

In the following sections, we will use different techniques to find larger shifts of *P* against *T* instead of one character at a time as in the brute force method without missing any matching substring of *T*. In particular, Knuth-Morris-Pratt algorithm uses partial matching information and skips over portions of the text that cannot contain a match, Rabin-Karp algorithm uses hashing by a large prime to skip over portions of *T*, and Boyer-Moore algorithm uses good suffix and bad character rules to decide the shift. These algorithms are discussed in the following sections.

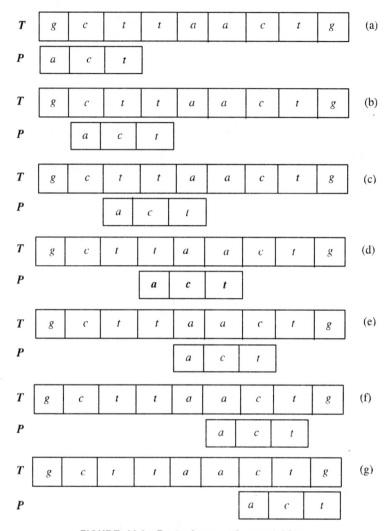

FIGURE 14.2 Brute force string matching.

Knuth-Morris-Pratt (KMP) Algorithm

KMP algorithm is based on a strategy of using the partial matching information and skipping over portions of the text that cannot contain a match. It also avoids checking characters in T that is already known to match a prefix of the pattern. Suppose we have noticed a mismatch at position i in the text, i.e., $T(i) \neq P(j)$, but the previous $j - 1$ characters of T match with the first $j - 1$ characters of P. Let Δ_j be the length of the longest prefix $P(1) P(2) \dots P(j - 1)$ that is also a proper suffix ending at $P(j - 1)$. One can avoid checking the characters that are already known to match with those in T. We only have to check the characters in T from i to $i + m - \Delta_j$ with the characters in P from Δ_j to m. Let us consider an example. Let P be the string $\alpha \, \beta \, \alpha \, \gamma \, \alpha \, \beta$ over the alphabet $\Sigma = \{\alpha, \beta, \gamma\}$. Δ_j is computed as shown in Table 14.1 for this pattern.

TABLE 14.1   Computation of Δ_j

j	1	2	3	4	5	6
$P(j)$	α	β	α	γ	α	β
Δ_j	0	0	1	0	1	2

How the search proceeds in KMP method is shown with an example in Figure 14.3.

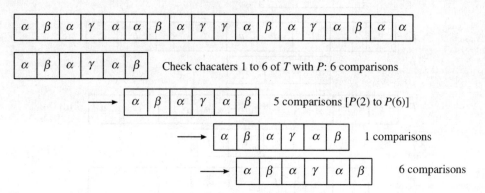

FIGURE 14.3   KMP string matching.

The following pseudocode for Knuth-Morris-Pratt algorithm tries to do this.

```
Procedure KMP_Matching (P, T)
    Array P(m),T(n),Delta(m)
    /*P pattern array, T text array, Delta array is updated in
    Form_Delta */
    m = |P|;
    n = |T|;
    i = 1;
    j = 1;
    Form_Delta(P, Delta, m);
Restart: While (j ≤ m and P(j) = T(i)) Do
    i = i + 1;
    j = j + 1;
    Endwhile
    If (j > m) Then
        Print("Matching");
        Return(i - m);
    Else
    /* Array Delta returned by Form_Delta Procedure, undefined
    values are treated as zero */
        If (j = 1) Then
            i = i + 1;
```

```
          Endif
            j = Delta(j - 1);
          If j = 0 Then
            j = 1;
          Endif
        Endif
        If (i ≤ n - m) Then
              Go to Restart;
            Else
            Print("No Matching");
        Endif
End KMP_Matching
```

The above code is incomplete without the definition of Form_Delta procedure. We now write pseudocode for Form_Delta procedure.

```
Procedure Form_Delta(P, Delta, m)
    Array P(m), Delta(m)
    /*P pattern array, Delta(j) is the length of the longest prefix
    of P(1)P(2) ....P(j) that is a proper suffix P(j - Delta (j)
    + 1)........ P(j) of P, Delta(j) < j for j = 2, ...,m */
    Delta(1)= 0;
    j = 0;
    For i = 2 to m Do
      While (j > 0 and P(j + 1) ≠ P(i)) Do
        j = Delta(j);
      Endwhile
        If (P(j + 1)= P(i)) Then
          j = j + 1;
        Endif
        Delta(i)=j;
    Endfor
End Form_Delta
```

The worst-case performance of Form_Delta procedure is $O(m)$ as the for loop in it is repeated maximum m times and the while loop is repeated less often. The KMP_Matching procedure can at most be repeated n times. KMP_Matching calls Form_Delta only once. So this matching algorithm's worst-case time complexity is $O(m + n)$. Regarding space requirement, KMP algorithm has $O(m)$ space complexity.

Rabin-Karp Algorithm

The Rabin-Karp string searching algorithm calculates a hash value for P, and for each m-character subsequences of T. If the hash values are unequal, the algorithm calculates the hash value for the next m-character subsequence of T. If the hash values are equal (we call it a hit), the algorithm will do a brute force comparison between the pattern and the m-character subsequence of T, as two different strings may have the same hash value. In this way, there is only one comparison per text subsequence, and the brute force is only used when the hash values are equal. The brute force comparison may establish exact matching (perfect hit) or mismatching of P with the current substring of T (spurious hit).

Let p denote the numeric value of P interpreted as a decimal number, and t_i ($1 \leq i \leq n - m + 1$) denote the numeric value in decimal of the substring $T(i) \ldots T(i + m - 1)$. We call a shift valid when $t_i = p$. If we are able to compute p in $O(m)$, and all of t_i values in total time $O(n)$, then we could decide all valid shifts in $O(n)$ time by comparing p with each of t_i's. p and t_1 can be computed in $O(m)$ time using Horner's method. We can compute t_{i+1} using value of t_i in constant time with the help of the following formula: $t_{i+1} = 10 \times (t_i - 10^{m-1} \times T(i + 1)) + T(i + m + 1)$. In this way, we never explicitly compute a new value. We simply adjust the existing value as we move over one character. If the scalar 10^{m-1} is pre-computed in $O(m)$ time, then each piece of computation for t_{i+1} takes constant number of arithmetic operations. p and all t_i for $1 \leq i \leq n - m + 1$ can be computed in $O(n + m)$ time. Hence we can find all occurrences of P in T in $O(n + m)$ time. Regarding space requirement, Rabin-Karp algorithm has $O(m)$ space complexity.

Each arithmetic operation on p taking constant time may not be acceptable. So we try to find an alternative. We use modulo q arithmetic for this. What should be the value of q to be used is an important issue. We use q as a large prime such that $10 \times q$ fits within one word of the computer. For an r-ary alphabet, we choose q so that $r \times q$ fits within a computer word. The recurrence relation used to compute t_{i+1} using value of t_i is rewritten as $t_{i+1} = (r \times (t_i - (r^{m-1} \bmod q) \times T(i+1)) + T(i + m + 1)) \bmod q$. Computation of p, t_i and other values using mod q arithmetic can all be done in $O(n + m)$ time. For large prime values of q, the spurious hits occur less frequently. We call a hit spurious if $t_i \equiv (p) \bmod q$ but $T(i) \ldots T(i + m - 1) \neq P(1)P(2) \ldots P(m)$. We give below the pseudocode for Rabin-Karp method.

```
Procedure RK_Matching (P, T, r, q)
    /* r is radix and q is a large prime */
    Array P(m),T(n) /*P pattern array, T text array*/
    m = |P|;
    n = |T|;
    k = r^{m-1} mod q;
    p = 0;
    t₁ = 0;
    For i = 1 to m Do
        P = (r×p + P(i)) mod q;
        t₁ =(r× t₁ + T(i)) mod q;
    Endfor
    For i = 1 to n - m +1 Do
        If (p = tᵢ)Then
            Count = 0;
            For j = 1 to m Do
```

```
            If P(j) = T(i + j) Then
               Count = Count + 1;
            Endif
         Endfor
      Endif
   If (count = m) Then
      Print("Pattern occurs", i);
   Endif
   If (i < n - m + 1)Then
      t_{i+1} = (r×(t_i - k×T(i + 1)) + T(i + m + 1))mod q;
   Endif
   Endfor
End RK_Matching
```

Suppose that P and T are strings over the alphabet $\Sigma = \{a, b, c, d, e, f\}$, and the decimal values of a, b, c, d, e, f are 1, 2, 3, 4, 5, and 6 respectively. Let $P = dae$, $T = abeadbefdae$, and $q = 13$. The Rabin-Karp method works as shown below:

We calculate the hash values $h(dae) = 12$, $h(abe) = 8$, $h(bea) = 4$, $h(ead) = 7$, $h(adb) = 12$, $h(dbe) = 9$, $h(bef) = 9$, $h(efd) = 5$, $h(fda) = 4$, and $h(dae) = 12$. In the brute-force method, we would have made $(n - m + 1) \times m = (11 - 3 + 1) \times 3 = 27$ comparisons but the Rabin-Karp method makes 13 comparisons as shown in Figure 14.4.

The worst-case time complexity of Rabin-Karp matching algorithm is dependent on the product $m \times (n - m + 1)$. What is the maximum number of times p is to be compared with the t_i values of the substrings of T? It is $m \times (n - m + 1)$. So the worst-case complexity of Rabin-Karp algorithm is $O(nm)$ for $m \ll n$. This, however, is likely to happen only if the prime number used for hashing is small. In more practical examples, it takes $O(n + m)$ time. Regarding space requirement, Rabin-Karp algorithm has $O(m)$ space complexity.

Boyer-Moore algorithm

Boyer and Moore proposed this algorithm in 1977. While the pattern P is slided along the text T in the left to right direction, this algorithm uses *right-to-left scan* of the pattern against the text. It shifts P left to right by more than one place in general when a mismatch occurs without missing any occurrence of P in T. For doing this, it uses two shift rules: *good suffix* and *bad character* shift rules. It uses the larger value out of these two shifts for checking whether $P = P(1)P(2) \ldots P(m)$ occurs in $T = T(1)T(2) \ldots T(n)$ at some position in the right-to-left scanning of T. While matching the characters of P with a substring of T, suppose we find $P(i) = x$ and $T(i + j) = y$ while the leftmost character of the pattern is aligned at $T(j)$. The previous characters $T(i + j + 1) \ldots T(j + m)$ of the text match with the characters $P(i + 1) \ldots P(m)$ of the pattern. The suffix shift aligns $T(i + j + 1) \ldots T(j + m)$ with its rightmost occurrence in P which is preceded by a character different from x. If this is not possible, it aligns the longest suffix of $T(i + j + 1) \ldots T(j + m)$ with a matching prefix of P. In bad character shift, it aligns the bad character $T(i + j) = y$ with its rightmost occurrence in P. Suppose y does not occur in P, then the first character of the pattern is aligned at $T(i + j + 1)$.

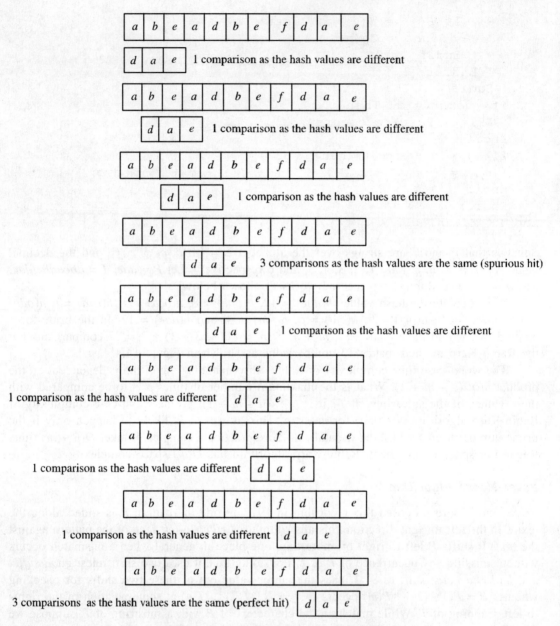

FIGURE 14.4 Rabin-Karp string matching.

The Boyer-Moore algorithm is known to be the most efficient string-matching algorithm when the pattern is relatively long and the cardinality of Σ is large. We first give a pseudo-code to calculate these two procedure-values and then that of the main Boyer-Moore algorithm.

```
Procedure Character_Last_Occurrence (P, m, α, k, B)
    Array P(m),B(m),α(k)
    /*P pattern, B array returns values, α alphabet array*/
    For j = 1 to k Do
      B(α(j))= 0;
    Endfor
    For l = 1 to m Do
      B(P(l)) = l;
    Endfor
End Character_Last_Occurrence
```

For $P = 23020202$ and $\alpha = \{0, 1, 2, 3\}$, $B(0) = 7$, $B(1) = 0$, $B(2) = 8$, and $B(3) = 2$. The B array contains information about the last occurrence of a symbol in P.

The following pseudocode for good_suffix is based on a modified version by Knuth and others for calculation of shift.

```
Procedure Good_suffix(P, m, G)
    Array P(m), G(m), V(m)
    /*P pattern,G array returns values, V array is used for
    computation of G, V has the property: V(m) = m + 1, V(j) = Minimum
    of i, where j < i ≤ m and P(i + 1) ... P(m) = P(j + 1) ... P(m +
    j - i) */
    For L = 1 to m Do
      G(L)= 2*m - L;
    Endfor
    j = m;
    k = m + 1;
    While j e" 1 Do
      V(j)= k;
      While k ≤ m and P(j) ≠ P(k)Do
        G(k) = Min(G(k), m - j);
        k = V(k);
      Endwhile
      j = j - 1;
      k = k - 1;
    Endwhile
    For L = 1 to k Do
      G(L)= Min (G(L), m + k - L);
    Endfor
    j = V(k);
    While k ≤ m Do
      While k ≤ j Do
        G(k) = Min (G(k), j - k + m);
        k = k + 1;
```

```
      Endwhile
         j = V(j);
      Endwhile
   End Good_suffix
```

The above procedure calculates G values using some auxiliary array V. Suppose $P =$ 23020202. The G values calculated by Good_suffix procedure are shown in Table 14.2.

TABLE 14.2 G values calculated by Good_suffix procedure

	1	2	3	4	5	6	7	8
P	2	3	0	2	0	2	0	2
V	8	4	5	6	7	8	8	9
G	14	13	12	6	10	6	8	1

```
Procedure Boyer_Moore_Matching (P, T)
   Array P(m), T(n) /* P pattern array, T text array*/
   m = |P|;
   n = |T|;
   Good_suffix(P, m, G);
   Character_Last_Occurrence(P, m, α, k, B);
   i = 1;
   j = m;
   While (i ≤ n - m + 1)Do
     k = i + j;
     j = m;
   While (j > 0 and T(k - 1) = P(j))Do
     j = j - 1;
     k = k - 1;
   Endwhile
   If (j = 0) Then
         Return("Pattern occurs in Text", k);
      Else
         i = i + Maximum{G(j), j - B(T(k - 1))};
      /*Chooses the larger amount of shift */
   Endif
   Endwhile
End Boyer_Moore_Matching
```

The Boyer-Moore algorithm has a worst-case time complexity $O(m)$ provided that the pattern does not appear in the text. When the pattern appears in the text, the Boyer-Moore algorithm has worst-case running time $O(n \times m)$. With randomly generated strings, the expected running time is sublinear. Figure 14.5 illustrates working of the Boyer-Moore

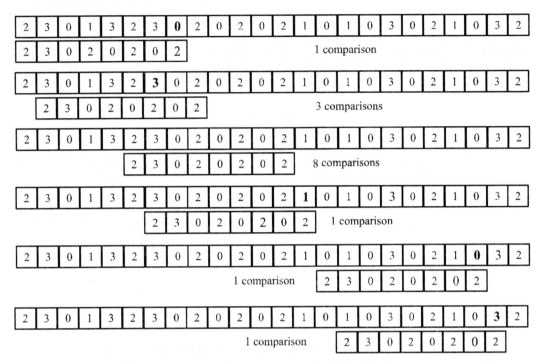

FIGURE 14.5 Boyer-Moore string matching.

algorithm. P and T are over the alphabet $\Sigma = \{0, 1, 2, 3\}$. The first bad character detected in T during the right to left scan is shown by bigger bold-faced character. The shift is decided either by using bad character heuristic or through good suffix, whichever is larger. The algorithm makes $15 (= 1 + 3 + 8 + 1 + 1 + 1)$ comparisons using these two heuristics, while a brute force method makes 136 comparisons for this T and P.

Simulation results with random texts over a moderately large alphabet indicate that the brute force algorithm takes the longest time, almost independent of the length of the pattern. KMP requires much less time than that of the brute force method, and the time is more or less independent of the pattern length. The Boyer-Moore method takes the least time but is sensitive to the pattern length. As the pattern length increases, time required for Boyer-Moore method decreases drastically.

Exact matching with suffix tree

Using the concept of prefix (different substrings starting from the first position) and suffix (different substrings ending at the last position), the exact string matching problem can be viewed as: Given a text T and a pattern P, the problem is to find a suffix of T such that P is a prefix of this suffix or to find a prefix of T such that P is a suffix of this prefix. Let $T = gcttaactg$ and $P = act$. The prefixes of T are g, gc, gct, $gctt$, $gctta$, $gcttaa$, $gcttaac$, $gcttaact$, $gcttaactg$. The suffixes are g, tg, ctg, $actg$, $aactg$, $taactg$, $ttaactg$, $cttaactg$, $gcttaactg$. After lexicographic sorting of these prefixes, we get $aactg$, $actg$, ctg, $cttaactg$, g, $gcttaactg$,

taactg, tg, ttaactg. Since *P* starts with *a*, we examine the two suffixes starting with *a* and we will find that *P = act* is a prefix of the suffix *actg*. So *P* appears in *T*. If *P* is not a prefix of any suffix, we conclude that *P* does not appear in *T*.

We append each suffix with $ at its end. The suffix tree so constructed is shown in Figure 14.6.

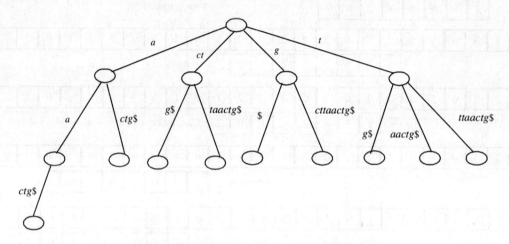

FIGURE 14.6   String matching with suffix tree.

The suffix tree can be used to solve the exact string matching problem. The time complexity of searching a suffix tree is $O(m)$ where *m* is the length of the pattern. Once the suffix tree of the text is constructed, it can be used for all patterns. This is an advantage of exact matching using suffix tree. There are $O(n)$ algorithms for constructing suffix trees. But, we must keep in mind that suffix trees occupy a large amount of memory if the texts are long.

14.2.2   Approximate String Matching

This deals with matching with bounded errors. Given a pattern *P*, a text *T*, and a positive integer *k* independent of *P* and *T*, we have to find substrings of *T* that differ from the characters of *P* in *k* places at most. This we call *k*_matching. Suppose *P = act,* and *T = gcttaactg*, and *k* = 1. *T* contains two 1-matching of *P*. If *k* = 2, then *T* contains three 2-matchings. Pseudocode for this problem is given as:

```
Procedure K_Matching (P, T, k)
    Array P(m), T(n) /* P pattern array, T text array*/
    K_match = 0;
    For i = 0 to n - m Do
        j = 1;
        Mismatch = 0;
    While (j ≤ m) Do
```

```
      If T(i + j) ≠ P(j))Then
         Mismatch = Mismatch + 1;
      Endif
      j = j +1;
   Endwhile
   If (Mismatch ≤ k) Then
         Print("K_match found");
         K_match = K_match + 1;
   Endif
   Endfor
   Print("Total K_match found =", K_match );
End K_Matching
```

The above algorithm is similar to the brute force approach and has the same time complexity. This problem can be solved using a suffix tree for small patterns only. An alternative is to derive all strings Q that can be derived from P by changing up to k characters of P, and then to search for Q in a suffix tree for T. Time to search for Q requires time proportional to the length of Q.

Dynamic programming approach

We discuss a different formulation of the approximate matching problem. Given two strings P and T, we want to decide how much they differ. Let $D(i, j)$ be the distance between the substring $P(1)P(2) \dots P(i)$ of P and the substring $T(1)T(2) \dots T(j)$ of T. This distance is defined as the minimum number of substitution, deletion, and insertion operations required for transforming one substring to the other. This distance is commonly known as the *edit distance*. The next section discusses more about edit distance. If $P(i) = T(j)$, then $D(i, j) = D(i - 1, j - 1)$. We assume that inserting a character into the substring of T to transform it to a substring of P is equivalent to deleting a character from P. For the sake of convenience, we perform the equivalent operation of character deletion from P instead of character addition to T. Without loss of generality, we assume that the sequence of operations involving the first $i - 1$ characters of P and the first $j - 1$ characters of T are operated on first. If the last operation is substitution of $T(i)$ with $P(j)$ in T, then $D(i, j) = D(i - 1, j - 1) + 1$. If the last operation is the deletion of $P(i)$ from P, then $D(i, j) = D(i - 1, j) + 1$. If the last operation is the deletion of $T(j)$ from T, then $D(i, j) = D(i, j - 1) + 1$. The edit distance is found by picking the minimum of these three possibilities. Finally, we write:

$$D(i, j) = \{D(i - 1, j - 1), \text{ when } P(i) = T(j)\}$$
$$= \text{Min. } \{D(i - 1, j - 1) + 1, D(i - 1, j) + 1, D(i, j - 1) + 1\}, \text{ otherwise}$$

and $\qquad D(0, i) = D(i, 0) = i$

This recurrence relation may be used to develop an algorithm to solve the approximate string matching problem in $O(nm)$ time.

14.2.3   Comparing Biological Sequences

Comparing base sequences of nucleotides and amino acid sequences of proteins are important to understand the evolutionary pathways. Sequence comparison is motivated by the fact that all living organisms are related by evolution. High similarity in sequence is usually indicative of functional or structural similarity. Species that are closer to each other should exhibit similarities at the DNA level. We decide similarities by aligning sequences.

In the case of nucleotides, one usually aligns identical nucleotide symbol (A, T, G, C). When dealing with proteins, alignment of two amino acids occur if they are identical or if one can be derived from the other by substitutions that are likely to occur during evolution in nature. Alignments are generally categorized into: local alignment and global alignment. Local alignment focuses on small lengths of the sequences, whereas global alignment focuses on the entire length of the sequences. How similar two sequences are generally measured by per cent identity, which is equal to the ratio between the number of positions containing identical symbols divided by the number of symbols in the longest sequence.

Let us see how the two strings HEAD and TAIL are related. We may convert HEAD to TAIL by a sequence of elementary operations. The elementary operations involve insertion of a symbol, deletion of a symbol, and substitution of a symbol by another. We transform HEAD to TAIL as: HEAD $\rightarrow$ TEAD $\rightarrow$ TAAD $\rightarrow$ TAID $\rightarrow$ TAIL. In the first step, we have replaced H by T, in the second, E by A, in the third, A by I, and in the fourth, D by L. We have used four elementary operations. We define *edit distance* between two strings as the minimum number of elementary operations required to transform one string to the other. If we confine to insertion and deletion operations forgetting substitution operation, then the edit distance problem is equivalent to the longest common subsequence problem discussed in Section 4.7 using dynamic programming. We allow gaps ('–') in biological sequence alignment. Consider the sequences *bd* and *abcd*. One possible alignment is $\begin{matrix} a\,b\,c\,d \\ -b-d \end{matrix}$. For the sequences *abcd* and *buc*, one possible alignment is $\begin{matrix} a\,b-c\,d \\ -b\,u\,c- \end{matrix}$. An optimized alignment tries to maximize matches of identical symbols in both sequences.

There are many alignments between two strings X and Y. Which one to prefer? To rank different alignments relatively, we introduce the notion of *scoring function*. To define this, we need to introduce two terms: *alignment matrix* and *edit graph*. An alignment matrix for strings $X = \{x_1, x_2, ..., x_n\}$ and $Y = \{y_1, y_2, ..., y_m\}$ is a 2-row matrix with maximum $m + n$ columns, 1st row contains the characters of X in order and the 2nd row contains the characters of Y in order, both may be interspersed with spaces and no column of the matrix contains spaces in both the rows. Columns that contain the same character in both the rows are called *matches*, while columns containing different characters are called *mismatches*. The columns of the alignment matrix containing one space are called *indels*, with the columns containing a space in the top row called insertions and the columns with a space in the bottom row deletions.

Consider the strings $X = GTATTGT$, and $Y = GTCATGC$ for alignment. A possible

alignment matrix is
$$\begin{matrix} 0 & 1\,2\,2\,3\,4\ \ 5\ 6\,7\,7 \\ X: & G\,T-A\,T\,T\,G\,T- \\ Y: & G\,T\,C\,A\,T-G-C \\ 0 & 1\,2\,3\,4\,5\ \ 5\ 6\,6\,7 \end{matrix}$$

It has five matches, zero mismatches. The alignment may also be represented as

$$\begin{pmatrix} 0 \\ 0 \end{pmatrix}\begin{pmatrix} 1 \\ 1 \end{pmatrix}\begin{pmatrix} 2 \\ 2 \end{pmatrix}\begin{pmatrix} 2 \\ 3 \end{pmatrix}\begin{pmatrix} 3 \\ 4 \end{pmatrix}\begin{pmatrix} 4 \\ 5 \end{pmatrix}\begin{pmatrix} 5 \\ 5 \end{pmatrix}\begin{pmatrix} 6 \\ 6 \end{pmatrix}\begin{pmatrix} 7 \\ 6 \end{pmatrix}\begin{pmatrix} 7 \\ 7 \end{pmatrix}$$

The numbering of the characters of the strings start from 1 and increases towards right; if a space is encountered the numbering does not change. The columns of the above matrix represent coordinates in a 2-dimensional $n \times m$ grid. The alignment is simply a path in this grid as shown in Figure 14.7. For our example, the path is from $(0, 0)$ to (n, m) represented as $(0,0) \rightarrow (1,1) \rightarrow (2,2) \rightarrow (2,3) \rightarrow (3,4) \rightarrow (4,5) \rightarrow (5,5) \rightarrow (6,6) \rightarrow (7,6) \rightarrow (7,7)$.

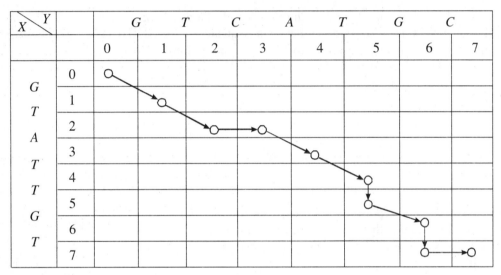

FIGURE 14.7 Path in the edit graph.

Given an alignment matrix or a path in the edit graph, the scoring function determines the quality of an alignment. There are many possibilities for the scoring function. We want to select a scoring function that gives higher scores to alignment of strings X and Y with more matches. The simplest approach is to score a column of the alignment with a positive number if the character in X is the same as the character in Y for a particular column, with a negative number if the two characters are different. The score of an alignment is the sum of the scores of all the columns of the alignment. In terms of the edit graph, this can be achieved by assigning a positive number (say +1) to the diagonal, negative number (say −2) to the horizontal (representing blank character in X) and vertical edges (representing blank character in Y) as shown in Figure 14.8. Using edit graph, the score of an alignment is the sum of the weights thus assigned to the edges in the edit graph path, every edge in the path corresponds to one column in the alignment.

Global sequence alignment

We consider global alignment of two sequences X and Y in this section. The problem is to find the best alignment of X and Y under a given *scoring matrix*. The scoring matrix is of

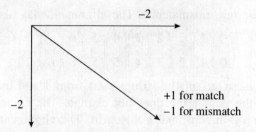

FIGURE 14.8   Edge weights in edit graph.

size $(k + 1) \times (k + 1)$, where k is the number of characters in the alphabet Σ. For nucleic acid sequence, k is 4, and for amino acid sequence, k is 20. To take care of the blank character in alignments, we add 1 to both row and column sizes of the scoring matrix.

Consider the prefixes $X(1)X(2) \ldots X(i)$ of X and $Y(1)Y(2) \ldots Y(j)$ of Y. Let the optimal alignment of these prefixes be denoted by $OA(i, j)$. We may write the following recurrence relations:

$$OA(i, j) = \text{Max} \begin{cases} OA(i-1, j) + s(X(i), \text{`}-\text{'}) \\ OA(i, j-1) + s(\text{`}-\text{'}, Y(j)) \\ OA(i-1, j-1) + s(X(i), Y(j)) \end{cases} \tag{14.1}$$

where $s(X(i), \text{`}-\text{'})$ represents the score of the column having $X(i)$ in $X$ and `$-$' in Y, $s(\text{`}-\text{'}, Y(j))$ represents the score of the column having `$-$' in X and $Y(j)$ in Y, and $s(X(i), Y(j))$ represents the score of the column having $X(i)$ in X and $Y(j)$ in Y.

If we assume that the matches are rewarded by +1, mismatches are penalized by $-\alpha$, and indels (space in alignment) are penalized by $-\beta$, the resulting score is equal to the number of matches $-\alpha$ times the number of mismatches $-\beta$ times the number of indels. The previous recurrence (14.1) may be rewritten as

$$OA(i, j) = \text{Max} \begin{cases} OA(i-1, j) - \beta \\ OA(i, j-1) - \beta \\ OA(i-1, j-1) - \alpha, X(i) \neq Y(j) \\ OA(i-1, j-1) + 1, X(i) = Y(j) \end{cases} \tag{14.2}$$

Using this recurrence relation, we write the following pseudocode for global sequence alignment. The problem of longest common subsequence discussed in Section 4.7 is similar to the global sequence alignment. In the following pseudocode, we use proper values of the parameters α, β to get the longest common subsequence. α and β values may be taken as 0, 0 or ∞, 0 respectively to adapt the algorithm for the common subsequence problem.

```
Procedure Global-Seq-Align(X, Y, n, m, α, β)
    /* α mismatch penalty, β penalty for indels */
    Character Array X(n), Y(m)
    String Array D(n, m)
    /* Array D helps us to trace back the path in the edit graph of
    the alignment using directions 'UP', 'LEFT', 'DIAGONAL UP' */
    Array OA(n, m)
    For i = 0 to n Do
      OA(i, 0) = 0;
    Endfor
    For j = 0 to m Do
      OA(0, j) = 0;
    Endfor
    For i = 1 to n Do
      For j = 1 to m Do
        If X(i) = '—' Then
          OA(i, j) = OA(i-1, j) - β;
            D(i, j) = 'Up';
        Else
        If Y(j) = '—' Then
        OA(i, j) = OA(i, j-1) - β;
            D(i, j) = 'Left';
            Else
            If X(i) = Y(j) Then
            OA(i, j) = OA(i-1, j-1) +1;
              D(i, j) = 'Diagonal Up';
            Else
            OA(i, j) = OA(i - 1, j - 1) +1;
              D(i, j) = 'Diagonal Up';
            Endif
          Endif
        Endif
      Endfor
    Endfor
End Global-Seq-Align
```

Local sequence alignment

The global alignment problem finds similarities between two strings on the whole. The score of an alignment between two substrings of X and Y in some biological applications might actually be greater than the score of an alignment between X and Y as a whole. As an example, we may cite *homeodomain*. This is the conserved region of *homeobox* gene (regulating embryonic development) over different species. An important issue is how to find this conserved area (local sequence alignment) and ignore areas that show little similarity. Let us consider the following strings for alignment. The local sequence alignment problem is to find the maximum similarity between the substrings of X and Y.

An example of global alignment with 8 matches is

X: $A\ T\ G\ C\ T\ T\ A\ A\ G\ G\ C\ T\ T\ A\ G\ C\ T\ A\ T$

Y: $A\ A\ G\ G\ C\ T\ T\ A\ G\ A\ C\ T\ A\ G\ C\ A\ T$

An example of local alignment with 12 matches is

X: $A\ T\ G\ C\ T\ T\ A\ A\ G\ G\ C\ T\ T\ A\ G\ C\ T\ A\ T$

Y: $A\ A\ G\ G\ C\ T\ T\ A\ G\ A\ C\ T\ -\ A\ G\ C\ -\ A\ T$

The problem may be stated as:

Given two strings $X = X(1)X(2) \ldots X(n)$, and $Y = Y(1)Y(2) \ldots Y(m)$, find the maximum similarity over all substrings $X(i)X(i+1) \ldots X(j)$ of X where $i < j$, and $Y(l)Y(l+1) \ldots Y(p)$ of Y where $l < p$. With reference to the edit graph, the problem of local sequence alignment corresponds to finding the longest among the paths between all possible pairs of vertices (i, j) and (l, p). The approach of finding the path lengths between every pair of vertices (i, j) and (l, p) in the edit graph and then selecting the longest one is inefficient. The time complexity of this approach is $O(n^4)$ as each of i, j, l, p is either of order n (or m).

By adding some additional edges of weight 0 to the edit graph, the local alignment problem can be reduced to finding longest paths from $(0, 0)$ to every other vertex. These zero weight edges make the source vertex $(0, 0)$ as a predecessor of every vertex in the edit graph providing a zero cost edge from $(0, 0)$ to any other vertex (i, j). With this modification, we can rewrite the recurrence (14.2) as

$$OA(i, j) = \text{Max} \begin{cases} 0 \\ OA(i-1, j) + s(X(i), \text{`--'}) \\ OA(i, j-1) + s(\text{`--'}, Y(j)) \\ OA(i-1, j-1) + s(X(i), Y(j)) \end{cases} \tag{14.3}$$

where $OA(i, j)$ represents the optimal alignment and $s(a, b)$ represents the score of a column containing a in X and b in Y. The longest value of $OA(i, j)$ over the entire edit graph represents the score of the best local alignment of X and Y.

Multiple sequence alignment

Multiple sequence alignment is alignment of three or more sequences. Biologically important patterns cannot be revealed sometimes by comparison of two strings in isolation. It becomes clear when many related strings are simultaneously compared. It is sometimes possible to arrange a set of related strings in a tree to demonstrate continuous changes along a path connecting two distant strings which by themselves show little pairwise similarity. The biological sequences may have some evolutionary relationship. Multiple sequence alignment helps in homology modelling, phylogenetic analysis, advanced biological data base searches.

Multiple alignments are used for proteins as well as DNA modelling programmes. It helps in predicting the secondary as well as tertiary structures of new sequences.

Let $X_1, X_2, ..., X_p$ be p strings of lengths $n_1, ..., n_p$ respectively over an alphabet Σ. We extend Σ to Σ' by including indel '—'. A multiple sequence alignment of the p strings is a $p \times n$ matrix, where n is the maximum of $\{n_1, ..., n_p\}$. Each row i of the matrix contains the characters of X_i in order with $n - n_i$ indels interspersed. No column of the matrix contains indels only. We define the score of a multiple alignment as the sum of the scores of the columns. The optimal alignment is that alignment giving maximum score.

Suppose we have only three strings X, Y, Z and we want to find the best alignment of these strings. Every multiple alignment of three sequences corresponds to a path in the corresponding three-dimensional edit graph. One could reach vertex (i, j, k) from any of the seven predecessors $(i - 1, j, k)$, $(i, j - 1, k)$, $(i, j, k - 1)$, $(i - 1, j - 1, k)$, $(i - 1, j, k - 1)$, $(i, j - 1, k - 1)$, $(i - 1, j - 1, k - 1)$ in the edit graph. We may write recurrence relation for dynamic programming approach to find the optimal alignment involving three strings as

$$OA(i, j, k) = \text{Max} \begin{cases} OA(i - 1, j, k) + s(X(i), \text{`}-\text{'}, \text{`}-\text{'}) \\ OA(i, j - 1, k) + s(\text{`}-\text{'}, Y(j), \text{`}-\text{'}) \\ OA(i, j, k - 1) + s(\text{`}-\text{'}, \text{`}-\text{'}, Z(k)) \\ OA(i - 1, j - 1, k) + s(X(i), Y(j), \text{`}-\text{'}) \\ OA(i - 1, j, k - 1) + s(X(i), \text{`}-\text{'}, Z(k)) \\ OA(i, j - 1, k - 1) + s(\text{`}-\text{'}, Y(j), Z(k)) \\ OA(i - 1, j - 1, k - 1) + s(X(i), Y(j), Z(k)). \end{cases} \tag{14.4}$$

Equation (14.4) can easily be converted to a pseudocode for multiple alignments of 3 strings. In the case of p sequences, the time complexity of the approach is $O(n^p)$. There are many suboptimal heuristics for multiple alignments. One approach is to compute all $^pC_2$ optimal pairwise alignments between every pair of strings and then combine these together to get multiple alignments close to the optimal ones. However, it is not always possible to combine optimal pairwise alignments into a multiple alignment. This is because of some pairwise alignments being incompatible. As an example consider the three strings $X = AAAACCCC$, $Y = CCCCGGGG$, and $Z = GGGGAAAA$.

Pairwise alignment of X and Y is:

X: A A A A C C C C ... ...

Y: ... ... C C C C G G G G

Pairwise alignment of Y and Z is

Y: C C C C G G G G ... ...

Z: ... ... G G G G A A A A

Pair-wise alignment of X and Z is

X: .... $A\ A\ A\ A\ C\ C\ C\ C$
Z: $G\ G\ G\ G\ A\ A\ A\ A$ ... ...

In this particular example, pairwise alignments cannot be combined into a multiple alignment. Another approach is greedy. The greedy approach selects the pair of strings with greatest similarity and merges them together into a new string, if necessary with gaps. A gap once introduced for alignment remains throughout the merging processes. Multiple alignments of p strings is reduced to $p - 1$ merging operations of most similar pair of strings at each step. There is no performance guarantee for the greedy approach. If the initial pair of strings is aligned in such a way that it becomes incompatible for later alignments through merging; the error in the initial steps propagates through the later stages. Moreover, quality of the scoring function used to define most similar strings can affect the quality of the resulting alignment.

14.2.4 Protein Identification Problem

Most of the proteins are identified through database search. The experimental mass spectra (obtained through separation of ions according to their mass to charge ratios under electromagnetic fields) are compared with the stored spectra of known proteins. The entry in the database that best matches with the experimental spectrum usually provides the sequence of aminoacids of the experimental protein. Many proteins undergo further modifications after its synthesis in a cell. These modifications may be permanent or reversible. These modifications include phosphorylation (combining of phosphate with an organic compound), glycosylation (enzymatic process that attaches glycans to proteins, lipids, or other organic molecules). Finding these naturally occurring modifications is an important open problem. Generating all modified proteins and searching for the experimental spectrum against this database leads to large combinatorial problem. The major difficulty is that two similar proteins P_1 and P_2 may have very different spectra.

We define a notion called *spectral similarity* that correlates well with amino acid sequence similarity. Spectral similarity decreases very quickly with the increase in the number of mutations. We now try to cast the problem as a dynamic programming problem. Let $X = \{x_1, x_2, ..., x_n\}$ be an ordered increasing sequence of integers. A shift β_i changing the last $n - i + 1$ elements transforms X to $Y = \{x_1, x_2, ..., x_{i-1}, x_i + \beta_i ..., x_n + \beta_i\}$ assuming shifts that do not alter the sequence of the elements of X. The k-similarity between X and Y is defined as the maximum number of elements in common between these two sets after k shifts. One may represent the sets $X = \{x_1, x_2, ..., x_n\}$ and $Y = \{y_1, y_2, ..., y_m\}$ as 0-1 arrays A and B of lengths x_n and y_m respectively. The array A contains n ones and $x_n - n$ zeros. The array B contains m ones and $y_m - m$ zeros. A shift $\beta_i < 0$ is simply a deletion of β_i zeros from A. A shift $\beta_i > 0$ is simply an insertion of β_i zeros in A. The spectral alignment problem is to find the edit distance between A and B with the elementary operations of deletions and insertions of blocks of zeros.

We define spectral product $X \otimes Y$ to be the $x_n \times y_m$ matrix with $n \times m$ ones corresponding to all pairs of indices (x_i, y_j), other elements being zero. The number of ones on the main diagonal describes the shared peaks count between spectra X and Y. The k-similarity problem is now defined as the maximum number of ones on a path through the matrix that uses at most $k + 1$ diagonals. The k-optimal spectral alignment is defined as the path that uses these $k + 1$ diagonals. For example, 1-similarity is defined by the maximum number of ones on a path through this matrix that uses at most two diagonals.

We try to attack the problem with the approach of dynamic programming. Let X_i be the i-prefix X and Y_j be the j-prefix of Y. Let $D_{ij}(k)$ be the k-similarity between X_i and Y_j such that the last elements of X_i and Y_j are matched. This amounts to the maximum number of ones on a path to (x_i, y_j) that uses at most $k + 1$ different diagonals of the matrix. We accept (i', j') and (i, j) as co-diagonal if $x_i - x_i' = y_j - y_j'$ and that $(i', j') < (i, j)$ if $i' < i$ and $j' < j$. We introduce a fictitious $(0, 0)$ element in the array with $D_{00}(k) = 0$ with the assumption that $(0, 0)$ element is co-diagonal with any other (i, j) element. We are now in a position to write the dynamic programming recurrence for D as:

$$D_{ij}(k) = \text{Max}_{(i', j') < (i, j)} \ D_{i'j'}(k) + 1, \text{ if } (i', j') \text{ and } (i, j) \text{ are co-diagonal}$$

$$= \text{Max}_{(i', j') < (i, j)} \ D_{i'j'}(k - 1) + 1, \text{ otherwise.}$$

The k-similarity between X and Y is given by $D(k) = \text{Max}_{ij} D_{ij}(k)$. The above approach leads to an algorithm for spectral alignment with $O(n^4 k)$ complexity. Let us try to have an algorithm with improved performance.

Let $\text{diag}(i, j)$ denote the maximal co-diagonal pair of (i, j) such that $\text{diag}(i, j) < (i, j)$. This implies that $\text{diag}(i, j)$ is the position of the previous one on the same diagonal as (x_i, y_j) or $(0, 0)$ if such a position does not exist. Let us write $M_{ij}(k) = \text{Max}_{(i', j') \le (i, j)} D_{i'j'}(k)$. The recurrence relation for $D_{ij}(k)$ can be rewritten as:

$$D_{ij}(k) = \text{Max}\{D_{\text{diag}(i, j)}(k) + 1, \ M_{i-1, j-1}(k - 1) + 1\}$$

and that for $M_{ij}(k)$ as:

$$M_{ij}(k) = \text{Max}\{D_{ij}(k), \ M_{i-1, j}(k), \ M_{i, j-1}(k)\}.$$

Using these recurrences for solving the spectral alignment problem leads to an $O(n^2 k)$ algorithm. However, this simple dynamic programming approach does not consider many details that make spectral alignment a difficult problem.

SUMMARY

In this chapter, we have introduced both exact and approximate string matching problems. The algorithms discussed for exact matching are brute force, Knuth-Morris-Pratt, Rabin-Karp, Boyer-Moore algorithms, and matching with suffix tree. In the latter part of the chapter, we have introduced the problem of comparing biological sequences. We have discussed about global sequence alignment, local sequence alignment, and multiple sequence alignment with dynamic programming approach. We have concluded the chapter with an outline of dynamic programming formulation of protein identification problem.

EXERCISES

14.1 Suppose $q = 13$ (for modulo arithmetic), $P =$ '153', and $T =$ '1332457394424' over the decimal digits $\{1, 2, 3, 4, 5, 7, 9\}$. How many hits does Rabin-Karp algorithm generate for this instance?

14.2 What is global sequence alignment? Find the best global sequence alignment of the strings $X = AAGTTCACGT$, $Y = GTACGATCG$. Assume the score: match = +1, mismatch = 0, and indels = −1.

14.3 Apply the KMP algorithm to the string matching problem where $P = 001201$, $T = 00100200220011201012200$, and the alphabet consists of $\{0, 1, 2\}$. Find the number of comparisons made in this instance of the problem.

14.4 Find an approximate matching of $T =$ HEAD, and $P =$ HALL. Assume that at most 3 characters may differ.

14.5 Design an algorithm for finding all occurrences of substrings of the text string T that is at most a k-approximation of the pattern string P.

14.6 Modify the basic Rabin-Karp algorithm to solve the problem. Given j pattern strings $P_1, P_1, ..., P_j$ each of length m, find all occurrences of these patterns in the text T.

14.7 Suppose the pattern P is of size $m \times m$, and the text T is of size $n \times n$. Find all occurrences of P in T by modifying one of the basic string matching algorithms.

14.8 Develop an algorithm to find all the 3-mismatch palindromes in a string of length n in $O(n)$ time.

14.9 Use edit graph to align 'HADON' with 'TALON'.

14.10 Two strings $A = A(1)A(2) ... A(n)$ and $B = B(1)B(2) ... B(n)$ are given. Design an $O(n)$ time algorithm to determine whether B is a cyclic shift of A.

14.11 The consensus of an alignment is a string of the most common characters in each column of a multiple alignment. Consider the following three strings X, Y, Z, where $X = ACTCGCATCGGT$, $Y = ACTCGACATCGGTAA$, and $Z = CTTCGCCATCCGTAC$. Find the alignment matrix and the consensus of the strings.

14.12 Find the predecessor nodes of vertex $(i_1, i_2, ..., i_p)$ in a p-dimensional edit graph.

14.13 For the following four strings, find all pairwise alignments and then combine them into multiple alignments.

$$X = ATAAGCTAGG$$

$$Y = TGCAGTTG$$

$$Z = CATTTAGG$$

$$W = AGCTAGAT$$

14.14 Apply greedy technique to make multiple alignments of the four strings in Exercise 14.13.

14.15 We are given c patterns $P_1, P_2, ..., P_c$, each containing m characters. The problem is to search for any one of these c patterns in the text T of length n. Modify the Rabin-Karp algorithm for this problem.

14.16 How many comparisons would the KMP algorithm make for the text and pattern given below?

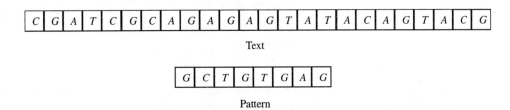

Text

Pattern

14.17 Rewrite the brute force algorithm that scans the pattern from the right to the left instead of left to the right.

14.18 Compute Δ_j table defined in Section Knuth-Morris-Pratt algorithm for the pattern of Exercise 14.16.

14.19 Modify the Rabin-Karp algorithm for the rectangular pattern of size $m \times m$ and a rectangular text of size $n \times n$, where $n > m$.

15

CONCLUSION

The primary objective in the previous chapters has been to acquaint the readers with the standard methods of algorithm design and using these methods in solving some common problems. Whenever one needs to design an algorithm for a new problem, one should think first to consider these methods for possible use. The methods we have discussed are divide and conquer, greedy, dynamic programming, approximation schemes, randomization approach, search tree approach based on branch and bound, etc. Most of the time, these approaches, in isolation or used in combination, may produce a satisfactory algorithm.

For defining the framework for analysis of algorithms based on the above-mentioned methods, we have introduced the common theoretical models like Turing machine, circuit model, RAM, PRAM, and BSP. We have shown how to analyze the algorithms in the framework of RAM model for the representative problems developed using the different methods. If for the problem at hand, one finds that more than one of the standard methods can be used, then the comparatively efficient one can be found through the time complexity analysis.

We have not discussed many specialized techniques designed to solve some specific problems efficiently, because this text is intended to provide a general background in algorithm design methods and analysis. Some of the topics not covered but find place in many other texts are number-theoretic algorithms, computational geometry algorithms, algorithms for matrix algebra, linear programming, etc. We have, however, devoted a chapter on graph algorithms based on graph searching.

An algorithm's performance may change depending on the data structure used. So we have devoted a few pages on outlining the common data structures. We have also discussed some advanced data structures. The time complexities of many of the problems may be formulated in the form of recurrence relations. An introduction has been given about how to solve recurrence relations. The chapter on 'A Bit of Theory' introduces the reader to the world of hard problems and how to characterize them.

There are many other approaches like artificial neural computing, simulated annealing, genetic algorithm, etc. for getting near-optimal solutions to many hard optimization problems in reasonable time. These techniques are being used for solving many practical problems.

We have devoted a chapter on genetic algorithm and discussed the main issues involved in solving a problem using genetic algorithm. We have shown how the genetic algorithm may be used to solve some representative problems like 0/1 knapsack, bin-packing, TSP and numerical function optimization.

By using many processors in parallel, an algorithm's running time can be reduced. Chapter 13 introduces the reader to parallel algorithms, the theoretical model for parallel processing, and the common interconnection networks. Parallel algorithms can be designed either within the framework of the different theoretical PRAM and BSP models or based on the bounded-degree network models. We have discussed some representative problems based on PRAM and bounded-degree network models. We refrained from discussing about associative algorithms, systolic algorithms, etc., because these algorithms are very specific and tied to the underlying architectures. Associative algorithms are used mainly for searching associative memory. Associative memory contains processing logic that can determine in parallel whether a given cell does or does not contain data having the given properties.

Systolic processors are a class of pipelined array architectures. Systolic algorithms schedule computations in such a way that a data item is not only used when it is input, but reused as it moves through the pipelines in the array. This results in balancing the processing and input/output bandwidths, especially in compute-bound problems that have more computation to be performed than they have input and output.

Keeping the scope of the book in mind, we have not attempted to bring in the topic of algorithm design in the distributed set-up, which is a more advanced topic and is better included in a second course on algorithm design. There are non-determinism, lack of knowledge of the global state, and global time frame in a distributed system. For a particular programme with the given input, a single computation is possible in a centralized system. But in a distributed system, many computations are possible because of non-determinism. The combination of lack of knowledge of global state, global time frame, and non-determinism makes the design of distributed algorithms an intricate craft, because the three aspects interfere in several ways.

In online computation, an algorithm must produce a sequence of decisions that will have an impact on the final quality of its overall performance. Each of these decisions is made based on the past events without secure information about the future. Many computational problems are intrinsically online in that they require immediate decisions to be made in real time. This, being an introductory book, we have not attempted to discuss the design and analysis of online algorithms. The topic deserves to be treated in an advanced book.

The discovery of quantum factoring algorithm in 1994 caused a great excitement. Many people expected a succession of interesting algorithms to follow. However, reality has not been that encouraging. The important quantum algorithms, known to offer substantial speed-up over the classical algorithms for the same problems, fall into one of three classes. The first class uses the Fourier transform to find periodicity. This class contains the factoring and discrete logarithm algorithms. The second class contains Grover's search algorithm, which can perform an exhaustive search of N items in $\sqrt{N}$ time. The third class consists of algorithms for simulating or solving problems in quantum physics. According to experts, it is quite likely that several new and significant algorithmic techniques remain to be discovered in quantum algorithms.

Asymptotic measure of time complexity of an algorithm does not give adequate information regarding the time required for an implementation of an algorithm. Details of the machine are not part of the model under which asymptotic time complexity is evaluated. More detailed considerations like effects of external memory, presence of cache, etc. should be part of the model for finding realistic estimate of time complexity. Experimental evaluation of algorithms referred as *Algorithm Engineering* is required for assessing realistic performance of algorithms. We need good design methods, analysis tools and elaborate testing and characterization of algorithms.

To take care of mother earth for sustenance of life, the paradigm of green computing for reducing greenhouse gas emission is the need of the hour. Greenhouse gases are those that can absorb and emit infrared radiation. Developing computing technologies that can effectively reduce energy consumption leading to significant reduction in Greenhouse gas emission is generally known as *green computing*. Energy-aware applications are gaining more and more attention. It is necessary to stress a *green metric set* for measuring and monitoring of energy consumed and wasted in computing. Some of the technological challenges in green computing are algorithmic in nature. The most obvious type of algorithmic problems arising directly involves managing power, energy and temperature as a resource. A long-term research goal is to build a toolkit of widely applicable algorithmic design and analysis techniques for power management problems. Long-term goal is to build a science of algorithmic power management to support the computing community's ability to abstractly reason out power, energy and temperature. Over the last several decades, time and space were the key computational resources. Computer science researchers developed many techniques for designing time and space efficient algorithms. Now one has to take into account the energy parameter of an algorithm in addition to time and space analysis. Some formal scheme which can take care of time, energy, space requirements of an algorithm has to be developed for this. Maybe we have to use measures like $E \times t^2$, where E is the energy consumed in carrying out a piece of computation in time t which is to be used as a measure of the efficiency of a piece of computation.

Reducing the voltage, which consequently lead to the frequency reduction, provides substantial saving in power at the cost of slower programme execution. Green computing is still in the initial stage as many methods, technologies, or standards are not mature enough. Computer system products of *green computing* are with high price. These are the major impediments to adoption of *green computing* on a large scale.

Appendix

MATHEMATICAL PRELIMINARIES

MATHEMATICAL FORMULAE/SYMBOLS REVIEW

A. Summation

(i) $\displaystyle\sum_{i=1}^{n} \{a + (i - 1)b\} = n\{a + (n-1)b/2\}$

(ii) $\displaystyle\sum_{i=1}^{n} i = n(n + 1)/2$

(iii) $\displaystyle\sum_{i=0}^{n} ar^i = a\left(\frac{r^{n+1} - 1}{r - 1}\right)$

(iv) $\displaystyle\sum_{i=1}^{n} i^2 = n(n + 1)(2n + 1)/6$

(v) $\displaystyle\sum_{i=1}^{n} i^3 = \{n(n + 1)/2\}^2$

B. Logarithms

(i) $\log_b xy = \log_b x + \log_b y$

(ii) $\log_b (x/y) = \log_b x - \log_b y$

(iii) $\log_b x^c = c \log_b x$

(iv) $\log_b a = \log_c a \times \log_b c$

(v) $b^{\log_c a} = a^{\log_c b}$

C. Floor and Ceiling Functions

Floor function: $\lfloor x \rfloor$ is the greatest integer less than or equal to x.

Ceiling function: $\lceil x \rceil$ is the smallest integer greater than or equal to x.

D. Some Common Sets

ϕ denotes the empty set

Z denotes the set $\{..., -2, -1, 0, 1, 2, ...\}$

R denotes the set of real numbers

N denotes the set $\{1, 2, 3, ...\}$

E. (i) $\displaystyle\sum_{k=0}^{n} {}^nC_k = 2^n$

(ii) ${}^nC_r = {}^{n-1}C_{r-1} + {}^{n-1}C_r, \qquad 1 \le r \le n - 1$

(iii) $\displaystyle\sum_{r=1}^{n} r\,{}^nC_r = n2^{n-1}, \qquad n > 0$

F. $\displaystyle\sum_{i=1}^{n} \frac{1}{i} \approx \ln(n) + \gamma$, where the Euler's constant, $\gamma \cong 0.577$

G. Fibonacci Numbers

$f_n = f_{n-1} + f_{n-2}, \; n \ge 2, \; f_0 = 0$ and $f_1 = 1$

H. Stirling's Formula

$$\left(\frac{n}{e}\right)^n (2\pi n)^{1/2} < n! < \left(\frac{n}{e}\right)^n (2\pi n)^{1/2}\left(1 + \frac{1}{11n}\right) \text{ for } n \ge 1$$

I. Ackerman's Function (Ack)

$\mathrm{Ack}(i, j) = j + 1, \; i = 0$

$\qquad\qquad = \mathrm{Ack}(i - 1, 1), \; i > 0, \; j = 0$

$\qquad\qquad = \mathrm{Ack}(i - 1, \mathrm{Ack}(i, j - 1)), \text{ otherwise}$

J. Generating Functions for Some Sequences

Sequence	Generating function
1, 1, 1, ...	$1 + z + z^2 + z^3 + \cdots = 1/(1 - z)$
1, c, c^2, ...	$1 + cz + (cz)^2 + \cdots = 1/(1 - cz)$
1, $2c$, $3c^2$, ... $(i + 1)c^i$, ...	$1/(1 - cz)^2$
$\binom{n}{0}, \binom{n}{1}, ..., \binom{n}{i}, ...$	$(1 + z)^n$

K. (i) For any event A, $0 \leq$ Probability$[A] \leq 1$.

(ii) For all A belonging to the sample space(S), $\sum\limits_{A \in S}$ Probability$(A) = 1$.

(iii) For any events A and B, Probability $[A \cup B]$ = Probability$[A]$ + Probability$[B]$ − Probability$[A \cap B]$.

(iv) The conditional probability of A given B is Probability $[A|B] = \dfrac{\text{Probability } [A \cap B]}{\text{Probability } [B]}$.

(v) The expected value $E(X)$ of a discrete random variable X is

$$E(X) = \sum_x x \ \text{Probability}[X = x].$$

L. Functions Used in Section 12.4.5

Unconstrained test functions:
UC–1: Rosenbrock's function

$$\text{Minimize } F(X) = \sum_{i=1}^{n-1} [(1 - x_i)^2 + 100(x_{i+1} - x_i^2)^2]$$

with $-5.12 \leq x_i \leq 5.12$, $i = 1, ..., n$. The function has a global optimum $F(X^*) = 0$ located at $X^* = \{1.0, 1.0, ..., 1.0\}$.

UC–2: Rastrigin's function

$$\text{Minimize } F(X) = 10n + \sum_{i=1}^{n} [x_i^2 - 10\cos(2\pi x_i)]$$

with $-5.12 \leq x_i \leq 5.12$, $i = 1, ..., n$. The function has a global optimum $F(X^*) = 0$ located at $X^* = [0, 0, ..., 0]$.

UC–3: Schwefel's function

$$\text{Minimize } F(X) = \sum_{i=1}^{n} \left(\sum_{j=1}^{i} x_j \right)^2$$

with $-100 \leq x_i \leq 100$. The function has a global optimum $F(X^*) = 0$ located at $X^* = [0, 0, ..., 0]$.

UC–4: Griewank's function

$$\text{Minimize } F(X) = \frac{1}{4000} \sum_{i=1}^{n} x_i^2 - \prod_{i=1}^{n} \cos\left(\frac{x_i}{\sqrt{i}} \right) + 1$$

with $-600 \leq x_i \leq 600$. The function has a global optimum $F(X^*) = 0$.

UC–5: Michalewicz's function

$$\text{Minimize } F(X) = - \sum_{i=1}^{n} \sin(x_i) \sin^{20}\left(\frac{i \cdot x_i^2}{\pi} \right)$$

with $0 \leq x_i \leq \pi$. The function has a global optimum $F(X^*) = -99.2784$.

Constrained test functions:
C–1:

$$\text{Minimize } F(X) = 5x_1 + 5x_2 + 5x_3 + 5x_4 - 5 \sum_{i=1}^{4} x_i^2 - \sum_{i=5}^{13} x_i$$

with variable bounds $0 \leq x_i \leq 1$, $i = 1, ..., 9$; $0 \leq x_i \leq 100$, $i = 10, 11, 12$ and $0 \leq x_{13} \leq 1$ and subject to the constraints:

$$2x_1 + 2x_2 + x_{10} + x_{11} \leq 10$$
$$2x_1 + 2x_3 + x_{10} + x_{12} \leq 10$$
$$2x_2 + 2x_3 + x_{11} + x_{12} \leq 10$$
$$-8x_1 + x_{10} \leq 0$$
$$-8x_2 + x_{11} \leq 0$$
$$-8x_3 + x_{12} \leq 0$$
$$-2x_4 - x_5 + x_{10} \leq 0$$
$$-2x_6 - x_7 + x_{11} \leq 0$$
$$-2x_8 - x_9 + x_{12} \leq 0$$

The function has a global optimum $F(X^*) = -15$ located at $X^* = (1, 1, 1, 1, 1, 1, 1, 1, 1, 3, 3, 3, 1)$.

C–2:

$$\text{Minimize } F(X) = x_1 + x_2 + x_3$$

with variable bounds $100 \le x_i \le 10000$; $1000 \le x_i \le 10000$, $i = 2, 3$; $10 \le x_i \le 1000$, $i = 4, ..., 8$ and subject to the constraints:

$$1 - 0.0025(x_4 + x_6) \ge 0$$
$$1 - 0.0025(x_5 + x_7 - x_4) \ge 0$$
$$1 - 0.01(x_8 - x_5) \ge 0$$
$$x_1 x_6 - 833.33252 x_4 - 100 x_1 + 83333.333 \ge 0$$
$$x_2 x_7 - 1250 x_5 - x_2 x_4 + 1250 x_4 \ge 0$$
$$x_3 x_8 - 1250000 - x_3 x_5 + 2500 x_5 \ge 0$$

The function has a global optimum $F(X^*) = 7049.330923$ located at $X^* = (579.3167, 1359.943, 5110.071, 182.0174, 295.5985, 217.9799, 286.4162, 395.5979)$.

C–3:

$$\text{Minimize } F(X) = (x_1 - 10)^2 + 5(x_2 - 12)^2 + x_3^4 + 3(x_4 - 11)^2$$
$$+ 10 x_5^6 + 7 x_6^2 + x_7^4 - 4 x_6 x_7 - 10 x_6 - 8 x_7$$

with variable bounds $-10 \le x_i \le 10$ for $i = 1, ..., 7$ and subject to the constraints:

$$127 - 2 x_1^2 - 3 x_2^4 - x_3 - 4 x_4^2 - 5 x_5 \ge 0$$
$$282 - 7 x_1 - 3 x_2 - 10 x_3^2 - x_4 + x_5 \ge 0$$
$$196 - 23 x_1 - x_2^2 - 6 x_6^2 + 8 x_7 \ge 0$$
$$- 4 x_1^2 - x_2^2 + 3 x_1 x_2 - 2 x_3^2 - 5 x_6 + 11 x_7 \ge 0$$

The function has a global optimum $F(X^*) = 680.6300573$ located at $X^* = (2.330499, 1.951372, -0.4775414, 4.365726, -0.6244870, 1.038131, 1.594227)$.

C–4:

$$\text{Minimize } F(X) = e^{x_1 x_2 x_3 x_4 x_5}$$

with variable bounds $-2.3 \le x_i \le 2.3$, for $i = 1, 2$; $-3.2 \le x_i \le 3.2$, $i = 3, 4, 5$ and subject to the constraints:

$$x_1^2 + x_2^2 + x_3^2 + x_4^2 + x_5^2 = 10$$
$$x_2 x_3 - 5 x_3 x_5 = 0$$
$$3 x_1^3 + x_2^3 = -1$$

The function has a global optimum $F(X^*) = 0.0539498478$ located at $X^* = (-1.717143, 1.595709, 1.827247, -0.7636413, -0.7636450)$.

C–5:

$$\text{Minimize } F(X) = x_1^2 + x_2^2 + x_1 x_2 - 14x_1 - 16x_2 + (x_3 - 10)^2$$
$$+ 4(x_4 - 5)^2 + (x_5 - 3)^2 + (x_5 - 3)^2 + 2(x_6 - 1)^2$$
$$+ 5x_7^2 + 7(x_8 - 11)^2 + 2(x_9 - 10)^2 + (x_{10} - 7)^2 + 45$$

with variable bounds $-10 \leq x_i \leq 10$ for $i = 1, ..., 10$ and subject to the constraints:

$$105 - 4x_1 - 5x_2 + 3x_7 - 9x_8 \geq 0$$
$$-3(x_1 - 2)^2 - 4(x_2 - 3)^2 - 2x_3^2 + 7x_4 + 120 \geq 0$$
$$- 10x_1 + 8x_2 + 17x_7 - 2x_8 \geq 0$$
$$-x_1^2 - 2(x_2 - 2)^2 + 2x_1 x_2 - 14x_5 + 6x_6 \geq 0$$
$$8x_1 - 2x_2 - 5x_9 + 2x_{10} + 12 \geq 0$$
$$-5x_1^2 - 8x_2 - (x_3 - 6)^2 + 2x_4 + 40 \geq 0$$
$$3x_1 - 6x_2 - 12(x_9 - 8)^2 + 7x_{10} \geq 0$$
$$-0.5(x_1 - 8)^2 - 2(x_2 - 4)^2 - 3x_5^2 + x_6 + 30 \geq 0$$

The function has a global optimum $F(X^*) = 24.3062091$ located at $X^* = $ (2.171996, 2.363683, 8.773926, 5.095984, 0.9906548, 1.430574, 1.321644, 9.828726, 8.280092, 8.375927).

BIBLIOGRAPHY

Aho, Alfred V., John E. Hopcroft, and Jeffrey D. Ullman, *The Design and Analysis of Computer Algorithms*, Addison-Wesley, 1974.

_____, *Data Structures and Algorithms*, Addison-Wesley, 1983.

Akl, S.G., *The Design and Analysis of Parallel Algorithms*, Prentice-Hall, NJ, 1989.

Alan Parker, *Algorithms and Data Structures in C++*, CRC Press, 1993.

Atallah, M.J. (Ed.), *Algorithms and Theory of Computation Handbook*, CRC Press, 1999.

Ausiello, G. et al., *Complexity and Approximation: Combinatorial Optimization Problems and Their Approximability Properties*, Springer-Verlag, 1999.

Berlioux, P. and P. Bizard, *Algorithms: The Construction, Proof, and Analysis of Programs*, John Wiley & Sons, 1986.

Berman, Kenneth A. and Jerome L. Paul, *Algorithms*, Cengage Learning, 2002.

Borodin, A. and I. Munro, *The Computational Complexity of Algebraic and Numeric Problems*, Elsevier Computer Science Library, 1975.

Brassard, Gilles and Paul Bratley, *Fundamentals of Algorithmics*, Prentice-Hall of India, 2004.

Cormen, Thomas H., Charles E. Leiserson, and Ronald L. Rivest, *Introduction to Algorithms*, 2nd ed., Prentice-Hall of India, 2004.

Daniel Pierre Bovet and Pierluigi Crescenzi, *Introduction to the Theory of Complexity*, Prentice-Hall, NJ, 1994.

Dasgupta, Sanjay, Christos Papadimitriou, and Umesh Vazirani, *Algorithms*, McGraw-Hill Companies, 2008.

David Harel, *Algorithmics: The Spirit of Computing*, Addison-Wesley, 1992.

Ellis Horowitz and Sartaj Sahni, *Fundamentals of Computer Algorithms*, Computer Science Press, 1978.

Even, S., *Graph Algorithms*, Computer Science Press, 1979.

Garey, Michael R. and David S. Johnson, *Computers and Intractability: A Guide to the Theory of NP-Completeness*, W.H. Freeman, 1979.

Goldberg, David E., *Genetic Algorithms in Search, Optimization, and Machine Learning*, Addison-Wesley, 1989.

Graham, R.L., D.E. Knuth, and O. Patashnik, *Concrete Mathematics*, Addison-Wesley, 1989.

Gusfield, Dan, *Algorithms on Strings, Tree, and Sequences*, Cambridge University Press, 1997.

Heileman, Gregory L., *Data Structures, Algorithms, and Object-Oriented Programming*, McGraw-Hill Companies, 1996.

Hochbaum, D.S. (Ed.), *Approximate Algorithms for NP-Hard Problems*, PWS Publishing, 1997.

Hopcroft, J.E. and J.D. Ullman, *Introduction to Automata Theory, Languages, and Computation*, Addison-Wesley, 1979.

Horowitz, Sahni and Rajasekaran, *Computer Algorithms*, W.H. Freeman and Company, 1998.

Hu, T.C., *Combinatorial Algorithms*, Addison-Wesley, 1982.

Johnsonbaugh, Richard, and Marcus Schaefer, *Algorithms*, Pearson Education, 2004.

Jones, Neil C. and Pavel A. Pevzner, *An Introduction to Bioinformatics Algorithms*, The MIT Press, 2004.

Juraj Hromkovic, *Algorithmics for Hard Problems*, Springer-Verlag, 2001.

Kleinberg, Jon and Éva Tardos, *Algorithm Design*, Pearson Education, 2006.

Knuth, Donald E., *The Art of Computer Programming, Volume 1, Fundamental Algorithms*, Addison-Wesley, 1968.

Kozen, Dexter C., *The Design and Analysis of Algorithms*, Springer-Verlag, 1992.

Kreher, D.L. and D.R. Stinson, *Combinatorial Algorithms: Generation, Enumeration and Search*, CRC Press, 1999.

Kumar, V., A. Grama, A. Gupta, and G. Karypis, *Introduction to Parallel Computing: Design and Analysis of Algorithms*, Benjamin/Cummings Publishing Company, 1994.

Kurt Mehlhorn, *Graph Algorithms and NP-Completeness*, Springer-Verlag, 1984.

Lawrence, Davis, *Genetic Algorithms and Simulated Annealing*, Pitman Publishing, 1987.

Leeuwen, Jan van, (Ed.), *Handbook of Theoretical Computer Science, Volume A, Algorithms and Complexity*, Elsevier Science Publishers, 1990.

Leighton, F.T., *Introduction to Parallel Algorithms and Architectures: Arrays, Trees, Hypercubes*, Morgan Kaumann, 1992.

Levitin, A., *Introduction to the Design and Analysis of Algorithms*, Pearson Education, 2003.

Michalewicz, Z., *Genetic Algorithms + Data Structures = Evolution Programs*, Springer-Verlag, 1994.

Minisky, M.L., *Computation: Finite and Infinite Machines*, Prentice-Hall, NJ, 1967.

Mitchell, Melanie, *An Introduction to Genetic Algorithms*, Prentice-Hall of India, 2004.

Papadimitriou, Christos H., *Computational Complexity*, Addison-Wesley, 1994.

Papadimitriou, Christos H. and Kenneth Steiglitz, *Combinatorial Optimization, Algorithms and Complexity*, Prentice-Hall of India, 2001.

Pevzner, Pavel A., *Computational Molecular Biology: An Algorithmic Approach*, The MIT Press, 2000.

Preparata, F.P. and M.I. Shamos, *Computational Geometry: An Introduction*, Springer-Verlag, 1985.

Purdon (Jr.), Paul Walton and Cynthia A. Brown, *The Analysis of Algorithms*, CBS Publishing, 1985.

Quinn, M.J., *Parallel Computing: Theory and Practice*, McGraw-Hill, 1994.

Rajeev Motwani and Prabhakar Raghavan, *Randomized Algorithms*, Cambridge University Press, 1995.

Robert Sedgewick, *Algorithms*, Addison-Wesley, 1988.

Sara Baase and Allen Van Gelder, *Computer Algorithms: Introduction to Design and Analysis*, Pearson Education, 2000.

Sipser, M., *Introduction to the Theory of Computation*, PWS Publishing Company, 1997.

Standish, Thomas A., *Data Structure Techniques*, Addison-Wesley, 1980.

Tel, G., *Introduction to Distributed Algorithms*, Cambridge University Press, 1994.

Tucker, A.B., Jr. (Ed.), *The Computer Science and Engineering Handbook*, CRC Press, 1997.

Vazirani, Vijay V., *Approximation Algorithms*, Springer-Verlag, 2001.

Weiss, M.A., *Data Structures and Algorithm Analysis*, Benjamin/Cummings Publishing Company, 1995.

Wirth, N., *Algorithm + Data Structures = Programs*, Prentice-Hall of India, 2005.

INDEX